A
DICTIONARY, ENGLISH AND SINDHI

A DICTIONARY, ENGLISH AND SINDHI

BY

CAPTAIN GEORGE STACK

Printed by Order of the Government of Bombay

GYAN

Published by

Gyan Publishing House
5, Ansari Road
Daryaganj, New Delhi-110002
Phone: 011-47034999, 9811692060
E-mail: books@gyanbooks.com

Distribution Network
gyanbooks.com
India, USA, Canada, UK, Australia, France

ISBN : 978-81-212-4287-5 (PB)
First Published, 1849

2nd Impression 2020

Printed at: Gyan Press, Delhi.

The book at your disposal is the edition of an old book originally published long back. The Text quality of this book may not be at par as compared to our other books but many readers approached us to reprint this important book so that it could satiate their hunger. We request all the readers of this book to help us to improve its quality by providing the necessary text of those pages which are not properly visible. Your valuable support in this case will be highly appreciated and acknowledged and our future readers will be benefitted immensely.

A DICTIONARY, ENGLISH AND SINDHI.

BY

CAPTAIN GEORGE STACK.

Printed by Order of the Government of Bombay.

BOMBAY:
AMERICAN MISSION PRESS.
T. GRAHAM, PRINTER.

M,DCCC,XLIX.

PREFACE.

In commencing this work, I aimed at nothing more than to shew the Sindhi significations of the English words, given in Kennedy's English and Maratha Dictionary, which I chose as containing a brief yet good list of the words in most common use in our tongue. Sir George Clerk, the late Governor of Bombay, having however, during his visit to Sindh in February 1848, examined the work so far as it was prepared, and recommended its being published on account of Government, I thought it best to make it as complete, as my limited time would allow, without, however, delaying its publication, which I was informed was required early. The first sheets were at once given to the Printer, but to those left in my hands I made additions and improvements, forwarding them down successively, as the Printer was ready for them, till all was completed. This will account for the work getting more and more full, as it advances. The additions made have more than doubled the original plan, Kennedy's Dictionary containing significations for only 5,500 English words. This gives those for about 12,000.

This work does not profess to give all the Sindhi, or Sindified, synonymes in use in the country; it shews only those most common, and generally understood. The Sindhi, like the Hindostani, borrows from the Arabic, the Persian, and the Sanscrit, to an extent only limited by the learning and fancy of the writer. It would have rendered the work confused and difficult to add all such words to it. Such of them have been given, as are in common use, and also all pure Sindhi words, that I have been able to meet with. I would note that there are many words in use in Lár or Lower Sindh, which are not known in the northern parts of the province, and vice versâ. Different classes too favor different terms--the Hindoos using many Sanscrit words unknown to the Musalmans, and the Musalmans many Arabic vocables spoken only among themselves. For this reason I have tried to put first in place the synonymes best known generally, and these will often be found to be words used in Hindostani. The others follow in order as they seem more or less common.

I have but rarely attempted to express the meaning of a word by a phrase. In preference to doing so, I have generally omitted English words expressing ideas, or being names of things peculiar to ourselves. Such phrases could only be used with safety by one already acquainted with the language, and one so acquainted would find little difficulty in forming them for himself.

I have chosen the Devenagari character to write the Sindhi words in, as being for many reasons the most suitable and convenient. To some of its letters, however, I have been obliged to attach marks to distinguish sounds peculiar to the Sindhi. The letters so marked are ग़, ज़. ट़, ड़, ड॒. द़, and ब़.*

I have had considerable difficulty in fixing the Orthography. Many of the words I have given will be found to be pronounced and written very differently by different persons. I have tried to choose the most common forms of spelling, or to follow the general manner of pronunciation, without at the same time going into actual vulgarisms; but my choice was very arbitrary, and it will doubtless be thought that I am often incorrect. One of the most common differences is in the infinitive of those Causal Verbs, which I have terminated in आइणु. This many make आअणु, and some too आणु; thus we have कराइणु, कराअणु, or कराणु, 'to cause to do;' but the first form only will be found in this work.† The ओ also, terminating many nouns and adjectives, is often pronounced as if ऊ, especially if it be preceded by ण. These differences, however the learner will readily notice for himself.

The contractions of grammatical terms, which I have used, are so few and apparent, that it seems needless to give any list of them. As this work is meant solely for those already acquainted with the principles of Grammar, I have not thought it necessary to point out the various parts of speech, or to distinguish the different kinds of verbs, except where it was needful to do so to avoid confusion.

I would beg to add now a few remarks, which will be found useful in consulting this work.

An adjective can always be expressed by using its corresponding noun in the genitive, and where the Sindhi possesses no other form for the adjective, I have left the English word out altogether. The affix

* The peculiarities of these sounds will be found explained in a Grammar now in the Press.

† The people to the South use आ very commonly where they to the North have इ

वारो, too, used with nouns in their inflected form, gives them an adjective signification. But I have seldom expressed such formations. The learner can readily form them for himself.

Our English adverbs, where derived from adjectives, I have rarely given separate from the adjective, which, unless it be such as is in Sindhi formed from a noun by affixing ई, वारो, or any other of the affixes signifying possession or relation, can also be taken adverbially; thus, हिउ चङो माडहूं आहे, 'this is a good man;' हिउ माडहूं चङो थो हले, 'this man acts well.'

The Infinitive Moods of all verbs are used as verbal nouns, and I have not therefore thought it necessary to repeat these under the Nouns. In such cases too, as the verbal noun has in Sindhi no other forms, I have left the English word out altogether.

Passive verbs are formed by inserting ज before the final णु of the active infinitive, the preceding consonant taking either a short i (इ), or becoming silent, as मारणु 'to beat,' मारिजणु or मार्जणु 'to be beaten.' This form of the verb, however, I have seldom given, except in a few cases where the Sindhi is irregular. A Sindhi passive, though, will sometimes be found used as the synonyme of an English neuter verb, especially if the neuter form be wanting in the Sindhi.

The rules for distinguishing the gender of Nouns are very simple. Every word in Sindhi ends in a vowel, and it points out the gender. These terminating vowels are अ, आ, इ, ई, उ, ऊ, and ओ. Nouns ending in उ and ओ are masculine; in अ and इ, they are feminine, as are also those terminating in आ, ई, and ऊ, unless where, from being the names of living male objects, they become masculine naturally. The Sindhi possesses no neuter. The few exceptions to this rule that will be met throughout this work, I have marked with an 'm,' or 'f' following the word to shew the genders. It must be borne in mind, however, that the first of these vowels, अ, when immediately following a silent consonant, is not expressed, being considered inherent in the consonant, and therefore all final consonants, which have no vowels written after them, should be sounded with अ, thus खट, s. f. 'a bedstead.'

Where an English word has many different significations, I have often given under it only the Sindhi synonyme for that most common, and referred for the others to corresponding words in other parts of the Dictionary.

In conclusion I would remark that this work does not in any way profess to be free from mistakes—that it is by no means complete, will be at once apparent. No Dictionary can be made full and correct at the first attempt—above all one of a language that has been so little cultivated by the people themselves as the Sindhi has been. Other duties too have prevented my giving to it all the labor and attention I would have wished. Defective as it is, it may however, be useful as a foundation for a more complete work in some future day. And meanwhile in connexion with other works, which it is expected will be shortly through the Press, it is hoped, it will be found of use by officers employed in this province in facilitating the study of the language—a knowledge of which is absolutely necessary to enable them to perform their duties with satisfaction and efficiency.

GEO. STACK, Capt.
Dy. Collector.

HYDERABAD, SINDH,
1*st. May*, 1849.

A

DICTIONARY,

ENGLISH AND SINDHI.

A

A or An. There is no article in the Sindhi language; the indefinite may sometimes be expressed by हिकिडो *one*.

To Abandon. छड़णु, फिटो करणु.

Abandoned, (*reprobate*). लुंड़ो, विअलु, खर्यलु, लोठ्यो.

Abandoning, Abandonment. तर्कु, तलाक, त्यागु.

To Abash. लज़ाइणु, शर्मांइणु.

Abashed. लज़ी, शिर्मिंधो.

To be Abashed. लज़णु, शर्मांइजणु.

To Abate (*neu.*). घटणु, लहणु, ढिरो-सांति-थिअणु.

Abatement, (*remission*). छूटि, छड़ति.

To Abbreviate. थोरो करणु, घटाइणु.

Abhorrence. किरांहत.

To Abide. टिकणु, रहणु, विहणु.

Ability, (*power*). सघ, ब़लु.

Able. सघाइनो. *See* Powerful.

To be Able. सघणु.

Ablution. सनानु, मसउ, वज़ू.

Abode. घरू, जाइ, हंधु, रहाश.

To Abolish. कढणु, बंदि-मौकुफु-करणु, ब्यारे ड़िभणु.

An Abortion, to occur. पेटु-बारु-कचो-किरणु. *See* To Miscarry.

Above. मथे.

Above-mentioned. मथेंचिओ, अग़ेचिओ.

To Abound. घणो थिअणू.

About, (*in place*). ओसेपासे, हेड़्हां-होड़्हां, (*in number*) खनु.

Abroad. ब़ाहरि.

An Abscess. फुडी, ग़ड़्हु

To Abscond. लिकी वञणु, भज़णु, गाइबु थिअणु.

Absence. नअचणु, नथिअणु.

In one's absence. परपुठि.

To be Absolved. मुखिरणु, छुटणु.

Absolutely. तमामु, बिल्कुलु.

To Absorb. चुहणु, पी वञणु.

Absorbed, (*in meditation*). लीनु, मगनु.

Abstemious. किरिअवारो, संजमी.

To be Abstemious. वातु रखणु.

Abstinence. किरी, परहेज, संजमु.

Abundance. घणाई, वाधि.

Abundant. घणो, जाम, जालारो, झझो, गाइबो, मुक्तो, मउ, रेलिछेलि, ब्रहूं, सर्सु, अमुंगिडो, जाल.

Abuse. गारि, सुखिनु, तवारू, विणो, वेणु.

To Abuse. गारि ड़िअणु *or* कढणु, तवारणु, वेणु-साडु-विझणु.

Abusive. कमीणो, मुँह जो गंदो.

Accent. सुरू, बोली, आवाजु, गलो.

To Accept. वठणु, मञणु, (*a bill of exchange*) सकारणु, *to write the acceptance* पुठि भरणु.

An Accident. कजा.

Accidentally. ओचितो, अचानक, अचाचेति, अणज़ाणी, अपाक.

To Accompany. गड़जी हलणु.

An Accomplice. भाईवारू, साथी, हम्राहु, सलाही, ग़ांदुडु, ग़ांढू.

To Accomplish. करणु, पुरो करणु, निवेरणु, निबाहणु, रसाइणु, साधणु.

To be Accomplished. पुरो थिअणु, निबिरणु, निबहणु, पुज़णु, रसणु.

To Accord (*neu.*). जुडणु, ठहणुं.

According to. मापकु, मूजिबि, सारू.

An Account. लेखो, हिसाबु, खंधो, पेटो.

On Account of. लाइ, वास्ते, काणि, कातरि, सांगि, सांगों.

Account, (*relation*). समाचारू, खबर, हकीकत.

To Account. लेखणु, ग़णणु.

An Accountant. लेखेवारो, हिसाबी.

An Account-book. वहो, (*of kinds*) खरिडो, कचो, खातो, रोजनामो.

To be Accoutred. जुडणु, जकणु. *See* To be equipped.

Accoutrements. हथिभारपल्हार, साजु.

To Accumulate (*act.*). मेडणु, गडुकरणु, सथणु.

Accurate. सही, ठीकु, सोडोनु.

Accursed. नालती, फिठ्कार्यो, नामुरादु.

Accusation. दावा, (*false*) चत्र, इल्केलु, अडी.

To Accuse. ड़ोहु लग़ाइणु, दावा करणु.

An Accuser. दांहीं.

To Accustom. हेरणु.

One Accustomed or habituated. हेराकु, हेरू.

The Ace point, (*on dice*). पंउं (*on cards*) पको.

An Ache. सूरू, पीड.

To Ache. डुखणु, सूरूकरणु.

Acid. खटो.

To Acknowledge. बासणु, मञणु.

To Acquaint. ज़ाणाइणु. *See* To Inform.

Acquaintance, (*with another*). सुञाणप, सेंधि, सनाखत, पचों, साञहि, वाकुफी, लिहो, लड्वटु. *See* Knowledge.

An Acquaintance. सही, सेंधों, पचेंवानु, मुलाकाती, साञारो.

To be Acquainted with, (*another*). सुञाणणु. *See* To know.

Acquainted with. ज़ाणाऊ, ज़ाणू, वाकुफु, भुंयों, सही, सूंहो, ज़ाणोई.

To Acquire. लहणु, पाइणु, पिराइणु.

Acquired. प्रापति.

An Acquisition, (*gain*). लाहो, फलु.

Across, (*over a river, &c.*). पारि, परिंभरि.

Across, (*athwart*). आड़ो, उरेबो, पासोंरो.

To Act (*act.*). करणु.

To Act (*neu.*). हलणु.

An Act. कमु, हाज, ग़ाल्हि.

Active, (*nimble, smart*). फुडूनु, चालाकु, तेजु, तिखो, खहुरो, झांझिरो, तखडु.

Active, (*in grammar*). सकर्मक.
Activity. फुड़्ती, झांझिराई, चालाकी.
To Add, (*put to*). गड़िजी, रखणु- &c. *See* To Affix, Join.
To Add up, (*an account*). जोड़णु, जोड़ु करणु, जुम्लो ड़िअणु, मिलाइणु.
Addition, (*of numbers*). जोड़ु, मीज़ानु.
Additional. वाधू, वधीक.
An Address, (*direction of a letter*). सर्नांमो.
An Adept. भड़ु. *See* Skilful.
To Adhere. चंबुड़णु, चहुटणु, लग़णु. *See* To Stick.
Adhesion. चीड़हालो.
Adhesiveness. चीड़्हु.
To Adjoin, (*be close to*). भरि सांलागीतो–हुअणु.
To Adjust, (*set in order*). सँवारणु, सुधारणु, ठाहणु, (*an account*) लाहणु, चुकाइणु, निबेरणु.
An Adjustment. निबेरो.
Admirable. उम्दो, ऊचो.
To Admit, (*suffer to enter*). अचणुड़िअणु, छड़णु. *See* To Confess.
Admittance. वाट, मोकल.
An Adopted-son. ड़िनलु पुटु.
Adoration. पूजा, भज़नु, सेवा, बंदगी.
To Adore. पूजणु, भज़णु, सेवणु.
To Adorn. सींगारणु, सँवारणु.
Adornment. सींगारू, सँवार्णी, हारूसींगारू.
To Advance, (*come forward*). अगेहलणु, वधी हलणु, (*money*) अगुवार-अगुवाट-ड़िअणु.
Advantage. लाहो, नफो, फाइदो, भलो, चङो.
Advantageous. सज़ायो, सथ्यायो. *See* Beneficial.

Adverse. उबतो, ऊंधो.
Adversity. विपति, आफति, कहरू, कुभु, औसरू.
Advice. सलाह, मस्लत, मतो, नसिअत.
To Advise, or give advice. सेखारणु, सलाह &c. ड़िअणु.
Adult. बोराकु, बालगु.
An Adze. वाहोलो.
Affable. मिलिणो, मिलूणो, खिलमुंहो.
An Affair. कमु, ग़ाल्हि, बाबु, मामिलो.
To Affect, (*act upon*). लग़णु, असरू करणु.
Affectation. चालो.
Affection. नीहु, नेहु, प्रीति, प्रेमु, पिआरू, भाउ, मोहु, लहु, हुब, आरू.
Affectionate. नेहो, प्रेमी.
An Affiancing. मङिणो, सङु.
A solemn Affirmation. साख.
To Affix. हणणु, लग़ाइणु.
To Afflict. डुखाइणु, ड़हणु, पीडणु.
To be Afflicted. डुखणु, पीड़जणु, ड़झणु.
Afflicted. डुखी.
Affliction. डुखु, सोसु, सोकु, रंजु.
Afoot. पेरें, पिआदो, पंधिड्यो, पेरिपिआदो, पेड्यो.
To be Afraid. ड़िज़णु, ड़रणु, कउखाइणु.
After. पोइ, पुजाणो, पुंभों, (*in pursuit of*) पुठ्यों, पुंभों.
After, *of the after part*. पाछाटो.
The Afterbirth. ज़रू, ओर, ज़ेरि, ज़ौर.
The Afternoon. पोयाडी, पेशी, मँझंदि, अग़ों.
Afterwards. पोइ, वरी.
Again. ब्रिहर, मोटी, वरी.
Against, (*placed against*). भर, सां, (*advancing in opposition*) ने.

Age. उमिरि, वही, आर्जा, ज़मु, सनु, ज़मार.

An Age. जुगु.

Aged, *of middle age*. करडवडु, कडांट्टु.

Agency, *(acting for another)*. वकालत, वकीली.

An Agent. *(factor)* गुमास्तो, *(delegate)* वकीलु, *(in grammar)* कर्ता*m*.

Aggrandizement. चड्हीचड्हंदी.

To be Agitated. उछिलणु, फथिकणु, तड्फणु.

Agitation. छोभु, उछल, विलोडो, झिग़ोडु. *See* Disturbance.

A little time Ago. महँदेरिडो, अग़ाहीं.

To Agree, *(assent)*. मञणु, बासणु, कबूलणु.

To Agree, *(be in concord)*. ठहणु, जुडणु.

Agreeable, *(pleasing)*. सुहांइंदो, *(congruous)* ठाहू.

Agreed. कबूलु.

An Agreement, *(compact)*. जाइजु, बोलु, अंजामु, वाइदो, करारु, कौलु, *(concord)* बणति, बणाउ, ठहाउ.

Agriculture. पोख, ब्रनोज्ञारी.

Ague. तपु, ब्ररो, *cold fit* सोभो, *tertian* त्रिभडु, त्रैंभों, *quartan* ट्रिभडु, ट्रैभों, *quintan* चोथडु. *See Fever.*

Ah. ओंह, हाइ, हुए, है.

Aid. इम्राहो, भर्थी, वाहर, सहाइता, हिमाइत.

An Aider. सहाइ*m*. इम्राहु, हामी, वाहुरू.

To Aim, *(at a mark)*. तकणु, चिताइणु.

An Aim. तक, चुस्त.

Air. वाउ, हवा.

The open Air. वाउखाई.

To Air, *(expose to the air)*. वाउ खाइणु, फकुगाइणु.

To take an Airing. सैलु-सैरु-टोरो-करणु.

Airy, *(trifling)*. हवाई, *(exposed to air)* वाउखों.

Alarm. हूक.

To be Alarmed. डिजणु. *See* To be Afraid.

Alas. ओंह, हाइ, होइ. *See* Ah.

Albugo. फुली.

An Alchymist. कीमांगरु.

Alchymy. कीमां.

An Alembic. कर्णफुलु.

Alert. सुजागु, सुचेतु, खबंदारु, फुड्तु.

To Alight. लहणु.

Alike. हिकजिहडो, बरोबरि, हिकजेहों, मटु, समानि.

Alimony. कावोनो.

Alive. जिभरो, हयातु.

All. मिड्योई, सभोई, सभु, कुलु, सज़ो, सारो.

Allegiance. आण, ड्राही.

An Alligator. मांगमंछु, वाघू.

To Allot. फांड्णु. *See* To Distribute.

Allotment. वंड्, विछ. *See* Share.

An Allowance, *(for maintenance)*. विरउ, *(deduction in an account)* मुजिरा.

Alloy. कसु*f*. गैरु, मठु.

Alloyed, *(metal)*. मरु, मठो, कसो.

All-spice. सीतलचीनी.

To Allure. धुतारणु, रेबणु, लोभाइणु, लालचाइणु, चट बंधणु, भर्माइणु.

Allurement. धुतार, रेबु, चट, वसु. *See* Enticement.

An Almanac. टिपिणो.

An Almond. बादामी.
The bark of the Almond tree. तुरी.
Alms. पिन, बीख, खैर्यात, ड़ानु, धर्मु, भिछा, बिख्या.
Aloes, (*wood*). अगरू, ऊदु.
Alone. हेकलो, छड़्हो, जको, यको, निवेकिलो.
Along with. साणु, सां.
Aloud. ज़ोर सां, ड़ाढ्यां.
The Alphabet. आइंवेटा.
Also. बि, पि, पिणि.
An Altar. वेड़ी.
To Alter. मटणु, मटाइणु, फेरणु.
Alteration. फेरू, फर्कु.
To be Altered. मटिजणु, फिरणु.
Altercation. कथ, गहपोह, चटाभेटी, रगिड़ो, रीड, रदबदलि.
Although. तोडे.
Alum. फिट्की.
Always. सदा, हमेशां, नितु, ब्राहोंई, ब्राहों.
An Ambassador. वकीलु.
Ambergris. अंबरू.
An Ambling pace. रलो, वचुडालु.
To lie in Ambush. छपी-लिकी-विहणु, छह मारणु, छपि करणु.
Amiable. सुलछिणो, सभागो, सुंहारो, सब्राझो, मुराद्वंदु, सधातूरो, सुहाबतु, समुरादो.
Amidst. विचि, विच में.
Ammunition. दारूगोरी.
Among. विचि, में, मंझि.
Amount. अंदाज़ु.
An Amulet. तावीज़ु, कौंचु, ताइथु, फुलु.
To Amuse. रिझाइणु, विंदुराइणु.
Amusement. खुशी, सुखु, अरामु, विंदुर.
Anarchy. विगोडु, रोलो.
An Ancestor. वड़ो, वड़िको, वड़ेरो.

An Anchor. ब्रिलो, नातारी, लंगरू.
To Anchor. ब्रिलो *etc.* विझणु.
Ancient. आग़ाटो, आदऊ.
And. एं, अंऊं, अंईं.
An Angel. मलाइकु, पार्खंदु, फिरिश्तो.
To Anger. चेडणु, छेडणु, चेडाइणु, संदाइणु, कल्पाइणु.
Anger. कावडि, ड़मरू, क्रोधु, रंजु, गुसो, खाण्णी, चिड, चंड़ालु.
An Angle. कुंड़.
Angry. रंजि.
To be Angry. ड़मिजणु, कावड्जणु, कल्पणु, क्रोधिजणु, चिडणु.
Anguish. साड़ु, लोछि, पीड, सूरू.
To suffer Anguish. लुछणु, पीड़्जणु.
An Animal. जीउ, जान्वरू.
A wild Animal. मिरू.
Animate. जंगमु.
Anise seed. वडुफ, सौंफ.
An Ankle. मुरो, गिर्यो.
Ankle ornaments, *of sorts.* कुनेपटो, घिंघिरा, *plural.* नूरो, पांजिबु, डी, छेरि.
Annihilated. फ़ना, नासु.
To Annoy. कडाइणु, खपाइणु, ड़नणु, रंजाइणु.
Annoyance. हलाखी, डुखु, दिकत, खेचरि, उपाधि.
Annual. व्रहँमाँहीं, वर्ह्योको.
To Anoint. मखणु.
The act of Anointing. मखु.
Another. ब्रिओ.
Another's. धार्यो, पराओ, वेग्यो.
To Answer. वराणी &c. ड़िअणु.
An Answer. वराणी, वरंदो, जबाबु.
An Ant. (*small*) किंउली, (*large*) माकोडो.
A body of Ants. माकडि.
A white Ant. उड़ोही.
Anterior. अग्यों, पेह्यों.

Antimony. सुर्मो, सोईरो.
The Anus. गुई, चुति, सुफ़िरो.
An Anvil. संदणि, संदाणि, अरणि.
Anxiety. फिकिरु, चिंता, उल्को, ग़-णती, उझादु, अर्मानु, विस्वासु, अंदेसो, ओसीडो, ओनो, ओन, हिड़िक.
To be Anxious. अर्माणिजणु, फिकिरु &c. करणु.
Any. को, कोई.
Apart. धार, जुदो, वखिरो.
To Apologize. माफु घुरणु.
To Apostatize. बिगिड़णु.
An Apostle. रसूलु. *See* Prophet.
Apparatus. साज़, सामानु, सरंजामु.
An article of Apparel. गंदो, लटो, लुग़िडो.
To Appear, (*seem*). सुझणु, ड़िसिजणु, भासणु.
Appearance, (*outward shew*). डेखु, ड़िसिणी, सूरत, सरूपु, शिकिलि.
To Appease. लाहणु, सांति-ढिरो-थधो-करणु, टारणु. *See* To Reconcile.
To Appertain. लग़णु, लाग़ाऊ थिअणु.
To Applaud. साराहणु, वखाणणु.
Applause. साराह, तारीफ, वखाण, उस्तुति.
An Apple. सूफु.
Apple-colored. सुफांओ.
To Apply, (*put or lay to*). लाइणु, लग़ाइणु.
To Appoint, (*settle*). ठाहणु, (*nominate*) मुकररु करणु, बिहारणु.
Appointed. मुकररु.
Appointment, (*assignation*). समन, ड़ाई. *See* Office.
To Apportion. फांड़णु. *See* To Distribute.
Apprehension, (*suspicion*). संसो, भर्मु, अंदेसो, सांग, भिर्मु, विस्वासु.
To Approach. ओड़ो-ओड़िडो-वेझो-अचणु.
Approved. कबूलु, पसंदि, कसि.
To be Approved of, (*to please*). वणणु, सुहाइणु, पसंदि अचणु, भाइ पवणु, कसि लग़णु, आउड़णु.
April, and part of May. वेसाखु.
Aqua-fortis. तिजाबु.
Aquarius, (*the Sign*). कुंभु.
Aquatic. पाण्यांरो.
An Aqueduct. कस्यो, कसी, कूर. *See* Canal, Water course.
Arab, Arabian, (*horse or dog*). ताज़ी.
Arable land, (*in cultivation*). आइटो, (*uncultivated or now brought under tillage*) नहूर.
To Arbitrate. पंचाइत &c. करणु.
Arbitration. पंचाइत, टिआकुडी.
An Arbitrator. टिआकुडु, अमीनु, मुन्सिफु.
An Arch. मिहिराबी, वंग.
An Archer. तीरंदाज़ु.
Archery. तीरंदाज़ी.
Arguing, Argument. तर्क, तकारु, बहसु, रदबदलि, वादु.
Aries, (*the Sign*). मेखु, मेषु.
Arithmetic. हिसाबु, लेखो,
To Arm. हथिआर बंधणु.
An Arm. बांह.
An Arm-ornament (*of kinds*). खेंज, ग़भो, ड़ोरिडो, पटो, बाजुबंदु, बांहों, बुकी, बोडोंड़ो, चूडि, बूंहरखी, ताइथु, बांहूटो.
An Armfull. भाकुरु.
The measure between outstretched Arms. पुरिहु.
Armour. जिरिह.
The Armpit. कछु, बगलु.
The Armpit piece in a dress. कछिडी, बग़्ली.

Arms. हथिआर, हथिआर पन्हार.

An Army. लश्करु, उर्दु, कटकु, फौज, *large* दलु.

Around. चौगिर्दि, चौधारी, चौफिरि, चौवटि.

To Arrange. सँवारणु, सुधारणु, ठाहणु.

An Arrangement. ठाहु, सिजिलि, बंदोबस्ति, जोडजक, सठो.

Arrears. बकाया, बाकी.

Arrest, (*restraint of person*). नजरबंदी.

One placed in Arrest. नजरबंदि.

To Arrive. पहुचणु, रसणु, अची *or* वञो-सहडणु, (*as goods*) ढुकणु.

Arrogance. मग्रूरी, अहंकारु, आकडि, अंधु, अभिमानु, ओजु, मदु, मानु.

Arrogant. मग्रूरु, अहंकारी, आकिडिओ.

An Arrow. तीरु, कानु, गजु.

An Arrow head. तुकी, *notch at the but-end* गोशो.

An Arsenal. कार्खानो.

Arsenic. संख्यो, *red* मन्छुरु.

Art, (*skill*). हुनिरु, कला, कारीगरी.

An Artery. रग़, नाडी.

Artful, (*cunning*). पुख्तो, पको. *See* Knowing.

An Artifice. छलु, मकरु, मिकिरु, होलो. *See* Deceit.

An Artificer, Artisan. कस्बी, कारीगरु.

The Artillery department. तोब्खानो.

An Artillery-man. तोब्ची, गुलंदाजु.

Artless, (*simple-minded*). भोरिडो, बोलोभालो, बोदिलो, भोरो, भोलो, साधु.

Artlessness. भोरिडाई, बोदिलाई, भोराई.

As, (*in such manner as*). जिंअ, जिएँ.

As, (*while*). जड्हीं.

As, (*such as, like as*). जिहडो, जेहो.

As large as. जेड़िडो, जेड़ो.

As long as, as far as. जेसोतोणी.

As many, as much. जेतिरो.

As yet. अञा.

Assafœtida. हिङु.

To Ascend. चड्हणु.

An Ascent. चाड्ही, चाड्हु.

To Ascertain. लखणु, सुधि–समाउ–लहणु, तहकीकु–सही–निस्रुकु–करणु.

Ashamed. फिको, शिर्मिंधो, पिशेमाणु, लज़ो, खिथुं.

To be Ashamed. लज़णु, पिशेमाणजणु, शर्माइजणु.

Ashes. रख, फुल्हरु, केरी, छाई, किरि, भसु *f.* छारु *f.*

Aside. पासे.

To Ask. पुछणु.

To Ask for. घुरणु, सुआलु करणु, मङणु.

Asleep. सुतो.

An Ass. गड़हु, खोतो, *young* खोदो, खोदिडो.

A wild Ass. गोर्खरु.

A keeper of Asses. बठारो, होर्वालो.

An Assault. हलाँ, जुलह, ढोडो, *a threatened assault* उलर. *See* Attack.

To Assay, (*coin*). पर्खणु.

An Assayer. पार्खू.

Assemblage. मेडु.

To Assemble (*act.*). गडु करणु.

To Assemble (*neu.*). मिडणु, गडु थिअणु.

An Assembly. मज्लस, सभा.

To Assent. मञणु. *See* To Agree.

An Assent. आंकार, आंइं; *humble forms of expressing assent* अख्युनि सां, अख्युनि ते, तयारू, हाज़ुरू.
Assiduity. सायो, धुनि, उज़्मु.
Assiduous. चुस्तु, उज़्मो.
An Assignation. समन, ड्राई.
An Assignment, (*on the revenues*). तन्खा.
The agreeing to the Assignment, or transfer of a debt, &c. मनोती.
To Assist. सहाइता, &c. करणु, पुठि भरणु.
Assistance. हम्राही, सहाइता, भर्थी, वाहर, मदत.
An Assistant. हम्राहु, पुठिभरू, साथी.
Assurance, (*confidence*). वेसाहु, निहिचो.
Asthma. दमु, साहु, जीक, उभो साहु.
Astonishing. अजबु, अजब, &c. जिहडो.
Astonishment. अजबु, विस, हैरत, अचुर्जु, इबिरत.
Astringent (*in taste*). कसारो.
An Astrologer. निजूमी, जोतिषी, जोसी, जोतिकी.
Astrology, Astronomy. जोतिषु, जोतकु, निजूम.
An Asylum. आसिरो, अझो, पखो.
At (*in*). मैं.
An Atheist. दहरी, नास्ती.
Athletic. मल्लु, सघो, पहिल्वानु, सघारो.
An Atom. रती, जरो.
To Attach, (*goods, &c.*). ठपो हणणु, टल्हणु.
An Attack. काह, जुलह, हक्ल, हलाँ, हलो, हम्लो.

A night Attack. रातहो.
To Attack. हलाँ-जुलह-करणु.
An Attempt. सायो, उज़्मु.
To Attend to, (*obey*). बुधणु, मञणु.
Attention. ड्रेसु, सुर्ति, सुचेती.
Attentive. हिकचितो, हेकमनो.
To be Attentive. जुटणु, दिलि लाइणु.
To Attract. छिकणु.
Avarice. लोभु. *See* Covetousness.
An Auction. निलामु.
The hall of Audience. कचहरी.
An Average. सरासरी.
To Avert. टारणु.
Averted. दफे.
An Auger. सराई, बर्मो.
Augmentation. वाधो, सर्सी, वाधि.
An Augurer. सौंणी.
Augury. सोणु. *See* Omen.
August, and part of September. बड्रो.
Aunt, (*father's sister*). पुफी, बुई, (*mother's sister*) मासी, (*father's brother's wife*) चाची, (*mother's brother's wife*) मामी.
Avocation, (*business*). कसबु, कमु, किर्ति.
Auspicious. सभागो, मंगलीकु, सगोरो, सदोरो, सुहारो, सोणाइतो, सगुणाइतो.
An Auspicious moment. महूरतु.
Authority, (*rule, power*). हुकूमत, पहुच, सगति. *See* Power.
Autumn. सरउ, कती, खरीफ.
The Autumn crop. कती, खरीफ.
To Await. वाट ड्रिसणु, तांघणु.
Awake. सुजागु, सुजाखो.
To Awake, (*act.*). जागाइणु.
Awful, (*terrible*). आफात, अघोरू.

An Awl. आर.
An Awn, or beard of corn. सिर.
An Awning. चंदो, साइबानु.
Awry (*crooked*). ड़िंगो, आड़ोटोड़ो.
An Axe. कुहाडो, तबर.
An Axle, Axletree. शोख, सराई.
Azure. आस्मानी.

B

To Baa (*like a sheep*). ब्राकारणु, ब्रेकणु.
A Babe, Baby. किकों, ब्रारू, ब्रालकु.
A Bachelor. कुंआरो, वांढो.
The Back. पुठि, पुठी.
The Back of a garment. पीछो.
The Back of the head. किआडी.
Behind one's Back. परपुठि.
To lie on the Back. पुठिअ भर पवणु, सैंओं पवणु.
Back (*again*). मोटी, वरी.
To Backbite. गिला करणु.
A Backbiter. गिलाखोरू.
Backbiting. गिला.
The Backbone. पुठि जो कंड़ो, करंघो, कण्घो.
The Backside. गुई, चुति;—a cheek of the B. चुतडु, दुड़ो.
Backwards. पुठोरो, उबतो.
Bad. बुछिडो, बुरो, मंदो, खराबु, बुछो, माडो.
Badness. मंदाई, बुछिडाई, &c.
A Bag. ग़ोथिरी, कोथिरी, खलीथो, (*of date mat*) पातु, पिंड़ो, (*of leather*) आछाडो, (*a fukeer's bag*) झोलो.
Baggage. मड़ो, शइशिकिलि.
Bail. जामिनी, जामिन्गीरी, खोलांदरी.
A Bailsman. जामिनु, जिमेदारु, जमानु, खोलांदरू.
A Bait. (*for fish*) ग़ाडु, (*for birds*) चूणो.
To Bake (*act*). पचाइणु.
A Baker. नान्वाई.
To Balance (*regulate scales, &c.*). काणि लाहणु, भहनु करणु.
Balance (*remainder*). बाकी, (*due in excess*) फाजिलो.
Bald. ठोड्हो.
A Bale. बारू.
A Ball (*to play with*). खेनो, खेन्हूडो, खेन्हो.
A Ball of thread. ढेरो, वेड्हो.
A Ball, or bullet. गोरी, गोली, तोरू.
A cannon Ball. गोरो, गोलो, तोरू.
The Ball of the foot. पबु.
A Ball of dough, butter, &c. चाणो.
A Ballad. गीतु, रागु.
A Balustrade. कटहडो.
A Bamboo. बांसु.
A Band (*for tying*). बंदु, पटो.
A Band (*of men*). गूलिरी, छुल्की, छुलिगो, (*of fukeers*) झुंडु, जमात. (*of thieves*) घलि, धाड, (*of musicians*) टोली.
A Bandage. पटो.
A Bandit. धाडेलु, फीरू.
To Banish. ड़ेह निकारणु, परड़ेहि कढणु.
Banishment. ड़ेहनिकारो.
The Bank of a river, &c. भरि, कपु, कंधी, ड़नी, कंठो, (*high*) कपरू, भिक.
A Bank of earth. दडो, (*dike*) कड, बंधि.
A Banker. सराफु, शराफु.
A Bankrupt. ड़ेवालो, खुटलु.
Bankruptcy. ड़ेवालु, ड़ेवालो, कंगणु, ड़ेवालाई.
A Banner. झंडो, नीशानु, बैरक.

A Bar. सराई, *(of a door)* ताडी.
Barbarian, Barbarous. झंगली, वाही, ठ्हरी.
A Barber. नाई, हजमु.
Barberries. जिरिश्क.
Barefooted. पेरें उघाडें.
Bareheaded. मथे उघाडो.
A Bargain. जाइज़ु, बोल.
A Barge. झम्टी.
The Bark of a tree &c. छिल, खल, छोड़ो.
To Bark *(trees)*. छिलणु.
The Bark of a dog. भौंक.
To Bark *(as a dog)*. भौंकणु, बहणु.
Barley. जउ.
Green Barley *(for cattle)*. खोइदु.
Of Barley. जाभो.
Barren *(a female)*. संढि, पछड, *(or land)* वांझ, *(a tree &c.)* खसी, सखिणो, ठल्हो.
The Barrenness of a female. संढिपाई, संढिपणु.
Base *(mean)*. नीचु, खुभारू, ओछो.
Bashful. लज़ारो, लज़ावानु, शर्माऊ.
Bashfulness. लज़, शरमु.
Basil. तुल्सी ; the leaf, दलु, ड़लु ; sweet basil, नाज़्बुई.
A Basin. चिल्मिची.
A Basket, *(various in form and material)*. खारो, खारी, सुंदु, सुंदिडो, टुक्रिणो, ड़ल्हो, चंगेलि, टोकिरो, दबकु, चंगारू, पिंड़ो, छबो, छली.
The Bass *(in music)*. खर्ज.
A Bastard. हरामी, हराम्ज़ादो.
A Bastion. बुर्जु, ठुलु.
A Bat *(the animal)*. चमिडो.
A Bat *(for playing)*. ड़ींको.
A Batch *(set)*. दफो.
To Bathe. विंह्जणु, धांइणु, सनानु करणु.
Bathing. सनानु, इश्नानु, तडु.
A Battalion. पल्टणि.
A Battery. मोर्चो.
A Battle. जंगि, जंगाहु, किलो.
A Battle-axe. तबर.
A Battle field. रिणु.
A Bawd *(procuress)*. धूती, भडुई.
To Bawl. दांह–वाको–करणु, बाकारणु, फाटणु, रडणु.
Bay-colored. कुमेदु, कुमेतु.
Bdellium. गुगुरू.
To Be. *(exist)* हुअणु, *(become)* थिअणु.
A Bead. मणिको, दाणो, गण्ढो.
A Beak. चुहुंब.
A Beam. काम, शह्तीरू, काठु.
The Beam of a balance. कानो.
A Beam of light. किरिणि, कनो.
To Bear. *(carry)* निअणु, *(support)* झलणु, थंभणु, *(suffer)* सहणु, जारणु.
A Bear. रिछु.
A Beard. ड़ाढ़ी, रीश, सुँहारी.
A Beast. जनावरू, जान्वरू.
A wild Beast. मिरू. *See* Wild.
A Beast of burden. वहिटु.
To Beat. मारणु, *(slightly)* झींगारणु, झींगार कढणु, *(severely)* कुडणु.
To Beat, *(as the pulse)*. हलणु, धवणु.
To Beat out, *(as metals)*. टपणु.
A Beating. मार.
Beatitude. मोखु, मुक्ति.
Beautiful. सुँहुणो, सुंदरू, हसीनु.
Beauty. सुँहुणाई, सुंह, सूंह, हुसिनु, सोभा.
Because of. वास्ते. *See* On Account of.
To Beckon. इशारो करणु.

To Become (*neu.*). थिअणु.
To Become (*befit*). जुग़ाइणु, सुँहणु, सुँहाइणु.
Becoming. लाइकु, जोगु, वडु, जुग़ाइतो, ठाहूको, ठाहू.
A Bed. पथर्णी, तूलि, (*with the couch*) सेज, (*on the ground*) पाथारी, (*of a river, &c.*) पेटु.
Bedding. हंधु, (*upper clothes*) दफु.
The foot of the Bed. पेरांदी.
The Bedhead. सेरांदी.
A Bed stead. खटोलो, मंजो, (*varieties*) खट, छपरखट, धौंरसरू.
To Bedust. लटणु.
A Bee. माखिअ जी मखि.
A Bee-hive, *or* Bee's nest. माखारो, छट्टो, मानारो.
A Beetle. टिंड्डिणु.
To Befall. पवणु.
Before. (*in front of*) साम्हो, साम्हो, साम्हुणे, रूबरू, अग़ियों, अगु में, (*in advance*) अग़े, महँदि.
Before (*in time*). अग़े, अगु में, पेहांई, महँदि, अग़ाहो.
A little Before. अग़ेरिडो, अग़िरो, महँदेरिडो.
To Beg, (*beseech q. v.*). लोलाइणु. *See* To Entreat.
To Beg (*alms*). पिनणु, गदाई करणु, मङणु.
A Beggar. पिनिणो, पेनारू, फकीरू.
Begging (*alms*). गदा, गदाई, पिन, बीख. *See* Entreaty.
To Begin. शुरू-आरंभु-करणु, सिटणु, मंड्णु.
A Beginning. शुरू, आरंभु.
To make a Beginning. पिडणुं.
On Behalf of (*another*). पारों, पारां.
To Behave. हलणु.
Behaviour. हलति, चालि, ढंगु, ढबु.
To Behead. सिसी वढणु.
Behind. पुठ्यों, पुठों, पुट्टते, पोइते.
A little Behind. पोईतांहें, पुहांओं.
Behind one's back. परपुटि.
To Behold. ड्सिणु. *See* To See.
A Belch. ओगिराई, ढ्कारू.
Belief. (*credit given*) वेसाहु, इतिबारू, (*theological*) सधां, सिदिकु. *See* Faith.
To Believe. वेसाहणु, सचु मञणु, विसाहणु.
A Bell. घंडु, घंटो, (*varieties*) घिंडिणो, खर्को, चडो, टलो, संघरू.
Bell-metal. कंझो, कुटि.
A Bellow. ट्राड़.
To Bellow. ट्ड़णु, रंभणु.
A pair of Bellows. धँवणि.
The Belly. पेटु, डोलु, ढिढु, (*of a pot*) भभरू.
To Belong. *The substantive verb* हुअणु *with the noun, standing for the possessor, in the genetive.*
Beloved. पिआरो, जानिनु, जानी.
Below. हेठि, हेठों, हेठां.
A Belt. चेल्हिबंदु.
A Bend. वरू, ड्रिंगु, टेकु, विंगु.
To Bend (*act.*) ड्रिंगो करणु, मोडणु, down निवडाइणु.
To Bend (*neu.*). वरणु, मुडणु, down झुकणु, निवणु, नूडणु, निउडणु.
Beneath. हेठि. *See* Below.
A Benediction. दुआ, आसीस.
A Benefactor. हित्कारी.
Beneficent. मिहिर्बानु, परमार्थो.
Beneficial. गुणाइतो, हित्कारी, गुणकारी. *See* Advantageous, Profitable.
A Benefit. (*favor*) थोरो, (*profit*) लाहो, फाइदो.

Benevolence. सज़णाई, नेकी, परमार्थुं.

Benevolent. परमार्थी; a benevolent person, सज़णु.

To be Benumbed. ठलिज़णु, ठंभिजणु.

Benzoin. लोबानु.

A Beryl. लसणो, ऐनुल्हुरू.

To Beseech. मिनथ &c. करणु, लीलाइणु.

Beseeching. मिनथ, नोजारी, वेनती, लीलिड़ाटीं, लील्डी.

Beside (*over and above*). सिवाइ, वाधू, धारीं.

Beside (*close to*). लग़ोलग़ि, सां, वटि.

To Besiege. वेड्हणु, घेरणु.

To Besmear, (*as a floor with mud-wash*). लिंबणु.

Bemearing, (*as a floor with a layer of mud &c.*). लेपणु, लेपो, पोचो, पोथो, भारोडो, चौंको.

A Besom. बुहारी, सुहारी.

To Bestow. ड़ेई ड़िअणु, बख्शणु.

A Bet. शर्त.

To Bet. शर्त हणणु.

Betel-leaf. पानु.

Betel-nut. सोपारी, सुंबो, (*varieties of*) चिकिनी, वाकुडी.

To Betray. द्रोहु करणु.

To Betroth *or* cause to Betroth. मङाइणु.

To be Betrothed. मङ्जणु.

A Betrothed girl. मङ.

A Betrothing. मङिणी,

Between. विचि, विच में, में.

To Bewail. भांहूं करणु. *See* To Lament.

To Beware. चेतणु, सँभालणु, साञाणणु.

Bewildered. मूड्हो, मुझुडो, हैरानु.

Bewilderment. मोंझारो, हैरानी.

To Bewitch. जादू &c. करणु.

A Bewitcher. जादूगरु, कामिणगोरु. टोणाई.

Bewitchment. जादू, कामिणु, टोणो.

Beyond. पर्यो, पर्येपासे, परे.

A Bezoar. जहरमुहुरो.

To Bid. चवणु.

A Bidding, (*order*). चयो.

A Bier. टट्टी.

Biestings, (*first milking*). पिसु, (*the next few milkings*) ब्ररही.

Big. वड़ो.

Bile. पितु.

The Bill of a bird. चुहुंब.

A Bill of exchange. हुंड़ी, (*duplicate*) पाँउठि, (*triplicate*) परपाँउठि, (*quadruplicate*) तडपाँउठिं, (*paid and cancelled*) खोखो.

To Bind. बंधणु.

The Binding a book. जुल्दबंदी, जुल्दबन्दी; the binding or cover, जुल्दु; different kinds of binding, बयाजी, मुकवा.

A Bird. पखी.

A Bird catcher. मारो.

Birth. ज़मु, जन्मु. *See* Childbirth.

A Birth-place. जन्मभुंइ, जन्मभुमि.

A Bit. टुकरु. *See* Piece, Scrap.

The Bit of a bridle. लगामु, (*of various kinds*) लसो, मोतीचूडु, कंड़ग्रारो, कंड़िरु, भत्याणु.

A Bitch. कुती.

A Bite. चकु, (*from a beast*) ड़ाढ्ह, (*of a snake*) ड़ंगु.

To Bite. चकु पाइणु, ड़ाढ्हणु, (*as a snake*) ड़ंगणु.

A Biter. चकिरु.

Bitter. कौडो.

Bitterness. कौडाई, कौडाणि.
To Blab. सलणु. *See* To peach.
A Blabber. चुगिलु.
Black. कारो, (*a horse*) मुश्की.
Somewhat Black, Blackish. कारांझिडो.
To grow Black. काराटिजणु.
A Black-guard. लुचु, लुचो, डुगानो, बांड़ो, लेख्यो. *See* Rascal.
Blackness. कारादुणि, काराणि, काराई.
A Black-smith. लुहरु, लुहारु.
A Bladder. मुट्टांगो.
The Blade of a knife, &c. फरु.
A Blade of grass. पनु.
The Blade-bone. फणि, हंझो.
Blameable. डुहारो, हर्फो.
Blame. ड़ोहु, हर्फु, (*imputation of a fault*) मयार.
To Blame. ड़ोहु &c. रखणु.
Blameless. बेड़ोहु, बेगुनाहु.
Bland. कुँअरो, गरिबु, मिठो.
Blandishment. नखिरो, नाजु, तालु, तानु, हावभाउ, चागु.
Blank. कोरो.
A Blanket. खथो, लोई, खथाई जोडो, कमरि.
A Blast. फूक, झुल्को, झूटो, झट्को.
A Blaze. मचु, भभटु, भभडु, भड़्क. *See* Flame.
To Blaze. ब्ररणु, भड़्कणु, भभूकणु, लहलहाइणु.
To Bleat like a sheep. ब्राकारणु, ब्रेकणु.
To Bleed (*neu.*). रतु-वहणु *or* ग़ाडणु.
To Bleed (*let blood*). सोर-फस्त-छोडणु.
A Blemish. ऐबु, औगुणु, दागु, कलंकु, कारंइं. *See* Defect.
To Bless. दुआ &c. करणु.
A Blessing. दुआ, आसीस.
Blind. अंधो, माजूरु, सूदासु, सूरो, अंधिडो.
Blind in one eye. काणो.
Blindness. अंधाई.
A Blister on the skin. फूक्रिणो, निफ, छालिणो, फोफींड़ो, छालो, फलूहो, फलूकिणो, लिफ.
A Block. अड़ो.
A Blockhead. भोंदू, बेवकूफु, मूढु, अहमकु, ठुठु, ड़हरो, जहलो, बुजू, बेअकुलु, हुडु, कुंदु, कुंदु, अनाडो, कुजटु, गँवारू, लटु, झब्लू, ड़ुडु, भूकड़ाडहो, भूकु, मूर्खु, बुजु, झबू, ग़हेलो, ग़ल्हो, जडु, बुंड़ो, मोंगो, विसो, ओडु.
Blood. रतु, लोहू.
Bloody, stained with Blood. रतोरत्नि.
A Blossom. फुलु, गुलु, (*of a fruit tree*,) बूरु,
To Blossom. खिडणु, फुटणु, फुलणु.
A Blot. चुटो, चिटो.
A Blotch. लसणु.
A Blow. धकु, मार, टोकर, ठोंसो, फहको, ठोक. *See* Box, Knock.
To Blow, (*as the wind*). लग़णु.
To Blow, (*with the breath*). फूकणु, (*with bellows &c.*) धँवणु.
To Blow, (*as a flower*). खिडणु, फुलणु, टिडणु.
To Blow the nose. नकु-सुंघणु, *or* सुण्कणु.
Blubber, (*fat of fish*). सोफो.
Blue. नीरो, माभो.
A Blunder. भुल.
To Blunder. भुलणु.
Blunt. मुड़ो, मुनो, बुंड़ो, लमो, लाभो, रूंड़ो.
A Boar. सुअरु.
A Board. फरहो, तख्तो,

Boarded (*a floor or ceiling*). तख्तापोशु.
To Boast. दम हणणु, पड़णु, मकंणु.
A Boaster. बटाकी, टर्डो, फटाकी.
Boasting, a Boast. पडु, लाफ, टडाई, मर्कु, दमु, बटाक, फटाक.
A Boat. बेडी, (*large*) बेडो, (*various kinds of boats*) झम्टी, जौरक, दंगी, नावक, डूंडो, डूंडी, कौंतल, बतेलो, सीतपुडो, मछुओ, सूही.
A Boatman. मोर्वहरू, मुहाणो, नाखुंओ.
A Bobbin (*weaver's*). नांणाड़ो.
A Bodice, (*various fashions of such*). चोली, गजु, अंगी, कंजुरी, पेपिनी.
A Body. जुसो, बुतु, देहि, सरीरू, बदनु, तनु.
A Body, or person (*familiar term*). जिअड़ो.
A headless Body. धडु.
The Body-cloth of a horse, &c. झुल.
A Body of individuals (*of any class*). राजु. *See* Band.
Of or pertaining to such a Body. राज़िको, राज़ाइतो, राज़ाणो.
To Boil (*neu.*). टुहकणु, उब्रिरणु, कढ़हणु, फफ्कणु.
To Boil (*act.*). उब्बारणु, टुहकाइणु, काढ़हणु, (*cook in water*) रँधणु.
To Boil up, or over. उभामणु.
To Boil, *or* be Boiled, (*cooked in water*). रझणु.
A Boil, *or* Boiling. उब्बारो, टुहको.
A Boil, *or* Bile. फुर्डी, दुंबिडो, रग़ाडडु, कोडो, ग़ाडडु, फिरूडो.
Bold. बेभओ, निर्भउ, बेपर्वाहु, निधडु, निधड़कु, हिमथभर्यो. *See* Courageous.
Boldness. बहादुरी, हिमथ, ठेंगेमड़ी, सत्था. *See* Courage.

A Bolster. विहाणो, सिराणो.
The Bolt of a door. ताडी.
To Bolt. ताडी-विझणु *or* पाइणु.
A Bond, (*tie*). बंधणु.
A written Bond. अंगुडो, कबूजु, खतु.
A Bond of agreement. कबूलिभत.
A Bone. हडु, हड़ो, हड़ी, (*of a fish &c.*) कंड़ो.
Bones remaining after the cremation of a body. फुलु, संखो, संखु.
Bony, full of bones. कंड़िरू.
A Book. किताबु, पोथी, पुस्तकु, पोथु, (*small*) गुटिको.
A bag or cover for a Book. पोटिडी, बोफिली.
A Book-binder. जुल्द बंधणवारो, मुजुल्दी.
A Boon. दानु, वरू, बक्शीश.
A Boot. मोजो.
Borax. सुहागो, कंगणखारू *f.*
Border. किनारो, कनी, अंदी.
To Bore. सलु-टुंगु-करणु, सलणु, (*pearls &c.*) विंधणु, (*the ear or nostril*) टोपणु.
To be Born. ज़मणु, ज़ापणु.
To Borrow. उधारणु, मङ्यो-उधारो-कर्जु-वठणु.
Borrowed. मङ्यो.
The Bosom. उरहु. *See* Breast.
Both. बई, बेई.
To Bother. खपाइणु, अकाइणु. *See* To Annoy.
To be Bothered. हलाखु-ककि-थिअणु.
A Bottle. शीशो, बुती.
The Bottom part of any thing. तरो, हेठु.
Of the Bottom. हेठ्यों.
Bottom (*power of endurance*). अथकाई.

A Bough. ड़ारू. *See* Branch.
Bound. (*tied*) ब्रधो, (*in bonds*) बंदि.
To be Bound. ब्रझणु, ब्रधिजणु.
A Boundary. दंगु, संधो, सोंभ, सोम, हद.
Boundless. बेहदि, अपारू, बेअंतु.
Bountiful. ड़ातारू, सखी. *See* Generous.
To Bow. निंवणु, नंवणु, निउडणु, नमणु, नूडणु.
To Bow down (*in reverence*). मथो टेकणु.
A Bow (*weapon*). सीड़, कमान.
A Bow-shot. तीर जो पंधु.
A Bow-string. जिहु, नारू.
Bowing. निउडत, निंवति, (*down in prayer*) सिड्दो.
A Bowl. कटोरो, वटो, फेलो, पिआलो, उठपेरो.
A Box. संदूक, पेती, (*small*) सूंगो, दबुलो, दबुलो, संदूकिडो, सुंगु, कूती.
A Box with the fist. लुग्तो, मुक, घुपितो, घूसो.
A Boy. छोकरू, छोकिरो, नींगरू, छुहिरू, ग़भुरू, छोकिराटु.
Boyhood. छोकिराई.
Boyish. छोकिराणो.
A Brace (*of birds*). ढुंगु.
A Bracelet (*various forms*). पहुंची, कंगणु, वाढोलो, कतिर्यो, चूडि, चूड़ो, कंगिणी, दस्तो, तोंकु, मंग्लो, मोरो, संघी, सिधबालो. *See* Arm ornaments.
Brackish. खारो.
A Brahman. बांभणु, ब्राह्मणु.
A Braid of hair in front. मींढी, मनहडो.
The Brain. मिञु *f.* मिखु *f.* मिज़, मज़ालो, मग़्ज़ु, मेज़ालो.

Bran. कतर *plu:*, तुह *plu:*, छाणु.
A Branch. टारी, ड़ारी, शाख, लाम
A Brand (*mark*). दागु, ड़ंभु.
To Brand. दागु ड़िभण, ड़ंभणु, दागणु.
A Branding instrument. ड़ंभिणी
Brass. पितलु.
A Brave man. सूरिहु, बहादुरू, सूमों. *See* Hero.
Of a Brave man. सूरिहाणो, सूर्माणो.
Bravery. सूरिहाई, बहादुरी, सूर्माई.
Bravo. शाबसि, वाहुवाहु, छाबसि, अश्कु.
To Bray. हींगणु.
Brazen. पेतिली.
A Brazier. ठांठारो.
Bread. मानी, रोटी, नानु. *See* Food.
Breadth. वेकिराई, वरू, पेटु, मोकरि.
A Breadth of cloth. ड़रू, तकु.
To Break (*act.*). भञणु, टोड़णु, तोड़णु, फोड़णु, (*a rope*) छिनणु.
To Break (*neu.*). भज़णु, टुटणु, (*as a rope*) छिजणु, (*as day*) फुटणु.
The Break of day. पिरिहफुटी.
Breakfast. नेरनि.
The Breast. छाती, उरहु, हिंओ, कोडो, सोनो.
Breath, साहु, दमु, पसाउ.
A Breeze. होर, तवार, हवार.
A Bribe. वढी, लबु, रूश्वत, शोणी.
To Bribe. वढी *etc.* ड़िभणु, लवणु.
One who takes Bribes. लपो.
A Brick. सिर.
A Brickbat. सिरोटो.
A Bricklayer. राजो.
A Brickmaker. सिरबंदु.
A Bride. कुंआरि, लाड़ी, वनी.
Of a Bride's family. कुंआरेतो.
One of the Bride's party. मात्री.
A Bridegroom. घोटु, लाड़ो, वनो, वरू, वनहडो.

Of a Bridegroom's family. घोटेतो.
The Bridegroom's party. ज़ञ.
One of the Bridegroom's party. ज़ान्नी.
A Bridge. बंधि, फुडि, पुलि, दमदमो.
A Bridle. कयांडी, लगामु.
Bright. ऊजलु, जोतिवारो, (*in color*) चहरो.
To Brighten (*make bright*). चिम्काइणु, चिल्काइणु, झल्काइणु.
To Brighten (*become bright*). चिम्कणु, चिल्कणु, झल्कणु.
Brightness. चमक, झल्क, ऊझलाई, कला, चिल्को, झल्को, भडक, चिल्काटु, चिल्कति.
The Brim of any thing. कनो. *See* Edge.
Brimful. भरपुरि, कनाकनि, टिम्टारु, तारातूरु, तारि.
Brimstone. गंद्रफु, गोगिडू, आव्लासारु.
To Bring. आणणु, वठी अचणु.
To Bring up. निपाइणु, पालणु.
To Bring forth. (*young*) ज़णणु, (*be delivered*) विआमणु.
A Brinjal (*vegetable*). वाङणु.
A Brink. भरि, कपु, कनो.
Brittle. ठाकुंभों.
Broad. वेकिरो, मोकिरो, कुशादो.
Broad-cloth. बनात.
Brocade. कीम्खाबु, जर्बफ़्तु, तासु.
Broken. भग़लु, भग़ो.
A Broker. दलालु.
Brokerage, *or* Brocage. दलालो.
A Brood of young birds. तुरु, झोलो.
A Broom. बुहारी, सुहारी.
Broth. रहो. *See* Soup.
A Brother. भाई, भाउ, अदो; elder brother, दादो.
A Brother-in-law. (*husband's brother*) ड़ेरु, ग़ोरो, (*wife's brother*) सालो, (*sister's husband*) भेणीविओ, (*wife's sister's husband*) संढू.
Brotherhood. भाईचारी, भाईबंदी, भाउराई, बिरादरी.
Brotherless. निभायो.
To Browbeat. साघणु, दबाइणु.
Brown. खाकी, फाख्ताई, भूरो, (*hair, complexion*) कको, भूरो, (*a horse*) समंदु.
A Bruise. चोट, धकु, रिणु, *See* Dint.
To Bruise. चिभाटणु, चिथाडणु, चिपणु.
A Brush made of hair. कूचो, वारोचो, (*for flies*) चौंरी, चौंरु. *See* Broom.
Brushwood. झतरि, झातरि.
Brutal. मिरूंभको.
Brutality. मिरूंपणु.
A Bubble. फोटो, फूकिणो, बुद्बुदो.
A Bubbling noise, (*as of a hooka in smoking*). बुड्को, बुड्बुडि.
A Bubby. बुबो, बुबी, (*small, of a girl*) डुकू.
A Bubo. वेलणि, ग़नरि.
A Bucket of leather. ड़ोल्वी, बोको, चडही, ड़ोलु.
A Buckle. जबानो.
A Bud. कली, मुखिरी, अखि.
A Buffalo. (*male*) पाड़ो, सानु, (*female*) मेंहि, मंझ, (*calf*) वछ. *See* Calf.
Of a Buffalo. माझो, माहो.
A Buffalo-herd. मेहारु.
A herd of Buffalos. मेहागु.
A Buffet. मुक. *See* Blow, Box, Slap.

A Bug. मुंघिणु.
Bugloss. गाजिबां.
To Build. अड़णु, जोडणु, ओसारणु.
To Build up, or close up, (*a door-way, &c.*). चुणणु.
A Building. अड़ावत, अड़ा, अड़ति.
A Bull. ढ़ांदु, ढग़ों ; a free bull, आनिरू, साणु.
A Bullet. गोरी, गोली, तीरू.
A Bullock. ढग़ो, ढ़ांदु, (*young*) वहुडों ; a plough bullock, हारी ; a pack bullock, पोठी, बारी ; one trained to a water wheel, नारी.
A Bullock-driver. ढ़ांदाई, ढग़ाई.
To Bully. सूटणु, झिण्कणु, दबाइणु.
A Bump. ग़ोड़हों.
A Bunch. छुगों.
A Bundle. ग़ंढिडी, हड, (*of clothes*) बुडकों, (*of grass, &c.*) गडों, बंदु, लड़.
A Burden. बारू.
A Burial-ground. सुकासु.
To Burn (*act.*). खांइणु, साडणु.
To Burn (*neu.*). बुरणु ; away (*be consumed*), खामणु, सडणु, जलणु.
A Burning ground. सरू, मसाणु.
To Burnish. मलणु, चिलकाइणु.
A Burnisher. तेविरो.
To Burst (*act.*). फाडणु, फेहणु.
To Burst (*neu.*). फाटणु, फिसणु, फुटणु.
A Burst of passion, &c. छुहो, झट्कों. *See* Fit.
To Bury. पूरणु, निहुरणु.
A Bush. बूडों, बूटो, वणु.
Business. कमु, हाज, कमुकाजु, काजु, धंधों, कमुं.
A Bustle, Bustling. हलचलि.
Busy. रुधो.
To be Busy. रुभणु.

But. पर, पण.
A Butcher. कासाई, नहरीवारू.
To Butt. थूनो–टकरू-हणणु.
Butter. मखणु.
Clarified Butter, or *Ghi*. गिहु.
Ghi &c. put into bread. मोइणु, मोणु; bread prepared with *Ghi*, &c. ग़ाभुओ, मोण्यो.
A seller of clarified Butter, or *Ghi*. गेही.
To Butter. पाराठणु.
A Butterfly. पोपटु.
Buttermilk. झणि, मही, छाछि, खटो, छाहि.
The act of Butting. थूनो, टकरू.
A Buttock. चुतडु, टुडो.
A Button. ब्रीडो, ब्रीडो, तुकिमों.
A Button hole, or loop for the button. फाही, फांदि, कडो.
To Buy. गिन्हणु, मुल्हि वठणु, खरिद करणु, विहाइणु, वण्जणु.
Buying. खरीद.
Buying and selling. ढ़ेनोलेतो.
A Buzz, Buzzing. भूंभूं, भूण्कार, भुण्भुणि, भुण्कों. *See* Hum.
By. (*denoting instrument*) सां, साणु, सें, (*cause*) करें, सें, (*agent*) खां, कनों.

C

A Cable. नोडु, (*for fastening boats*) पग़ाहु.
A Cage. पिञिरो.
A flat Cake, of flour (*of various kinds*). रोटी, मानी, टिकी, ढ़गिडो, लुची, पूरी, फुलको, ढ़ग़ाडु, उफिराटो.
A thick Cake. रोटिलो, रोटु.
A Calamity. आफति, विपति, घाणी, बला, मुसीबत, आपदा.

To Calculate. ग़णणु, सारणु, लेखो करणु.
Calculation. ग़ण्ती, लेखो, हिंसाबु, सार.
A Caldron. देगि.
A Calf. गाबो; buffalo's (*male*), कूंहो, पाड़ो, (*female*) वछ, पाड़ी.
The Calf of the leg. बुकी, पिनी.
A Call. सडु, हकल, सड़ो, कोठो.
To Call. कोठणु, सड़णु:
To Call out. दांह-रडि-करणु. *See* To Bawl.
Callous. ड़ाढो, सख़्तु.
A Calm. निवाई, गविरो, घुट.
To Calm. लाहणु, सांति करणु. *See* To Appease.
To grow Calm. ठहरणु.
Calmness. सांति, ठहर.
To Calumniate. ड़ोहु-लेउ-लग़ाइणु.
Calumny. लेउ, लीभ, तूफानु.
Cambric. नैन्सुखी, जगन्नाथी.
A Camel. (*male*) उठु, ड़ाघो, लेडो, (*female*) उठि, ड़ाची, लेडी, (*young suckling*) गोरो, गौरो, तोडो, (*of various ages*) माजादु, मजाकु, धपडु, ट्रिहाणु, कँवाटु, छटु, दोकु, दुअकु, चौगो, नेशु, अमोंशु.
A strong Camel. बुग्दी.
A riding Camel. महरी, सांड़िणी.
Of a Camel. ओठो.
Camel's hair. मिलिस.
A Camel-man. ओठारू, जतु.
A Camel-rider. ओठी.
A Camp. उडदु.
A Camp-follower. उड्दाई.
A Campaign. मुहीम.
Camphire. कपूरू.
A Canal (*of various sizes*). वाहु, वंगो, वंझी, वाहुडु, कूर, कूल, कस्यो. *See* Water course.
The tail part of a Canal. पुछिडी.
A Canal-digger. खाम्डिओ.
A Canal-measurer. खाच्रू.
Canal-digging. खाटी.
To Cancel. मेटणु, फेरणु, रदि करणु.
Cancer (*the Sign*). कर्कु.
Candid. सँभोँ, सुधो.
A Candle. शमा.
A Candle stick. शमादानु.
A Cane. *See* Reed, Rattan, &c.
A Cannon. तोफ.
A Cannon-ball. गोलो, गोरो, तीरू.
A Canopy. चंदो, साइबानु.
A Cantonment. देरो, लश्करू.
A Cap. टोपी, टोपु, (*pointed, of a fukeer*) दलकु, ताजु.
Capable. रजाऊ, रसाकारू. *See* Fit.
Capital (*stock*). मूडी, मूरू.
Capricious. पूरारो, मौजी, लहरी.
Capricorn. मकरू.
To Captivate. झलणु, बंदणु, (*the understanding or affections*) वसि करणु, मोहणु.
To be Captivated. फसणु.
A Captive. बंदी.
Captivity. झल, बंदु, कैदु.
A Car. गाड़ी.
A Caravan. साथु.
A Caravansary. सराहि.
A Carcase. लोथ, ढूंढु. *See* Corpse.
To Card (*cotton*). पिञणु, (*with the fingers*) तुंबणु.
An instrument (*a bow*) for Carding. पिञणि.
A Carder of cotton. पीञारो, कासाई.
A pack of Cards, or the game. गंजिफो.
One Card of a pack. ताकी.

Care. (*carefulness q. v.*) संभाल, संभार, सांढ, टहोड, तांति, सोघाई, (*heed, regard*) सांगों, पर्वाह, गर्ज, सांग, गूंदरू, उल्को.

To Care for (*heed*). उल्को करणु, साङाहणु.

To have Care. संभालणु, साङाहणु, चेतणु.

To take Care of. सांढणु, सोघे-संभाले-रखणु, सहेडणु, तातणु, सांभणु, जांकणु.

Free from Care. अगूंदिरो.

Requiring Care, Carefully. भवाइतो, भवहथीकेां.

Careful. खबर्दारू, सुचेतु.

Carefulness. सहेड, सांढ, जतनु, सांभ, खबर्दारी. *See* Care.

Careless. बेखिओ, गाफिलु.

Carelessness. गाफिली, बेसाङाहो, अचेताई.

Caresses, Caressing. लाडु, चुमाचाटी, हाउभाउ, पिआरू.

A Carpenter. वाढो, डुखणु, सूटहड़ु.

A Carpet. गिल्मु, फरासी, फर्शु, ट्पड़ु, गालीचो, गिआलो.

Carriage (*for conveying*). वहिटुवाडो.

A Carrot. गजर, गजर पिताई, सिंधी गजर; pickled carrots, आहुरी, कुर्कुटो.

To Carry. खणणु, ढोइणु.

To Carry away. खणी वञणु, निभणु.

To Carry through. निभाइणु. *See* To Complete.

To Carry on. हलाइणु. *See* To Conduct.

Expense of Carrying. खणाणी, ढुआणी, ढुआई.

A Cart. छकिड़ो, गाड़ो, गाड़ी.

A Carter. गाड़ेवानु.

A Cartridge-box. किस्बत.

To Carve (*cut out*). उकिरणु, खोटणु.

A Case in law. मामिलो.

A Case. (*cover*) खानो, (*of cloth*) पोशु, छँव, (*over merchant's stores*) बार्दानो.

Cash. रोकिड़ो, रोकु, रोकडि, नगदु, नग्दी.

To Cash a bill. भरणु.

A Cashewnut. खाज़ो.

Cassia, lig. तज.

Cassia, fistula. अमल्दासु.

The leaf of the Cassia laurus. कमालपटु.

To Cast (*throw.*) हणणु, उछिले-उछिलाए-हणणु.

To Cast away. फिटो करणु, उछिलणु, उछिलाइणु.

To Cast (*metals*). पल्टणु, ढारणु.

Cast in a mould. पाल्टू.

A Cast (*tribe*). जाति.

Of good or high Cast. जातीरो.

The Castle at chess. रुखु.

The Castor oil plant. हेरणु.

To Castrate. (*a man*) खोजो करणु, (*brutes*) खसी-कुटु-करणु.

A Cat. बिली, फूस्नो, मिनो, फूसी.

A Catamite. गांडू, गुयरू, चुतु, भ्रोटणु.

To Catch. झलणु, (*as a thing falling*) झटणु.

Cat-gut. जिडु, नारू.

A Caterpillar. सूबटु.

Cat's-eyed. शेरो, शिमिरो.

Cattle. ढोर *plu.*

A Cattle-pen. वाडो, वथाणु. *See* Pen.

Cavalry. अस्वार *plu.* सवार *plu.*

A Cave. गुफा, चुर.

A Caviller. बहझो, कदी, जिदी.

A Cavity. पोरू.

To be Caught (*to stick, or be ensnared*). फासणु, फसणु, अड़णु.

A Cause. सबबु, वास्तो, कारणु.

To Cause. कराइणु. When this verb is used governing another, it is expressed by putting the latter into its causal form.

Causelessly. नाहकु, दादेनइस्तादे, हरूभरू, खामखाइ.

A Cause-way. ब्रंथि.

To Cauterize. ड़ंभणु, दागणु.

A Cautery. ड़ंभु, फुलु.

Caution, Cautiousness. सुर्ति, साड़ाह, सुचेती.

Cautious. सुचेतु, सुर्तो, ग़ागू.

To Caw. कांकां करणु.

To Cease (*act.*). बसि-बंदि-करणु.

To Cease, (*neu.*). बसि-बंदि-थिअणु, दिही वञणु.

A Ceiling. छिति, छति; various kinds of ceilings, तखतापोशु, चादरपोशु, मुसत्ता, तीलीदारू.

Celebrated. नामूसवारो, नामो, नामवरू, नामदारू. *See* Famous.

A Cellar. बुहुरो, (*for hiding things in*) गुझट.

Per Cent. सैकिड़ो.

A Centipede. सौपेरो, कनसोपारी.

The Centre. विचु, दुनु.

Centuple. सऊणो.

A Century. सदी.

A Ceremony (*religious rite*). क्रिआ, क्रिआकर्मु, पूजापाठु.

Certain. जाई, सही, तकारू, निहिचे, तहकीकु, चिटो, खुतो.

Certainly. अलबत, जरूरु, हरूभरू, अवसि, मड़हीं, मुकररु. *See* Certain.

A Certainty. निहिचो, पक, काथो, नेमु.

Cerumen. कन जो मरू.

Chaff. बुहु, (*husk of different grains*) तुह, बुरी, बुहो, बुहीं, डुही.

Chaffering. रीड़पीड.

A Chain. जंजीरू, संघर.

A Chair. कदेल, गदेल.

Chalk. खड़ो, खेड़ी.

A Chamber. कोठो, कोठी.

Chance. कजा.

By Chance. ओचितो. *See* Accidentally.

To Change. मटणु, मटाइणु, फेरणु.

A Chaplet of flowers. सिहिरो.

A Chapter. बाबु, अध्याउ, ध्याउ.

Character. नांउ, (*good*) आबिरूइ, पति.

Charcoal. कोइला *plu.* अङर *plu.*

A Charge. (*accusation*) दावा, (*false*) चब, अड़ो.

Charge (*trust*). जिमो.

In Charge. हवाले, बिले, जिमे.

Recommending to one's Charge. पर्न, पारत, सुपारत.

Charitable. धर्मी.

Charity. दानु, ड़ानु, धर्मु, बीख, खैरात.

Given in Charity. धर्माऊ, खैरांती.

A Charm. मंत्रु, मंडु, मंटु, फीणो, मोहिनो, टोटिको, इसिमु. *See* Amulet.

To Charm. मोहणु, (*as a remedy*) झाड़णु.

A Charmer. मांड्रो. *See* Bewitcher.

Charming. सुहाईंदो, मोहनु.

Chaste. सती, जती.

Chastisement. सेखति, मार.

Chastity. सतु, जतु.

Chat. गाल्हि. *See* Talk.

To Chatter. बकणु, झकणु, जखणु, टौंकणु, बड़बड़ाइणु, लवणु.

A Chatterer. जखी, झकी, बकवादी, बक्बक्यो.

Chattering. च बोलो, चौबोलो, चिभों-भिभों, टांटां, टॉको, लर्लरि, सुर्पुरि, बक्बकि, बड्बडि, लड्लडि.

Cheap. सहांगो, *(fallen in price)* मोडो.

Cheapness. सहांगाई, सुकरू, मोडो,

To Cheat. ठग़णु. *See* To Deceive.

A Cheat. ठगु, ठग्बाज़ु, ढोंगी, ड्रोही, गिदरू, धपाई.

To be Cheated. ठग़ाइणु, ठग़िजणु.

Cheating. धपो, धोंधो, गिदी, धोखो, धोपो. *See* Deceit.

To Check *(restrain)*. झलणु, अट्-काइणु, रोकणु, पलणु.

A Check. झल, अट्काउ, रोक.

Check *(at chess)*. शह.

Checkmated. मातु.

A Cheerful person. खुशिजिभडो, खुश्दिली.

The Cheek. ग़लु, गिटो, मिट.

A Cheese. पनीरु.

Chess. शतंजि.

A Chess-board. बिसात.

The Chest. उरहु, छाती.

Chestnut *(a horse)*. बोरु.

To Chew. चबणु, चबाडणु.

The noise made in Chewing. चबूकों.

To Chide. छीभणु, झिण्कणु, दड्को ड्रिभणु.

Chief. वड़ो.

A Chief. सर्दारु, पर्यो मुसु, चडो मुसु, सर्कर्दो, रैसु, सिर्दारु, सिर्ताजु, *(among traders)* मुखी, *(of fishermen &c.)* कलांतिरी.

A Child. ब़ारु, ब़चो, ब़ालकु, विभाउ, *(as still wanting discretion)* महसूमु, भलडु.

Child-birth. विभमु. *See* Lying in.

Child-hood. बारपणो, छोकिराई, ब़ाराई.

Childish. ब़ाराणो, छोकिराणो.

Childless. निपुटो.

One having many Children. ग़भोराडो.

To grow Chill. ठरणु, सिभाटिजणु.

A Chimney. बुखारो, गुजारो.

A Chin. खाड़ी, ठोडो.

China-root. चोब्चीनी.

China-ware. चीनी.

A Chink. चीरु.

Chints. छीट.

A Chip. टोटो.

The Chirping of a bird. तंवार.

A Chisel. रंबो, रंबी; a large kind of chisel, पतासो रंबो.

A Choice. इख्त्यारु.

Without Choice. अवसि, बेवसि.

To Choke *(act.)*. घुटणु, ब़ूसाटणु, घोघो ड्रिभणु.

Cholera morbus. वबा.

To Choose. धुणणु, चूंढणु, पसंदि करणु.

A Chooser. धूणो, चूंडो.

To Chop. वढणु, चिथणु, चिचिरणु, ड्रिरणु, *(straw)* कुतिरणु, टुकणु.

Chopped straw. कुतिरि.

A Chord *(string)*. तार.

A Churn, or pot used as such. चाड़ी, कुनो.

To Churn. विलोडणु.

A Churn-staff. मांधाणी, मथिभडो.

Cinnamon. दारचीनी.

A Cipher *(mark for nothing)*. बुडो.

A Circle. चकरु, चकिरी, पिडु, दाइरो.

A Circuit. फेरु, वरु.

To Circumcise. तुहिरणु.

Circumcision. तोहरू, तहोरू, तुहिरू, सुनत, सथिरी.
The operator in Circumcision. बुभो.
A Circumference. घेरो, गलि, गिर्दो.
Circumspect. ग़ाणू. *See* Cautious.
A Circumstance. ग़ाल्हि.
Circumstances (*state*). हवालु, हालु, ड़सा.
Circumvention. पेचु, वरू, दब्बो, अग़वंधी, बाजी.
A Citron. तुरंजु.
A City. शहरू, नगरू.
A Claim. दावा, (*false*) चत्र, अड़ी, इश्केलु.
A Claimant. दांहो, (*false*) चत्रिरू, चत्रारो.
Clamour. गोड़ु, हुलु, लुड़, गोगाउ. *See* Outcry.
To Clamour. गोड़ु &c. करणु.
A Clang, Clangour. ठकुठकि, ठड़्की, ठकाठुकी, ठकाउ.
Claret-colored. सोसिनो.
To Clasp. झलणु, दबे वठणु.
A Clasp-knife. चाकू.
A Class (*order*). दफो.
A Claw. नँहुँ, चंबो.
To Claw. नँहँडुणु, रहँडुणु.
Clay. चीकी मिटी, (*for plaster*) भंजू.
Clean. सफा, साफु, फुटिरो, ऊजलु.
To Clean. सफा &c. करणु.
To Clean by rubbing. माञणु, मलणु.
To Clean grain. छड़्हणु, छंड़ुणु.
Cleanliness, Cleanness. सफाई, ऊजलाई.
Clear. साफु, सफ़ा, फुटिरो, (*not confused*) चिटो.
Clear-spoken. सलंजिबानु.
To Clear up (*the weather*). ओका-णणु, हीउ खणणु.

The Clearing up of the weather. ओचीडो.
A Cleft. ड़ारू, फांउ.
Clemency. ब्राझ, रहमु, दया.
Clement. ब्राझभर्यो, रहमी, दयालु.
A Clerk. महरड़ु, कारिगरी, लेखारी.
Clever. भड़ु.
A Clew of thread. ढेरो.
A Clew (*trace*). सगु, ड़सु.
Climate. वाउपाणीm.
To Climb. चड़्हणु.
A Climber. चाड़्हो.
To Clip. कतिरणु.
A Cloak. गुंधिगु, लबादो.
A Clod. भितरू, खड़ो.
A Clocking hen. कुड़्कि कुकिड़ि; her nest of eggs, आरो.
To Close (*act.*). पूरणु, वराए छड़्णु, बंदि करणु, ढेकिड़णु, लग़ाइणु.
To Close (*contract the hand, eyes, &c.*). भीड़णु, ब्रूटणु, मिटणु.
To Close (*neu.*). लग़ी-पूर्जी-पवणु, बंदि थिअणु.
Close (*near*). लग़ोलगि, लाग़ोतो, भरि सां.
Close (*dense, thick,*). घाटो, गहरो.
Closeness of weather. घुट, काड़्हो, ड़ेभो. *See* Sultriness.
Closeness (*from want of ventilation*). गुफो.
Cloth. कपिड़ो, (*woollen*) बनात.
To Clothe. ढकाइणु, पहराइणु.
A Cloth merchant. बजाजु.
Clothes. कपिड़ा *plu.* लुग़िड़ा *plu.* गंढु *plu.* *See* Apparel.
A suit of Clothes. वग़ो, पोशाख.
A Cloud. ककरू, बदलु, बादलु, मेघु; a light cloud, उब्र.
Cloudiness. झुड़ु, झुड़ालो, सारंगु.
Cloudy weather. लसी, लसु, रुहो.

A Clove. लांगु.

To be Cloyed. ढ्राइजणु, ढ्रापणु. *See* To be Satiated.

A Club. लठि ; various kinds of clubs सोटो, धुको, लोड्रू, घोत्रारो, कुतिको, डंड़ो; (*of iron*), गुर्ज.

A Cluster of grapes, *&c.* छुगो, गोशो.

A Clump of trees. हुडी, खोड्डी.

To Coagulate. ज़मणु.

A Coagulator for milk. संवाणु.

A Coal. (*live*) टांड़ो, जाग़िनो, अ-ङ्गरू, (*dead*) कोइलो, अङरू.

Coarse. खहुरो.

A Coat. कुर्तो, गिड़ो.

Cobbling. गंढिणी.

A Cobweb. ज़ारो.

Cochineal. किर्मिची.

A Cock. कुकुडु.

A Cockade. तुरो.

A Cockroach. तिड़ो, मकिडी.

The Cockscomb flower. कलंगो.

A Cocoanut. नाइरू, नारेलु.

The kernel of a Cocoanut. गोरो, कोपिरो.

One half of a split Cocoanut. ड़ूंघो.

The fibres round a Cocoanut. का-ब्रारु.

The Codpiece in drawers. ब्रची.

Coffee. काहू, भुनु.

The Cog of a wheel. अरो.

A Coil. वरू, पेचु.

Coin, Coinage. छिको, जर्ब.

Cold (*adj.*). थधो, सर्दु, सीतलु.

Cold (*sub.*). सीउ, थधि, सर्दी.

A Cold. थधि, लेसु, (*in horses*) सर्गीरू.

The Cold season. सिआरो.

To grow Cold. ठरणु.

Coldness. थधाई, थधाणि, सर्दी.

The Collar of a garment. गिरेबानु.

A dog's Collar. पटो.

To Collapse. भीड़जणु, कूमाइजणु.

To Collect (*act.*). गडु-कठो-हेकां-दो-करणु, मेडणु.

To Collect (*debts, &c.*), उग़ाडणु, वसूलु करणु.

Collected. जमा, गडु, हेकांदो.

To be Collected. मिडणु ; (*debts, taxes, &c.*) उग़िडणु.

Collecting, Collection. उग़ाड, ओ-ग़ाहो, ओग़ाडि, वसूलु, तहसील.

A Collector of taxes. तहसीलदारु; of outstanding debts, उग़ाड़ू, ओ-ग़ाह्यो.

A Collector-ship. तहसीलदारी.

Collyrium. सोईरो, सुर्मो.

Coloquintida (*bitter apple*). टूहु.

A Colour. रङु, वरनु.

To Colour. रङणु.

A Colt. वछेरो.

A Comb. फणी, फणोटो.

A Comb-maker. फणीगरु.

To Comb. फणी ड़िभणु.

To Come. अचणु.

To Come out. निकिरणु.

A Comet. चोट्यरु-चोट्यांओ-पुछड़-गु-तारो.

Comfort. तसलाई, धीज़ु, सुखु.

Comfortable. सुखी, सुख्यो, सौखो.

In Coming and going. इंदडिवेंदडि, ओटमोट.

A Command. हुकुमु, आग्या.

To Command (*order*). हुकुमु करणु, फर्माइणु.

A Commander. सर्दारु. *See* A Chief.

Commendation. शाबसि, साराह. *See* Praise.

A Commentary. टीका, शरहु.

Commerce. वकाती, वणिजुवापारू.

A Commission (*paper conveying authority*). सनद, दस्तावेज़ु.

To Commit, or do. करणु.

Common. आम.

A Companion. साथी, संगी, संगती, बेली.

Company (*fellowship*). मेलु, सुह्बत, संग, संगति.

Company (*an assembly*). मज्लस, *See* Band.

To Compare. भेटणु, मुकाबिलो करणु, टकिराइणु, सारणु.

A Comparing, Comparison. भेट, मुकाबिलो.

In Comparison with. लेखे, अग्यां, करे.

A Compartment (*partition*). खानो, घरू.

A pair of Compasses. पर्गारू, पल्कारू.

Compassion. रहमु, बाझ, दया, मया, रहमाई.

An object of Compassion. बाझारो.

Compassionate. बाझभर्यो, रहमो, दयालु, रहमाइतो.

Competition. रीस.

A Competitor. रीसारो.

A Complainant. दांही, फर्यादी.

A Complaint. दांह, फर्यादु.

A false Complaint. चब, अडो, इक्केलु.

Complete. पूरो. *See* Entire.

To Complete. निबेरणु, चुकाइणु, पुज़ाइणु, निछोडणु, उकिलाइणु.

Completed. तमामु.

To be Completed. निबिरणु, उकिलणु, चुकणु, पुज़णु.

Completely. तमामु, पटिअ, फटि, मूरि.

Completeness, Completion. निबेरो, निछोरो, ओडकु.

Compliments. सलामु.

To Compose. (*to form*) जोडणु, करणु, (*as an author*) चवणु, कविता करणु. *See* To calm.

To Compound. गडणु, मिलाइणु.

Compounded. गाडुड, गाडुओ.

To Comprehend. समुझणु, परूडणु, बुझणु.

Comprehension. समुझ, परूड, अकुलु.

To Compress. दबणु, थन्हणु, सथणु, सिथणु.

To adjust by Compromise. टोडणु, लाहणु.

Compulsion. जोरु, ज़ादाई.

A Comrade. साथी, संगति, गांढुड.

To Conceal. लिकाइणु, लुकाइणु, दबणु.

Concealed. गुझो, तलु, दबु, पोशोदो.

To be Concealed. लिकणु, छपणु, दबोजणु.

A Concealer of another's faults. ढकणु.

Self-Conceit. टिंड़ि.

Conceited. टर्डो, सिफिलो.

To Conceive. दिलि में आणणु, समुझणु.

To Conceive in the womb. दुकिजणु, पेट सां थिअणु. *See* Pregnant.

Conception (*notion*). सुधि, समुझ, समाउ, खुर्क.

Concern (*business*). वास्तो, कमु.

Concern (*care*). सांग, गूंदरू. *See* Care.

A Conch. संखु, नादु.

To Conclude. निबेरणु, पूरो करणु.

The Conclusion. छेहु, ओडकु, अंतु, निछेडो, पुज़ाणो.

In Conclusion. नेटि, आखरि.
Concord. मेलु, बणति, ठहाउ.
A Concubine. सुरेति, सुरेतिणि, विहार्यल.
Condition (*state*). हालु, हवालु, ड़सा, रूइ, रूइदादि, सूरत, रूबकारि.
A visit of Condolence on a friend's decease. पर्चाणो, ज़ाणाणो.
Conduct (*behaviour*). चालि, हलति.
To Conduct (*manage*). हलाइणु, निभाइणु, करणु.
A Cone. चोटु.
A Confection (*of fruits*). मुर्बो.
Confectionary. मिठाई.
A Confectioner. हल्वाई.
A Confederate. हम्राहु, साथी. *See* Accomplice, Comrade.
A Conference. जवाबुसुआलु, सलाह.
To Confess. बासणु, मञणु.
A Confident. सुहागी.
To Confide. विसाहणु.
Confidence (*trust*). वेसाहु, इतिबारु, पर्तीति, भरोसो, भर्वसो.
Confidence (*boldness*). दिल्जाई, तसलाई.
To Confine. बंदि-कैदि-करणु.
Confirmed (*ratified*). बहालु.
To Confiscate. खाल्से-जब्त-करणु, फुरणु.
To Conform to. सारू &c. हलणु, मञणु.
Conformable to. सारू, माफ़कु, मूजिबि.
Confounded (*perplexed*). हैरानु.
To Confront. साह्मणे-मुक़ाबिले-करणु.
To Confuse (*disorder*). उबतो सुबतो &c. करणु. *See* To Perplex.
To be Confused in mind. मथो फिरणु, मुझणु.

Confusion. बखेड़ो, मॉझि, मॉझारो, रोलो, गड़बड़ि, लुडु.
In Confusion. इस्तिविस्ति, उबतोसुबतो, अगपोइ, गांऊंमांऊं.
To Confute. कूड़ो-काइलु-करणु.
To Congeal (*neu.*). ज़मणु, ज़ापणु.
To Congeal (*neu.*). ज़माइणु, जाराइणु.
A Congratulation. वधाई, वाधाई, मुबारख.
Congressus venereus. जमाउ, भोगु, फैलु.
A Conjecture. अट्कल, तक.
To Conjecture. अटकलणु.
Connexion. मेलु, सन्बंधु, वास्तो, लागापो.
A Conniver in a theft. गांढुड़ु.
A Connoisseur. सुज़ाणु, खांदो.
To Conquer. फतिह करणु, खटणु, जीतणु.
A Conquest. फतिह, जीत.
Consanguineous. हिकरतु.
To be Conscious (*to know*). ज़ाणणु.
Consecration. थापना.
Consent, or assent. आंकार.
To Consent. वासणु, मञणु, कबूलु करणु.
A Consequence (*effect*). फलु, गुनु.
Consequence (*importance*). सांगो, भउ.
To Consider. ग़णणु, तकणु, विचारणु, पहणु, रिथणु.
Considerate. ग़ाणू.
Consideration. ग़ण्ती, विचारु, तक, पहु, मथ, रिथ, तपास, ग़णतोर.
Consolation. तसलाई, दिल्जाई, दिल्दारी, धीर्जु.
Conspicuous. पधिरो, जाहिरु, प्रघटु, रोशनु.
Conspicuousness. जाहिरो, पधिराई.

Constant *(faithful)*. सचो. *See* Firm.

Constantly. भेरेभेरे, वरोवरो, हरहर, हरघडो, पलपलि, घडोघडो, वेरवेरि, हर्दमु. *See* Continually.

Consternation. ड़हकारू. *See* Dread.

Constipation of the bowels. कबज़ी.

To Consult. सलाह &c. करणु, पहणु, पहु पचाइणु.

A Consultation. सलाह, ग़ल्ती, मसलत.

To Consume *(act.)*. खपाइणु.

Consumption. खापो, खर्चु.

Consumption *(the disease)*. सिल.

To Contain. धरणु, झलणु.

To be Contained. माइजणु, समाइजणु, मामणु, मापणु.

The expressing Contempt for any one. फिट्कार, नालत.

Exclamation of Contempt. फिटि, हेटि, फेटि.

To Contend. विड्हणु, झग्डो–झेडो–करणु, *(to vie)* रोस करणु.

Content, Contented. राजो, संतोखो.

Content, Contentment. सबुरू, संतोखु.

Contention. झग्डो, झेडो, करहि, चटाभेटी. *See* Quarrelling.

The Contents of a book. तक्कि-रो, पनोतिरी.

To Contest. *See* To Contend.

Contiguous. वेझो, वेझिडो, ओड़ो, ओड़िडो.

Contingent Expenses. मथखर्चु.

Continually. नितु, हमेशां, सदा, हरहर. *See* Always, Constantly.

Continuance. टिकाउ, तग़ाउ.

To Continue. रहणु, टिकणु.

A Contract. बोल, मकादो, मोकातो, मुटो.

By Contract. बिल्मुक्तो.

To Contract *(draw in)*. सोड्हो करणु, घटाइणु.

To Contract *(bargain)*. बोलणु.

A Contractor. मक़ातेदारू.

To Contradict. ग़ाल्हि भञणु *or* उथिलाइणु.

Contradicting, Contradiction. उथिलाणी.

Contrary. उबतो, ऊंधो, *(as wind)* अवलो, थणाभो.

A Contrivance. हिक्मत, ढंउं, ड़ौलु, जुग़ति, चतुराई.

To be Convenient. ठहणु, वणणु.

Conversant. सहो, ज़ाणू, वाक़ुफु.

Conversation. बोलाचालो, जवाबुसुआलु, ग़ाल्हिबोलि, ग़ाल्हिमुहाडि.

To Convey *(by trips)*. ढोइणु. *See* To Carry.

To Convict. साबितु करणु.

To be Convinced. ठीकु-पको-समुझणु, निहिचे करणु.

To Coo. बग्बगोतू करणु.

A Cook. रसोयो, रांधाऊ, रांधो, बोर्चो.

To Cook. रंधणु, पचाइणु.

To be Cooked. पचणु, रझणु.

A Cook-house. रंधिणो, बोर्चोखानो, खाणांड़ो, भंड़ारो.

The act of Cooking. रंधिणी.

Pay for Cooking. रंधाणी.

To Cool *(neu.)*. ठरणु, थधो थिअणु.

Cool air, &c. थधिकार.

Cooling *(adj.)*. ठारू, ठारू.

A Cooling beverage, or application. थाधलि.

Coolness. थधाणि. *See* Coldness.

Copious. घणो, झझो, वड़ो. *See* Abundant.

Copper. ट़ामो.

Copper-money. पैसो.

Copper-rust. जंगालु.

A Copper-smith. ठांठारो.

Copperas. हीराकसु, आमिणु.

To Copulate. जहणु, जमाउ-भोगु-करणु, चोदणु.

To be Copulated. जभणु, जहाइणु.

Copulation. जमाउ, भोगु.

A Copy (*transcript*). उतारो, नकुलु.

A Copy (*to write after*). खाको, मश्क.

To Copy. उतारणु, नकुलु करणु.

Coquetry. चागु, चांलो, हाउ, हाउभाउ, नाजु, नखिरो.

A Coquette. चागुलो, नखिरेली.

Coral. गुणोटो.

The Coran. कुरानु, मुसाफु.

Cord. नोडो, ड़ोरो, ड़ोरि, (*of mung*) जोट़ो.

The Core. अणी, अंदरू, हडु, पितो.

Coriander seed. धाणो.

A Cork. बुंजो, ड़टो.

To Cork. ड़टणु.

Corn. अंनु. *See* Grain.

A Corn merchant. अंनवणजारो.

A Corn (*on the foot*). ककिरो.

A Corner. कुंड़.

A Cornelian. अकीकु.

The Coronation of a king. राजतिलकु.

Corporeal. देहिधारी.

A Corpse. मुड़दो, मेथु, पिराणो, पिराणो, लोथ, मड़हु.

Corpulency. थुल्हाई, माचि.

Corpulent. थुल्हो, डुढ्टो, दौंसो, मतारो, ड़टोमुटो, यटो.

To Correct (*amend*). सोधणु.

Correct, Correctly. ठीकु, सहो, रइ, रासि, दुरुस्तु, वहवारू, लेखाइतो, सोड़ोनु, सुबतो.

Correction (*punishment*). सेखति, सजा.

To Correspond (*tally*). टहणु. *See* To Fit.

Correspondence (*among merchants*). लिखापड़ही, भलावणी, आड़त, वहवारू, वहीवाट.

A merchant's Correspondent. भलोण्यो, आड़तिओ.

To Corrupt (*deprave*). खारणु, फिटाइणु.

To Cost. लहणु.

Costiveness. कबुजो.

Cottage. राउति. *See* Hut.

Cotton. कपाह, कपह, (*of a fine kind*) नर्मो.

Of Cotton. सोटो.

A pod of Cotton. फुटी.

The Cotton plant. वँउँणु.

A Cotton carder. पोञारो. *See* To Card.

To clean Cotton. टाणणु.

The instrument for cleaning Cotton. अटी.

A Cotton-seed. ककिडो.

A Cotton-seller. कापाहि.

A Couch. खटोलो, सेज, सेजा. *See* Bedstead.

To Couch in ambush. छपि करणु, छह मारणु.

A Cover. ढकणु, ढकिणी, ढकु, सर्पोसु, (*of cloth*) छँव, पोशु, (*to a hooka top*) ढूलु.

A Cover (*shelter*). अड, ओट, ढक, अझो.

To Cover. ढकणु, कजणु.

To Cover in (*to roof*). छाइणु.

To Cover (*with dirt, &c.*). भरणु.

A Covering (*dress q. v.*). ओछणु.

A Coverlet *(of various kinds)*. सबडि, रली, गोदिडो, रजाई.

To Covet. ब्राझाइणु, सिकणु.

Covetous. ब्राझारो, लालिची, लोभी, हिर्सी.

Covetousness. हब्रछ, लाल्चि, लोभु, हिर्सु.

A Cough. खंघि, खंङ्कार.

To Cough. खंघणु.

A Council. मज्लिस, सभा.

Counsel *(advice)*. सलाह, ग़ण्तो, मतो, मस्लत, पहु, मथ.

A Counseller. सलाही, मस्लती.

To Count. ग़णणु, सारणु.

The Countenance. मुंहु, मुहांडो, चिहिरो.

Countenance *(protection)*. हिमाइत.

Counterfeit. कूडो, खोटो.

The act of Counting. ग़ण्तो, सार, ग़णति.

Countless. बेशुमारु, अणग़णति. *See* Innumerable.

A Country. भुँइ, मुल्कु, ड़ेहु, ड़ेसु.

A foreign Country. विलाइत, परड़ेसु, परड़ेहु.

One's native Country. वतनु.

Of one's native Country. वतनी.

The Country *(opposed to town)*. ब्रहराडो.

Of the Country *(opposed to town)*. ब्रहरतू.

A fellow Country-man. वतनी, ड़ेही.

A Couple. जोडो, जोडी.

In Couples. ब्रब्र, ब्रेजडि, (*cattle so joined*) सल्हडु.

To Couple *(animals)*. सल्हाडणु.

A Couplet. बैतु.

Courage. सूरिहाई, बहादुरी, सूर्माई, छातो, दिलेरी.

To take Courage. सतणु, सन्या मंडणु.

To lose Courage. सत्या छडणु.

A Courageous man. सूरिहु, मर्दानो, बहादुरु, सूर्मो, दिलेरु.

Of a Courageous man. सूरिहाणो, सूर्माणो.

A Courier. कासिदु.

A Court of audience. कचहरी, दर्बारि.

A Court-yard. अङणु, आग़ंधु, सहनु.

Courtesy. आदरु, मानु, भाउ, खातरि.

A Courtier. दर्बारी.

A Cousin. (*father's brother's son*) सौटु, (*father's sister's son*) पुफाटु, (*mother's brother's son*) मारोटु, (*mother's sister's son*) मासातु.

A Cow. ग़ँउँ, गांइ, गऊ, दग़ी.

Of a Cow. ग़ाभी.

Cow-dung. छेणो, ग़ोहो, बोसो, छेणु.

A dried cake of Cow dung. थाफ, छेणो.

Cow's urine. ग़ोंटु.

A Cow-herd. ग़ांरु, धनारु, धरारु.

A Coward. कांइरु, गांड़ू, भाज़ूकडु, गीदो, नामर्दु.

Cowardice. कांइराई, गांड़ूपणु, नामर्दी.

A Cowrie (*used as money*). कोड़ी.

A seller of Cowries. कोड़ियरु.

A Crab-fish. कांकिडो.

A Crack (*fissure*). फोड, ड़ार, चीर, फोटि, सीर.

A Crack (*sound*). ठकाउ, कड़काउ.

To Crack, or split (*act.*). चीर &c. विझणु, भजणु.

To Crack, or split (*neu.*). टुड़कणु, टिड़कणु, फुटणु.

To Crack the fingers. ठकाउ कदणु.
A Cracker (*squib*). फटाको.
A Cradle. पींघो, हिंदोरो.
To Cram. दब्रणु, सथणु, थन्हणु.
The Cramp, Crampiron. गिढी.
To be Cramped (*affected with cramp*). आकिड़जणु.
A Crane (*bird*). बगु, बगुलो.
The Craw, or crop of birds. गुजो.
To Crawl. रिड़हणु, रेंड़ूही पाइणु, सिरणु.
The Crawling of an infant. रेंड़ूहो.
To Creak. चीकणु.
A Creaking noise. चीकाटु, चीचाटु, चींचीं, रोंगटु, चींघटु.
Cream. छटो, थरु.
A Crease (*plait*). सरु.
To Create. खल्कणु, सिर्जणु, रचणु, उपाइणु.
Created. पैदा.
Creation. रचना.
The Creator. कर्तारु, सिर्जणहारु, उपाइणहारु, खालिकु.
A Creature. जीउ, जिअडो.
Credible. वेसाह जिहडो.
Credit (*credence*). वेसाहु.
Credit (*honor*). पति, साख, सचारी, पैज.
On Credit or tick. उधारो, ओधरि ते.
The Credit side (*of an account*). आगति, जमा.
Credits (*assets*). ओधरि, लहणो.
To enter in the Credit side (*of an account*). आगति करणु.
To allow Credit (*for any thing in account*). मुजिरा ड़िअणु.
Creditable. सुपत्यो, मातिबरु.
A Creditor. लहणेदारु, लहण्यातु.
A Creek. खाड़ी.
To Creep. रिड़हणु, सुरणु.
A Creeping plant. वलि.
A Crest. मोड़ु. *See* Cockade.
A Crevice. चीर.
A Cricket (*the insect*). तिड़ो, तिड़ि.
A public Crier. होकाई.
A Crime. ड़ोहु, गुनाहु, अपिराधु.
Criminal. डुहारो, ड़ोही, गुनहगारु, अपिराधी.
A Cripple. मंड़ो, पिंगुलो.
Crippled in hands. टुंड़ो; from want of hands, ठूंठो.
To Croak. टांटां करणु.
Crooked. ड़िंगो, फिडो, विंगो.
Crookedness. ड़िंगाई, फिड़ाई, विंगाई.
The Crop (*of a bird*). गुजो.
A Crop (*of a field*). बनो, पोख; a first crop, नेरो; an after crop from the same seed, बांठ, लाभु.
To Cross over. लंघणु.
To sit down Cross-legged. पल्थी मारणु.
A Cross-road. चौवाटो.
Cross (*peevish*). तोसिरु. *See* Perverse.
A Crow. कांउं, कांगु; young, अलु; a female crow, कांविली.
A Crow-bar. चंजूरु.
A Crowd. मेड़ु, ठटु, गोड़ु, पोह, पोहट, घम्झानु, भीड, मेडाको, गपागपि, गपागोह, गड्गाहु, गाहटु, गाइलो.
The Crowing of a cock. ब्रांग.
The Crown (*of a deity or bridegroom*). मुकिटु, मुटिकु.
The Crown of the head. कापारु, केपिराटी, चोटी; of a hat, चंदो.
To Crown. पग बंधणु.
A Crucible. कोठारी.

Crude. कचो.
Cruel. निर्दई, बेरहमु, कठोरू.
Cruelty. बेरहमी.
A Crumb. भोरू; the crumbs, भोरि.
To Crumble (*act.*). भोरणु.
To Crumble (*neu.*). भुरणु.
To Crumple. चुंज इणु.
A Crupper. दुंबूची; of a camel-saddle, पुछड़ंगु.
To Crush. चिपे विझणु.
To be Crushed. चिपजणु.
A Crust. खल; of bread, छिलुरू.
A Crutch. घोडी.
To Cry (*weep*). रूंअणु, ओछिंगा-रणु. *See* To Proclaim.
To Cry out. रडणु.
The act of Crying. रूंभणु, रोजु, रूंभणाई.
Addicted to Crying. रूंभणो.
Crystal. बिलोरू.
Cubebs. कबाबचोनी.
A Cubit. हथु.
A Cucumber. ककिड़ी, पाती, बादि-रंगु, वंगो.
The Cud. ओग़रि, ओग़ार.
To chew the Cud. ओग़ारणु, उग़ा-रणु.
Cudgel. धुको, लठि, सोटो, लोड्ह. *See* Club.
A Cue (*hint*). इशारो, ड़सु.
A Cuff (*slap*). चमाट, लपाट, चपाट, थपड, तमाचो.
Culpable. डुहारी.
To Cultivate. पोखणु, आबादु करणु, वसाइणु, वलणु.
Cultivated. आबादु.
Cultivation, Culture. पोख, ज़मीनारी, आबादी.
A Cultivator. हारी, कुड्मी. *See* Husbandman.

Cumin-seed. जीरो, (*varieties of*) सुरहो जीरो, साओ जीरो, पुलाड्जीरो, (*black do.*) कारा जीरो.
Cunning. (*crafty*) पको, पुखूतो, ड़ाढो, छली, (*skilful q. v.*) चतुरू.
Cunning. (*skill*) चतुराई, (*artifice q. v.*) ठग्बाजी.
A Cup. पिआलो, कटोरो, वटो. *See* Bowl.
A Cup-board. दरी.
Cupidity. लालिचि, हबुछ, लोभु.
A Cupola. कुबो, गुंबजु.
A Cupping instrument. सिङो, रूमो.
To Curdle or Coagulate (*neu.*). ज़ापणु, ज़मणु.
Curds. धौरो, डुधु; a thick lump of curds, फुटो, दिगु. *See* Milk.
Curds and whey. डुधा पाणी, छिविरि.
To break into Curds and whey (*neu.*). फिटणु, खरणु.
To Cure. (*a person*) छुटाइणु, चङो &c. करणु, (*a disease*) लाहणु. *See* Well.
To be Cured. चङो &c. थिअणु, छुटणु.
A Curiosity. तोफो, सूखिडी, टोलु.
A Curl. वरू, घुंड़ो.
Currency. चलणु, चलति.
The Current of a river. वहुक, वहु, तिख, छड्ह, सीर. *See* Stream.
A Currier. चमारू, ढेढु, मोचो.
A Curry-comb. खर्खिणो, खर्खिडो.
A Curse. पिट, परातो, डुरिह.
To Curse. पिटणु, परातो &c. ड़िअणु.
A Curtain. पड्दो.
Musquito Curtains. महारि.
A Curve. ड़िंगु, वरू, विंगु, ढेकु.
A Cushion (*pillow*). विहाणो, तूलु, तकिओ.
A Cushion for sitting on. गादि.

A Custard apple. सीनाफलु.
Custody. जिमो, हथु.
Custom (*habit*). रीति, चालि, दस्तूरु, हलति, चलनि, रीतिभांति, भ्रिनि, हलोचली, मामूलु, रसम, -पर्वेज, परिवर्ज, वर्जीस, शरह.
Custom (*on goods*). महसूलु, इजारो.
Contrary to Custom. कुरीतो, बेदस्तूरि.
A collector of Customs. इजारदारु.
A Custom house. मराहि, मड़ो.
Customary. रीताइतो, मामूली, वर्जाइनो, नीताइतो.
A Customer. बुकी, खरीदारु, आसामी.
A Cut (*incision*). वढु, छेहु, टुको, चुटो.
A Cut on the body from a blow. फाडु.
To Cut (*act*). वढणु, कपणु, कतिरणु.
To Cut (*as insects do cloth*). टुकणु, कुतिरणु.
To Cut out clothes. विउटणु, व्रिहटणु.
To Cut up meat for cooking. बनारणु.
A Cutlass. तरारि.
The act of Cutting. वढिणी.
A Cutting (*slip for planting*). कलमु.
A Cymbal. झांझु, कंझी, छेणो, तालु.
A Cypress-tree. सरवु.

D

A Dagger. कातो, खंजरु, कटारी.
Daily. तारोक, ड़िहाडो, ड़िंहींड़िंहुं, नितु.
Daily pay or allowance of food. रोजीनो.
A Dainty, or delicacy. खूर्मो, मलीदो.
Dalliance. खिलखुशी, हाउभाउ, हाउ.
A Dam in a canal. जकु, छहो.
Damage. जिआनु, टोटो, घाटो, हाञि, नुख्शानु.
To be Damaged. खरणु, जिआनु &c. थिअणु.
Damp (*adj.*). आडोको, आलो, पाण्याठो.
Damp, Dampness. पिम, पाण्वठु, आलाणि, आडोकाई, (*from the ground*) पोसलि.
To be effected by Damp. पिम्जणु, सेलापिजणु, गोडिजणु.
A Dance. नाचु.
To Dance. नचणु.
A Dancing boy. नाचू.
A Dancing girl. कञिरी.
A band of Dancing boys. टोलो.
A band of Dancing girls. ताइफो.
To Dandle. लुडइणु, कोड़ाइणु, नचाइणु.
The act of Dandling. कोडु, लाडु.
Dandruff. बफो.
Danger. जोखो, खतिरो, जोखमु भउ.
Dangerous. जोखाइतो, खौफाइतो, भवाइतो, भवहथीको.
To Dangle. लडणु, लटूकणु.
Daring. हिमथभर्यो, निधड़ु, निधड़ूकु.
Dark. ऊंधाओ, अंधारो, अंधेरो, ऊंदाहो.
Dark colored, Darkish. कारांझिडो.
The Dark, Darkness. ऊंधइ, अंधारो, अंधूकारु, मेर, अंधारु, ऊंदाहो, ऊंदाही, ऊंदाहि.
Darkness from a dust storm. धुंधूकारु.
Deep Darkness. बिबऊंदाहि, भिभ.
A Darling. लाडुलो, सिकीलधो, ढोलणु, लालु, लालनु, लुडणु, मिठू, पपनु, ढोलो, दादुलो, मिठणु. *See* Fondling.

A Darn, Darning. तुनु, तुञु, रफू.
To Darn. तुनणु, तुञणु.
A Darner. रफूगरू.
To Dash. खणी-हणणु or फिटी करणु.
A Date (*time*). तारीक, मिती.
A Date tree. खजी. *See* Palm.
The Date fruit. (*general term*) पिंड़, कतल, खुर्मो, खजूरि, (*varieties*) खारिक, जारिख, ड़ौको, छुहारो; a half date, अखड़ु, आभिओ.
The juice of the Date. दोसो.
The Datura plant. धातूरो.
Daubed. हाणो.
A Daughter. धिउ, धिअ, निआणी, कन्या.
A Daughter-in-law. नुंहु, नुंह.
The Dawn of the day. पिभांति, भींभिकों, पिरिह, ढकी, पिरिहफुटी, असुरू, वड़ो वेलो.
To Dawn. पिरिह फुटणु.
A Day. ड़ींहु, ड़िंहु, (*the 24 hours*) ड़िहाडो, ड़िहाडो, रोज़ु.
A Day of the lunar fortnight. तिथि.
Of the Day. ड़िंहोको, ड़िंहूणो.
To Day *or* this Day. अजु
Of to Day. अजोको, अजूणो.
In a Day or two. अजु सुबह.
The Day before yesterday. ट्रिओ-ड़िंहु.
The Day after tomorrow. परिंहं.
The fourth Day in advance. तैंहिं-परिंहं, तरिंहं, अरिंहं.
A Day-book. कचो, खरिडो.
To Dazzle (*neu.*). तिर्विरि करणु.
Dead. मुओ, मो.
Deadly. कातलु.
Deaf. ब्रोडो.
Deafish, *or* somewhat Deaf. घ-ब्रिरो.

Deafness. ब्रोडाई.
Dealing (*trade*). ड़ेतीलेती, वहवारू, लहु.
Dear (*beloved*). पिआरो. *See* Darling.
Dear. (*costly*) महंगो, महांगो, (*risen in price*) सझिउ, चड़ंदु, आकिरो.
Dearness. महंगाई, गिरानी, महांगु, (*a rise in price*) सझाई, आकिराई.
A Dearth. डुकरु, डुकारु, कहतु.
Death. मौतु, कालु, मर्णो. *See* Decease.
The angel of Death. जमु, कालु.
The point of Death. सकिरात, अंतिकालु.
Deathless. अमरु.
A Debauchee. लंगोताडो, लंडो, लांगछोटो.
A Debt. कर्जु, ड़िभणो.
Debts, Debits. पेटि, ड़िभणो.
A Debter. ड़िभणेदारू, कर्जदारू, कर्जी, ड़ेज़ुगारू, ड़िअणातु.
The Debtor side *of an account*. नांइ, वासुलु.
To Decamp. लड़णु.
A Decay, Decaying. ग़ारो.
To Decay. ग़ारणु, सडणु.
Decease. चलणो, हलाणो. *See* Death.
Deceit. ड्रोहु, दगा, दगाबाजी, छलु, छहल, फितूरू, दोलाबु, ठग़ी, घातु, फिरेबु, खिरेबु, कपटु, खोटु, पर्पंचु, वेसाहघाती. *See* Dissimulation.
Deceitful. ड्रोही, छली, दगाबाज़ु, दोलाबी, ठगु, कपटी, फिरेबी, ठग़बाजु, वेसाहघाती.
To Deceive. ठग़णु, ड्रोहणु, छलणु, भुलाइणु, ड्रोहु &c. करणु.
A Deceiver. ठगु, ठोग़ी, ड्रोही. *See* Deceitful.

December & part of January. पोहु.
To Decide. ठहराइणु, निबेरणु, ठोकु करणु.
To be Decided. ठहरणु.
Decision. निबेरो.
A Declivity. लाहो.
A Decoction. काढ़हो.
To Decorate. सींगारणु.
Decoration, Decorating. सींगारु.
To Decrease. घटणु, लहणु.
A Decree. हुक़ुमु.
Decrepit. जईफु, हीणो.
To Deduct. लाहणु, कटणु, काटणु, वजह करणु.
A Deducting, Deduction. कट, लाथि, काट.
A written Deed. सनद, दस्तावेजु, कबज़ु, (*of acquittance*) फारखंती, (*of agreement*) कबूलिअत, (*of lease*) पटो.
Deep. ऊन्हो, तारि.
Deep in color. ग़ूढ़हो, घाटो, गहरो, चहरो.
A Deep sleep. अघोर-गहरी-निंड, ग़हर.
A Deer. हरणु.
A hog-Deer. फाढ़हो.
Defamation. खुभारी, गिला, निंदा.
A Defamer. गिलाखोरु, निंदकु.
A Default (*neglect*). कोताही.
A Defeat, Defeating. हार.
To Defeat. जीतणु.
To suffer Defeat. हारणु, हाराइणु.
A Defect (*blemish*). ऐबु, विंग, वोक.
Defective. घटि. *See* Deficient.
A Defence. बचाउ, रख, रछा, पनाह.
To Defend. बचाइणु, रखणु.
A Defendant. जदाबडींदडु, मुदई.
A Defender. वाहि, रखवालु, रछकु.
To Defer. रखणु.

Deference. रखिणी, लिहाज़ु, खातिरि.
A Deficiency. खोटि, ऊणाई, कोताही, सोसि, हुफी.
Deficient. ऊणो, घटि, कोतहु, कसो.
To be Deficient. खुटणु, घटणु.
A Defile, or strait. लकु, दरो.
To Defile (*pollute.*). असुचि-पलीतु -करणु, (*by supping or lapping*) चिटारणु, लकणु, जूठो करणु.
Definite. सँओं, साफु, सफा.
Deformed. कोझो, बेड़ोलो.
To Defraud. ठगणु. *See* To deceive.
To Degenerate. खरणु.
Degree (*rank*). मरातिबो, दर्जो, जाइ. *See* Stage, Step.
Dejected. उदासु, उब्राणिको, बेदिलि.
Dejection. उदास, उब्राणिकाई.
A Hindoo Deity. देवता, ड़ेवता, ड़ेउ, ठाकुरु.
The Deity. (*Mussulman*) अलाहु, खुदा, (*Hindoo*) ईश्वरु, भगवानु.
Delay. अवेल, गिसिरि, देरि, गेसरि, फुर्सत, वेर, वेरम, चिकुं.
With Delay (*late*). चिकों.
Delay (*allowed for payment, &c.*). रखति, लह.
To Delay (*act.*). देरि &c. कराइणु, सीडाइणु, अट्काइणु.
To Delay (*neu.*). सीडणु, ओसीड़जणु,
The act of Delaying. सीडापो, सीड.
To Deliberate. ग़ाणणु, रिथणु, विचारणु, पहणु.
Deliberately. ड़िसीवाइसी, दीनादास्ती, ज़ाणीवेणी.
Deliberation. ग़ाण्ती, विचारु, सलाह, रिथ.
A Delicacy. *See* Dainty.
Delicate. (*in constitution*) नाज़ुकु, (*nice*) मलूकु.

Delicious. सवादी.

Delight. खुशी, रीझ, जशनु, जौंकु, बहार, भनंदु, बिलासु, हुलासु.

Delighted. खुशि, सरहो, निहालु.

Delightful. *See* Pleasing, Charming.

To Delineate (*mark out for painting &c.*). लीकणु, अंगारणु.

Delirium. बेहोशो, खुश्की.

To Deliver in charge. सौंपणु, हवाले करणु, सुपारणु, पर्नणु.

To Deliver (*save*), तारणु, बचाइणु, उधारणु.

Deliverance. छोट्कारो, छोट्को, खलासी.

To be Delivered (*of a child*). विश्रामणु.

A Deliverer. छोटाऊ.

A woman's Delivery. विश्रमु.

To Delude. ठगणु, भुलाइणु, भमाइणु.

A Deluge. बोड्बोडां.

To Deluge. बोड्बोडां करणु.

A Delusion. भिर्मु, फिरेबु.

A Demand (*claim*). दावा, छिक.

To Demand (*to claim*). घुरणु, छिकणु.

Demand (*for purchase*). खापो, खपु, घुर्ज.

To be in Demand. खपणु.

To lessen in Demand. मठो–माठो–थिभणु.

To Demolish. ढाहणु.

A Demon. जिनु, देउ, भूतु, राकसु, वीरू, (*female*) मम, बाभ.

The Den of a wild beast. डुरि.

A Denier. मुकिरू.

Dense. घाटो, गहरो.

To Deny. नाकर करणु, नमञणु, भलणु, मुकिरणु, नाकारणु.

To Depart. वञणु, रवानो थिभणु, उसहणु, सिधारणु.

Dependence (*as of a dependent*). मोथाजी.

In Dependence (*on another*). ताबे, भाहिर.

To be Dependent. काणि कढणु.

A Dependent. ताबेदारू, अधीनु, कूंजिडो, कांयारो, काण्यातो, मोथाजु,

A Depilatory. नूरो.

A Depopulated. सुञो, फिटो, उजडु.

Deportment. ड़ेखारो. *See* Conduct.

To Depose from office. तडे कढणु.

To Depose (*give evidence*). शाहिदी ड़िभणु.

A Deposit. धरावत, भमानत.

To Deposite. सैंपि–भमानत–रखणु.

The Deposition of a witness. इजहारू.

To grow Depraved. खरणु, बिगिड़णु, फिटणु.

Depredation. फुरि, फुर्फार, लुटि.

A Depredator. फौरू.

Depth. ऊन्हाई, ऊन्हाणि, भोभरू.

A Deputy. नाइबु.

To Deride one. फलाणे ते खिलणु.

Derision. पबो, खिल, ठठोली, मश्किरी, चेड.

To be Derived. निकिरणु.

To Descend. लहणु.

A Descendant, Descendants. भोलाधु, वंसु.

A Descent, Descending. लाहो, लहु, लाहु.

To Describe (*explain*). निर्वारू करे चवणु.

A Desert. थरू, बरू, रुञ, रिणु.

To Desert. छड़े–भज़ी–खिस्की–वञणु.

A Deserted village. पढु.

A Deserter. भगलु.

To Deserve. लाइकु थिभणु.

A Design (*purpose*). दिलि, इरादो, मुराद, निअत.
To Design. दिलि &c. करणु.
Designedly. ज्ञाणोबुझो. *See* Purposely.
Desire. इछा, खाइश, रुचि, सध, दिलि, चाउ, चाह, मनिसा.
To Desire. इछा &c. करणु.
To Desist from. छड़णु, बसि करणु.
Desolate. सुञो, उजड़ु, वैरानु, बिड्वांडु, सुञ.
To Desolate. उजाड़णु, फिटाइणु.
Desolation. सुञ, वैरानी, सुञाई.
Despair. नाउमेदी, निरासाई.
To Despair. आस-उमेद-छड़णु, सहसाइणु.
Despairful, Despairing. नाउमेदु, निरासु.
To Despatch (*send off*). रवानो करणु, ड्रिआरे मोकिलणु *or* मुँजणु.
To Despatch (*perform*). निबेरणु.
Despicable. नीचु, फिट्कार्यो, ओछो.
To Despise. न ग़णणु.
Destiny. नसीबु, भागु, तालिहु, बख्तु, कर्मु, प्रापति, प्रालभि, लिख्यो, लेखु, भाणो.
Destitute (*in want of, wanting*). सखिणो.
Left Destitute. बेवाह, निधण्को, अबालो.
To Destroy. नासु &c. करणु, विञाइणु.
Destroyed. नासु, फना, चटु, चपड्-चटु, चौड़ु, विनासु.
To be Destroyed. नासु &c. थिअणु, फिटणु.
Destructible. फानो.
Destruction. नासु, फना, खराबो.
Destructive. नासुकंदड़ु, जिआन्खोरू.
To Detach. धार करणु. *See* To Separate.

A Detachment. दफो, गुलिरी.
A Detail, Detailing. विचूड, विडुरो.
To Detail. विचूडणु.
To Detain. अट्काइणु, रोकणु, झलणु.
Detention. अट्काउ, रोक, झल.
To Deter. ड्रेजारणु.
A Determination. ठहराउ.
To Determine. ठहराइणु, ठाहणु.
To be Determined. ठहरणु.
To Detest. बुछां भांइणु.
Detraction. गिला, बद्नामी.
Detriment. जिआनु, टोटो, छोओ.
To Devastate. फिठाइणु, सुञो करणु.
Devastation. फुर्मार.
To Deviate. बाहरि हलणु.
A Device. ढंउँ, जुग़ति. *See* Contrivance.
The Devil. शैतानु.
Of the Devil, Devilish. शैतानी, शैतानिको.
Devil's tricks, Devilment. शैतानी.
To Devise. ढंउँ *&c.* करणु. *See* Device.
Devoid. रहितु, बे.
To Devolve (*neu.*). अचणु, पवणु.
To Devote. घोरणु, वारणु, कुरबानु *&c.* करणु.
Devoted or what is Devoted. कुरबानु, फ़िदा, घोर, सदिको.
A religious Devotee. (*Mussulman*) फकीरु, दर्वेशु, कलंदरु, (*Hindoo*) बेखदारी, भगतु, त्यागी, various sects; (*Mussulman*) सूफी, मदारी, (*Hindoo*) सन्यासी, नाँगो, खाकी, उदासी, बैरागी, जोगी, सेविड़ो, जंगमु.
The abode of a Devotee. (*Mussulman*) दाइर्यो, तकिओ, (*Hindoo*) टिकाणो, धर्मिसालि, मढ़ी.

Devotion. बंदगी, भग़ति, ध्यानु, जपु.
Austere Devotion. जोगु, समाधि, तपु, तपस्या.
Devout. निमाज़ी, संतु, साधु.
Devout ceremonies. सेवापूजा, कर्मु.
The Dew. माक, विल्ह, माट्टु.
The Dewlap. कमरि.
Dexterity. कारीगरी, सुघडाई, भडाई, चालाकी.
Dexterous. कारीगरू, सुघडु, चालाकु.
Diagonally. उरेबी.
A Dialect. ब्रोली.
The Diameter. पेटु.
A Diamond. हीरो.
A Diarrhœa. दस्त *plu.* अतिसारू.
To have a Diarrhœa. पेटु हलणु *or* छुडणु.
Dice. ढारा *plu.*
A Dictionary. लुगति, नाममाला, कोशु.
Die (*color*). रङ्गु; a die for the hair, केसु.
A Die for gaming. ढारो.
To Die (*color*). रङणु.
To Die (*expire*). मरणु, फौतु थिअणु, रजा-समउ-करणु, चलणु, गुजिरणु.
A Dier. खट्टी, खुहुंबाट्टी, (*of blue*) नोरीट्टी, नोरोली.
Diet. खाजु, खाधि, खोराक.
To Differ. न ठहणु *or* मिलणु, तफावतु *&c.* रखणु.
To cause to Differ (*or fall out*). फिटाइणु.
A Difference (*distinction*). फेरू, तफावतु, फर्कु.
A Difference (*falling out*). डुफेडु, अणमेलु, अणबणति.
To cause a Difference (*or falling out*). डुफेडु *&c.* विझणु.
Different. बिओ, धार.
Difficult. औखो, मुश्किलु, डुहेरो, अहंजो, अवलो, कटनु, डुख्यो.
A Difficulty. औखु, औखी, औखाई, औखति, अहंजु, अहंजाई, मुश्किलु.
With Difficulty. मसमस, मसाँ, मसें.
To Diffuse. पखेडणु. *See* To spread.
To be Diffused. पखिडणु.
To Dig. खणणु, खोटणु.
To be Digested. फञणु, पचणु, भुचणु, हजमु थिअणु.
Digestion. हजमु.
Dignified. शानाइतो, आबाइतो, मानाइतो.
Dignity. शानु, वड़ाई, आबु, उमिराई.
A Dike (*mound*). बंदु, बंधु, बंधि, कड, पुल्शाही.
Dilapidated. ढ़ठो.
Dilatory. गेस्लिओ, गेसियलु.
A Dilemma. मोंझारो, गंडु. *See* Perplexity.
Diligence. सायो, धुनि, जतनु.
Diligent. चुस्तु, उज़मी.
To Dilute. मठो करणु.
To Diminish. घटाइणु.
Dimity. झमटी.
Dimness. झांविराई, झांई, धुंधु, धुंधकारू.
Dim-sighted. झांविरो.
A Din. ठकाठुकी, ठकूठकि.
To Dine. खेणु &c. खाइणु.
A Dinner. खेणु, खाइणु, मानी, रसोई.
A Dint. चिबु, कुबु, चिपु, घुबु, झिकु, चुघु.
Dinted. चिबो, झिको.
To Dip (*act.*). ब्रोडणु, टुबाइणु.
A Dip. ब्रोडो, टुबी.
Direct. सँधो.
To Direct (*point out*). डसणु, डेखारणु.

To go Direct. साम्हो वञणु.
Direction (*indication*). ड़सु.
In Direction of (*towards q. v.*). पारि, ड़िसि, तर्फि, पासे.
The Direction of a letter. सर्नामो.
A Dirge. पारू.
Dirt. मेलु *f.* गंदु, बुहरू.
Dirtiness. मेराणि, मेराई.
Dirty. मेरो, गदिलो, मलीनु, चिकड़ु.
Somewhat Dirty. मेरांझिड़ो.
To Dirty. मेरो &c. करणु, लुड़णु.
To grow Dirty. मेरो &c. थिअणु, लुड्ज़णु.
To be Disabled. जड़ो थिअणु.
Disadvantageous. बेफ़ाइदो, अनयार्थो.
To Disagree. न ठहणु.
Disagreeable. अणसुहाइंदो, अणठाहू.
Disagreement. अणबणति, अणठाहु. *See* Difference.
To Disappear. गुमु-गैबु-गाइबु-थिअणु.
To Disappoint. उमेद भञणु, निरासु करणु.
Disappointment. नाउमेदी, निरासाई.
To Disapprove. नापसंदि करणु.
A Disaster. बला, आफति. *See* Calamity.
To Disavow. न मञणु, न बासणु.
To Disbelieve. बेमहु न करणु.
To Discard. कढी छड्णु.
Discernment. सुञाण, स्याणप, सुर्ति.
A person of Discernment. सर्तो, सुज़ाणु, स्याणो.
A Discharge (*dismissal*). मोकल, जवाबु.
A written Discharge of a debt, &c. फार्खती.
To Discharge from service. कढणु, जवाबु ड़िअणु.
To Discharge a debt. पीचाइणु, पिआरणु, भीचाइणु.
To Discharge (*as fire arms*). छोड़णु.
To be Discharged (*a debt*). पीचणु, भीचणु.
To be Discharged from service. मोकूफु थिअणु, निकिरणु.
A Disciple. सिखु, चेलो, सेवकु, खादिमु.
To Disclose. उघाड़णु, ड़ेखारणु, छुली विझणु, सलणु, फोल्हणु, उपटारणु.
A Disclosure, Disclosing. उपट, उपटार, उघड़.
To Discolor. रङु विञाइणु.
Discomfiture. हार.
Discomfort. कशालो, ड़ाखिड़ो, हलाखो.
To be Discontented. अरहो-बेराजी-थिअणु.
To Discontinue. बसि करणु, छड्णु.
Discord. अणमेलु, अणबणति.
To Discover (*find out*). गोले कढणु, फोल्हणु.
A Discovery. फोल्ह.
Discount. वटो, लाथि, वटा, (*taken for a flaw in coins*) पाड़ो.
To Discount a bill. हुंड़ी ग़िन्हणु.
To Discourage. ढिरो करणु. *See* To Dishearten.
Discourse. गाल्हिबोलि, ताति, पचार. *See* Talk.
Discredit. बद्नामी, अजसु.
Discreet. ग़ाणू.
Discretion. ग़ण्तो, साञाह.
To arrive at years of Discretion. सामाइजणु, संभालणु.
To Discriminate. सुञाणणु, सही करणु.
A Discus. चकरू.

To Discuss. ग़ाल्हि ग़ागणु, सलाह क-रणु.
Disdain. निरादरू.
A Disease. आज़ारू, रोगु, मर्ज़ु, डु-थारि.
To Disembark (*act.*). लाहणु.
To Disembark (*neu.*) लहणु, उल-हणु.
To Disengage. छोडणु.
To be Disengaged. छुटणु, (*at leisure*) वांदो–वाल्हो–वेल्हो–आजो–नि-कमो–निवेकिलो–थिअणु. *See* Idle.
To Disentangle. समुझाइणु.
To Disfigure. बेड़ोलो करणु.
Disgrace. खुआरी. *See* Dishonor.
To be Disgraced. खुआरू थिअणु.
Disgraceful. खुथारिअभर्यो, बेमानो, बेआबो.
Disguise. सांगु, बेखु, वेसु.
To Disguise. सांगु &c. करणु.
Disgust. सूग, किराहत, किरिभ.
To affect with Disgust. बुछां ल-ग़णु.
A Dish (*varieties*). थालु, थारू, थाल्ही, थारी, रिकेबी, पाटि, ढंगारी, फेली, तबकु, तबाकु, ठांठि, पाटोडो, सिणिक.
A Dish with cover. ढाकुंभों, मुखबो.
A Dish of meat. थांउ.
A chafing Dish. (*metal*) मंगलु, (*earthen*) कुलु.
To Dish up meat. वधणु, पड्छणु, प-रोसणु.
To Dishearten. संशो पाइणु. *See* To Discourage.
Dishonest. कुपत्यो, बेपत्यो, बेईमानु, कुसतो.
Dishonesty. कुपति, बेईमानी.
Dishonor. खुआरी, बेआबी, बेआब्रुई.
To Dishonor a bill. नाकारणु.

Dishonorable. बेआबो, बेमानो.
The Dishonoring a bill. नाकारी.
Disinterested. बेगर्जो.
To Disjoin. उखेडणु, उखोलणु.
A Disk. टिको.
To Dislike. न भांइणु, न घुरणु, न वणणु.
To be Dislocated. उखिडणु, निकि-रणु.
Dismay. डुरु. *See* Dread.
To Dismiss from service. तडणु, कढणु.
Dismissed, Discharged. मोकूफु.
A Dismission. मोकल, जवाबु, मोकूफी.
To Dismount (*neu.*). लहणु, उलहणु.
Disobedient. होड़ो, निजसु.
To Disobey. न मञणु.
Disobliging. बेशायो, बेफैजो.
Disorder (*of things, affairs, &c.*) रोलो, गंडुगोडु, गड्बडि. *See* Confusion, Disturbance, Sickness.
In Disorder. उबतो सुबतो, इस्तिविस्ति.
Dispassionate. थधो.
To Dispatch (*accomplish*). निबेरणु.
To Dispatch (*send off*). डिआरे-मोकिलणु *or* मुँजणु, रवानो करणु.
To Dispel. विञाइणु.
To Disperse (*neu.*). कुणोकुणो थि-अणु. *See* To Scatter.
Dispirited. उदासु, उञाणिको, बेदिलि.
To become Dispirited. अमांणिजणु.
To Display (*exhibit*). डेखारणु, ज़ा-णाइणु.
To be Displeased. नाखुशि–बेदिलि–खस्तो–थिअणु, डुमांइणु, विचिरणु.
Displeasure. डमरू, रंजु, खस्ताई.
At one's Disposal. हथि, वसि, इख्-तिआरि.
Disposition of mind. सुभाउ, तबह, मिज़ाजु, लछणु, पिकारू.

Good Dispositioned. सुळछिणो, सभागो, सब्राझो, सुभा तूरो. *See* Amiable.

Ill-Dispositioned. कुलछिणो, बेलछिणो, कुधो, कुवाटो.

A Dispute, Disputing. होड़, बहशु, तक्रारु, रदबदलि, झिद, कदु, जिदि, हुज्जत.

To Dispute. होड़िजणु, मुदो पाइणु.

One who Disputes or cavils. बहशी, होड़ो, जिदो, कदो, झिदो.

Disquiet, Disquietude. बेआरामी, लुछ, लोछि. *See* Restlessness.

To be Disquieted. अमांणिजणु.

Disregard. बेपर्वाही; silent disregard, कनलाटार.

To Disregard. न ग़णणु, नटाइणु, लाटारणु.

Disregardful. बेपर्वाहु, अलगर्जो.

Disrespect. बेइजती, निरादरु, बेअदबी.

Dissatisfaction. अरहाई.

To be Dissatisfied. अरहो-बेदिलि-बेराज़ी-थिअणु.

To Dissemble (*neu.*). अंदरब्रहरी &c. करणु. *See* Dissimulation.

A Dissembler. अंदरब्रहरो, खोटो.

Dissension (*disagreement q. v.*), अणबणति. *See* Contention.

Dissentient. नाक़बूलु, अणठाहू.

To be Dissimilar. हिकजिहड़ो न हुअणु.

Dissimilarity. फेरु. *See* Difference.

Dissimulation. अंदरब्रहरी, ब्रिभाई, खोटु, कपटु. *See* Deceit.

To Dissolve or melt (*act.*). ग़ारणु.

To Dissolve or melt (*neu.*). ग़रणु.

Dissolute. लांगछोटो, लांड़ारो, लंडो.

Distance. पंधु, तफावतु, वेचो.

At, or to, a Distance. परे, डूरि.

To be Distant. परे हुअणु

Somewhat Distant. डूरांहों, डूरांहों, परांहों, पर्तांहों.

The more Distant. पर्यो.

To Distil (*liquor, act.*) छिकणु, चिकाइणु.

To Distil, *or* be Distilled. चिकणु.

Distilled. Single, छिक; double, दुआस्तो; treble, टिआस्तो.

A Distilled liquid. अर्कु.

A Distiller. कलालु.

A Distillery. बठो.

Distinct. (*different*) धार, जुदा, (*clear*) चिटो, सफा.

A Distinction. फेरु, तफावतु.

Distinctness. चिटाई, सफाई.

To Distinguish (*note difference*). सही करणु.

To Distinguish (*one's self*). मल्हाइणु.

To Distort. मरोड़णु.

Distracted. हैरानु, हलाखु, बेजारु.

Distraction. हैरानी, बेजारी.

To Distrain. झलणु.

Distress. डुखु, सूरु, रंजु, कशालो, अँहँजु.

To Distress. डुखाइणु, रंजाइणु, कल्पाइणु.

Distressed. रंजि, डुखी, (*for means*) तंगी.

To be Distressed. डुखणु, कल्पणु.

To Distribute. वंड़े-विर्छे-विराहे-फांड़े-ड्रिअणु.

A Distribution. फांड़िणी, वंड़, विर्छ, विरह.

A District. जिलो, मुल्कु.

Distrust. बेवेसाही, संसो, शकु, गुमानु.

A Disturbance. झिगोड़ु, विगोड़ु, घम्सानु, रोलो, बखेड़ो.

Disunion. अणमेलु, जुदाई.
To be Disunited. धार थिअणु, फिटणु.
A Ditch. खाही.
A Dive. टुबी.
To Dive. टुबणु, टुबी ड़िअणु.
A Diver. टुब्रयरू, टोबो.
Diversion (*sport*). रांदि, खुशी. *See* Sport, Amusement.
To be Diverted (*amused*). विंदुरणु.
To Divide. विराहणु, वंड़णु, विर्छणु, फाड़णु.
A Dividend. सतिमी, फाड़िणी. *See* Division.
Divination. फाल, परीछा, रमलु.
Divine. खुदाई, ईश्वरी.
A Division, Dividing. विर्छ, वंड़, विरह, फाड़िणी, भाङो. *See* Share, Compartment.
A Division of an Army. दस्तो.
A Divorce. तलाक.
A Deed of Divorce. तलाक्नामो.
To Divulge. छुली विझणु, फोल्हणु.
A Dizziness. फेरी, चकरू.
To Do. करणु.
Docile. चएदारू, सुधातूरो.
Docked (*tail cropt*). लंडो.
A Doctor. तबीबु, हकीमु, वैदु.
A Doe. हरिणी.
A Doer. कंदरू.
A Dog. कुतो; various kinds of dogs, गुलिरू, पिस्तो, भचरू, तोजो, लुचु, खालु, ड़बो, खटरू.
A Dog's collar. पटो.
A Doll. गुड़ी.
A Dome. कुबो, गुंबजु.
Domestic. घराणो, घरू.
Dominion. अमलु, राजु, हुकुमु.
A Donation. बख्शीश, इनामु.
To be Done. किजणु.
A Door. दरू, दर्वाजो, दरो; (a door) made of wicker, ब्रटोंओं; of plank, ताकोंओं.
A wicker Door or gate. ब्रटुं.
One side of a double Door. ताकु.
A Door-frame. चौंकु.
A Door-keeper. दर्वानु, ड़ेढीवानु.
A Door-post. ब्रांही.
A Door-way. बुंभो.
The top of a Door-way. सर्दरू.
Dorsers for a camel. कजाओ, पाल्णो.
A Dose. फकी, सुती.
A Dot. बुडो, बिंढ़ो, टुब्को, नुख्तो. *See* Spot.
Dotage from age. ब्राहतिरी, ब्राहतयाई.
A Dotard. बाहतयो.
Double. ब्रोणो, ब्रिटो, दुहुरो.
The Double. ब्रोणि.
To Double. ड़ूणाइणु, ब्रोणो &c. करणु.
Doubling, making Double. ब्रोणाई.
Doubt. शकु, वस्वसो, गुमानु, भिर्मु, संसो.
To Doubt. शकु &c. करणु.
Doubtful. शकी.
Doubtless. बेशकि.
A Dove. कबूतडु, (*various kinds*) पारेलो, ग़ेरो, खुमिरी, रोहेलो.
Dove-colored. फाख्ताई.
Dough. ग़ोह्युलु अटो, (*made up in a ball*) चाणो, लेयो.
A Dower, a Dowry. ड़ाजो, ड़ाजु, ड़ेजु
The giver of a Dowry. ड़िअण्यातु
Down on the chin. रेह.
Down, Downward (*adv. and prep.*) हेठि.
To go or come Down. लहणु.

Down the river, with the stream. लाव्हारो.
To become Downcast. मुँहु लहणु, हपणु, होस्जणु.
Downward (*adj.*) हेर्ठों.
To Doze. पिनिकी खाइणु.
Dracunculus. वारो.
A rough Draft of a letter. मुसौदो. *See* Draught.
To Drag. गिहिरणु.
Dragon's blood. बस्तासुर्खी, होरादखिनी.
A Drain. चरी, चरू, मोरो, कसी.
To Drain out (*water*). ग़ाडणु.
Draining. ग़ाड.
A Draper. बजाजु.
A Draught (*in drinking*). ढुकु.
A medicinal Draught. सुतो, शर्बतु.
A Draught on a banker. हुंडी, पुर्जो, अंगुडो.
To Draw, or pull along. गिहिलणु, छिकणु.
To Draw a picture. कढणु, चिटणु.
To Draw a line. पाइणु, विझणु, कढणु.
To Draw, *or* Draw up, (*a bill &c.*). लिखणु.
To Draw, as plaster does. चिकाइणु.
To Draw in (*contract*). सोड्ही करणु, भीडणु, (*from outside*) अंदरि करणु.
To Draw out. कढणु.
To Draw up. मथे छिकणु.
A pair of Drawers. सुथण, कांच.
The waist-string of Drawers. अग़ठु.
A Drawn sword. उघाडी तरारि.
Dread. भउ, डपु, ड्रिजु, डेजो, डाउ, ड़रू, उड़िको.
To Dread. ड्रिजणु, ड़रणु.
To cause one to Dread. डेजारणु.
Dreadful. भैवारो, खौफाइतो.
A Dream. सुहुणो, सुपनो, खाबु.
Dregs. फोगु.
A Dress. पोशाख, वगो, ओछणु. *See* Clothes.
A Dress of honor. सरोपाहि, (*given by a priest*) पखर, पाखर.
To Dress (*one's self*). कपिडा करणु *or* पहरणु.
To Dress (*another*). पहराइणु, ढकाइणु.
Dried. सुको.
Any thing Dried and hard. ठोठु.
In the state of being Dried. फकुरो.
A Drill or auger. सराईं, बर्मो.
To Drink. पिअणु.
Drinkable. पिअणजिहडो.
A Drinker. पिआकु.
Drinking (*sub.*). पिअणी.
To Drip. ग़डणु, टिमणु.
To Drive (*act.*). काहणु, हकिलणु.
To Drive away. लोधणु, हकिलणु, तडणु.
A Driver. काहो.
To Drizzle. फुड्फुडि लाइणु.
A Drop. टेपो, बूंद, फुडी, फुडो, ग़ाडो, चुआको.
To Drop (*fall in drops.*) ग़डणु, टिमणु.
To Drop (*fall*). किरणु, किरी पवणु, (*as fruit from a tree*) छणणु.
A Dropping. टिमटिमि, ग़ाड.
The Dropsy. जलंधरू.
Dross. खाधि, मठु, कसु *f.* गेरू.
A Drove. धणु, जबुं.
Drought. अणोठि, औसरु, अवसरु, सुक.
To Drown (*act.*). बोडणु.

To Drown (*neu.*) बुड़णु.
Drowned. गर्कु.
Drowsiness. निंडु, ऊंघाई.
Drowsy. निंडाखिडो, निंडाखो.
To be Drowsy. निंडु &c. अचणु, निंडाइजणु.
To Drudge. ग़हणु.
A Drug. दवा, मशालो.
A Druggist. पसारी.
A Druggist's stores. पसारू.
A Drum (*varieties of such*). दुहुलु, ढोलक, मिर्दंगु, धुकड़ु, भेरि, दमामो, दमरू, दुहुलिडो, नगारो, पखवाज, बमु, ढोल.
A Drummer. दुहुलारी, धोंकिडो, नगार्ची.
A Drum-stick. डंकौ.
Drunk. खिओ, मस्तु, नशई, चर्यो; dead drunk, अलूटु.
To be Drunk. खिओ &c. थिअणु.
A Drunkard. कैफी, पिआकु, शराबी.
Of a Drunken man. मस्ताणो, मस्तानिको, मस्तिको.
Drunkenness. नशो, मस्ती, मस्ताई.
Dry. सुको.
Dry and hard. सोटु.
Dry (*plain*). रूखो.
To Dry (*act.*). सुकाइणु.
To Dry (*neu.*). सुकणु.
To become Dry in milk (*as a cow*). विहुकणु.
The Drying up, of ground after wet. सोकहडी, फकुराई; of a crop from want of water, सोकिडो, सोकि, तई.
Drying, Dryness. सुकाई, सुकाणि.
The Duce, or Deuce, at cards. त्रिको; or dice, दूओ.
A Duck. बदक, (*wild*) हंझर, नीली.
To Duck (*act.*). टुब्राइणु.

A Due (*right*). हकु.
To be Due. ड़िभणो *or* लहणो थिअणु.
To have Due. लहणणु.
A Dug or teat. थुंजो, थणु. *See* Nipple.
Having large Dugs (*adj*). थुबिरि.
A Dull person. ढिरो, बेहोशु, मोंगो.
Dull, (*as a fire, light, trade, &c.*). ढिरो, झको.
Dumb. गुंगो.
Dumbness. गुंगाई.
A Dun, or Dunner. छिकाऊ, छिकू, छिकंदडु.
To Dun. छिकणु.
A Dunce. कुंदु. *See* Blockhead.
Dunning (*sub.*). छिक.
Dung. (*of cow or buffaloe*) छेणो. *See* Cowdung. (*of horse, mule &c.*) लिड़ि, (*goat's, hare's &c.*) फोलिडी, फेड्णो, पोलिडी, (*camel's*) गिसो, (*bird's &c.*) विठि, (*hawk's or pigeon's*), पखाल, (*man's*) गुंहु. *See* Excrement.
Orbicular Dung of cattle. लेडूणो, फोलिडो, पोलिडो.
Dung, used as manure. ज़मु, भाणु.
A Dunghill. अरूडी.
A Duplicate. मुसनो, (*of a bill of exchange*) पाउंठ.
Duplicity. त्रिभाई, अंदरबहरी, खोटु. *See* Deceit.
Durability. जटा, जटाउ, तग़ाउ, हंढ़.
Durable. हंडाऊ, हंडिणो, जटाऊ, टिकाऊ.
During. में.
The Dusk. अंधेरो.
Dust. खेह, धूडि, लट, दज, मिटो, खाकि, धुधुडि, बुसिडि.
To Dust. छंडणु.

A Dusting. छंड्कार, छंड्कौ.
Duty. कमु, धर्मु.
Duty on goods. महसूलु, इजारो.
A Dwarf. ज़ामिडो.
Dwarfish. मँधिरो, बिंदिरो.
To Dwell. टिकणु, रहणु, विहणु.
A Dweller. वेठलु, रहाकू.
A Dwelling. रहाश, रहाशत.
To Dwindle away. सुसणु, हपणु.
Dying (*expiring, adj.*). मर्णोगु.
The act or manner of Dying or coloring. रङ्गिणी.
The expense of Dying or coloring. रङ्गणी.
Dysentery. अतिसारु.

E

Each. हिकिडो हिकिडो, सभि.
Eager. शौंकी, उब्रहरो, तकिडो.
Eagerness. शौंकु, उब्रहराई, सिक, तकडि, उबहर.
An Eagle. उकाबु, परमारु.
The Ear. कनु.
The lobe of the Ear. पापिडी.
A stoppage in the Ear. ताडो.
An instrument for cleaning the Ear. छिंघ, कन खोट्रिणी.
To bore the Ear. टोपणु.
Ear cropt, or one without ornaments in the Ears. बुटो.
Ornaments for the Ear (*varieties*). दुरु, केवटी, पनिडो, लुड्को, कुंढलु, झुमकु. कुर्क, ब्रिलिडो, ग़नु, ढ़ेढी, छली, चंद्रसेनो, वाली, मुर्की, चंबुलु, ढ़ेउढी, तनडो, नस्वो, बुंदिडो. मत्ररु, बुंदी, वींढी, चंगुलु.
Ear-wax. मरु *f.*
An Ear of grain. संगु, सिटो, फसु; in different stages in growth, चौंकु, ड़िढो, गल्फाडु, नेसरु, जीउ, ड़ोघो, खीरो, आभू, ड़ड़रु, पकी.
Earlier. अग़ेरो.
Somewhat Earlier. अगेरिडो, महंदेरिडो.
Early. सवेल, सवेर, सवेलो, सवेरे, सांझुरु.
Somewhat early. सवेलाँहों, सवेरिडो, सवेडांहो.
Early (*a crop*). पेशिरसु.
Early morning. वड़ोवेलो, सुभू, सुभूमर्दानी.
To Earn. कमाइणु, खटणु, उपाइणु.
Earnings. कमाई, खट्यो.
Earnest-money. सूथो, बयानो.
Earth (*soil.*). मिटी.
The Earth. जहानु, दुआ, जग़टु, लोकु.
Earthern-ware (*the substance*). ठिकरु. *See* Potsherd.
A seller of Earthern ware vessels. ठेकिरी.
An Earthquake, to occur. धर्ती धुड़णु *or* धुब्रणु.
Ease. सुखु, आरामु, राँहत, सरहाई, फरहत.
Ease (*facility*). सँहँजाई, सौखाई, सौखति, सवलाई.
At Ease, Easy. सौखो, सुख्यो, आसूदो, अयासी.
To be at Ease. करार्जणु.
To Ease nature. टोरोफिरणु.
Easily. सहजें.
The East. उभिरंदो, ओभरु, पूरबु.
Easterly, Eastern. उभिरंयो.
Easy, (*not difficult*). सँहँजो, सौखो, सुख्यो, सुथिरो, सवलो. *See* At Ease.
To Eat. खाइणु, खिअणु, ड़ल्हणु.
Eatable. खाज़िरू.
To be Eaten. खाज़णु, (*as by insects*) सुर्जणु.

An Eater. खाऊ.
The Eaves of a house. छजहरो, लुई.
The Ebb-tide. आलुडु, भाठो.
To Ebb. आलुडणु.
Ebony. आबूसु.
Ebullition. जोशु, भभ्को.
An Echo. पर्लाउ.
An Eclipse. ग्रहणु.
To be Eclipsed. गिरहजणु.
Economy. सर्फो, सांगुसर्फो. *See* Frugality.
An Eddy. कुनु, घुमिरो.
The Edge (*margin*). किनारो, कंधी, कनो, कपु, अंढो, वटि.
The Edge of a blade. धार, मुँहु, रउ; of a web of cloth, ढ़ुंदि.
An Edging for a garment. मग्ज़ो, मिजाफु.
To Educate. पढ़ाइणु, सेखारणु.
An Eel. गोज.
To Efface. मेटणु, लाहणु.
To be Effaced. मिटणु.
An Effect (*consequence*). फलु, फाइदो.
To have an Effect. असरु करणु.
Of no Effect. अकयार्थो, बेफाइदो.
To be Effected. सरणु, थिअनु.
Effeminate. जालाणो, जनानो, जोयो, रनजातोडो, रनजात्यो.
Efficacious. सजायो, सक्यार्थो, सफलो.
An Effort. सायो, उज़मु.
An Egg. आनो; the white of an Egg, सुफेदी.
The Egg plant. वाङणु.
Eight. अठ.
Eight per cent. अठोतिरो.
Eight fold (*adj.*). अठूंणो.
The Eight fold. अठूंणि.
Eighteen. अर्डहं.
Eighteenth. अर्डहों.
Eighth. अठों.
The Eighth figure, or number. अठो.
The Eighth day of the lunar fortnight. अठंईं.
Eightieth. असीभों.
Eighty. असी.
Eighty-one. एकासी.
Eighty-two. ब्रिआसी.
Eighty-three. ट्रिआसी.
Eighty-four. चोरासी.
Eighty-five. पंजासी.
Eighty-six. छहासी.
Eighty-seven. सतासी.
Eighty-eight. अठासी.
Eighty-nine. उणानवे.
Either (*of two*). हिक्रिडो.
Either (*conj.*). जां, तोडे.
The Elbow. ठूंठि, इरिक.
Elder. वडो.
An Elder. वडेरो, मोभी.
Eldest. पेड्यों, पेड्यौं.
To Elect. चुणणु. *See* To Choose.
An Electuary. माजून.
Elegance. सोभा. *See* Beauty.
Elegant. सुहुणो, मोचारो, उम्दो, ऊचो. *See* Nice.
An Elegy. पारु, मर्शो.
An Element. ततु, भूतु, अनासिरु.
An Elephant. (*male*) हाथी, (*female*) हाथ्याणी.
The trunk of an Elephant. सूंढि.
An Elephant driver. पीलवानु.
An Elephant goad or hook. कुंढो, गड्बागु.
An open litter for riding on an Elephant. हौदो; a covered litter, हंबारी.
To Elevate. चाड्हणु, मथे करणु.
Elevation. ड्रेघु, ड्रिघाई.

Eleven. यारँहं, कारँहं.
Eleven fold (*adj.*). याहूंणो.
The Elevenfold. याहूंणि.
Eleventh. याहीं.
The Eleventh figure or number. याहों.
The Eleventh day of the lunar fortnight. ग्यारिसि. एकाड़सी, काहीं, याहीं.
An Elk. गोइनु.
Eloquent. चर्ब्रटु.
Else (*pro. other*). ब्रिओ.
Else (*adv. otherwise*). नत.
Elsewhere. ब्रिएहंधि.
To Elude. गुसाइणु. *See* Evade.
Emaciated. होणो, डुबिरो, कड़ंगु, खीणु, ग्रंड़ो.
Emancipated. आजो. *See* Free.
Emancipation. छोट्कारो, छोट्को, मोखु.
An Embankment. बंधि, बंदु, बंधु.
To lay an Embargo on goods. ठल्हणु.
To Embark (*act.*). चाड़्हणु.
To Embark (*neu.*). चड़्हणु.
Embarrassment. जंजलु, मांझि. *See* Perplexity.
An Embassador. वकीलु, एल्ची.
To Embezzle. खाई-ग़िहो-वञणु, फब्राइणु.
To be Embezzled. पचणु, फब्रणु, भुचणु.
Embezzlement. खाड़ो, खुर्दिबुर्दि.
An Embrace, Embracing. भाकुरु, ग़िराहुटिडी, ग़िराहुटी, ब्रखु.
To Embrace. भाकुरु &c. पाइणु *or* विझणु.
An Embrasure. मारो.
To Embroider. भरणु.
Embroidered. चिकिमी, भर्थूं.
An Embroiderer. चिकिन्दोनु, जदोंजु, कार्चोबु, कुंढीदोजु.
Embroidery. चिकिमु, चिकिनु, भर्थु.
An Embryo. गर्भु, ग्रभु.
An Emerald. जमुरदु, पनो.
Eminent. जसी. *See* Famous.
To Empale. सूरी ड़िअणु.
An Emperor. महाराजु, बाछा. *See* King.
To Employ. कमि लाइणु *or* लग़ाइणु.
To be Employed. जुंबणु, लग़णु. *See* To be Engaged.
Busily Employed. घणवाखुतो, रूधो.
Employment. कमु, कमुकाजु, हाज.
To Empoverish. सखिणो करणु.
Emptiness. पाल्हाई, वेल्हाई, ठल्हाई.
Empty. ठल्हो, पाल्हो, वांदो, खालो, वेल्हो, सखिणो.
To Empty. ठल्हो &c. करणु.
Emulation. रीस.
Emulative, Emulous. रीसारो.
Enamel. मीनो; a red kind of enamel, पर्पूरो.
Enamelled. मीनाकारी.
Enamelling. मीनाकारी; a kind of enamelling, सवादिकारी.
To Enamour. मोहणु, वसि करणु.
To be Enamoured. वसि थिअणु, फसणु, अट्कणु.
To Encamp. मैजल विझणु, लहणु.
An Encampment. मैजल, देरो.
An Enchanter. जादूगरु, कामिण्गोरु.
Enchantment. जादू, कामिणु, टोणो.
To Encircle. वेड़्हणु, घेरणु.
Encircling. वेड़्हु, घेरो.
To Enclose. वाड़ि-लोड़्हो-विझणु *or* ड़िअणु.
An Enclosure. वाड़ो, वेड़्हो.
To Encounter (*act.*). मुहाड़ो करणु.

To Encounter (*neu.*). साम्हों थि-अणु, टकिरणु, भिड़हणु.

To Encourage. दिलासो &c. ड़िअणु, सत्या मंड़ाइणु.

Encouragement. दिलासो, दिल्जाई, दिल्दारी, तसलाई, धीर्जु, खातर्जमो.

To Encroach. दखलु करणु.

An End (*extremity*). मुहुंडो, मथो, सिरो, मुँहु.

End (*conclusion*). ओड़कु, अंतु, छेहु, आखरि, तोड़ु.

End (*finishing*). निबेरो, निछोड़ु.

To End (*act.*). निबेरणु, निछोड़णु, पूरो करणु.

To End, be Ended. निबिरणु, निब-हणु, पूरो थिअणु.

To no End. अजयाथो, बेफाइदो.

Endearment. चचुलाई, लाडु.

An Endeavour. सायो, उज़मु.

Ended. पूरो.

Endive. कासिनी.

Endless. बेहदि.

To Endorse a bill. (*in selling*) वि-काउ लिखणु, (*in accepting*) पुठि भरणु.

Endurance (*continuance*). तग़ाउ, टिकाउ, जटाउ, बकाउ.

The property which causes Endurance, or lastingness. सतु.

To Endure, or last. तग़णु, ज-टणु.

To Endure, or suffer. सहणु, झ-लणु, जारणु.

Enduring (*sub. brooking*). जर्णो, खांदि.

Enduring (*patient*). खांदीरो.

An Enemy. दुश्मणु, वेरी.

Of an Enemy. दुश्मणाणो, दुश्मण्को, वेर्याणो, वेर्को.

Energy. सत्या, हिमथ.

To be Enfeebled. वेसघो-हीणो-नि-सतो-थिअणु.

To Engage (*enter upon*). जुटणु.

To Engage (*a servant*). रखणु, धा-रणु, बिहारणु.

To Engage (*contract*). ब्रोल्णु.

To be busily Engaged. रुभणु.

An Engagement (*agreement*). जा-इजु, ब्रोलु, वचनु, वाइदो, अंजामु. *See* Fight.

To Engender. पैदा करणु, उपज़ाइणु.

English. अंग्रेजी.

An Englishman. अंग्रेजु.

To Engrave. उकिरणु.

An Engraver. वींझरू.

An Enigma. पिरोली, गुझारत, बुझा-रत.

To Enjoin. हुकुमु करणु, समुझाइणु. तागीद करणु.

To Enjoin. सुखु &c. लहणु *or* पा-इणु, भोगणु, माणणु.

Enjoyment. सुखु, मजो, खुशी, सवादु, ऐशु, भोगु.

One fond of sensual Enjoyment. ऐशी.

To Enlarge. वधाइणु.

Enmity. वेरु, दुश्मणी, अदावत, लाग़.

Enough. बसि, घणो, झझो.

To Enrage. काविड़ाइणु, ड़मिराइणु.

To Enrich. साओ &c. करणु, रज़णु. *See* Rich.

To Ensue (*neu.*). थिअणु, निकिरणु.

To Entangle. गंड़णु, मुँझाइणु, फसा-इणु.

To be Entangled. मुँझणु, फसणु.

An Entanglement. मोंझि, मोंझारो, गंड़ु.

To Enter. पिहणु, घिड़णु.

To Enter (*in registering*). दाखिलो करणु.

To Enter upon a business. घिडणु, पेहु-इथु-विझणु.
An Enterprise. मुहीम.
To Entertain *(divert)*. रीझाइणु, विंदुराइणु. *See* To Engage.
An Entertainment (*at table*). मिड्मानी, मिझाणी.
To Entice. धुतारणु, रेबणु, भर्माइणु, लोभणु, लोभाइणु, लाल्चाइणु.
Enticement. धुतार, चट, रेबु, बमु, चडहु.
An Enticer. रेबी, चटिरू, धुतारू, धुतिरू.
Entire. सज़ो, सारो, पूरो, सभु, सभोई, समूरो, सबंस्तो, साबितु.
Entirely. सारो &c. *as above*, सभों, बिल्कुलु, बरोबरि, तमामु, पटिअ, सरासरि.
Entrails. ओझिरो, आंडो, गुजो; of a fish, बोरी.
Entrance (*admittance*). वाट, मोकल, वञणु.
An Entrance (*door way*). बुंभो, दरू.
To Entrap. फासाइणु.
To Entreat. लिलाइणु, मिनथ, &c. करणु.
An Entreating. मिनथ, नीज़ारी, विननी, लीलिडारी, लिल्डी.
An Entry (*into any place*). अचणु.
An Entry for register. दाखिलो.
To Entwine, Envelop. वेडहणु.
An Envelope. लिफाफो, सर्नामो.
Envious. खामिखाधो, साडेखाधो.
To be Envious. सडणु, डझणु, जलणु, खामणु.
The Environs of a town, &c. पसिगराई.
To Enumerate. हिकु हिकु करे चवणु.
Envy. हूस, खामि, सडणि, साडो, साडु, जलणि, जल्णी.
To Envy. हूसणु.
An Epicure. सवाद्खोरू.
An Epidemic disease. मरी, ओथडि, वबा, वफा.
The Epilepsy. मिर्घी, मरी.
Equal. बरोबरि, हिकजिहडो, हिकजेडो. मटु, समानि, तुलि.
Equal in age. सर्तो, जेड़ो.
To Equal, or be quits with. पाड्णु.
Equality. बरोबरी, हिकजिहडाई, जेड़ाई, *(the being quits)* पाडझाड.
Equilibrium, Equipoise. सँवाई.
To be Equipped. संभिरणु, संवहणु, जुडणुजकणु.
Equitable. हकी, सचो, वाजिबी. *See* Just.
Equity. हकु. *See* Justice.
An Era. संवतु, सनु.
To Eradicate. पटणु, कढणु.
To Erase. उखहणु, लाहणु, मेटणु, (*by scraping*) खुडणु.
Erect. उभो, खडो.
To Erect or build. अड़णु, गंड़णु, जोडणु.
To Erect (*place upright*). बिहारणु.
To Err (*do wrong*). भुलणु, ड़ोहु करणु.
An Error. भुल, भोलि, भोलो, ड़ोहु, खता.
To Escape. भजो-खिस्की-छुटो-वञणु, बचणु.
Especially. घणो.
Espousals. मङिणो.
An Essence. सारू, मग्जु, ततु, तंतु.
To Establish. विहारणु, जोडणु.
To Esteem. लेखणु, ग़णणु, भांइणु.
An Estimate. तक, कथ, रिथ.
To Estimate. तकणु, कथणु, रिथणु, लेखणु.
By Estimate. अठिसठो.

Et cetera. वगैरा.
Eternal. नितु, काइमु, सति.
Eternally. सदा, हमेशां, नितु.
Ethics. नीति.
To Evacuate. छड़णु, वांदो-पाल्हो-खाला-करणु.
To Evade, or practice Evasion. टारणु, गुसाइणु, टुल्काइणु, टाटमाइणु, नटाइणु.
One who Evades. गोझरू, गुसाऊ, गोमिरू, नाटाऊ.
Evanescent. फानी.
To Evaporate *(neu.)*. सुकणु, खपणु.
An Evasion, or Evading. टार, गोहो, गहु, गोश्नाथ, टालो, कांइं.
Even *(level, &c.)*. बराबरि, सँभों, हिकजिहड़ो. *See* Equal.
Even, even so much as. मूरिगो, निग़णो. *See* also Although.
An Even number. बधी.
The Evening. सांझी, टिकर, शाम, निमाशाम, संझां, संझो.
Evenness. सँवाई.
An Event (*incident*). गाल्हि, कमु.
Ever (*at any time*). कड़ही. *See* Always.
Every. सभि, कुलु, सभुकोई.
Evidence (*testimony*). साख, शाहिदी. *See* Witness.
Evident. पधिरो, जाहिरू.
Evil *(Adj.)*. बुछिड़ो, मंदो.
Evil (*Sub.*). बुछिड़ाई, मंदाई.
Evil-minded. खोटो. *See* Malevolent.
A Eunuch. नाजिरू, खोजो.
A Ewe. रिढ, घेटी, दुंबी.
Exact, Exactly. ठीकु, दुरुस्तु, पूरो.
To Exaggerate. वधीक-वाधू-ग़ाल्हाइणु.
To Exalt. निहालु-सर्फिराजु-करणु. *See* To Raise.
An Examination. पर्ख, जाच, आज़्मुदो, परीछा. *See* Inquiry.
To Examine. पर्खणु, जाचणु, आज़्माइणु. *See* To Investigate, Inquire, Inspect.
An Example. मिसालु, द्रिष्टांतु.
To Exasperate. चेड़ाइणु, चेड़णु.
To Excavate. खोटणु.
To Exceed. वधीक &c. करणु.
Exceeding bounds or what is needful. वधि, वधीक, वाधू, सर्सु.
Exceeding, Exceedingly. घणो, तमामु, ड़ाढो, अतंति, निपटु.
To Excel. सर्सु-भड़ु-हुअणु.
Excellence *(superiority)*. उम्दाई, ऊचाई, ऊचाणि, मोचाराई, सर्साई. *See* Goodness.
Excellent. उम्दो, ऊचो, मोचारो, खासो, चोखो, कसर, सर्सु. *See* Good.
Except. सिवाइ, धारां, धारे, रे, बाझों, विना.
To Except. धार रखणु, छड़णु.
Excess. वधिक. *See* Superfluity.
Excess due on a running account. फाजिली.
One who commits an Excess. अशिरो.
Excessive. घणो. *See* Exceeding.
Exchange, Exchanging. मटसट.
Exchange (*discount*). मटा, वटो.
An Exchange (*what is given*). एवजु, एवजी, बदरू.
In Exchange. बदिरें, बदरि, एवजि.
To Exchange. मटणु.
To Excite. मचाइणु, दुखाइणु, चोरणु.
To be Excited (*a quarrel*). मचणु, दुखणु.

An Exciter of quarrels. छेणाभोरू फिब्रती.

To Exclaim. दांह-रडि-वाकी-करणु.

To Exclude. बाहरि रखणु, वांजणु.

To Excoriate. खल उथेडणु.

An Excoriation. गाठी.

The Excrement of man. गुंहु, कि-रिस्की, झाडो, (*thin*) तीक.

A lump of Excrement. लेंडो.

An Excrescence. गंढि, गोड्हो.

An Excuse. उजिरू, सबबु.

An Execration. पाराती. *See* Curse.

To Execute (*perform*). बजाइ आ-णणु, करणु. *See* To Perform.

Exempt, Exempted. माफु.

Exemption. माफी.

Exercise (*practice*). इस्तमाली, अ-भ्यासु, ड़ाखिडो.

Exertion. सायो, उज़मु, मिहनत.

An Exigence. औखु. *See* Difficulty.

To Exist. हुअणु, रहणु, जिअणु.

Existence. हयाती.

To Expand (*act.*). पखेडणु, उप-टणु, पसारणु.

To Expand (*neu.*). पखिडणु, पसि-रणु. *See* To Swell.

Expansion. वेकिराई, मोकिराई, गे-लि, फेलाउ, पसारो.

To Expect. वाट ड़िसणु, उमेद &c. रखणु.

An Expectant. आसाऊ, आसावंतु, उमेदवारू.

Expectation (*hope*). आस, उमेद, (*looking for*) हिड़िक, ओसीडो.

To Expectorate. खांघारणु.

An Expectoration. खांघार ; phlegm discharged, खांघारो.

An Expedient. ढंउं, वझु, विलो, उ-पाउ. *See* Remedy.

Expeditious. जल्दु, (*a person*) झां-झिरो, (*an act*) सिघो. *See* Quick.

To Expel. तडणु, कढणु.

To Expend. खपाइणु, खर्चणु.

To be Expended. खपणु

Expenditure, Expense. खापो, खर्चु, खपति, खपु.

Expensive (*extravagant*). वडखर्चो. *See* Dear.

Experience. पर्खं, आज़्मुदो, दकु.

Experienced. भडु, पको.

An Experiment. पर्खं, आज़्मुदो.

An Expert person. भडु, सुघडु, का-रीगरू, पको.

Expertness. भडाई, पकाई, सुघडाई.

An Expiation. पुनइचरणु, कफारत.

To Expire. मरणु. *See* To Die, To End.

To Explain. समुझाइणु, पधराइणु, निर्वारू करणु.

An Explanation. इज़हारू, विहुरो,

Explicit, Explicitly. चिटो, सफा-साफु.

An Exploit. कारिस्तानु.

To Explore. सुधि लहणु. *See* To Examine, Search.

Export, Exporting. नेकालु, नेकासु, नेखनि.

To Expose. उघाडणु.

Express, Expressly. साफु. *See* Explicit.

An Express (*courier, letter, &c.*) खेप्यो.

Charge for an Express. खेप.

To Express (*squeeze out*). पीडे-निपुडे-कढणु. *See* To Represent, Utter.

To Extend. वधाइणु. *See* To Spread.

Extension. वधाऊ.

Extensive. वड़ो. *See* Wide.
Exterior, External. ब्हर्याँ.
To Exterminate. पाड़ू पटणु.
Exterminated, Extinct. नासु, फना, चट्टु, चपड्चट्टु.
Extermination. नासु. *See* Destruction.
To Extinguish. विसाइणु, उझांइणु, (*a lamp only*) गुलु-वड़ो-करणु.
To be Extinguished. विसामणु, उझामणु.
To Extirpate. पाड कढणु.
To Extort. पीड़े वठणु.
Extra. वधीक. *See* More.
To Extract. कढणु, उखेड़णु.
Extraordinary. अजबु.
Extravagant. उड़ाऊ, लुटाउ, खापाऊ.
Extremely. तमामु. *See* Exceedingly.
The Extremity (*end*). सिरो, मुड्डो.
To Extricate. छड़ाइणु, कढणु.
Exuberance. वाधि. *See* Superfluity.
Exultation. खुशी, रीझो. *See* Delight.
The Eye. अखि, नेणु, चश्म.
The Eye of a needle. नाको, पाखो.
The dark spot of the pupil of the Eye. वनी, माणिकी.
The Eye-ball. तारो.
An Eye-brow. भिरूं.
One-Eyed. काणो.
The hair of the Eye-lash. पिंबिणी.
An Eye-lid. छपरू, पलक.
Gum or mucus of the Eye. पिचो.
To become sore, the Eyes. अख्यूं उथणु.
The Eye sight. निर्ति.
An Eye twinkling. अखिछिंभ, पलक.

F

A Fable. इंदकथा *See* Story.
The Face. मुंहु, मुखु, चिहिरो, मुहड़ि.
A wry Face. मेछ, मुच्को, मोडो.
To make Faces. मेछूं *&c.* ड़िअणु.
Face to Face. आमोसाम्हो, मुखामुखी.
With Face downwards, on its Face मुंह भर.
With Face upwards. सँभो, पुठिभर
Facility. सौखु, सवलाई सै खाई, मँहँजाई
Facetious. चचाई. *See* Jocular.
A Factor. गुमाश्तो.
Factorship. गुमाश्तिगीरी.
To Fade away. कुमाइजणु, गरणु, सड़णु.
To Fade (*as colors*). फिरणु, फिको झको-थिअणु.
To Fag. वहणु, गहणु.
A Fagot. फोड़ाठी, टोटो, बुंड़ो, काठी.
To Fail (*fall short*). खुटणु.
To Fail (*miss, miscarry*). गुसणु
To Fail (*as a crop*). न थिअणु.
A Failing (*defect*). ऐबु, वोक, औगुणु. *See* Deficiency.
To Faint. टकिजणु.
Faint (*weak*). मांदो, गेरो.
To grow Faint. विसामी वञणु.
A Faint, Fainting. टकरु, गशो.
Fainted, in a Faint. गशु, बेसुधि.
A Fair. मेलो, मेड़ो.
Fair (*just*). सचो, सँभो, वाजिबु.
Fair (*complexion*). गोरो, भूरो.
Fair (*wind*). सणाओ, साज़ो, सवलो.
Fairness (*honesty q. v.*). सचाई, सँभाई, (*of complexion*) गोराई, भूराई.
A Fairy. परी.

Faith (*religious belief*). दीनु, धर्मु.
Faith (*trust*). ईमानु, निभत, सधा, (*trust in God*) तौंकल.
Faithful. सचो, ईमानी, निमकहलालु.
Faithless. कूडो, बेईमानु, निमकहरामु, बेसाहधातो, बेवफा.
Faithlessness. कूडाई, बेईमानी, निमकहरामी, वेसाहधाती.
A Falcon. शाहबाज़ु.
A Falconer. बाज़दारु.
To Fall. किरणु, पवणु, (*as leaves, fruit, &c.*) छणणु.
To Fall or abate (*as a flood, wind, &c.*). हलणु, मुडणु, छिज़णु.
To Fall (*as a building*). डहणु.
To Fall on, Fall out, *See* To Attack, To Quarrel.
A Fall, or declension of the flood in the river. छिनहडो.
The time of the Fall of the flood. सांधारो.
A Fall in price. मोडी.
Fallen in price. मोडो.
A Falling off. कोताही.
Fallow land. आइठो; old Fallow land, विसाणो.
False. कूडो, खोटो, कुलालु.
A Falsehood. कूडु.
Falseness, Falsity. कूडाई.
To Falter. हब्कणु, अट्कणु, हट्कणु.
Fame. नामूसु, नाँउं, नामु, नामाचारु, नाम्वारी, नाम्तारी, जसु, हाक, हाकार.
A Family (*household*). घरु, आकहि, कुडुमु, कुटिमु, कुटभु, टब्बरु, कबीलो, अयालु, साघरि.
Family (*race*). निआति, नुख, पथरु, कूम, आकहि, कुलु, अल, गोटु.
Of high Family. घराइतो, घराणी, आकाद्यो, कलाइतो.
One who has a Family. घरबारी, ब्चडवालु, कबीलदारु, सधिरो, अयालदारु.
A Famine. डुकारु, डुकरु, कहतु, कालु.
To Famish (*neu.*). बुख, मरणु.
Famous. नालेरो, हाकार्यो, नामकिर्यो, उजारो, नाम्दारु, नाम्वरु, नामी, नाँइचड्यो, जसी.
A Fan (*small*). विञ्णी, पखो, (*large*) विञ्णो, पखो, (*suspended*) झलो, झूलोणी.
To Fan. विञ्णो हणणु, वाउ करणु.
Fanciful. गुरारो, ओकातो, लहरो.
A Fancy (*foolish conceit*). पूरु, उमघु, कुडु, खिआलु, रीचकु, बुद्बुदो, बुदिकी.
To Fancy (*imagine*). भांइणु, समुझणु, शक्जणु, गुमान्जणु.
A Fang. नेशु. *See* Tusk, Claw.
Far. परे, डूरि.
How Far. केतिरो पंधु.
Fare (*food q. v.*). खेणु.
Fare (*for conveyance*). चाड्हाको, भाडो.
Farewell. अलहतुहारि, अलहुवाही.
A Farm. ब्नी, आइठो, पनो.
To Farm, or take on lease (*revenue*). मकातो खणणु.
A Farmer. मुखादिमु, ज़िमीदारु, ब्न्यरु. *See* Husbandman.
A Farmer of revenue. मकातेदारु.
A Farrier. नाल्बंदु.
A Fart. टिटु, गोजु, वाइडो; a dead fart, फुस.
To Fart. टिटु *&c.* छिडणु.
Farther. परांहीं, डूरांहीं.
Farthermore. अगा बि. *See* Also, Besides.
A Farting. टोटीं, टूंटूं, ढूंढूं, ढेढीं

To Fascinate. मोहणु, वसि करणु.
Fascinating (*adj.*) मोहिणो, मोंहु.
Fascination. मोहणु.
A Fashion. ढँढ, ड्रौलु, ड्रांउ. *See* Form, Custom.
To Fashion. घड़णु.
Fashionable. रीताइतो. *See* Customary.
A Fast. रोज़ो, सोकहडो, लंघणु, विर्तु, फाको.
To Fast. रोज़ो-विर्तु-रखणु, लंघणु, &c. कढणु or करणु.
Fast (*firm*). ड़ाढो, पुख्तो, सोघो, हथोको. *See* Quick.
To Fasten. बंधणु, गंढणु.
A Fastening. बंधणु.
Fasting since the morning (*adj.*). नेरानो.
Fastidious. मिजाज़ी.
Fat (*subs.*). वह, चर्बी.
Fat (*adj.*). थुल्हो, डुढिटो, ड़टोमुटो, मतारो, यटो, जटो, मुठ्को.
To grow Fat. मचणु.
Fate. नसीबु, तालिहु, किस्मत, बख्तु, भागु, कर्मु, नेति, प्रापति, प्रालभि, थिभणी, भाणी, लिख्यो, होणहारी, हुअणी, लेहु.
Ill-Fated. निभाग़ो.
A Father. पिउ, बाबो, अबो, पिता.
A Father in law. सहुरो, ठकुरू.
One's Father in law's family. साहुरा *plu.*
A wife's Father's family (*so called by her*). पेका *plu.*
The Father in law of one's son or daughter. सेणु.
Fatigue. थकु, चोकिडो.
To Fatigue. थकाइणु.
To be Fatigued. थकणु, कुड़णु, खुहिजणु.
One easily Fatigued. खुह्यलु, थकलु.
Fatness. माचि, थुल्हाई, थोल्हि.
To Fatten (*act.*). मचाइणु.
To Fatten (*neu.*). मचणु.
A Fault. भुल, ड़ोहु, हर्फु, खता.
To lay one's Fault on another. ठिकरू भञणु, ड़ोहु रखणु.
Faultless (*innocent*). बेड़ोहु, बेगुनाहु, (*perfect, complete*) पूरो, (*sound*) बेऐबो.
Faultlessly. बेगुनाहि, बेड़ोहि.
Faulty (*guilty of a fault*). ड़ुहारो, ड़ोही, हर्फी, (*defective*) घटि.
Favour. मिहिर्बानी, थोरो, फज़ुलु. *See* Kindness.
Favourable (*wind*). सणाओ, सवलो.
Favouring, Favouritism. पासि, वंटिप, पास्खातरि, रिआउ. *See* Partiality.
A Favourite. दादुलो, सुहाग़ी.
A Favourite wife. सुहाग़िणि.
A Fawn. ब्रठिडो.
Fawning. लिबास, ललोपतो.
Fear. ड्रपु, ड्रिजु, ड्रेजो, भउ, ड़रू, ड्राउ, तर्सु, उड़िको.
To Fear. ड्रिजणु, ड़रणु.
To cause Fear. ड्रेजारणु.
Fearful (*causing fear*). खौफाइतो, कड़ो, करूड़. *See* Timorous.
Fearless. बेभओ, निधड़ु, निधड़कु, निर्भउ, निसंगु, बेपर्वाहु.
Fearlessnes. बेभवाई, बेपर्वाही.
A Feast. जुञु, मिझाणी, मिज्मानी, मज्लस, झुग़िलु.
A brahmin's or fukeer's Feast. थानसुधि, जगु, दलु, भंड़ारो, ओछउ, कुण्को, जोड़ु, तिलु.
To Feast (*entertain*). मिझाणी करणु.
A Feat. कारिस्तानु.

A Feather. खंभु, पख, पखु.
Featherless. अणखंभो, लुसु, गोडू.
The Features (*face*). मुहांडो.
February and part of March. फागुणु.
A Fee. लागो, लाग, मिन्हताणो, अब्वाबु. *See* Perquisite.
Feeble. बेसघो, अघो, निसतो, हीणो. *See* Weak.
Feebleness. बेसघाई, अघाई.
Feebly. मठो, ढिरो.
To Feed (*eat*). खाइणु, (*as cattle*) चरणु.
To Feed (*another*). खाराइणु, (*cattle*) चारणु.
To Feel (*neu.*). लगणु.
To Feel (*try by touch, &c.*). छुहो डिसणु, सही करणु.
To Feign. मिंहु-बहानो-करणु.
To deceive by Feigning. मिंहाइणु.
A Feint. छलु, भुलाओ.
To Fell. केरणु, केराइणु.
The Felloe of a wheel. वंग.
A Fellow (*match q. v.*). जोडु. *See* Companion, Partner, Equal.
Fellowship. संगति, संगु.
Felt (*subs.*). नौदु, नमँदु, नाओ, नाई.
A maker of Felt. नौदाई, नौदो.
A Female. माद, मादी. *See* Feminine, Woman.
The Female apartments. जनान्खानो, ड़ेढी.
Feminine. जालाणो, (*gender*) स्त्रीलिंगु, मुअनिसु.
A Fen. भुब्रणि.
A Fence (*hedge*). लोड्हो, वाडि, पँझरू, मुहाडो, पल्वाडो, कंधी.
A Fencer. पल्थेबाजु.
The art of Fencing. पल्थो.
Fennel. सुआ.

Fenugreek. मेथी; the seed, हुर्बो.
To Ferment (*neu.*). मचणु.
To Ferment (*act.*). मचाइणु.
Ferocious. करूडु, कडो.
A Ferry. पतणु.
A Ferryman or Ferry boat. पातिणो.
Ferry money, Ferriage. पतणु.
Fertile. आबादु, वसँदडु.
Fertility. आबादी, वसँदी.
To Fertilize. वसाइणु, आबादु करणु.
To Fester (*as a sore*). पचणु.
A Festival. थिभुं, पर्भु, वड़ो ड़िंहु, बारहमाहों ड़िंहु, ड़िंणु, ईद, तिहाडो.
Festivity. शादी, शाद्मानो, काजु, काजुं, मंगलाचारू.
To Fetch. आणणु, खणी अचणु.
Fetid. किनो.
Fetidness. किनाई.
To Fetter. नैलु, &c. विझणु *or* पाइणु.
Fetters. नैलु, नेलु, जोल.
A Feud. झेडो, चटाभेटी. *See* Contention.
A Fever. तपु, तापु, ब्ररो, बुखारू.
An intermittent Ferver. वारे-जोतपु. *See* Ague.
A prevailing Fever. तपति, तपावलो.
A slight Fever. तौंस, कणिस.
The cold fit in Fever. सीभो.
To be seized with Fever. तपिजणु.
Few. थोरो, थोरिडो.
A Few. की.
Some Few. कींक, कीथोरो.
Fewness. थोराई, थोरिडाई.
A Fibre. तंदु *f.*
Fickle. चंचलु, चल्विलो.
Fickleness. चल्विलाई.
A Fiction. कूडी गाल्हि, ड़ंदकथा.
Fidelity. सचाई निमकहलाली.
Fidgety. चल्विलो, हर्कती.
Fie. छि, छो, थू.

A Field. इनी, खेट्टु, तकु
A Field of battle. रिणु.
Fierce. तुंदु, करुँर्ो.
Fierceness. तुंदी.
Fieriness. करुाई, तिखाई.
Fiery. तिखो, करुंो, कौडो.
Fifteen. पंद्रहँ, पंध्रां.
Fifteenth. पंध्रों, पंद्रहों.
The Fifteenth day of lunar fortnight (*after new moon*). पूनँईं, पूनँउँ *f.* पूरणमासी, (*after full*) अमास.
Fifth. पंजों.
The Fifth day of lunar fortnight. पँजँईं.
Fifty. पंजाह.
About Fifty. पँजाहो.
Fifty-one. एकवंजाह.
Fifty-two. ब्रावंजाह.
Fifty-three. टेवंजाह.
Fifty-four. चोवंजाह.
Fifty-five. पंज्वंजाह.
Fifty-six. छावंजाह.
Fifty-seven. सत्वंजाह.
Fifty-eight अठ्वंजाह.
Fifty-nine. उणहठि.
A Fig. अंजोरू.
The sacred Fig tree. पिपिरू.
The Indian Fig tree. बड़ु.
A Fight, Fighting. जंगि, झेडो, वेड्हि, किलो.
To Fight. विड्हणु.
A Fighter. वेड्हू.
Figure (*form*). ड़ौलु, सूरत, (*statue, image*), पुतिली, मूरति.
A Figure (*number*). अंगु.
A Filbert nut. फंदक.
A File (*the instrument*). रवास, कनंहि
A File of papers strung. पुभडो.

To File (*abrade*). रवासणु.
Filial. पुट्राणो.
Filings. बूरो, चूरो.
To Fill. भरणु.
A Fillip. ठोंगो, फिड़िक.
A Filly. वछेडी, बिहाणि.
A Film. छटी, थरी.
To Filter (*act.*). छाणणु,
Filth. मैल, गंदु, (*stinking*) किनु.
Filthiness. मेराई, मेराणि, गंदाई.
Filthy. मेरो, गदिलो, मलोनु, किनो, गलोज़.
A Fin. खंभुडि, खंभुडो.
Final. पोंगों.
To Find (*obtain*). लहणु, (*with its object as nom:*) लभणु, मिलणु, (*to perceive*) ड़िसणु.
To Find out. गोले-फोल्हे-कढणु, सुधि लहणु.
Fine (*subtile*). सन्हो, सन्हिडो. *See* Elegant, Excellent.
A Fine. चटी, ड़ंडु.
To Fine. चटी &c. वठणु.
Fine drawing. तुनु, तुञु.
Fineness. सन्हाई.
A Finger. आङुरि.
The fore-Finger. ड़सिणी आङुरि.
The middle-Finger. विचीं आङुरि.
The ring-Finger. बाच.
The little-Finger. चीच.
A Finger's breadth. अङुरू.
To Finish. निबेरणु, पुज़ाइणु, चुकाइणु, पूरो करणु.
To be Finished. पुज़णु, निबिरणु, पूरो-तमामु-थिअणु, उकिलणु, चुकणु.
A Finishing. निबेरो. *See* Conclusion.
Fire. बाहि, आगि, ज़रो; a great fire, मचु; a fire of smoke, दूंहों.
To Fire, or set on Fire. बाहि ड़ि-

अणु, साडणु. *See* To Cauterize.
To Fire as a gun. छोडणु.
To be Fired as a gun. छुडणु, छुटणु, छुट्कणु.
A Firebrand. चुआंती, उमाडो, उमडु.
A Firefly. टांड़ाणो, खुड्खुवोतो, खड्खटु.
A Fire place. आग़ोठो, चुल्हि, चुल्हो.
Firewood. काठ्यूं *plu.* ब़ारणु.
Fireworks. आतश्बाजो, (*varieties*). फटाको, कुपो, चादर, टोटिको, टोटो, नरी, नरो, बागु, मातावु, माताबी, सूसूरी, हवाई, विछूं.
Firm. ड़ाढो, पको, पुख्तो, सोघो, काबू.
To make Firm (*as a post*). खोडणु. *See* To fix.
To be Firm or fixed. खुपणु, फहकणु.
Firmly. ड़ाढ्यां.
Firmness. ड़ाढाई, पुख्ताई.
First (*adj.*). पेन्ह्यों, पन्ह्यों, पेह्यों, अग़ियो.
The First, adding a quarter. सवांओं; adding a half, ड़ेढुंओ.
First (*adv*). पेहीं, पेन्हीं, परीदे, अग़हीं.
First born. पेह्यांतु, पेह्योंठो.
A Fish. मछो; a large fish, मछु.
To Fish. मछी मारणु.
Smelling of Fish, (*adj*). खिखो.
A Fishy smell. खिख, खिखी, खिखाई.
A Fish bone. कंड़ो.
A Fisherman. मेउ, मुहाणो; *of Pulla*, माछुरु; his pot, माटो.
Of a Fisherman. मेअको, मुहाणको.
A Fishery. मिआणी.
A Fishhook. कुंढी.
A Fishmonger. माछी.
A Fishwoman. माछ्याणी.
A Fissure. ड़ारु, फोड, डरिडु. *See* Crack.
A Fist. मुठि, मुक.
A Fistful. मुठि.
Fisticuffs. मुकामुकी.
A Fistula. नासूरु, (*in uno*) भगंदरु.
A Fit, as of epilepsy. झूटो.
A Fit of passion. जकु, जलु. *See* Burst.
Fit. लाइकु, जोगु, मुनासिबु, बावु, मडाइतो.
Fit for nothing. की न थिओ. *See* Useless.
To Fit. ठहणु, जुडणु. *See* To Become.
Fitness. लाइकी.
Five. पंज.
The figure Five. पंजो
Fivefold. पंजूंणो.
The Fivefold. पंजूंणो.
To Fix (*apply, fasten*). लाइणु, हणणु, लग़ाइणु, विहारणु, खोडणु, खुपाइणु, फहकाइणु.
To Fix (*settle*). ठाहणु, अंजामु करणु.
To Fix the price of any thing. चुकाइणु.
To be Fixed (*fastened*). लग़णु, विहणु, फहकणु, खुपणु.
Flabbiness. फेफाई.
Flabby. फेफो, फफसु.
A Flag (*ensign*). झंड़ो, नीशानु, वांवटो, बैरक, मर्वल.
A Flag (*stone*). फरहो, तख्तो
A Flag-staff. छडुह.
A Flagon. घुघो, सुराही, झारो, कुजो, भभुई.
A Flame. लाट, ज़िभी, ओरांभो, भभडु, भभटु.
A Flank. पासो, ब़ाहीं

To Flap the wings. खंभ साहणु.
A Flash, Flashing. चिम्कौ, झल्कौ.
To Flash. चिम्कणु, झल्कणु, खिंवणु.
Flat (*as a dish*). तराखिडो, तरासिडो, तराशौ, तान्हिडो, तांघिडो, तांघो.
Flat (*level, prone*). सँऔं, (*as a slip of wood*) पटेदारू, चिपिरौ.
Flat-bottomed (*as a bowl, &c.*). वेठडो.
To Flatten. चिपणु.
Flattened. चिपो.
To Flatter. खुशामदि *&c.* करणु.
A Flatterer. खुशामदिड्यौ.
Flattery. खुशामदि, ललोपतो, लिबास.
Flatulency. वाई, बादी.
Flatulent. वादी.
Flavour. सवादु, मजो, रसु, लजत, चाश्नी, सुआउ, साउ.
A Flaw (*in a rupee*). कैजु. *See* Crack, Defect.
Flax. सिणी.
To Flay. खलणु, चमु लाहणु.
A Flea. कारिडो.
Fleawort. इसंगरू.
To Flee. भज़णु.
A Fleece. पुठो.
Fleet. छुहो, तिखो. *See* Swift.
A Fleet. बहरू, नवाडो.
Flesh. माहु, माँसु, गोस्तु, (*Hindoo terms*) सारिणो, सागु, लाल भाज़ी.
A lump of Flesh meat. सुधु, दगलु, बेरो; a bit of do. सुधी सुंढी. *See* Piece.
Flexible. कुंभरो, मुडिणो.
A Flight, Fleeing. भज़ि, भाज़डि, भाज़ि. *See* Flying.
To put to Flight. भज़ाइणु.
Flighty (*capricious*). पूरारो, ओकाति.

To Fling (*act.*). उछिलाइणु.
A Flint. चक्मकु, गोटी.
To Flit (*migrate*). लडणु.
To Float (*neu.*). तरणु.
To Float, or be carried along in the stream. लुडहणु.
A Float, (*raft q. v.*) तुरहो.
A Flock of sheep or goats. धणु, वलरू, अजडु, जबुं, टोरो, खेरि.
A Flock or flight of birds. वलरू, झारि, संघर.
To Flog. चहबुकु *&c.* हणणु, ढुनणु.
A Flood, (*rise in river*). बरहरो, लडहो. *See* Inundation.
A Flood, Flooding, or overflowing. उथल, बोडि, मोक, लेट, सेलावु.
To Flood. बोडणु.
To be Flooded. बुडणु.
To be in the state of Flooding or overflowing. लेटणु, उथिलणु.
A Flood gate. मोरी.
A Floor. तरू, पटु, धर्ती.
Flour. अटो, (*fine, wheaten*) मैदो, (*of pulse grains*) बेसणु.
To Flourish. वसणु, साभो-आबादु-थिअणु.
Flourishing (*adj.*). साभो, हर्यो, आबादानु.
To Flow. वहणु.
A Flower. गुलु, फुलु.
A Flower (*in embroidery*). फुली, बूटी, बूटो.
To Flower. फुलणु. *See* To Blow.
Flowered (*as on embroidery*). फुल्कारो.
Flowered silk. गुल्दोज़ु, खुदिबाफु.
A Flower garden. फुल्वाडी, गुल्कारी.
A Flower woman. बकारिणि, फुलारिणि, भार्याणी.
Fluent. सलंजिबानु.

A Flute. मुर्लों, बांसुरी.
To Flutter. फड़्कणु.
To Fly, or cause to Fly. उड़ाइणु.
To Fly (*neu.*). उड़ामणु, उड़णु, उड़िरणु.
A Fly. मखि.
A large Fly. मखो.
A dog or horse Fly. ॿगाई.
A dung Fly. ड़ांदिडो.
A Flying or Fly. उड़ारी.
A Foal. वछेरो, ॿिहाणु.
To Foal. विभामणु.
Foam. गजी, झॻ, कफ, गफ.
Fodder. चारो, गाहु.
A Fœtus. गर्भु, ॻभु.
A Fog. लुडाटु, लुडु, धुंधु, रूई.
Foil (*gold or silver leaf*). वर्कुं, (*of brass*) पनी.
Foil (*under precious stones*). ड़ाकु.
A Fold for sheep. भाणो. *See* Pen.
A Fold or double. तहु.
To Fold. वेड़्हणु, विलोटणु, तह करणु.
Fold (*affixed to numerals*). ऊणो.
Foliage. सबूज़ो, सब्ज़ो, सावकि.
Folk. माण्हूं, माड़्हूं.
To Follow (*go after*). पुठ्यों-पुभों-हलणु. *See* To Obey.
A Follower. पुभलगु. *See* Dependant.
Followers. संगति.
Folly. बेवकूफी, बेअकुली, इआणप.
To Foment (*with warm lotions*). सेकणु, टकोरणु, (*dissension*) दुखाइणु, मचाइणु.
A Fomenter of quarrels. फिन्ततो, फितिनो.
Fond (*affectionate*). नेहो, कोड़्यो.
To be Fond of (*with object as nom.*). वणणु.
A Fondling (*darling*). ढोलणु, लालनु, लाड़ुलो, ढोलो, सज़णु, ज़ानिबु, दिल्बरु, मिठणु. *See* Darling.
Fondness. हुब, दिलि, नेहु, नींहु, रुचि.
Food. खेणु, खाइणु, खाधो, कूतु, खोराक, खिभणु, खाज़ु, मानो, रोटी, रसोई, दाणोपाणी, रोचो, खाधि, भुॻिति.
Food of birds. चोगु, चोॻो.
A Fool. मूर्खुं, बेवकूफु, अहमकु, चर्यों, ड़ुडु, अनाडो, भौंदू, खेथियों.
Foolish, of a fool. अहमकाणो, मूर्खांणो, खेथियांणो, चर्यों.
A Foot. पेरु.
The Foot of a table, chair, &c. पाभो.
The Foot, or bottom, of a bed. पेरांदी.
The ball of the Foot. पबु.
On Foot. पंधिड्यों, पेड्यों. *See* A foot.
A Footman. पिभादो.
A Footmark, Footstep. पेरु, पेरो, रंदु.
A Footpath. चारो, पेचिरो.
A Footstool. मंजी, संदली.
A Fop. नटुंभों, टांइरो, टिंडिरूं.
Foppery. टिंडि, टोप, टांइँ, ठिॻ.
For (*on account of*). काणि, वास्ते, लाइ.
For (*on the part of*). पारां.
For (*the dative sign*). खे.
Forage. गाहु, चारो.
To Forbear. खांदि &c. करणु, पाण खे झलणु.
Forbearance. खांदि, सबुरु, खिमा.
To Forbid. पलणु, मनह करणु, झलणु, रोकणु, वारणु.
God Forbid. खुदा न करे.
A Forbidding. पल, झल, मनिह.
Force. जोरु, ड़ाढाई.
With Force or violence. ड़ाढो, ड़ाढ्यां.
By Force, Forcibly. हरूभरू, हुकुमों, जोरें.

To Force. हलभल &c. कराइणु, &c.

A Ford. लांघो.

To Ford. पेरें लंघणु.

Fordable. लांघो, तांघे.

Fore. अग्यों, महँद्यो.

The Fore-castle of a boat. अग़ेलि.

A Forefather. वड़िको, वड़ो.

The Forehead. निराडु, निडुं, निराडो, पेशानी, लिलाटु.

The Hindoo sectarial mark on Forehead. तिलिकु, टीको.

An ornament for the Forehead. ड़ाणी.

Foreign. विलाइती.

A Foreign country. विलाइत, परदेसु, परड़ेहु.

A Foreigner. परदेसी, परड़ेही, विलाइती.

A Foreman. लाकुडो, दरोग़ो.

Foremost. अग़वाणु, पन्द्यों, महँद्यो, *See* First.

The Forepart. अगु.

To Foresee. अग़्में, डिसणु.

Foresight. अग़ जो ग़ण्ती.

The Foreskin. खोलो.

A Forest. ब्रेलो, वनु.

Of a Forest, Forester. ब्रेलाई, ब्रेलारी.

To Foretell. अग़्में, चवणु

Forge (*form*). घड्णु.

A Forgery (*forged writing*). जालु, कूडो अखरु.

To Forget. विसारणु.

Forgetful. वेस्त्रिओ, वेसारो, विसूडो.

Forgetfulness. वेसरि, विसूडाई, भुल.

To Forgive. माफु करणु, बक्शणु, छडणु.

Forgiveness. बक्श.

To be Forgotten. विसिरणु, भुलणु.

A Fork (*furcation*). ब्रिहंग.

Forked (*a stick, &c.*). ब्रिहंगो, ब्रिल्हांगो.

A Forked stick for moving thorns, &c. ब्रिभानी.

Forlorn. निधण्को, अवालो.

Form (*shape*). ड़ोलु, ढंउ, सूरत, शिकिलि, घाटु.

Of good Form or figure. ढँवाइतो.

To Form. जोडणु, घडणु, ठाहणु.

Formality. आदरभाउ.

Formation. जोड, घडिणी.

To be Formed. जुडणु.

Former. अग्यों, अग़णो, अग़णिको.

Formerly. अगे, पेहांई, अगहों, अग्में, महँदि.

Formidable. ड़ाढो, सख्तु. *See* Dreadful.

Formless. बेड़ोलो.

To Fornicate. जमाउ करणु. *See* To Copulate.

Fornication. हरामु. *See* Congressus Venereus.

The wages of Fornication. भाडि.

A Fornicator. जिनाही, लांगछोटो.

To Forsake. छडणु, फिटो करणु.

A Fort. कोटु, ग़डहु, ग़ड्ही, किलो.

The keeper of a Fort. किलेदारु.

Forthcoming. मौजूदु, हाज़ुरु.

Forthwith. हाणेई. *See* Now, Quickly.

Fortieth. चालीहों.

A Fortification. आलम्पनाह.

Fortitude. धीर, धीजुं, दिलेरी. *See* Courage.

A Fortnight. ब्रिहफ्तो; the lunar fortnight, पखु, पछु.

Fortuitously. ओचितो.

Fortunate. वड़भाग़ो, भाग़भर्यो, सभाग़ो, बख्तावरु, सदोरो.

Fortunately. चङो.
Fortune. नसीबु, भागु, बख़्तु, तालिहु, कर्मु.
Fortune (*possessions*). धनु, दौलत. *See* Riches.
One who brings good Fortune. सुपेरो.
Ill Fortune. बद्रुख़्ती, निभागु.
One who brings ill Fortune. कुपेरो.
A Fortune-teller. सामुद्री.
Forty. चालीह.
About Forty. चाल्झारो.
Forty-one. एकेतालीह.
Forty-two. ब्राएतालीह.
Forty-three. टेतालीह.
Forty-four. चोएतालीह.
Forty-five. पंजेतालीह.
Forty-six. छाएतालीह.
Forty-seven. सतेतालीह.
Forty-eight. अठेतालीह.
Forty-nine. उण्वंजाह.
Forward (*impudent, q. v.*). गुस्ताकु.
Forward, Forwards. अगे़, महँदि.
A little Forward. अगे़रो, अगे़रिडो, महँदेरिडो.
A Fosse. खाहो.
To Foster. निपाइणु, पाळणु.
A Foster brother. खीरेतो भाउ.
Foul. गंदो, मेरो; (wind) *See* Unfavorable.
Foul tongued. मुँह जो गंदो, कमीणो, रजालो.
To Found. जोडणु, बंधणु, ठाहणु.
To be Found. मिळणु, लभणु.
A Foundation. पोढि, बिनाह, मंड़ाणु.
To Founder (*sink*). बुड़णु.
A Fountain (*spring*). सेमो, चश्मो, (*a jet*) फुहारो.
Four. चारि.
The number or figure of Four. चौंको.
And Four or with Four (*prefixed to hundreds*). चोडो, चोरोतरु.
Four (*collective number*). चौंकिडो, चौंकु.
Four (*per cent*). चोरोतिरो.
Four cornered. चौकुंड्यारो, चौकुंड़ो.
Four fold (*adj.*). चऊंणो.
The Four Fold. चऊंणि.
Four footed. चैपिरो.
Fourteenth. चोडहँ.
The Fourteenth day of the lunar fortnight. चोड्हों, चोड़हों.
Fourth. चोथों.
The Fourth day of the lunar fortnight. चोथि.
A Fourth part. चोथाई, चोथि. *See* A Quarter.
A Fowl. कुकिडु.
A Fox (*male*). लोवड़ु, लूकडु, (*female*) लोंबिडी.
Fragile. भज़िणो, टाकुंओं,
A Fragment. टुकिरू. *See* Piece.
Fragrance. सुरहाणि, खुश्बो, खुश्बुंई, सुगंधु, हुग़ाउ.
Fragrant. सुरहो.
Frail, *See* Fragile, Weak.
The Frame of a door, window, &c. चौंकु.
To Frame. करणु. *See* To Form.
Frank. साफ़ुदिलि, निर्मलु, निहकपटु.
Frankincense. लोबानु, कुंदिरू, सिँहतकुंदिरू.
Fraud. ड्रोहु, छलु, पपंचु, दगा, दगाबाजी, खोटु, ठग़ो, दोलाबु, मकरू. *See* Deceit.
Fraudful, Fraudulent. खोटो, दोलाबो, छली, पपंची. *See* Deceitful.
A Freak. खिभालु. *See* Fancy.

A Freckle. तिरू, *(from small pox)* सिभरी.
Free. आजो, संकरू, खलासु.
Free to act as one wishes. रजाराणो.
To Free. छडुणु, छुटाइणु.
To be Free. छुटणु.
Freedom. छोट्कारो, छोट्को, खलासी.
Freedom from care. अगूंदिराई.
To Freeze. ज़मणु.
Freight (*hire*). भाडो, खणाणो, नूलु.
Frequently. घणा भेरा *or* घुमिरा.
Fresh. ताजो, सज़रू, अज़ोको.
Freshness. ताजाई, सज़राई.
To Fret (*vex*). खिज़णु. *See* To Rub.
Friction. गहणी.
The mark caused by Friction. गाठि, गोसो.
Friday. जुमो, थारूं, थांवरू, शुक्र.
Fried. भुगो.
To be Fried. भुज़णु.
A Friend. सेंधो, दोस्तु, दोस्तारू, यारू, सज़णु, टोलु, दोसु, टोल्यो, साञारो.
Of a Friend, Friendly. दोस्ताणो, सज़णको.
Friendless. बेदोस्तु. *See* Destitute.
Friendship. दोस्ती, याराणो, यारी, सेंधि, सज़ण्याई, पर्चो, मेलापु, मेलु, सलूकु.
A Fright. डेजो, डहकारू, डिजु, डपु, डाउ, धकाउ.
To Frighten. डेजारणु, टाहणु.
To be Frightened. डिजणु, डरणु, दहल्जणु.
Frightful. खौफाइतो. *See* Fearful.
A Fringe. झालरि.
A Frisk. ठेंगु, टपो.
To Frisk. टपणु, ठेंग &c. डिभणु, कुज़णु.
Frisking, Friskiness. टिंगिट्पो, टपिणी, कुडु.
A Frith of the sea. घारो, खाड़ो, नारो.
Frivolous. हल्को, हवाई, अजायो.
A Frog. डेड़रू, (*small*) डेड़िरी.
Frolicsome. टपिणो, कुड़िणो
From. खां, खों, थां, थों, कनां, ड्हों, गनां.
From in. मों, मझों; from on, तां, तों, उतां उतों.
From within. अंदिरों; from without, ब्रहरों.
The Front. अगु, आगो, मुहगु, मुहडु.
In Front. अगे, रूबरू, सामुहों, साम्हुणो, साम्हुणे, साम्हों, आड़ो.
A little in Front. अगभरो, अगांहों, महँदेरिडो.
A Frontier. संधो. *See* Boundary.
Frost. पारो.
Froth. गजो, झग, फीणु, गफ.
To Froth. गजो &c. करणु.
Froward. कुधो, होड़ो, ऐथिरो, औथिरो.
A Frown. घुंडो, घुंडु, टिउडी, सूंढु.
To Frown. घुंडु &c. पाइणु, भूकणु.
To Fructify. (*bear fruit*) फरणु, फलणु.
Frugal. सर्फाई, जुगतो, संजमी
Frugality. सर्फो, सांगुसर्फो, जुगिति, संजमु.
Fruit. फलु, फरू, मेवो.
A basket of Fruit. डालो.
A Fruit-seller. बाकिरी.
Fruitful. फरवारो, फलवारो.
Fruitless (*a tree, &c.*). सखिणो, निफलो, खसी.
Fruitless, Fruitlessly (*vain*). निफलो, अजायो, अविर्थो.

To Frustrate. भञणु, भञ्किडो, विझणु.
To Fry (*act.*). भुञणु.
To Fry (*neu.*). भुज़णु.
A Frying. भुञिणो.
A Frying pan. तई, कड़ाही, कणाहो.
Fuel. ब्रारणु.
Fugitive. भाज़ूकडु, भज़िणो.
To Fulfil. पाडणु, पूरो करणु.
To be Fulfilled. पडणु, पूरोथिअणु.
Full. पूरो, (*filled*) भर्यो.
Fulness. पूराई.
Fume (*vapour*). ब्राफ, दूँहों.
Fun. खिलखुशी, कोडु, रौंशो.
A subscription Fund. चंदो, फोडो, चोरो. *See* Capital.
A Funeral pile. चिख्या.
Funeral rites. क्रिआकर्मु.
Funny. रौंशांभों.
To Furbish. मलणु, चिल्काइणु.
A Furbisher. तेविरो.
A Furlough. मोकल.
A Furnace. खूरो, खूरी.
Furniture. काठोडि.
A Furrow. जाट़, ओड.
Further. परांहों, ड़ूरांहों.
To Fuse. ग़ारणु, पघारणु.
Fusion. ग़ार्णी, ग़र्णी.
To get Fusty. बुसिजणु, ट़किजणु.
A Fuss. रोलो, बखेड़ो.
The Future tense. इस्तक़्बालु, भविष्यति.
In Future. अग़ते.
The Future, Futurity. अगु.
Fy. छि, छी, थू,

G

Gabble, gabbling. बक्बकि, टोंटों, टर्टरि, लर्लरि, फड्फडि. *See* Chattering.
To Gabble. बकणु, बड्बडाइणु, जखणु, झकणु. *See* To Chatter.
The Gable-end of a house. जंड़ो.
To Gad. रूलणु.
A Gadder. रोलाकु, रोलु, रोलाकडु.
Gain. खट्यो, लाहो, नफो, फाइदो, लाभु, फलु, वाधारो, किफात. *See* Advantage.
To Gain. खटणु, कमाइणु, मखणु, वटणु, पिराइणु.
Gainful. नफाइतो, लाहाइतो, खट्याइतो.
Gait. चालि, टोर, गति, हलिणी.
A Gaiter. झाड़ूलो.
Galangal. पानवाड.
A Gale (*of wind*). वाच. *See* Storm, Passion.
The Gall. पितु.
The Gall-bladder. पितो.
A Gall-nut. माभो.
A Gallop. सिरारो.
To Gallop (*neu.*). मैदानु ड़िभणु, पिडु पाइणु *or* ड़िभणु, ड़ोकणु.
To Gallop, (*act.*). मैदानु-पिडु-ड़िआरणु, ड़ोकाइणु.
To Gamble, game. जुआ खेलणु.
A Gambler or Gamester. जूआरी.
Gambling. जुआ.
To Gambol. ट़पणु, ठेंगड़िभणु.
A Gambol. ठेंगु, ट़पो. *See* Frisking.
A Game. बाज़ो, रांदि, (*as being won or lost*) लिंडु.
Game (*prey*). शिकारू.
A Gaming house. जुआखानो, फडु.
The Gamut. सर्गमु.
A Gang. टोलो, गूलिरी. *See* Band.
A Gang of thieves. धलि, धाड; one of do. धाडाई, धाडेलु; an attack from do. धाड़ो.
A Gaol. बंदीखानो, कैद्खानो.

A Gap. खडह.
To Gape. वातु फाडणु. *See* To Yawn.
A Garb. पोशाख. See Clothes.
A flower Garden. फुल्वाडी, गुल्कारी.
A fruit Garden. बागु, बागोचो, हुडी.
A Garden cf vegetables, sugar cane, &c. पुडो.
A Gardener. बागाई, आराई, माली.
Gargling, gargle. गुरूडो.
The sound made in Gargling. गड्गडि.
Garlick. थूम.
A Garment. लटो, गंदो, लूगिडो. *See* Clothes.
A Garner. भांडो, अंबारू.
A Garnet. याकूतु.
To Garnish. सींगारणु.
A Garrison. चौंकी.
Garrulous. घणग़ाल्हाओ. *See* Loquacious.
A Gasp. घुट्को.
A Gate, gateway. दर्वाजो, दरू.
To Gather or collect (*act.*). गडु करणु, मेडणु.
To Gather (*pluck*). छिनणु.
To Gather (*pick up*). चूंडणु.
To be Gathered together. मिडणु.
A Gatherer. चूंडो.
A carpenter's Gauge. खत्कशु.
Gauge. धूड्कपूरू.
Gay (*blithe*). रौंशाई. *See* Merry.
Gayety. खिल्खुशी, रौंशो, तमाशो.
To Gaze. निहारणु, तकणु.
To Geld. कुटु *&c.* करणु.
Gelt. कुटु, खशी.
A Gem. जवाहिरू, जँव्हँरू, रतनु.
The Sign Gemini. मिथुनु.
A Gender. जिनिस, लिंगु.
A Genealogy. वंसावली, सुजिरो.
General (*adj.*). घणो, आम.
Generally. घणोकरे.
To Generate. उपज़ाइणु, उपाइणु.
A Generation (*single succession*). पीडो, पुठि.
The parts of Generation (*male*). लनु, लौडो, टटो, खाझो, काडु, (*female*). चुडू, पोकु, चूचि, तोतो, गांड़ि.
Generosity. सखावत, ड़ातारी.
Generous. दिलिखुल्यलु, ड़ातारू, दाता, सखी, जामडुु, सतो.
Genethliacks. जातकु.
Genius. बुधि, अकुलु.
Gentle (*meek, affable*). गरीबु, मिलिणो, सांतोको, निंवंदडु. *See* Mild.
Gentle, gently. झको, झीणो, ढिरो, आरास्तो, आरास्ते, धीरे, होयां, होरे-होरे.
A Gentleman. साहिबु, अमीरू.
Of a Gentleman, gentlemanly. साहिबाणो.
Gentleness. गरीबी. *See* Humility.
Genuine. सचो, खरो, नातिकु.
Genuineness. सचाई.
A Germ. सलो. *See* Sprout.
A Gesture, gesticulation. तालुपखालु, (*as a sign*) इशारो, रम्ज.
To Get (*act.*). वठणु, लहणु, पाइणु. *See* To Obtain.
To Get (*become*). थिअणु.
To Get before. अग्रो लंघे वञणु.
To Get down. लहणु, उलहणु.
To Get on, or along (*neu.*). हलणु, गुजिरणु, निबहणु, टुरणु.
To Get up (*rise*). उथणु, (*mount*) चड्हणु.
To Get by heart. यादि–वर्जिबान–कंठि–करणु.
To Get out of the way. सिरणु.
A Ghost. प्रेतु, भूतु.

A woman's Ghost. प्रेतिनी, भूतिनी.
A Giant. टॅंगु.
Gibbosity. कुब्राई, कुबु.
Gibbous. कुब्रो.
A Gibe. टोंक, तानो, चाणक, तर्क.
Giddiness. भाणि, भांउटी, फेरी, चर्खु.
To be Giddy. मथो फिरणु.
A Gift. बक्शीस, दानु, ड़ानु, ड़ाणु, इनामु, इम्दादु.
A deed of Gift. बक्शीसनामो.
To Giggle. खिलि खिलि लाइणु.
To Gild. मुलिमो करणु.
Gilding. मुलिमो.
The Gill of a fish. कली.
Ginger (*dry*). सुंढि, (*green*) अदिरक.
A Ginjall (*kind of gun*). जजार.
To Gird the loins. संधिरो-कमरि-बेठि-बंधणु.
A Girdle (*for waist*). बोछणु, लूंगो, पट्को.
A Girl. छोकरि, छोकिरी, नींगिरी, नींगिरि, छुहिरी.
Girlish. छोकिर्याणो.
Girth (*circumference*). गेलि.
A saddle Girth. तंगु.
To Give. ड़िभणु, बक्शणु.
To Give back. मोटाइणु, वराइणु.
To Give forth or out (*publish q. v*). ज़ाणाइणु.
To Give up. छड़णु.
To Give way. मुडणु, हटणु.
To cause to Give. ड़िआरणु.
To be Given. ड़िजणु.
A Giver. ड़ेंदड़ु.
The Giving. ड़िभणी, ड़िभणु.
A Gizzard. गुज़ी.
Glad. खुशी, सरहो, राजी, निहालु.
To Gladden. खुशि &c. करणु, रीझाइणु.

Gladness. खुशी. *See* Delight.
To Glance (*as a ray of light*). झल्को ड़िभणु.
To Glance (*strike obliquely*). उथिडणु.
Glare. दभो, दहो.
Glass. शीशो, कायो, काभो, कचु.
Of Glass, glassy. शीशांओं.
Glazing (*put on earthen ware*). काशी.
A Glazer of earthen ware. काशीगरू.
A Gleam, Gleaming. चिम्को, चमक, टिम्को.
To Glean. चूंड़णु.
A Gleaner. चूंड़ो.
To Glide (*flow gently*). वहणु.
To Glide, or slip away. खिस्कणु, सिर्कणु.
To Glimmer. टिम्कणु.
Glitter, glittering. चिम्को, चिम्काटु, चिल्को, चिल्काटु. *See* Brightness.
To Glitter, glisten. चिम्कणु, चिल्कणु.
Gloom. धुंधु.
Glorious. तेजसी, तेजवानु, पर्तापी.
Glory. तेजु, पर्तापु, धाको.
Gloss, Glossiness. चिल्को, चिल्कति, लसाई.
Glossy. लसो.
A Glove. दस्तानो.
To Glow. बखणु, चिम्कणु.
Glue. सिर्सु, थंभणु.
To Glue. सिर्स सां चंबुडाइणु. *See* To Stick.
To Glut. ढ़इणु.
Glutinous. चीड़्हालो, चीड़्हारो.
A Glutton, gluttonous. पेटोलो, पेटोडो, पेटी, पेटिरू, ड़ालिड़ो, खाऊ, वड़खाऊ, वड़कूतो, डूनु, पेटार्थी.

A Gnat. कूति. *See* Musquitoe.
To Gnaw. चब़णु, चब़ाडणु.
To Go. वञणु, इलणु, उसहणु, जुलणु, वुड़्हणु.
To Go back. मोटणु, वरणु.
To Go down. लहणु, उलहणु.
To Go into (*enter*). पिहणु, घिडणु.
To Go into (*be contained in*). माइजणु, समाइजणु, मामणु, मापणु.
To Go off, (*a gun*). छुडणु, छुट्कणु.
To Go out (*issue*). निकिरणु, (*be extinguished*) विसामणु, उझामणु.
To Go round. फिरणु.
To Go up. चड़्हणु.
A Goat. ब़किरो, पहु, पहरू; a species of do. बरी. *See* Kid.
A he Goat. ब़करू, ब़किरो,
Of a Goat. ब़ाकिरो.
Goat's hair. ड़ास.
Of Goat's hairs. ड़ासी.
A Goat herd. ब़किरारू.
A Go-between. विचवारो, वेचुओ, वेचो.
To Gobble up. हाऊहाऊ करे खाइणु.
A Goblet. आब्खोरो, गड़ूं, आबो. *See* Bowl.
God (*Mahomedan*). खुदा, अलाहु, रबु, (*Hindoo*) भगवानु, परमेसरू, ईश्वरू, नारायणु.
God forbid. खुदा न करे.
God grant. खुदा करे.
God guard you. अलहुवाही, अलहतुहारि.
God knows! अलाजे, वलआलमु.
A Goddess. देवी.
Godly (*pious q. v.*) दीन्दारू, धर्मी.
Going and Coming. ओटमोट, अचणुवञणु.
Gold. सोनु.
Cloth of Gold. तासु.
Gold leaf. वर्कु.
Of Gold (*work*). Gold colored. सोनहरी.
Gold thread. जरी.
Golden. सोनो.
A Goldsmith. सोनारो, माईअपोटो.
A Gong. घड्यालो, घड्यालु.
Gonorrhœa. पर्मेलु, पर्मेहु, सुजाखु.
Good (*adj.*). चङो, मोचारो, भलो, खासो, खूबु, चोखो, ओघो, कसर, नेकु, सखर, सफिरो. *See* Excellent.
Good (*profit*). चङो, भलो, चङाई, भलाई, खैरू.
Pretty Good. चङेरिडो, चङेरो.
Good for nothing. निकमो, निकारू. *See* Useless.
Of Good disposition, goodnatured. सुलछिणो, सुभातूरो. *See* Disposition.
Good natured. चङमुर्सी.
Goodness. नेकी, मोचाराई, चङाई, भलाई.
Goods. शइवइ, वथुसिथु *f.* मालु, अटालो, अस्बाबु, मड़ी, रासि, वसुलो. सामानु, आजिको, अथणु, भिटाओ.
A wild Goose. हंजु.
A Gourmand. चटो. *See* Glutton.
To Govern. राजु *&c.* करणु, हुकुमु हलाइणु.
Governance, Government. राजु, साहिबी, अमलु, हुकुमु, बाछाई, राजाई,
The Government (*state*). सर्कारि.
A Governor. हाकिमु, नवाबु.
A Governorship. नवाबी.
A Gouge. नैंहो.
A Gourd. कदू; a species of do. तुंबो.
A Gown. वेश्वाज, घघो.
Grace (*favor*). क्रिपा, फजुलु.
To Grace. सुंहणु, सोभणु.

Graceful, Gracefully. सुहुणो, मोचारो, ओधो.

Gracious. क्रिपालु, मिहिबानु. *See* Kind, Merciful.

Gradually. होयीं होयीं, वहंदे वहंदे, वही वही.

To Graft. पेवंदी करणु.

Grain.. अंनु, अनाजु, दाणा (*plu.*), धान्ु.

A Grain. दाणो, कणो, कणिको.

Grain, boiled, dry. कुहर (*plu.*); a seller of ditto, कुहरी.

A Grain merchant. अनवण्जारो.

A Grain seller. अनविक्यो.

Grainless. बेअंनो, ठल्हो. *See* Barren.

Gram. चणो.

Of Gram. चणांओं.

Roasted Gram. भुग्रिडो; boiled Gram, तलूणो.

A parcher of Gram. भोग्रिडो, दांहों.

A Grammar. व्याकरणु.

A Grammarian. व्याकरणी.

A Granary. भांड़ो, अंबारू.

One in charge of a Granary. अंबादारू.

Grand. *See* Great, Illustrious, Splendid.

A Grand daughter. (*male line*) पोटी, (*female line*) ड़ोहिटी.

A great Grand daughter. (*male line*) पडपोटी, (*female line*) पडड़ोहिटी.

Grandeur. शानु, ठाटु, ठासु, ठाहु.

A Grandfather. (*paternal*) ड़ाड़ो, (*maternal*) नानो.

A great Grandfather. (*male line*) परड़ाड़ो, (*female line*) परनानो.

A great great Grandfather. (*male line*) तडड़ाड़ो, (*female line*) तडनानो.

A Grandmother. (*paternal*) ड़ाड़ी, (*maternal*) नानी.

A great Grandmother. (*male line*) परड़ाड़ी, *female line*) परनानी.

A Grandson. (*male line*) पोटो, (*female line*) ड़ोहिटो.

A great Grandson. (*male line*) पडपोटो, (*female line*) पडड़ोहिटो.

A great great Grandson. (*male line*) तडपोटो, (*female line*) तडड़ोहिटो.

A Grant. दानु, इनामु.

A Grant of land. जागिर; the holder of such, जागीदारू.

To Grant. ड़िअणु, बक्शाणु.

A Grape. ड़ाख, अंगूरू.

To Grasp. दबे झलणु, सोघो झलणु.

A Grasp of the hand. पंजो, चंबो.

A Grapnel (*small anchor*). ब्रिली, नातारी.

Grass. गाहु, (*of kinds*) डुभु, छबर, टांपु, ड़ोर, मँधिभडो, लुलिरू, खिह, कलु, बेकह, ड़िनुही, ग़मु, चीहो, लंबु, मखिणी, कूणो, व्ररू, सिणु, ब्रटुं, साविडो, सांभों, ड़ंगिणी, मांधाणो, ग़ंढीरू, ड़ामणु, मलोरिडो, किरांझु, ब्रेरणु, भचटी, भुर्टु, पुभांटु, कलूरो, कांहीं.

Land rich in Grass. खथडि.

An instrument for scraping up Grass. रंबो.

A Grass cutter. गाहो, गाह्यो.

Of a Grass-cutter. गाहिको.

Grassy. गाहेरो.

To Grate (*act.*). गहणु.

Grateful (*pleasing*). सुहांइंदो.

To feel Grateful. थोरो-गुणु-मञणु.

A Grater. रोही.

Gratification. खुशी.

To Gratify. खुशि करणु, तुसाइणु.

Gratis. मुफ्तु, उँहेंइं.

Gratuitous, Gratuitously. अजायो, मुफ्तु.
Grave, Gravely. ग़रो, गंभीरु.
A Grave. कबर, ग़ोर, बुठी, समाधि.
To Grave. उकिरणु.
A Grave-yard. मुकामु.
Gravel. ककिरा *plu.*
The Gravel. ककिरी, पहणी, पथिरी.
Graveness, Gravity. ग़राई.
Gravy. लास, शुर्वो, रसु.
Gray (*a horse*). सुर्खो; iron gray, गरो.
One with Gray beard or head. करडवढु, कर्डांटु.
To Graze (*neu.*). चरणु.
To Graze (*act.*). चारणु.
The Grazing of a forest. पनचरी.
Hire for Grazing. चाराणी.
Grease. सणिभु, वह.
To Grease. मखणु.
Greasiness. सण्भाई.
Greasy. सण्भो, चिकडु.
Great. वड़ो.
As Great. जेड़ो; so Great, तेड़ो; how Great? केडो; so Great, हेड़ो.
A Great deal or many. घणो. *See* Much.
Greatness. वड़ाई.
Greediness. बुख.
Greedy. ज़र्को, बुख्यो, बुख्यतु, हब्छी. *See* Gluttonous.
Green. साभो, सब्ज़ु.
A brownish Green. मोडों.
Greenness. सावकि, सावाई.
Greens. साभोसागु, साईभाज़ो, सागु.
Grief. ग़मु, डुखु, सोगु, अफ्सोसु, सोसु. *See* Mourning.
A Grievance. डुखु.
To Grieve (*afflict*). डुखाइणु, ड़हणु.
To Grieve (*mourn*). ग़मु *&c.* करणु.
Grieved. डुख्यो, दिल्गीरु, रंजि.
A Grimace. मेछ, मुच्को, मोडो.
To Grin. ड़ंद कढणु.
To Grind in a mill. पीहणु, (*coarsely*) ड़रणु, घर्डणु.
To Grind on a grind stone. गहणु, घोटणु.
A Grinder (*tooth*). ड़ाढ, हेड.
The act of Grinding (*corn*). पीहणी.
The charge for Grinding (*corn*). पीहाणी.
To cease Grinding at a mill. उढारणु.
A flag for Grinding on. उर्सी.
A Grind stone. रोही, सिराणि.
To Gripe. दबे झलणु. *See* To Grasp.
The Gripes. पेचु, मरोडो, वकडु, वटु.
Gristle. ड़िपो.
To Groan. कंझणु, चिंघणु, काकिडाइणु, कंझिकणु.
A Groaning. कंझिकंझि, चिंघाचिंघि, कंझिकार.
A Grocer. पसारी.
Groceries. पसारु.
The Groin. नरो.
A Groom. सईसु.
To Grope. मनाडणु.
Groping. मनाड, इथोराडो.
In the Gross, by the Gross. उको, ब्रैथो. *See* Lump.
A Grove. खोड्हो, झमटु, आराडो.
The Ground. धर्ती, जिमीन, भुंइ, पटु.
To Ground (*run aground*). लग़णु.
Groundless, Groundlessly. अजायो, मुफ्तु.
Grounds (*dregs*). किटो, तरो.
To Grow (*increase*). वधणु, उसिरणु, उपिडणु.

To Grow (*be produced by vegetation*). थिअणु, उपज़णु.
To Grow (*become*). थिअणु.
To Growl. गौंरणु, गिरणु.
Growth. वाधि, ओपड, ओपड़ु.
A Grub. किंर्भौं.
A Grudge. खौंस, अकसु. *See* Enmity.
Gruel. भतु, रब्र, आश.
Gruff. रुखो.
Gruffness. रुखाई.
To Grumble. कुर्कुरि-झौंझौं-विकिविकि,-करणु, कुर्कणु.
A Grumbler. विकिविक्यो, कुर्कुर्यो, कुर्किणो.
To Grunt. हुड़िको करणु, हुड़िकणु.
A Guana. ग़ोह.
A Guard. चौंको, पहरो. *See* Watchman.
To Guard. रख करणु, तातणु, संभालणु.
To be on one's Guard. खबदारु-पुख्तो,-थिअणु.
A Guardian. वारिसु, कारिणी, झालू, राखो.
Guarding. रख, संभाल. *See* Watching.
A Guava. जैतूनु, जामु.
A Guess. अटकल, उन्मानु.
To Guess. अट्कलणु.
A Guest. मिहमानु, मिंह्मानु.
To Guggle. गड्गडि करणु, भभ्कणु.
A Guggling. गड्गडि, भभ्को.
Guidance, Guiding. सूंहांई, अगुआई.
A Guide. सूंहों, अग़वाणु, अगुओ, महँदारु.
To Guide. वाट लाइणु.
Guile. ड्रोहु, दोलाबु. *See* Deceit, Cunning.
Guileful. दोलाबो, ड्रोही. *See* Deceitful, Cunning.
Guileless. निह्कपटु, विसूडो, विसूडलु, साधु. *See* Simple.
Guilt. ड्रोहु. गुनाहु.
Guiltless. बेड्रोहु, बेगुनाहु, बेड्रोहो.
Guilty. डुहारी, गुनहगारु, ड्रोही.
A Guinea worm. वारो.
A Guitar. तंबूरो, दंबुरो, सितार.
The Gullet. निर्घटु, निडी.
A Gulp, Gulping. ग़ोत, तिक.
Gum Arabic. खौंरु.
Gum melted for sticking with. गोंइंदु, खाम्णी.
To Gum up a letter. खामणु.
Gum-lac. लाख.
A Gum (*of the mouth*). महर.
A Gun. बंदूक, दंबूक, तुफ़ाक. *See* Cannon.
A Gun-barrel. नरी.
A Gun-lock. चक्मकु.
A Gun-match. जाम्की.
The Gunnel or Gunwale of a boat. ग़ड्ह, अध.
A Gunner. तोब्चो, गुबार्चो.
Gunpowder. दारूं.
A manufacturer of Gunpowder. धिड़ाई.
A Gun-stock. कूंदाकु.
A Gurgling. गड्गडि. *See* Guggle.
A Gust of wind. खहो, छुहो.
A Gut. आंड्रो.
A Gutter. मोरी.
Gysum. चीरोली.
A Gyration. फेरो. *See* Turn.

H

Ha! हा, आहा.
A Haberdasher. सुरह्यो, सुरहो.
A Habit. हेर, आदत, टेव, खोइ, परि.

Habits, Customs. पाह, चालि, भीति. *See* Custom, Way.

A bad Habit. इलत.

A Habitation. *See* Abode.

To Habituate. हेरणु.

Habituated. हेराकु, हेरू, हेराइतो.

To become Habituated. हिरणु.

To Hack. ड़ड़िरणु, चिथणु.

A Haft. ग़नु.

An old Hag. ब्रभि, मम.

A Haggler. रीडारो.

A Haggling. रीडिपीडि. *See* Altercation.

A Hail-stone. ग़ड़ो.

A Hair. वारु, केसु.

Matted Hair. जटा, वुजु, लिट.

Downy Hair on the face. रेह.

The Hair on one's limbs. लुंभ, ज़ति, वुर.

The Hair of back of head. किआड़ी; (*a little higher up*), कांगु; of crown of head, चोटी; of front part of skull, ड़ाड़हूं; of the temples, चूणो, लैंणो, कलमु; of the privities, कुचो, झांट.

A twist in the Hair. भौंरी.

Hair smoothed angularly over each side of the forehead. ब्रटुऑं. *See* Braid.

Hair of head tied up in lump. वांगूड़ो, चोटो.

The line made by parting the Hair. सींधि.

Camel's Hair. मिलिस.

Goat's Hair. ड़ास.

Hairless. लुसु, खुसु, खुसिरो.

A Hairy man. भुचु, भूचु.

Half. अधु.

One and Half. ड़ेढु; two and Half, अढाई; three and Half, साढा ट्रे; and so on prefixing साढा to four, five, &c.

One and Half (*proportional adj.*). ड़ेढूंणो, ड़ेढो. *See* One, Two.

One Half more (*of one of an aggregate number*). साढु.

Half of a *dumri* or of a *guz* in land measure. अधिड़ी.

Half a *pice*. अधेलो.

A Half rupee piece. आधिऑ, अधेली.

One Half (*per cent*). अधोतिरो; one and a half (*do.*), ड़ेढोतिरो.

Half (*in composition*). अध.

Half finished. अधूणो, अधोगाबिरो, अधोखारो, अधगोदो, अधोखो.

A Half sharer. अधोअधि m.

A Half brother. (*by father's side*) माठ़ेजो–माट्रेयो-पेइतो–भाउ, (*by mother's side*) माइतो भाउ.

Half worn out. अधोराणो, अधचुब्यो.

To Halloo. सडु करणु.

A Halo. पिड़ु.

A Halt for rest. वेसाँइं, वेसाँहिं. *See* Rest.

To Halt (*stop*). विहणु, ठहरणु, मेजल विझणु.

To Halt (*limp*). लडाइणु, मंड़ाइणु.

A Halter. (*for horses*) वाग़, ड़ोर्वाग़, (*for camels*) महार.

To Halter or tie with a Halter. वाग़णु.

A Halting place. मैजल.

To Halve. अधोअधि-ब्रअध-करणु.

By Halves, in Halves. अधुअधु.

A Ham. रान.

To sit on the Hams. गुइअभर विहणु.

A Hamlet. वहणु, वाँहणु, वसीं, वसँदी.

A Hammer. मतिर्को, (*a goldsmith's*) चोरिसो.

To Hammer. ठोकणु, हणणु.
A Hamper. खारो. *See* Basket.
A Hand. हथु, दस्तु.
A Hand breath. चपो.
A pair of Handcuffs. हथोड्यूं, *plu:*
To tie the Hands behind. पछोड्-की-चौखंभो-बंधणु.
At Hand. मौजूदु.
In one's Hands or power. हथोको.
The full of both Hands joined. बुकु.
The full of one Hand open. लप, चुरू.
The full of one Hand contracted. मुठि, चंगुलु.
A Handkerchief. रूमालु.
A Handle. गनु.
The Handle of a sword. मुठि, कब्जो, कब्ज़ो.
To Handle. हथु लाइणु. *See* To Touch.
Handless. ठठो.
A Hand-mill. जंडु, चकी.
Handsel (*first sale*). बुहुणी.
Handsome. सुंहुणो, खूब्सूरत, मोचारो, सुंदरू, दर्सनी, ओपो.
Hand-writing. खतु, लिखति.
To Hang (*neu.*). लड्कणु, लट्कणु.
To Hang (*act.*). टंगणु, लट्काइणु, लड्काइणु, टेडणु.
To Hang (*execute*). फाहो ढ़िअणु, सूरिअ चाड़्हणु.
To let Hang down loosely. ढारणु.
To Happen. थिअणु, पवणु.
Happiness. सुखु, कल्याणु, आरामु, खैरखो, मंगलु, आनंदु, खैरू.
Happy. सौखो, सुख्यो, सुखो, आसूदो, खुशि, भयासो, अनंदि, जौंको.
To Harass (*worry*). अकाइणु, हलाखु-ककि-करणु, रंजाइणु, रोआइणु. *See* To Fatigue.
To be Harassed. अकणु, ककि-हलाखु-थिअणु.
A Harbour. बंदरू.
Hard. ड़ाढो, सख्तु, कठनु, (*through dryness*) सोटु.
Hard baked. सोकु.
To Harden (*act.*). ड़ाढो करणु, (*congeal*) ज़माइणु, ज़ाराइणु.
Hardly (*scarcely*). मसें, भञा. *See* with Difficulty.
Hardness. ड़ाढाई.
Hardy. सख्तु, राठोडु, ड़ाढो.
A Hare. सहो, सह्युड़.
A Hare's form. रूघ.
A Harem. जनान्खानो, ड़ेढी, ड़ेउढी.
A Harlot. कस्बिआणी, खोबिली, कञिरी.
Harlotry. कसबु.
Harm (*injury*). जिआनु, हात्रो, नुक्शानु. *See* Crime.
To Harmonize (*neu.*). ठहणु.
Harmony. हिकतालु, शम. *See* Concord.
Harness of a horse. संजु.
A Jew's Harp. चंगु, मोचंगु.
A Harrow. सांइरू.
To Harrow. सांइरू ड़िअणु.
Harsh. ड़ाढो, कडो, कठोरू.
Harsh to the taste. कसारो.
Harshness. ड़ाढाई.
Harvest. फसुलु, लाबारो.
To Hash. चिथणु, चिचिरणु.
A Hasp. कडो.
Haste. तकडि, उब्रहर, उब्रहराई, हब्रिरि, हँगुतिर्का, हैब्रिरि.
Hasty. उब्रहरो, तकिडो, अभोरो. *See* Quick, Impetuous.
A Hat. टोपी, टोपु.

One who sells Hats, or who wears one. टोप्यरू.

A Hatch. तूरू. *See* Brood.

To Hatch, or sit on eggs. छार *or* आरे ते विहणु.

A Hatchet. कुहाडो.

Hate, Hatred. वेरू, दुश्मणी, खारू, खौंस.

To Hate. बुछो-बुछिडो-भांइणु, वेरू *&c.* करणु or रखणु.

To Have. रखणु; also the substantive verb, हुअणु, with the agent in the dative.

Haughtiness. हटु, मग्रूरी, दिमागु. *See* Pride.

Haughty. हटीलो, दिमागी. *See* Proud

To Haul. छिकणु, ताणणु.

A Haunch. रान.

A Hawk (*varieties*). female, बाजु, शिकिरो, बाशो, शाहीन, बहरी, तुर्मिची, शहबाजु, कुही, चरगु, सोचाणो, बैसिरो, लगडु; male, जुरो, कोहिलो, चिपक, चर्गेलो, बहरोन्नचो, चटुओ, कुहेलो, बशोन, झगडु.

A Hawker of wares. घोर्ड्यो, घोरारो.

The Hawking wares. घोर.

Hay. गाहु.

Hazard. जोखो. *See* Danger.

Hazardous. जोखाइतो. *See* Dangerous.

A Haze. लुडाटु, रूई. *See* Fog.

He. हिउ, ही, हू, हो, हे, ए; indicating or distinguishing, इहो, उहो.

A Head. मथो, सिरू, मुंढी.

The Head distinct from the body. सिसी, सिरी.

The Head of an arrow, spear, &c. फरू.

The Head of a bed. सेरांदी.

To raise the Head. गाटु-कंधु-खणणु.

Headless. बेसिरो.

A Head-long person. हुडु.

The Head man of a village. पर्यो *or* चडो-मुर्सु, सखरू, अर्बाबु, ज़ामोटु, रैसु. *See* Chief.

A Head man among artizans and merchants. मुखो, चौधिरी.

A Head stall. सर्वांग़.

Head-strong. होड़ा, गहिरू, अहँडु. *See* Obstinate.

To Heal (*act.*). छुटाइणु. *See* To Cure.

To Heal (*neu.*). छुटणु, सुकणु.

Health, Healthfulness. चङभलाई, निरोआई, सिंहत, निमिराई.

Ill Heath. नाचङाई. *See* Sickness.

Healthy. निरोयो, चङो.

A Heap. ढेरू, ढिगु, दडो, खोडु, गुंदु, गंजु, दिडो, राहि, सथो, थहो, थहो.

A small Heap. ढिगो, खोडो.

The Heaps of grain collected for assessment. खरी; one among such, ज़ारि.

A Heap of dirt. अरूडो.

To Hear. बुधणु, सुणणु.

Quick of Hearing. कननि जो सलो.

Dull of Hearing. घब्रिरो.

The Heart (*vital muscle*). दिलु, हिँआँउ, हिँओ, हांउ.

The Heart (*mind*). दिलि, हिँआँउ, हिँओ.

To lose Heart. हिँओ लाहणु, हिमथ छड़णु.

To take Heart. सलणु, सत्या मंड़णु, हिमथ भरणु.

By Heart (*by rote*). बर्जिबान, कंठि.

Hearth money. चुल्हुं *plu.*

Heartily. दिल्यां, दिलसां.

Heat. ताउ, तउ, गर्मी, कोसाई, तपति, तपसि, तांग्डी.

A blaze of Heat. ज़र.

Prickly Heat. आरांयूं *plu.*

To Heat (*act.*). तपाइणु, ताइणु, कोसो करणु, सेकणु.

To Heat (*neu.*). तपणु, कोसो थिअणु.

To be in Heat. (*a bitch*) कतिजणु, (*a cow &c.*) वहुजंणु, मुहार्जणु, (*a mare*) मिहिजंणु, वडुजणु.

Heaven. बिस्तु, सर्गु. *For* "The Heavens," *See* Sky.

Of Heaven, Heavenly. बिस्ती, सर्गी.

Heaviness. ग़राई, ग़ौराई, ग़ौराणि.

Heavy. ग़रो, ग़ौरो.

A Hedge. लोड्हो, वाडि, पैंह्रू, मुहाडो.

A Hedgehog. ज़ाहो.

To Heed. बुंधणु, मञणु.

Heed. गूंदरू, साञाह. *See* Care.

Heedful. ग़ाणू, साञाहू.

Heedless. बेगूंदिरो, गाफिलु, ग़हेलो.

Heedlessness. बेगूंदिराई, गाफिली, ग़हेलाई.

The Heel. खुडी.

To spur with the Heel. अडी हणणु.

To sit on the Heels. ओकिडू विहणु.

The Heel ropes of a horse. पछाडी.

The Hegira. हिजिरी.

A Heifer. वहुडी.

Height. ओभरू, डुघु, डिघाई.

An Heir. वारिसु, कारिणी.

Heirless. बेवारिसु.

Hell. दोजकु, नरकु, नरगु.

Hellish. दोजकी, नरकी,

A Helm. सुखानु.

A Helmsman. सुखानी.

A Helmet. होलु.

Help. हम्राही, सहाइता. *See* Assistance.

To Help out food. वंड्णु, वर्ताइणु. *See* To Distribute, To Assist.

A Helper. हम्राहु, पुठिभरू. *See* Aider.

Helpless, Helplessly. बेवसो, बेवसि.

A Helpless creature. निधण्को, बेचारो, निधरू. *See* Forlorn.

Helplessness. अणसरंदी, बेवसी, लाचारू, लाचारी.

To Hem (*give a hem*). हूंगारणु.

A Hem. बुहो, ओटो.

A running Hem for a string. उबिड़णो.

Hemiplegy. अधंगु.

Hemp. सिणी.

The Hemp plant (*cannabis sativa*), or drug formed from it. भंग, (*of a strong kind*) बादांनो; the tops or fructification, गांजो; an exudation of the leaves, चसुं.

A Hen. कुकिडि.

Hence (*from this place or time*). हितां, हितों, इथां, इथों, इतांहीं, इतांहों. *See* Therefore.

Her. हुन जो, हिन जो.

Herbage. सब्जो, सब्ज़ी, सावकि.

A Herd (*of animals*). धणु, छांग, गोरमु, टुडु, ब्रलेदो, गोहरि, वलरू, टोड्हो, गलो, वगु. *See* Flock.

A Herdsman. धनारू, धरारू. *See under* Cow, Buffaloe, Goat, and Sheep.

Here. हिते, हिति, हेड़े, हेड़्हां, हेड़्हों, इते, इथे.

Here and there. हेड़ेहोड़े, ओसेपासे.

Hereafter. पोइ.

Hereditary. मौरसी.

A Heretic. काफरू.

A Heritage. मोरासि, वर्सा.

A Hermaphrodite. खदिडो.

A Hermit. मुनी, लाहूती. *See* Devotee.
A Hermitage. गुफा.
Hernia. छिकी.
A Hero. सूरिहु, सूर्मो, जोधो, वर्यामु, मांझी, सूरो, पहिल्वानु, गाजी, वीरू, मथेरू.
Of a Hero, Heroic. सूरिहाणो, सूर्माणो, वीराणो.
Heroism. सूहांई, सूर्माई, बहादुरी, पहिल्वानी.
A Heron. कंगु, बगु.
To Hesitate. हट्कणु, भट्कणु.
To Hew. वढणु.
To rough-Hew in shaping. तरणु.
Hexagon. छकुंडो.
A Hiccouch. हिड्किी.
Hidden. गुझो. *See* Concealed.
A Hide. छोडो, खल.
A Dealer in hides. छोडाई.
To Hide (*act.*). लिकाइणु, लुकाइणु, छपाइणु.
To Hide (*neu.*). लिकणु, लुकणु, छपणु.
Hide and Seek. लिकलिकोटो.
A Hiding place. गुझट.
Hideous. करूडु, ड्रेजारींदडु.
Higgledy piggledy. उबतो सुबतो, उबतडि सुबतडि, अगोपोइ.
High. ड्रिघो, ऊंचो, (*wind*) ड़ाढो, जोरारो, तिखो.
On High. मथे.
The Highlands. उपरू.
A Highway. दगु. *See* Road.
A Highway-man. वाटमारू.
A Hill. टकरू, जबलु, डूंगरू.
Of the Hills. टाकिरू, छापिरू, जबली.
A Hillock. टकिरी, डूंगिरी.
A Hilly desolate country. रोहु.
A Hilt. मुठि, कब्जो. *See* Handle.
Hinder (*adj.*). पोयों.
To Hinder. झलणु, अट्काइणु, रोकणु.
Hinderance. झल, रोक, अटिक, अट्काउ, भगो, मनिह. *See* Impediment.
A Hindú. हिंदू, वाण्यो, किराडु, महतो.
Of a Hindú. हिंदुको, वाणिको, महतिको.
A Hinge. नरूमाद, नरूमादक.
A Hint. इशारो, सुरू, ड़हनाई.
To Hint. इशारो ड़िभणु.
The Hip. दुड़ि.
To carry on the Hip (*a child, &c.*). कछ - हंज - कुछिडि - चेल्हि - चूडि - खणणु.
Hire. भाडो, किराओ. *See* Rent.
To Hire. (*procure for hire*) भाडणु, (*a servant*) रखणु, बिहारणु.
Hired. भाड्यतु.
His. हुन जो, हि जो, (*with indication*) तँहिंजो, संदुसि.
The Hiss, or Hissing of a snake. फूकारो, फूकार.
To Hiss. फूकारणु.
A History. तारीख.
To Hit (*a mark*). चुटणु. *See* To Strike.
Hither. हिते, हेड़े, हेड्डां, हेड्हों. *See* Here.
Hitherto. अञा-हाणे-तांई. *&c.* *See* Till.
Ho! ओ, अरे, अडी.
To Hoard. सथणु, सथु करणु.
To be Hoarse. घिघाइणु.
Hoarse, Hoarsely. घघो, घिघो, गिगो.
Hoarseness. घिघाई.
A Hoe. कोड़रि, (*wooden*) पाहोडी.
One who works with a Hoe. कोड़ार्यो.

A Hog. सुअरु, सोरु.
A Hog deer. फाड्हो.
To Hoist. खणणु, चाढ्हणु, हाकारणु,
Holcus saccharatus. जुअरि, जुआरि, (*different varieties*) माछिडो, कारतुही, गुगुंलो, ग़ाढ्ही, खिलणि, धुतिणी, रहमाई, सदा गुलाबु, अलख, जनपुरि, अछिडी, सठिडी, पांदपुसाडी, कोड़िडो, रतुल, मिठिडो, कारिडो, त्रिटिड़ी, चिब्रोतुरी, सतुर, रतिडो, रहजादो, कुंढिडो, साविडो, बग्दार. *See* Juwari.
Holcus spicatus. ब्राझरि, ब्राझिरी, ब्रांझिरी.
A Hold, Holding. झल.
The Hold of a boat. गंबटु.
To Hold (*grasp*). झलणू. *See* To be contained.
To Hold out (*stretch forth*). पखेरणु, डिघो करणु, वधाइणु.
A Hole. टुंगु, सलु, ग़िखुं, (*large*) ब्रिघंलु.
Full of Holes, or with a Hole. टुंगिरु.
A Hole, or pit, in the ground. खड़. खड़खूबो, चुढो, ड़रो, ड़रिड़ु, चरो.
A Hole made by housebreakers. खाटु, संधि.
The Hole of an animal. ब्रिरु, ड़रि,
Holiness. पाकाई, पवित्राई.
Holla. अडे, अडो, अरे, रे.
Hollow. पोगो, फोफो.
A Hollow (*hollow place*). पोरु.
A Hollow in which water lies. ढोरो.
Hollowness. पोराई, पोराणि.
A Hollow-way. सिरिंघ.
A Holly-hock. गुल्खैरो.
Holy. पाकु, पवित्रु.
A Holy person. साधु, फकीरु, सांईंलोकु, संतु.
A Holyday. मोकल or छुटिअ जो डिंहु. *See* Festival.
Home. घरु.
At Home, Homewards. घरि.
Home-bred, Home-made. घरेचो, घराणो, घरेतो.
A Homicide (*the act*). खूनु, विणाहु.
A Homicide (*the person*). खूनी, विणाही.
A Hone. रोही.
Honest. सचो, सुपत्यो, ईमानी, सचारु. सत्यावानु, साखाइतो.
Honestly. साखाइतो, सुपत्यो. *See* Honest.
Honesty. पति, आंट, कारि, ईमानु, सँवति, सत्या, सचारी, साख.
Honey. माखी.
The Honeycomb. मेणु.
Honor. (*dignity*) मानु, आबु, आबिरूइ, (*sense of honor*) पति, साख, सीलु, सीरु.
Honor (*chastity*). सीलु, सतु.
To Honor. मानु *&c.* ड़िअणु.
To Honor a bill. सकारणु.
Honorable. साऊ, सतो; *or* honorably, मानाइतो, साखाइतो, सुपत्यो.
A Hood for an ox, &c. अखिओ, खोपो, अख्याडी.
The Hood of a hawk. टोपी.
The Hood of a snake. फणि.
A Hoof. खुरु, सुंबु
One toe of a cloven Hoof. खुरांड़ी.
A Hook. कुंढी, (*large*) कुंढो.
A Hoop. चकरु.
A Hookah (*varieties*). चिलिम, हुको, कलो, गुगिंली, दस्ती, नरेलो, सर्कल्याणु, झझरि, बुलारि, चामेलो.
That part of a Hookah containing tobacco and fire. टोपी, फुलु;

the pipe below do, गोइ; that part connecting the tube with the Hookah bottom, ड्टो.
A Hookah snake. नड़ु, बुलारू.
Hoot (*inter.*). फिठि, हेठि, फेठि.
Hooting. फिठ्कार.
To Hop on one foot. चड्ही करे-खुड्योखणि-कुड्यो-हलणु.
Hope. आस, उमेद, भरोसो.
To Hope. आस *&c.* रखणु.
Hopeful, in hopes. आसाइतो, आसाऊ, आसावंतु, उमेदवारू.
Hopeless. निरासु, नाउमेदु.
Hopelessness. नाउमेदी. *See* Despair.
The Hopper of a mill. दञो.
A Horn. सिङु.
A musical Horn (*various kinds*). नसिंगो, नफील, तुरी, कर्नाइ.
Horned, having large Horns. सिङिरू.
Hornless. ठोड्हो, मोड़ो.
A Hornet. ढुंभू.
A Horsocope. वेला, कुंड़ली, जन्मपत्री.
Horrible. ड्डिजारींदडु, ड्डिजु, ड्डींदडु. *See* Fearful.
Horror. हैबत, हौलु. *See* Dread.
A Horse. घोडो; at different ages, ड्रिहाणु, सलुं, दौकु *or* दुभकु, चौसालु, पांजार्यलु.
On Horseback. सुआरू. *See* Horseman.
A Horse-breaker. कारिसुआरू.
Horse-breaking. कारिसुआरि.
A Horse-cloth. झुल.
Horse-dung. लिड़ि.
Horse-furniture. संजु.
A Horse-keeper. सईसु.
A Horse-laugh. ट्हकु, टहटह.
A Horse-man. सुआरू, स्वारू, असवारू, इस्वारू.
Horse-man-ship. सुआरि, चड़्ही. *See* Riding.
A Horse-shoe. नालु, नैलु. *See* Shoe.
Hospitable. मिह्माण्दारू.
A Host (*great number*). दलु.
A Hostage. ओल.
Hostile (*of an enemy*). दुश्मणाणो, दुश्मण्को, वैर्याणो, वैरो.
Hostility. वैरु, दुश्मणी.
Hot. कोसो, गर्मु, ततो.
Hot (*as pepper*). तिखो, कड़ो, कौड़ो.
The Hot season. ऊन्हारो, आड़्हडु.
To grow Hot. तपणु.
A Hovel. भुंगो, झूपिड़ो.
A Hover, Hovering. लामारो.
An Hour. घड़ी, घंटो.
A House. घरू, जाइ, हवेली, इंधु, (*of different forms*) बंगुलो, लांढी, सुफो, चौंरो. *See* Hovel, Shed, Cottage.
The men's part of a House. ओताक.
A fine House. महलु, महलातु.
A store House. भांड़ो, कोठो.
House and property. झुगो, घरू.
A House-breaker. संधिरू.
A Household. साघरि, घरबारू. *See* Family.
Household goods. वसुलो, वथुसिथु.
A House-holder. सघिरो, घरबारी, ग्रिहस्तो.
House-rent. मस्वाड.
The House-top. खुडु.
How (*in what way*). किअं, किहडे दस्तूरि.
How far. केतिरोपंधु.
How large, or great. केडो.

How many, or much. केतिरो, घणो.
How often. केतिरा भेरा.
How small. केड़िडो.
To Howl. ऊनाइणु, ऊनाडणु.
A Howling. ऊनाई, ऊनाड.
A Hubbub. गोडु, हुलु, लुडु.
A Huckster. सुरह्यो, मह्यांडो.
A Huff. रोसामो, रोसु.
A Hug. गिराहुटिडो. *See* Embrace.
To Hug. गिराहुटिडो पाइणु.
The Hum of bees, a top, wheel, &c. घूंघूं, घूंघटु, रूंरूं. *See* Buzzing.
Human. माण्हिको, माण्हुआणो, मड्हिको, माड्हुआणो.
A Human being. मानुखु. *See* Man.
Humanity (*man's nature*). माण्हुअपो, माण्हिपाई, मण्हिपो. *See* Kindness.
Humanity (*the human state*). मानिखो.
Humble. गरीबु, गरीबाणो, गारीबो. *See* Meek.
To Humble. निवाइणु, घटाइणु, झकाइणु, हपाइणु.
Humbled. ढिरो, झको.
Humidity. आलाणि, आलाई.
Humility. निवडत, निआजु, निहठी, निंवति, निहठाई, गरीबाई.
Good-Humored. खुशिजिअडो, खुश्दिलि.
Humor (*mood*). तब्रह, मिजाजु. *See* Moisture, Wit, Whim.
The Hump of a hump back, &c. गुकु, कुबु.
The Hump of an ox. कूंहटु, कांधो, कूहो, ग़नि, गूंबटु.
A camel's Hump. थूहो.
Hump-backed. कुब्रो, गुको.
A Hundred. सउ, सैकिडो.

A Hundred and one. एकोसउ, एकोतसंउ, सउ हिकु.
A Hundred and two. ब्रिडोसउ, ब्रिरोतसंउ, सउ ब्र.
A Hundred and three. ट्रिडोसउ, ट्रिरोतसंउ, सउ ट्रे.
A Hundred and four. चोडोसउ, चोरोतसंउ, सउ चारि.
A Hundred and five. पंजोसउ, पंजोतसंउ, सउ पंज.
A Hundred and six. छहोसउ, छहोतसंउ, सउ छ.
A Hundred and seven. सत्योसउ, सतोतसंउ, सउ सत.
A Hundred and eight. अठ्योसउ, अठोतसंउ, सउ अठ.
A Hundred and nine. नडोसउ, नडोतसंउ, सउ नवं.
A Hundred and ten. ड़होसउ, ड़होतसंउ, सउ ड़ह.
A Hundred fold. सऊंणि.
A Hundred thousand. लखु.
Hundredth. सउयों, सउओं सैओं.
Hunger. बुख.
To Hunger, be Hungry. बुखायो-बुख्यो- हुअणु, बुखाइजणु, बुख लगणु.
To Hunt. शिकारु करणु.
Hunting (*adj.*) A Hunter. शिकारी.
Hunting (*sub.*). शिकारु, आहेडो.
A Hurdle. किडो.
A Hurricane. तूफानु, दूफानु, वाच.
A Hurry. तकडि, उब्रहराई, हैब्ररि. *See* Haste.
In a Hurry, Hurriedly. तकिडो, उब्रहरो.
To Hurry (*neu.*). हड्बडाइणु, तकडि &c. करणु, हैब्रराइणु.
A Hurt. चोट, धकु, सट.

To Hurt. झोरणु. *See* To Injure, To Pain.
Hurtful. जिआन्खोरू, हात्रू.
Hurtfulness. जिआन्खोरी.
A Husband. मुसुं, भतारू, पइ, कांधु, घरवारी.
The duty of a Husband. मुसांई, मुसिंपाई, मुसिंपणु, कांधिपाई.
A Husbandman. हारी, कुड्मी, ब्रन्यरू.
A body of Husbandmen, &c. राजु.
Of or appertaining to a Husbandman. हारिको, कुड्म्याणो, कुड्मिको.
Husbandry. हारिअपो, कुड्मिअपो, हारिअपाई.
Hush! माठि. *See* Silence.
A Husk. खल, छिल.
The Husk of grain. तुहु. *See* Chaff.
To Husk. छिलणु.
A Hut. भुंगो, भुंगो, झुपिडी, चौंरो, झुपिडो.
To be seized with Hydrophobia. हड्किजणु. *See* Mad.
A Hyena. चराखु.
Hymeneal. विहांइतो.
A Hymeneal (*song*). सिठिणो, हेरो, सिहिरो.
The Hypochondres. कुखि.
Hypocrisy. खोटु, कपटु, ब्रिआई, पाखंडु.
Hypocrite. ठोंगो, पाखंड़ी, कुंगिरू.
Hyssop. जूफा.

I & J.

I. आँउं, आँ, मां.
To Jabber. *See* To Chatter.
A Jackal. (*male*) गिदड़ु, (*female*) गिदाडी.
A Jacket. गिड़िलो, कमिरी, पुठो.
To become Jaded. विचणु. *See* To be Tired.
A Jail. बंदिखानो, कैदखानो.
To Jam. सथणु. *See* To Cram.
January, and part of February. मांघु.
A Jar (*vessel*). कूलो, मर्तिबानु, *See* Flagon.
Jasmine. चंबेली.
The Jaundice. साई, कामिणु, जकांनु.
The Jaw, Jawbone. ज़ाड़ो, ज़ाड्ह, हड्ब्राठ.
A Jay. चांहि.
An Ibex. सरहु.
Ice. पारो, बर्फ.
An Ichneumon. नोरू.
An Idea. खिआलु, फुर्णो.
Identical. उहोई, साग्यो, सागूणो.
Identity. साग्याई.
Idiocy. चर्याई, मस्तानाई. *See* Madness.
Idiom. रीति, वर्ज, वर्जीस, मुहाविरो. *See* Custom.
An Idiot. मस्तानो, चर्यो, देवानो, बाँविरो. *See* Fool.
Idiotic, of an Idiot. चर्याणो, मस्तानिको, मस्तिको.
Idle. बेकर्मो, बेकार्यो, निखमिणो, रोलु, रोलाकु. *See* Disengaged, Unemployed, Lazy.
Idleness. बेकारी, निखमिणाई.
An Idler. आरिसो, रोलु, रोलाकु.
An Idol. मूरति, बुतु.
An Idol temple. ठाकुर्दूआरो, दुआरो, मंदरू, बुत्खानो.
An Idolater. मूरतिपूजु.
Idolatry. मूरतिपूज़ा.
Jealous (*of another's success*). सड़्यलु, साडेखाधो, खामिखाणो. *See* Suspicious, Envious.

Jealousy. साड़ो, खामि, जल्णो, पज़ारो. *See* Suspicion.
To Jeer. टोकणु. *See* Ridicule, Taunt.
A Jerk. उछल.
To Jest. ठठोली, &c. करणु, खिलणु.
A Jest, Jesting. ठठोली, पत्रो, चथरि, मश्किरी, मजाक, ठठो.
A Jester. मश्किरो, पत्राई, ठठोलु.
A Jet, Jet d'eau. फुहारो.
A Jew. यहूदी.
A Jewel (*gem*). जंव्हरु, जवाहिरु, रतनु.
A Jewel (*personal ornament*). ग़हु, ग़हणो, जेवरु. *See* Ornament.
A Jeweller. जवाहिरी.
Set with Jewels, Jewelled. जड़ाऊ.
Jewel settings. जड़ाउ.
To set Jewels. जड़णु.
A setter of Jewels. जड़्यो.
The Jew's harp. चंगु, मोंचंगु.
If. जेकड़हीं, जेकर, जे, कर, हूंद.
If not. नत.
Ignoble. अदिनो, की न जिहड़ो, नीचु, कुजात्यो.
Ignobleness. अदिनाई, नीचाई.
Ignominious. बेमानो, खुआरिअ भर्यो, बुछिड़ो.
Ignominy. खुआरी.
Ignorance. इआणप, अणज़ाणाई, अज़ाणाई.
Ignorant. अणज़ाणु, अज़ाणु, अबोझु, इआणो.
Ignorantly. अणज़ाणी.
An Iguana. ग़ोह.
To Jingle. छिण्कणु, छिम्कणु.
A Jingling. छिण्काटु, छिण्को, छिम्को.
Ill (*bad q. v.*). बुछिड़ो, (*in composition*) कु.
Ill (*sick q. v.*). नाचड़ो.
Ill-behaved. कुवाटो, कुरीतो, कुपेरो.
Ill-behaviour. कुवाट, कुरीति, कुपेराई.
Ill-bred. अढंगो, कुढंगो.
Ill-fated. निभाग़ो, निदोरो, चंड़ो.
Ill-formed, Ill-shaped. बेड़ोलो, कुढङ्गो.
Ill-fortune, Ill-luck. निभाग़ाई. *See* Fortune.
Ill-temper (*a child's*). तीसो.
Ill-tempered. तीसिरु.
Ill-timed. कुमहलो, कुवेलो.
Ill-will. खौंस.
To bear Ill-will. खौंसणु.
An Ill-wisher. मंद्खाहु, मठपुरो.
Illegal, Illegally. बेशरा, बेकाइदो.
Illiterate. अणपड़्यो.
Illness. नाचड़ाई, बेमजाई, लड़ाई.
To Illume, Illuminate. रोशनु-सोझिरो-करणु.
An Illusion. भिर्मु, खिआलु, माया, छलु.
An Illustration (*simile*). बयानो, अर्थाउ, ओखाण, द्रिष्टांगु.
Illustrious. नाम्दारु, जसी, उजारो.
Im (*neg. prefix*). अण, अ, बे, ना.
An Image. मूरति, पुतिलो.
Imaginary. दिल्यों ठाह्यलु.
Imagination. खिआलु. *See* Fancy.
To Imagine. भांइणु. *See* To Fancy.
Imbecile. हीणो, पोड़्हो. *See* Impotent.
Imbecility. हीणाई, पोड़्हाई.
To Imitate. नकुलु–चालि–करणु.
An Imitation. सांगु, नकुलु, (*of sounds*) लाति.
An Imitator. नकुली.
Immature. कचो.
Immediately. हाणेई.
Immense. *See* Great, Infinite.

To Immerge, Immerse. टुबाइणु, बोडणु.
Immersed (*in thought, &c.*). गर्कु, गल्तानु, मघनु, लीनु.
Immersion. बोड़ि, बोड.
Immoderate, Immoderately. बधीक. *See* Great, Excessive.
Immodest, Immodestly. बेलज़ो, बेलीहो. *See* Shameless.
Immodesty. बेलज़ाई, बेहयाई.
To Immolate. घोरणु, सदिके *&c.* करणु. *See* Sacrifice.
Immoral, Immorally. कुलछिणो, कुनीतो, लांड़रो.
Immortal. अमरु.
Immoveable. अचलु, काइमु, अणहलु.
Immunity. छुटि, माफी.
Immutable. अणमोटु.
To Impair. *See* To Injure, Lessen.
Impartial. बेरिआउ, बेरिआओ.
Impatience. बेसबुरी, उब्रहराई.
Impatient. बेसबुरो, उब्रहरो, अधीरो.
To Impede. अट्काइणु, झलणु.
An Impediment. झल, रोक, अट्काउ, विघिनु.
To Impel. कराइणु, हलाइणु, लाइणु.
Imperfect. अणपूरो, घटि, अधोखारो. *See* Half-finished.
An Imperfection. *See* Defect.
Imperishable. अविनासी.
Impertinence (*insolence q. v.*). शोखाई.
Impertinent (*insolent q. v.*). शोखु.
Impetuosity. हूडाई.
Impetuous. हूडु, अझलु.
Impetus. जोरु.
Impiety. बेदीनो, अधर्मु.
Impious, Impiously. बेदीनो, बेदीनु, अधर्मी.
To Implant. विहारणु. *See* To Fix.
An Implement. औजारु.
To Implicate. फासाइणु.
Implicit (*full*). पूरो, तमामु.
To Implore. वेनती करणु, लीलाइणु.
Impolite. रुखो.
Import (*meaning*). मुदाउ, मत्लबु, भाउ, हाशो, हार्दउ.
Import, Importation. आवति, आमदनी.
Import, Importance. भउ, सांगो, भोलो.
Important. वड़ो, ग़ोरो, भवाइतो.
Importunate, An Importuner. चंबुडु, जिजा, चिचिडु, छेकू, छेकाऊ, शिक.
To Importune. वचुडणु, चंबुडणु, छिकणु.
Importunity. वचुड, छिकताण, कुचकुचि, छिक, ताण.
To Impose. रखणु.
To Impose on. ठग़णु, छलणु, फसाइणु.
Imposition, Imposture. दल्बो, पर्पंचु, छलु. *See* Deceit.
Impossible. अणथिअणो, अणहुअणो, नथिअणो, अणहोणो.
An Impossibility. अणहोणो, नथिअणो.
An Impostor. ठगु, ठोग़ो. *See* Deceiver.
Impotence (*wanting manly powers*). नामर्दी, खदिडाई. *See* Weakness.
Impotent (*wanting strength*). बेकुअतो, बेसघो, बेजोरो, असमर्थु. *See* Weak.
Impotent (*without manly powers*). नामर्दु, खदिडो, कआरासी, होजिडो.
To Impoverish. खुहाइणु, सखिणो करणु.

To Impound. टकणु.
Impregnable. अणटोड़ु.
To Impregnate, Improlificate. टु-काइणु.
To Impress, Imprint. ठपणु, जबंणु, हणणु, छापणु.
An Impression (*stamp*). निशानु, ठपो, छाप.
An Impression (*effect*). असरु.
To Imprison. बंदि-कैदि-करणु, झलणु, पूरणु.
Imprisonment. बंदु, कैदु, झल.
Improbable. नथिअणजिहडो.
Improper, Improperly. नालाइकु, बेवडो, बेमुनासिबो, नाशास्तो, बेजाइ.
An Impropriety. नालाइकी, बेवडाई.
To Improve. उपिडणु, चड़हणु, चङो थिअणु.
An Improvement. चङाई, चाढूहो, सर्साई, ओपडु.
Improvident, Imprudent. अणग़ाणू, बेसाङाहो.
Imprudence. बेसाङाही.
Impudence. बेअदबी, शोखाई, ड़ोठाइ, बेहयाई. *See* Insolence.
Impudent. बेअदबु, शोखु, ड़ोठु, बेहया. *See* Insolent, Shameless.
An Impulse of the mind. पूरु. *See* Fancy, Force.
Impure. ओठो, नापाकु, हरामु, असुधि, पलीतु, छुतो, अपविटु.
Impurity. ओठाई, नापाकाई, नापाकी.
To Impute. लाइणु, रखणु.
In (*prep*). में, मंझि, अंदरि.
In (*neg. prefix*). अ, अण, बे, ना, न.
Inability. अघाई, बेवसी.
An Inaccuracy. भोल, गलति. *See* Incorrectness.
Inactive. ढिरो, खुझलु.
Inadmissible. नमञण जिहडो.
Inadvertence. अचेताई, अणज़ाणु.
Inanimate. निर्जीउ, जड़ु, थांवरु.
Inapplicable. अणठहिणो.
Inarticulately. अँऊँगँऊँ.
Inattention. ग़हेलाई, गाफिली.
Inattentive. ग़हेलो, ग़ल्हो, गाफिलु.
Inauspicious. निभागो, नहसु.
Incalculable. अग़णति, असंखु, बेशुमारु, अणग़णति.
An Incantation. मंडु, मंटु, मंत्रु, फीणो. इसिमु.
To become Incarnate. औतरणु.
The Incarnation of a deity. औतारु, अवतारु.
Incautious. अचेतु. *See* Careless.
Incense. वासु, धूपु.
To Incense, or perfume with Incense. वासणु, धूपणु.
An Incensory. वासाडो, वासूडो.
Incessantly. सदा. *See* Continually.
An Inch. तसू.
An Incident *See* Affair, Accident.
An Incision. छेहु. *See* Cut.
To Incite. दुखाइणु, मचाइणु.
Incivility. बेअदबी. *See* Rudeness.
An Inclination (*desire*). सध, खाहिश, चाह, अहल, मनु, मनिसा.
To Incline (*lean*). लडणु, अड़लणु, लेटणु.
Inclining. *See* Sloping, A Slope.
To Include. आणणु, गड़णु.
Including, Inclusive of. सूधो, साणु, सूधो.
Incombustible. अजरु.
Income, In-coming. आवति. *See* Revenue.
To Incommode. अँहँजाइणु.
Incommodious. अँहँजो.
Incomparable. अणमटु, अणजोड़ु.

Incompatible. अणठाहू, अणठहिणो.
Incompetency. नालाइकी.
Incompetent. नालाइकु, अजोगु.
Incomplete. अणपूरो, अधोखारो. *See* Half-finished.
Inconsiderate. बेकिआसु, अलबेलो, अलगर्जो.
Inconsistency. अणमेलु, बेजोडाई.
Inconsistent, Incongruous. बेजोडो.
Inconstant (*in affection*). बेवफा, कूडो. *See* Fickle.
Incontinence. लंगोताडाई, लांगछोटाई.
Incontinent. लंगोताडो, लांगछोटो.
Inconvenience. अँहँजु, अँहँजाउ.
Incorrect, Incorrectly. गलति, ड़धि, असुधि.
Incorrectness. भोलो, ड़धि, गलति.
Incorrigible. निर्जो, कुतेपुछु.
Incorruptible. अणग़ारू.
An Increase. वाधि, वधाउ, वाधो, सर्सी, चडु, चाड़ु.
To Increase (*neu.*). वधणु, वीझणु.
To Increase (*act.*). वधाइणु, विझाइणु.
Incredible. अणवेसाहो.
Incredulous. अणमञू, बेवेसहु.
To Incur. पाण ते आणणु.
Incurable. बेइलाजु, बेइलाजो.
Indebted. (*under obligation*) काण्यातो, कांयारो, (*in debt*) कर्जी.
Indecent, Indecorous. बेलज़ो, उभाडो. *See* Shameless.
Indeed. सचु, तह कीकु.
Indefatigable. अविर्चु, अणविर्चु, अणविर्चो.
Indefinite. बेकेतो, बेकायो, बेठीको, बेनेमो.
To Indemnify. छोओ &c. भरणु. *See* Loss.
Independence. मुख़्त्यारि, वेमोथाजो.
Independent. बेकाण्यो, मुख़्त्यारु, मुख्यारू, रजाराणो, पाणभरो.
Indeterminate. *See* Indefinite.
An Index (*to a book*). पनोतिरो, तक्तिरो.
Indian corn. मकाई, मकाइणि, मकी.
To Indicate. ड़सणु, ड़ेखारणु.
Indication. ड़सु.
Indifference. बेपर्वाही, अलगर्जाइ, अलबेलाई.
Indifferent. अलगर्जो, अलबेलो, बेपर्वाहु, बेपर्वाहो.
Indigence. तंगी, सुक. *See* Poverty.
Indigenous. ड़ेही, ड़ेसी.
Indigestible. कुपचु, बदूहजमु-मो.
Indigestion. बदहजमी, अजीरणु.
To be Indignant. डुर्माइणु, मत्थां भांइणु. *See* Angry.
An Indignity. बेआब्रुई, निरादरी, बेपत्याई.
Indigo. नीरू.
Of Indigo. नीरांओं.
Indiscreet, Indiscreetly. बेसाञाहो, अणसांगो, बेसाञहु-हो.
Indiscriminately. बेसाञाहो, अंदिलस.
Indiscrimination. बेसाञाही.
Indispensable. जरूरू.
Indisposed (*unwell*). नाचङो, बेमजे, नाताजो. *See* Sick.
Indisposition. नाचङाई. *See* Sickness.
Indisputable, Indisputably. बेहुजतो.
Indistinct, Indistinctly. अणचिटो.
An Individual. ज़णो, शख्सु. *See* Man.
Indivisible. अणवंडिणो.
Indolence. आरिसु, आलिसु, नेस्ती. *See* Laziness.
Indolent. आर्सी, आलिसो, थधो, नसुनि वको. *See* Lazy.

To Induce. कुच्कुचि करे कराइणु, सेखारणु.
Indulgence. भारो, भारू.
Indulgent. *See* Fond, Kind.
Industrious. मिन्हती, उज़मी
Industry. मिन्हत, उज़मु.
Inebriation. शराबिपणो. *See* Intoxication.
Ineffectual, Inefficacious. बेफाइदो, अजायो. *See* Vain, Futile.
Inequality. घटिवधाई, नंढवड़ाई.
Inestimable. अमुलु.
Inevitable. अटरू.
Inevitably. जाई, खामखा.
Inexhaustible. अखुटु, अणखुटु.
Inexperience. अणहेर, अणवाकुफी.
Inexperienced. अणहिर्यलु, अणहिर्यो, अणवाकुफी.
Inexpert. अणभडु, कचो.
Infallible. अगुसु.
Inexpressible. अकहु, अकथु.
Infamous. गिलारो, खुआरू.
Infamy. अजसु, निंदा, खुआरी, बद्नामी, गिला.
Infancy. किकाई, गींगाई.
An Infant. किको, गींगो, ब्रारिडो, ब्रारू, ब्रालकु, ब्रचो.
Infantile, Infantine. किकाणो, गींगाणो.
Infantry. पिआदि.
To grow Infatuated. चयों थिअणु, छकनु थिअणु. *See* To be Enamoured.
To Infer. ज़ाणणु, सहि करणु.
Inferior. (*in excellence or value*) निसुं, अझको, घटि, (*in place*) हेठि.
Inferiority. निसांई.
Infernal. नरकी, दोजकी.
Infertile. *See* Barren.
An Infidel. काफरू.
Of an Infidel. काफराणो, काफकों.
Infinite. अपारु, अनंतु.
The Infinitive (*in grammar*). मस्दरि.
Infirm. होणो. *See* Weak.
To Inflame. ब्रारणु. *See* To Kindle.
To be Inflamed. ब्ररणु, सडणु, तपणु.
Inflammation. ताउ.
To Inflate (*neu.*). फुलणु, फुंड़णु, आभामणु.
To Inflate (*act.*). फुंड़ाइणु, फुलाइणु.
Inflexible. अणमुड़, अमुडु.
To Inflict. ड़िभणु, विझणु.
To Influence. छिकणु; this verb is generally expressed by giving to that following its causal form.
To Inform. ज़ाणाइणु, जताइणु, चिताइणु, खबर &c. ड़िभणु, आगाहु करणु.
Information. खबर, समाउ. *See* Knowledge.
An Informer (*accuser*). जूण्यतु, चुगिलु.
Informing (*accusing*). जूणी, चुगिली.
Infrangible. अणटुटु.
To Infringe, भञणु. *See* To Break.
To Infuse. भरणु, विझणु.
Ingenious. (*inventive*) हुनिरेलो, हिक्मती, हुनिराइतो, (*of curious design*) हुनिराइतो.
Ingenuity. हुनिरू, हिक्मत.
Inglorious. बेजसी.
An Ingot. लुसिरी, रेणी.
An Ingrate. गुणचोरू, बेगुणो.
Ingratitude. गुणचोराई, बेगुणाई.
To Inhabit. *See* To Dwell.
An Inhabitant. रहाकू, वेठलु, रहू, रहाशी.
An Inhabited place. वसँउँ, वसिंह.

An Inheritance. वर्सो.
Inhuman. अणमाण्हिको. *See* Cruel.
Inhumanity. बेरहमी.
Initial. पह्रों. *See* First.
To Inject. अंदरि विझणु.
Injudicious. अणग़ाणू, बेसळाहो.
An Injunction. तागीद. *See* Command.
To Injure. जिआनु *&c.* करणु, झोरणु.
An Injurer, Injurious. जिआन्खोरू.
Injury. जिआनु, नुक्सानु, हाँणि, हात्रो. *See* Detriment.
Injustice. अन्याउ, नाहकु, अंधेरू, बग्दादु.
Ink. मसु *f.*
Daubed with Ink. मसुहाणो.
An Inkling. ज़ाणु, भासु.
An Inkstand. मसु *f.*
Cotton, &c. put into an Inkhorn. नाओ.
An Inlet (*place of ingress*). वाट. *See* Entrance.
Inner, Inmost. अंदियों.
Innocence. (*freedom from guilt*) बेड़ोहो, (*artlessness*) भोराई, भोरिड़ाई, बोदिलाई.
Innocent. बेड़ोहु, बेगुनाहु, (*simple q. v*) भोरिडो.
Innocuous, Innoxious. बेजिआनु–नो.
Innumerable. बेशुमारू, अणग़णति, असंखु.
To Inoculate. सीतला जो टुको ड़िअणु, सीतला कढणु.
Inodorous. बेबोयो.
Inoffensive. गरीबु, बेड़ोहो. *See* Innocuous, Simple.
Inopportune, Inopportunely. बेमहलु–लो.
Inquietude. चिंता. *See* Disquiet, Anxiety.

To Inquire, पुछणु, पुछणुग़ाछणु.
An Inquiry, Inquisition. पुछाग़छा, पुछाग़छ, ओखड़ोख, पुछा.
Insane. चर्यो, बाँविरो, सौदाई, मतिवालो.
Insanity. चर्याई, सौदाउ.
Insatiate, Insatiable. बेढ़ओ.
To Inscribe. *See* To Write, Engrave.
Inscrutible. अगमु.
An Insect. जीतु.
Insects bred in grain. सुरो.
An Insect destructive to grain, wood, &c. घुणो, सीवी.
Insect eaten (*corn*). सुर्यलु. *See* To be Eaten.
Insecure. बेहथीको, अणसोयो, अणपुख्तो.
Insecurity. बेहथीकाई, अणसोयाई.
Insensibility. बेहोशी, गेराई, सुंन, गुंगझोडि.
Insensible. बेहोशु, बेसुधि, गेरो.
To Insert. अंदरि विझणु.
Inside. अंदरि.
The Inside. अंदरू.
Inside-out. उबतो, उबतोसुबतो.
Of the Inside. अंदियों.
A little way Inside. अंदिरांहों, अदरांहों.
Insignificant. हल्को, बेकारू, बिर्थो.
Insincere. कूडो, कपटी.
To Insinuate (*introduce*). पिहारणु, घेडणु.
Insipid. फिको, बेसवादो, बेलजतो.
Insipidity. फिकाई, फिकाणि.
To Insist. होड़ *&c.* करणु. *See* Obstinacy.
To Insnare. फासाइणु.
Insolence. गुस्ताकी, शोखाई, मचुलाई, ड़ीठाई.

Insolent. गुस्ताकु, शोखु, मचुलो, ड्रीठु.
Insolvent. खुटलु. *See* Bankrupt.
To Inspect. चकासणु, जाचणु. *See* To Examine, Look at.
Inspection. चकास, जाच.
Inspiration (*divine*). आकासवाणी.
To Inspissate. घाटो करणु.
Instability. बेबकाई, बेतग़ाई.
To Install. विहारणु.
An Instalment (*in payment*). किस्त, खुंधी.
An Instance (*example q. v.*). मिसालु.
An Instant. पलु, लहजो, दमु, खिण. *See* Moment, Eye-twinkling.
Instantly. ठहफह, तुर्तु, चट्पटि, झट्पटि.
Instead. बदरि, बदिरों, एवजि, जाइ.
The Instep. पेर जी पुठि.
To Instigate. कुमति ड्रिअणु, सेखारणु. *See* To Incite.
To Instil. थोरो थोरो करे विझणु.
To Instruct. सेखारणु, पड्हाइणु.
Instruction. सिख्या, सिख, तालीम.
An Instructor. सेखारू, सेखारींदडु.
An Instrument (*tool q. v.*). ओजारू.
A musical Instrument. साजु, वाज़ो.
Through the Instrumentality (*of persons*). हथां, हथों, मार्फत.
Insufferable, Insupportable. अणसहिणो.
Insufficient. अणपूरो, घटि.
An Insult. गिला, निंदा, निरादरू, बेआब्रुई.
Insurance. वीमो.
To Insure. वीमो लाहणु.
Insurgent. याकी.
An Insurrection. झेडो, फितिनो.
Integrity. सचाई, सचारी, ईमानु. *See* Honesty.

The Intellect. बुधि, अकुलु, होसिलो, होशु, ग्यानु. *See* Understanding.
Intelligence (*news*). खबर, समाउ, सुधि, खबरचार, समाचारू. See Knowledge.
An Intelligencer. खाबिरू.
Intelligent. स्याणो, सञोझो, चतुरू, सुघडु, सुज़ाणु, खांदो.
Intemperate, Intemperately. वधि, वधीक, वाधू.
To Intend. इरादो &c. करणु or रखणु.
Intense. ड्राढो.
Intent, Intently (*adj.*). हिकचितो, हेकमनो.
Intent, Intention. इरादो, दिली, निअत, खिआलु.
Intentionally. ज़ाणीवाणी, ज़ाणीवेणी, ज़ाणीबुझी, ड्रिसीवाइसी.
Intercalary (*month*). अधिकु, लुंडु, डुतीकु, पुरूसोतमु.
To Intercept. वाट में झलणु.
An Intercessor. शफी, वेचुओ.
Intercourse. प्रीतिपर्चो, अचणुवञणु.
To Interdict. ममिह करणु, झलणु.
Interest (*of money*). व्याजु, लाभु, मितो, सूदु. *See* Advantage, Good, Concern.
At Interest. व्याज़ेरू.
Self-Interested. गर्जाऊ, गर्जाई.
To Interfere. दखलु करणु, विच में पवणु, हथु विझणु.
An Interim. विथि. *See* Interval.
Interior, Internal. अंदिर्यों.
Intermarriage. कनोवटी.
To Intermeddle. *See* To Meddle, Interfere.
Intermedial, Intermediate. विचों.
Interminable. *See* Boundless.
Intermission. विछोटी, विथि, छेटी. *See* Pause.

Intermittent. वाराइतो. *See* Ague, Fever.

To Intermix, Intermingle. *See* To Mix.

To Interpose (*act*). वेचुभो विझणु. *See* To Mediate.

Interpretation (*translation*). तर्जिमो. *See* Meaning.

An Interpreter. तर्जिमानु.

To Interrogate. पुछणु, पुछणुग़छणु, पुछा *&c.* करणु.

Interrogation. पुछा, पुछग़छ. *See* Inquiry.

To Interrupt. रंड़णु, रंड़ाइणु, गाल्हिवढणु, अट्काइणु.

Interruption. रंड़, भग़ी, भंगु, भञ्किडी.

An Interstice. संधो, वेचांदरू, वेचो. *See* Interval.

To Intertwine. *See* To Intwine.

An Interval. विचु, विथि, संधो, अंतिरो, विछोटो, वेचो, छेटी.

Interval (*term given for payment, &c.*). खुणु, मुदो.

To Intervene. विचि अचणु.

An Interview. मुलाकाति.

To have an Interview. गड्जणु.

The Intestines. आंड्रो. *See* Entrails.

An Intimacy. याराणी, एकाई, हिकिडाई. *See* Friendship.

An Intimate friend. हालभाई.

To Intimate. ज़ाणाइणु. *See* To Inform.

To Intimidate. दड्को ड्रिअणु, डेज़ारणु, दब्राइणु.

Intimidation. दड्को, दब्राउ.

Into. मँझि, में.

Intolerable. अणसहिणो.

To Intoxicate. मस्ताइणु.

Intoxicated. मस्तु, खिओ, नशई. *See* Drunk.

To become Intoxicated. मस्तिजणु.

Intoxication. मस्ती, मस्ताई, नशो, मस्तानाई, मस्तानी.

Intractable. दन्तुहेड़ो, वेचयो. *See* Obstinate.

Intrepid. वेभभो, निधडु, वड़जिगिरो. *See* Bold.

Intrepidity. वेभवाई, वड़जिगिराई, निधड़ाई. *See* Boldness.

Intricacy. मोंझारो. *See* Perplexity.

Intricate. मूड्हलु, मुझलु, मुझूडो.

To Intrigue. ढंडँ लाइणु. *See* To Plot.

To Intrust (*give in charge*). सौंपणु, पर्नणु, अमानत-धरावत-रखणु. हवाले- जिमे-करणु, सुपारणु.

Intrusted. पर्तो.

Intrusting. पर्न, सौंप.

To Intwine. वेड्हणु, वकुडणु, वचुडणु.

To Invade. चड्हणु.

Invalid. *See* Useless, Sick.

To Invalidate. निकमो करणु, भञणु.

Invaluable. अमुलु.

An Invasion. चड्ही, काह. *See* Attack.

To Inveigle. चट-चल्तो-बंधणु. *See* To Entice.

To Invent. ठाहणु, रचणु, कढणु.

An Invention. ठाहु, रचना.

An Inventor. ठाहू.

An Inventory. चिठो, यादास्त.

Inverse, Inverted. उबतो, ऊंधो.

To Invert. उबताइणु

To Invest. *See* To Clothe, Install, Besiege.

To Investigate. उपटारणु, जाचणु, चक्रासणु.
An Investigation. जाच, जाचाई, पुछग़छ, पुछाग़छा, ओखड़ोख, चक्रासणु.
Invincible. अजीतु.
Invisible. अणडिसिणो, गैबी.
An Invitation. दावत, धामो, नोतिरी, कांढ, नेंड्र.
The messenger who delivers an Invitation. नेंड्रो, कांढो.
To Invite. दावत &c. करणु, मानो चवणु.
To Inundate. बोडणु.
An Inundation. ब्रोड, बरहरो, उथल, लेट. *See* Flood.
To Involve. फसाइणु, गंडणु.
Involuntarily. पाण्हेई.
To Inure. हेरणु.
Inutility. निक्रमाई. *See* Uselessness.
Inward, Internal. अंदिर्यों.
A Jockey. कारि सुभारू.
Jocose, Jocular. मश्किरी, खिलिणो, चर्चाई. *See* Merry.
To Jog (*neu*). डुगाइणु.
A Jog-trot. डुग.
To Join (*act. put together*). गंढणु.
To Join (*neu.*). लग़णु, मिलणु.
Joined, Jointly. गडु.
A Joint. गंढु, संधी, पेवंदु, संधु.
The space between two Joints in a cane. गुरी.
A Joist. काम.
A Joke, Joking. ठठोली, पञ्ञो, मश्किरी, ठठो, खिल, चथरि, चर्चो, मजाक.
A Joker. मश्किरी, पञ्ञाई, मजाकी.
A Jolt, Jolting. धड्को, लोड़ो.
To Jolt. लोड़णु, धोड़णु.
A Jostle, Jostling. धिको, धेल्हो.
To Jostle. धिकणु, धेल्हणु.
A Jot. जरो, तिरू.
A Journal (*merchant's*). रोज़्नामो.
A Journey. सफरू, मुसाफिरी, पंधु.
A day's Journey. मैजल.
Provision for a Journey. समरू, तोशो.
To Journey. पंधु *&c.* करणु.
Joy, Joyfulness. खुशी, आनंदु, जशनु, हुलासु, जौंकु.
To Joy. खुशि &c. थिअणु.
Joyful. खुशि, आनंदी, जौंकी, बहारू. *See* Glad.
Irascible. तिखो. *See* Passionate.
The Iris (*flower*). सोसनु. *See* Rainbow.
Irksome. डुख्यो.
Iron. लोहु.
Of Iron. लोहांओं.
Irrecoverable. अणलभु-भो. *See* Irremediable.
Irregular, Irregularly. बेदस्तूरी, बेरीती, बेकाइदो, कुनीतो, बेड़ोलो, अग़ेपोइ.
An Irregularity. बेरीती, बेड़ोलाई.
Irreligion. बेदीनी, अधर्मु, बेधर्माई, बेधर्मी, बेदीनाई.
Irreligious. बेदीनो-नु, बेधर्मी.
Irremediable, Irreparable. बेइलाजो-जु.
Irresistible, Irrestrainable. अझलु.
Irresolute. ब्रिचितो.
Irresolution. ब्रिचिताई.
To Irrigate. रिजाइणु.
Irrigation. रेजु, रेणो, पेजु, पेज़ो.
Irritable. चिडिणो. *See* Passionate.
To Irritate. रंजाइणु, चेडणु, रीडाइणु, संदाइणु. *See* To Anger.
To be Irritated. चिड़णु, कल्पणु, To be Angry.

Irritation. चिड, चेड.

An Irruption (*hostile*). काह. *See* Attack.

An Island. टापू, दीपु, ब़ारी, बेटु, ब़ेटारो, केटो, ब़ेलारो.

To Issue (*neu.*). निकिरणु.

It. हू, हो, हे, हो, ऊं, ए.

The Itch. किरँहिँ, खहर, खारिस, खही, खाज़ि, सुर्णो, खहि.

To Itch. किरँहिँ &c. करणु.

An Itching. सुसुरि, सुर्णो.

An Item (*in an account*). रकम.

A Judge. मुन्सिफु.

To Judge. परखणु. *See* To Examine.

Judgment (*decision*). तज्वीज. *See* Understanding, Sentence.

The Judgment day. क्रिआमत जो ड़ींहु.

Judicious. ग़्याणू. *See* Wise.

A Juggle, Juggling, Jugglery. चिश्मबंदो, बाजोगरी.

A Juggler. बाजोगरू.

Juice. रसु, पाणी.

Juicy. रसोलो, तरि.

The Jujube tree. ब़ेरि.

The Jujube fruit. बैरू, (*various kinds*) मकाई, सूकी, ज़ाडूरो, सिंधो; ripe on the tree, गोक.

The stone of the Jujube. खखिडो. दखिडो.

July and part of August. सावणु, स्राणु.

To Jumble (*act.*). गंडु-गंडुगोडु-करणु.

A Jump, Jumping. टपो, कुडु, छालु, टिपु, ठेंगु, पंबही.

To Jump. टपणु, कुड़णु.

Junction. मेलु, जोडु.

June and part of July. आखाडु.

Junior. नंढो.

The Juniper tree. अहुबेरु.

A Jungle. झंगु.

Ivory. आजु.

A worker in Ivory. आजोगरु, चूडोगरु.

Jupiter (*the planet*). विरस्पति, विस्पति, मुश्तरि.

Jurisdiction. हुकुमु, अमलु, हाकिमी.

Just, Justly. हको, निभाई, वाजिबी, *See* Honest, Upright, Correct.

Just now, a little ago. सवेरिडो. अग़इडो, अग़भरो. *See* Exactly, Merely, Near.

Justice. आचारु, निआउ, गोरु, हकु, दादु, अदालत, शरा, तोरो, धर्मु.

Juvenile. See Young, Youthful.

Jowarí. जुआरि. *See* Holcus saccharatus.

Green Jowarí for feeding cattle. खीरो.

A sweet stalk of Jowarí. ग़नो.

A kind of Jowarí with sweet stalks. तुरी.

A kind of Jowarí with insipid stalks. कांगडु.

K

To Kaw. कांकां करणु.

Keen. तिखो.

Keenness. तिखाई.

To Keep. रखणु, धरणु. *See* To Guard, Detain, Obey, Fulfill, Maintain, Restrain, Last.

A Keeper. राखो, रखूवालु, वाही, झालू. *See* Guardian.

The act of Keeping. रख, रखिणी. *See* Charge, Watching.

The charge for Keeping. रखाणी.

A Kernel. मग्जु, ग़भु.
A Kettle drum. नगारो, दमामो, भेरि.
The beater of a Kettle-drum. नगार्ची.
A Key. कुंजो.
A Kick. (*with the toes*) थुड़ो, (*with sole of foot*) लत, (*backward of an ass*) इट.
To Kick. थुड़ो-लत-हणणु.
A Kicker. लतिरू.
A Kid. छेलो, लेलो, हुल्वाणु; of 11 or 12 months old, (*male*) पाठुरू, पाठो, (*female*) ऐठ, पठ.
A Kidney. बुकी, गुड्दी.
To Kill. मारणु, कुहणु. *See* To Slaughter.
A Killer. मारू.
A Killing. मारो, घातु. *See* Slaughter, Murder.
A Kiln. खूरो, खूरो, (*potter's*) निहांई.
Kind (*adj*). मिहिर्बानु, वडाइतो, उपकारी.
Kind (*sort, q. v.*). जिनिस, किसिमु, जाति, भाँति, बिरह, वझु.
Of what Kind. किहडो.
To Kindle (*act.*). दुखाइणु, बारणु. *See* To Light up.
To Kindle, be Kindled. दुखणु, बरणु.
Kindness. मिहिर्बानी, मिहिर, एछिपो, वडु, चङाई, भलाई, भालु, उपकारू, हितु, क्रिपा, दया, गुणु, नेकी. *See* Favor.
Kindred. बिरादरी, भाईचारो. *See* Relationship.
Kine. ढोर *plu.*
A King. बाद्शाहु, बाछा, पाछाहु, राजा, महाराजु.
A Kingdom. बाद्शाही, पाछाई, राजु.
Kingly. बाद्शाही, राजसी, राजाणो.
Kinsfolk. *See* Kindred.
A Kinsman. माइटु, मिटु, सको, छिलेरहमु.
A Kiss. चुमी, मिठी, मिठिडी, चशी.
To Kiss. चुमणु.
A Kissing. चुमिणी, चुम्चुमि.
A Kitchen. रंधिणी, बोर्चीखानो. *See* Cookhouse.
A Kite. सिरिणि, हिल.
A paper Kite. पतंगु, लगडु, सिरिणि, गुड़ो, कागिडो, तुकल, भकिंणी, नांगिर्णी.
A Kitten. पूंगो, पूंगिडो.
A Knack. ढँउँ. *See* Art, Contrivance.
A Knave, Knavish. मिकिरेली, मकरी, छली, अठेरो, नरानाकु. *See* Rogue.
Knavery. मकरू. *See* Deceit.
To Knead. गोहणु, मलणु.
Kneading. गोह, मलिणी.
The Knee. मूनो, गोड़ो.
To Kneel. मूननि or गोड़नि भरविहणु.
To Kneel, and sit on the heels behind. गोड़ा खोडे विहणु.
The Knee-pan. ढकिणी.
A Knife. कपु, कातो, छुरी. *See* Penknife.
A Knight (*at chess*). घोडो.
To Knit. उणणु.
A Knob. डुंडो, बूंबु, (*on a rough stick*) अंगु *f*.
A Knock. ठोक, ठोकर, ठोंसो, पछँड़, पछाड.
The sound of a Knock or Knocking. ठुड्को, ठड्को.
To Knock (*act.*). ठोकणु, ठड्काइणु, ठुड्काइणु. *See* To Strike.
To Knock about. गींदाइणु.

To Knock down. केरणु, केराइणु.
To Knock off or away. उथेड़णु, उथोड़णु.
To Knock together (*neu.*). ठहकणु, ठुङ्कणु.
To Knot. गंढि डिभणु.
A Knot. गंढि; kinds of ditto. चा-पहि, गाबेगंढि, ड़ेढगंढि, अधुगंढि.
A running Knot. सिर्किणी, सेरिणी.
Knotty. गंढिरू.
To Know. ज़ाणणु. *See* To Recognize.
Knowing (*cunning*). पक्रो, पुख़्तो, स्याणो, ड़ाढो, हरीफु, तरीनाकु. *See* Skilful.
The Knowing for certain. चिटाई, पकाई.
Knowingly (*purposely, q. v.*). जाणीवाणी, ड़िसीवाइसो.
Knowledge. सुधि, समाज, खबर, वाकुफी, कल, समक, परो, गमि, भास, मालिमो, सनाखत, लख. *See* Acquaintance, Learning.
Known. मालिमु, ज़ातलु, पधिरो.
A Knuckle. टिणी.
A Kos. कोहु, ग़ाहू.

L

Laborious. (*diligent, toilsome*). मिह्नती, (*toilsome*) मिह्नताइतो, मिह्नताणो.
Laboriously. मिह्नताइतो.
Labour. पोर्ह्यो, मिह्नत, पतोड, मजूरी. *See* Toil.
To Labour. पोर्ह्यो, *&c.* करणु, वहणु.
To Labour laboriously. ग़हणु.
To be in the pains of Labour. संभालणु.
A Labourer. कमो, पोह्यतु, मजूरु.
A canal Labourer. खाम्डिओ.
A pressed Labourer. वेगारी, छेडो; a body of ditto, छेड.
A Labyrinth. भवझड़. *See* Maze.
Lac (*the dye*). लाख.
Of Lac, dyed with Lac. लाखी.
Gold Lace. गोटो, धनिक, किनारी, चकिरी.
To Lacerate, Lack. *See* To Tear, Want.
Lacker. रोगनु.
A Lad. ग़भिरू, लास्यारू. *See* Boy.
A Ladder. चर्णी, ड़ाकणी, पोडी.
To Lade. लड़णु, (*a boat*) भरणु.
Laden. भर्थू.
A Ladle (*varieties*). केवी, कण्छो, कड्छी, डोई, चमचो, करंड़ी, टिपिडी, वधिणो, ड़ोइलो, कफगोरू.
A Lady. ब़ाई, बीबी, साहिबु.
A Lake. ढंढ.
A lamb. (*male*) घेटो, हुलवाणु, (*female*) घेटी.
Lame. मंड़ो, लड़ो.
To Lame. मंड़ो करणु.
Lameness. मंड़ाई, लड़ाई.
To Lament. ओंहू, *&c.* करणु, रूअणु पिटणु.
Lamentation. ओंह, हाइहाइ, दांह रोह, कूक.
A Lamp. ड़िभो, चरागु, (*varieties*) पील्सोजु, शमादानु, ड़िभाटो, फानूसु, ड़िभालु, जोति.
A hanging Lamp. कंदील.
Lamp black. कजलु, फुलो.
A Lance. भालो, नेजो.
A Lancet. नस्तर.
Land. धर्ती, भुंइ, थलु, जिमोन. *See* Country.
Land and water. जलथल, जलुथलु.
New Land fit for tillage. नह्वर.

Land under tillage. आइठो.
By Land. सुकी, खुश्की.
To Land (*act*). कंधिअ ते लाहणु.
A Landholder. जिमोदारू. *See* Farmer.
A Landing place. तडु, घाटु.
A good Landing place. सुतडु.
A bad Landing place. कुतडु, औतडु.
A Land tax. ढल, राजरू, महसूलु.
A Lane. घिटी, घटी, ग़ली.
A Language. बोली, भाषा, ज़बान.
Languid. आरिसी. *See* Lazy, Weak.
To Languish. ग़रणु, हथिजणु, हथामणु, सुसणु.
A Lantern. शमादानु.
Lantern jawed. चिब्रिरो.
The Lap. हंज.
The Lap or skirt. फाड़.
To Lap (*in drinking*). लकणु.
To Lap over as edge of cloth. (*act.*) वराइणु, (*neu.*); वरणु.
Large. वड़ो. *See* Plentiful.
Somewhat Large, too Large. वड़ेरो, वड़ेरिडो.
Largeness. वड़ाई, वड़ाणि.
A Lark. अगनु, जलु, चंडूलु.
Lascivious. शह्वती, कामी. *See* Lewd.
A Lash, Lashing. सट्को, चहबुकु, चाबुकु.
The Lash of a whip. पुछिडी.
To Lash. चहबुकु हणणु, सटणु. *See* To Beat.
To Lash as clothes in washing. पछाडणु, सटणु.
A Lass. ग़ाभिरू.
Lassitude. आरिसु, सुस्ती.
A shoemaker's Last. कालिबु.
Last (*adj.*). पोयों.
Last (*month, &c.*). अग़्यों, गुजियों, अग़ूणो, महँडूणो, महँड्यों.
Last night. वेई राति, काल्ह राति.
Last year. परू.
Of Last year. परोको.
At Last. नेठि, ओडकि, आखरि, निदानु.
To Last. जटणु, झलणु, तगणु, हलणु, हंडणु.
Lasting (*adj.*). जटाऊ, तगाऊ, हंडाऊ, हंडिणो, झालू.
Lastingness. जटा. *See* Durability.
Late (*with delay*). चिरों. *See* Last, Recent, Modern.
To be Late. देरि करे अचणु *or* वञणु, *&c.*
Laterally. पासारो, पासीरो.
A Lathe. जंड्रो.
A Lather. गजो. *See* Froth.
The Latter part. पोउ, पोछो.
Latter. पोयों (*of the latter part*) पाछाट्रो.
Lattice work. पिञिरो.
Latticed, Lattice worked. पिञिरांओं.
To Laud. साराहणु. *See* To Praise.
A Laugh, Laughing. खिल. *See* A Horse-laugh.
Much and loud Laughing. टहकिडो.
To Laugh. खिलणु, पाञोहणु, टहकणु.
Laughable. खिलिणो.
Laughter (*merriment*). खिलखाब्रारी, खिलखुशी, खिल्को.
Lavish. लुटाऊ, खर्चाऊ, लोटू.
To Lavish. लुटाइणु, उड़ाइणु.
To Launch (*act.*). घेडणु.
A Law. काइदो, कानूनु.
The Mussalmán Law. शरा.
Human Law. तोरो.

Lawful. कानूनी, शरई.
Lax. ढिरो, थधो. *See* Loose, Gentle.
Laxity. ढिराई. *See* Looseness.
To Lay (*place*). रखणु, धरणु. *See* To Settle.
To Lay a wager. शर्त हणणु.
To Lay (*an egg*). लाहणु, ड़िभणु.
To Lay hold. झलणु, वठणु.
To Lay out. खर्चणु. *See* To Expend.
A Layer. तहु, पुड़.
A Layman. संसारी, ग्रिहस्तो.
Lazily. ढिरो, मठो. *See* Lazy.
Laziness. आरिसु, आलिसु, सुस्ती, सुस्ताई, नेस्ती, सूंमत, टोटोपणो, कांइराई, थधाई, ढिराई.
Lazy. टोटो, सिल्यो, आर्सी, आलिसी, सूंमती, कांइरू, थधो, ढिरो, सुस्तु.
Lead. शीहो.
Red Lead. सिंधुरू.
White Lead. सुफेदो.
To Lead (*act.*). अगुभोथी हलणु.
A Leader. सिदारू, सिर्ताजु, सर्खेलु. *See* A Chief.
To Leaf. पन कढणु.
A Leaf. पनु.
A young fresh Leaf. मोर्डो.
The Leaf of a book. पनो, वर्कु, पर्तु, वंदु, फर्दु, पत्रो.
The Leaf of a door. ताकु; of a table, तकु.
Gold or silver Leaf. पनी, वर्कु.
Leafless. ठुंडु, ठोड्हो.
Leafy. पनिरू.
A Leak in a boat, &c. ड़ंगो.
To Leak. टिमणु, चुभणु, सिमणु, वहणु.
Leakage, Leaking. सेमो, सिम.
Leaky. टिमिणो, सिमिणो.
To Lean. टेक-अर्क-ड़िभणु, अहलणु. *See* To Incline.
Lean. डुबिरो, पउणो, पतिरो, सन्हो, माडो, हीणो, अभरो, खीणु.
Leanness. डुबिराइ, हीणाई, पउणाई, माडाई.
A Leap. टपो, कुडु, टंगु, उछांगु, छालु, टिपु.
To Leap. टपणु, कुड़णु.
A Leaper. टपिणो, कुड़िणो, टापू, टपिरू.
To Learn. सिखणु, पढ़हणु.
To Learn, or acquire knowledge (*neu.*). सिंडणु.
Learned. पढ़्यो, विद्यावानु, पंड़ितु.
Learning (*knowledge*). इल्मु, विद्या, विद्या.
A Lease. मोकातो, पटो.
On Lease. मोकाते.
A deed of Lease. पटो.
Least. सभ खां नंढो.
At Least. तड्हीं बि, त बि.
Leather. चमु, खल.
Of Leather, Leathern. चामिलो.
A worker in Leather. ढेढु, मेघिवाडु, मोची, चमारू.
Leave. मोकल, रूक्सत, छुटी.
To get or take Leave. मोकिलाइणु.
To Leave. छड़णु, फिटो करणु. *See* To Cease.
To Leave food. ओबारणु.
To Leave out. छड़णु. *See* To Pass over, To Skip over.
Leaven. खमीरू.
Leavings of food. जूठि, ओबरि, पसांदो.
A Lecher, Lecherous. हरामी, जिनाही, लंड़ो, लांड़ारो, लंगोताडो, लांगछोटो, जाहू.
Lechery. हरामु, लंड़ाई.
To Lecture (*act.*). समुझाइणु.
A Led horse, or one to spare in travelling, &c. कौंतलु.

A Leech. ज़ौर, ज़रू *f.*
A dozen of Leeches. खाड़ी.
To Leer. अख्यूं फिर्डाइणु.
Left (*not right*). खब्रो, ड़ाओ.
Left-handed. खाब्रुड, ड़ाव्रुड.
To remain Left. वचणु, उबिरणु, बाकी रहणु.
A Leg. ज़ंघ, टंग, लत.
The Leg of a table, &c. पाओ, पायो.
Long-Legged. ज़ांघो.
Legal. कानूनी. *See* Lawful.
A Leger. खातो.
To enter in the Leger. खतणु, खताइणु.
Legerdemain. चिश्मबंदी.
Legitimate. हलाली. *See* Just, Right.
A Legume. फरी.
Leguminous. फर्यांओं.
Leisure. पाल्हाई, वांदाई, वेल्हाई, वांदिकाई, फुर्सत, निख्मिणाई, निवेकिलाई.
At Leisure. पाल्हो, वेल्हो, वांदो. *See* Disengaged, Idle.
Leisurely. होर्यां, धीरे, आरास्तो.
A Lemon. लीमों.
Lemon colored. लीमाई, लीमांओं.
To Lend. मङ्यो-उधारो-कर्जु-ड़िअणु.
Length. ड्रेघु, ड्रिघाई, लाम.
A Length of time. मुदत.
At Length. नेठि. *See* At Last.
To Lengthen. ड्रिघो करणु.
Leniency, Lenity. कुंभराई, नर्माई.
Lenient. कुंभरो, नर्मु.
Leo (*the sign*). सिंघु.
A Leopard. चीतो.
A Leper, Leprous. कोढ्हो.
The Leprosy. कोढ्हु.
Less. घटि, थोरो. *See* Low, Short.
Somewhat Less. उंभालो, उंभालेरो, लाठेरो, लाठेरिडो.
A Lessee. मकातेदारू.
To Lessen (*neu.*). घटणु, हघणु, हघामणु, सुसणु.
To Lessen (*act.*). घटाइणु, हघाइणु, झकाइणु, सोसणु, सुसाइणु.
Lessened in force, beauty, color, &c. झको, ढिरो, मठो.
A Lesson. सबकु, संथा.
Lest. मतां.
To Let (*allow*). ड़िअणु. *See* To Hinder.
To Let on hire. भाडे ड़िअणु.
To Let go. छड्णु. *See* To Liberate.
A Letter (*epistle*). खतु, चिठी, लिखति. *See* Note.
A Letter of the alphabet. अखरू, अछरू.
A Levee. दर्बारि.
Level. सँभों, सूधो, बरोबरि.
To Level, or make Level. संदिरणु.
Levelness. सँवाई, सँवति, सूधाई.
Levity. *See* Lightness.
To Levy. गडु करणु, मेडणु. *See* To Collect.
Lewd. लांड़ारो. *See* Lecherous.
Lewdness. लांड़ाराई. *See* Lechery.
A Liar. कूड़ो, कुसाख्यो.
Liberal (*munificent*). ड़ातारू, ड़ातो, दाता, दातो, सखी, शखो, खर्चाऊ. *See* Generous.
Liberality. ड़ातारी, ड़ाति, शखा, सखावत.
To Liberate. छड़णु, छुटाइणु, आजो करणु.
Liberation, Liberty. छोट्कारो, आजाई. *See* Freedom, Leave.

At Liberty to act as one pleases. रजाराणो. *See* Independent.

Libidinous. लांड़ारो. *See* Lecherous.

Libra (*the sign*). तुलु, तुला.

To Lick. चटणु.

Licorice. मिठोकाठी, मुलठी; an extract of Licorice, रबूसुस.

A Lid. पुडु, ढकु, ताकु. *See* Eyelid.

A Lie. कूडु, कुसाख.

To Lie, or tell a Lie. कूडु ग़ाल्हाइणु *or* चवणु.

To Lie down. सुम्हणु, लेटणु, पोढणु.

To Lie hid. लिखो विहणु.

In Lieu. बदरि, बदिरों, एवजि, पारों, जाइ.

Life. जीउ, साहु, जानि, दमु, प्राणु, प्रानु, जिंदु *f.* सासु.

Life (*existence*). हयातो.

Life's term. अवधि. *See* Age.

Lifeless. बेजानो, बेजीउ. *See* Inanimate, Dead.

Life-time. ज़मार, उमिरि, वहो, आर्जा.

To Lift. खणणु.

To be Lifted. खज़णु.

Light (*brightness*). सोझिरो, सुझंदो, सुहाउ, सहाओ, सहाई, रोश्नाई, रोशिनी.

A Light. ड़िओ, जोति.

Light (*lucid*). सहाओ.

Light (*in weight*). हल्को, हीरो, हरिडो. *See* Easy.

Light, Lightly, (*slightly.*) उच्चातिरो, मथाछिरो, मथछिरो.

To Light or give Light to. सोझिरो *&c.* करणु. *See* To Illuminate.

To Light or become lit. ब्ररणु, दुखणु.

To Light or cause to Light. ब्रारणु, दुखाइणु. *See* To Illuminate.

To Light up, or begin to blaze. लहकणु.

To Light up or cause to blaze. लहकाइणु.

To Light up, or make bright (*coals*). पज़ारणु.

To Light or alight. लहणु, उलहणु.

Lightly, (*unpressed as in filling in grain, salt, &c.*). उफूंगिडो, मथाछिरो. *See* Light.

Lightness. हल्काई, हीराई, हरिडाई.

Lightning. विजु *f.* खिवणि.

The Lights, or lungs. फिफिड़.

Like. वांग्यां, वांगे, वांगु, वांगुरु, जिहडो, जेहो, पारो.

This Like. इहडो.

That Like. उहडो.

What Like. किहडो.

To Like. भाइणु, चाहणु, वणणु with agent in the dative. *See* To Please.

A Likelihood. ड़ौलु, बझु, आकारु.

Likeness (*similarity*). हिकजिहडाई. *See* A Picture.

Likewise (*in like manner*). उएँ, उँअ, उहडो. *See* Also.

A Liking. सध, दिलि, सिक. *See* Inclination.

A water Lily. कूणी, भलु; its seed, नापो; fruit, कुमु; roots or tubers, लोडहु, लोड्हो, खोरोली. *See* Lotus.

A Limb. उजिबो, लिङु, बाज, अंगु.

A Lime. लीमो.

A sweet Lime. नारंगी.

Lime. सेड्ही, चुनु.

A Lime kiln. सेड्हिअ जी खूरी.

A Limit. संधो, सींअ, दंगु, सीम, हद, पारु, इंडो, इढो, कडो.

To Limp. मंड़ाइणु, लङाइणु.

A Line. लीक, ओड, सिट, लीको, लीह.

A separating Line. बत.
A Line of verse, or writing. तुक.
A Line (*row*). कतार, सिफ.
Lineage. कुलु, ओलादु, वंसु *f.* बुणु, गोटु.
A Lineament. ओत्रह, उहुत्राणु.
To Linger in sickness. नुडणु.
Lining. अस्तरु.
A Link of a chain. कडो. *See* Tie.
A Link (*torch*). मशालु, ड़िभाटी, खड्गी.
A Link-boy. मशाल्ची.
Linseed. इल्सी.
The Lintel of a door. ओडो.
A Lion. शींहु, केहरि *m.*
A Lioness. शींहणि.
A Lip. चपु.
One with large Lips. चपिरु.
To Liquify (*neu.*). ग़रणु, पघिरणु.
Liquid (*adj.*). पट्टिडो.
To Liquidate. पिआरणु, पीचाइणु, पुज़ाइणु.
Spirituous Liquor. दारू, शराबु, कैफु, मदु. *See* Distilled.
Liquorice. मिठीकाठी, मुलठी.
Liquorice juice. रब्सूसु.
A List. चिठी, यादास्त, ब़ीजकु.
List (*border of cloth*). थडी, कनी.
To Listen. बुंधणु, ओनाइणु, सुणणु, कनु ड़िभणु.
To Listen stealthily. कनिडो–कन्सो–ड़िभणु.
One who Listens stealthily. कनिडाई.
Literal. अखिरी, लबूज़ो.
Lithrage. मुर्दासंगु.
Litigation. रग़िडो, मामिल्रो.
A Litigious person. मामिलाई, रगिडाई. *See* Quarrelsome.
The Litter of a stable. ओलडु.

Little (*in quantity*). थोरो, थोरिड़ो.
Too Little (*in quantity*). उँआलो.
Little (*in size*). नंढो, बिंदिरो, मिंधिरो, मंधिरो, लाठो.
Too Little or somewhat less (*in size*). नढेरो, नंढेरिडो, लाठेरो, लाठेरिडो.
A Little. थोरो, जरो, जरोभोरो, कीं, ज़रिडो.
Some Little. कींक.
Littleness. नंढाई, लाठाई.
To Live. जिभणु. *See* To Get on.
Livelihood. गुजिरानु, गुजरु, रोज़गारु, उपिरासो.
The Liver. जेरो, जिगरु.
The Liver and Lights. जेरांड़ो.
Living (*subs.*). गुजरु, गुजिरानु, गुजारो. *See* Livelihood.
Living (*adj.*). जिअरो. हयातु.
A Lizard (*varieties*). किरिडो, चिचो, किरिडो, सांड़ो, गिलोई, ग़ोहीरो.
A Load. बारु, लड़.
A man's Load. भरो, (*borne on back*) पुठारक; half or one side of a camel or bullock load, अडो.
To Load. लड़णु.
To Load (*a gun, boat, &c*). भरणु.
A Loadstone. चिमकपहणु, चिमकु.
A Loaf of bread. रोटिलो, मानी.
A Loan. उधार, कर्ज़ु.
On Loan. उधारो, मङ्ज़ो.
To Loathe. बुछो-बुछिडो-भांइणु.
The Lobe of the ear. पापिड़ी.
A Lock. कुफ़ुं, जंड़ो.
A Lock of hair. चग़. *See* Tuft.
To Lock. कुफ़ुं &c. ड़िभणु or पाइणु
A Locust. मकडु.
A flight of Locusts. माकडि.
Lofty. *See* High.
A Log. बुंडु.

Logic. तर्क.

A pain in the Loins. चुक. *See* Waist, To gird the Loins.

Loneliness. हेकलाई.

Lonely, Lonesome. हेकलो, हेकल-वसूडो.

Long. ड्रिघो.

Somewhat Long or Longer. ड्रिघे-रो, ड्रिघेरिडो.

Long (*time*). घणो.

As Long as. जेसी-ताईं or तोणो, *&c.* *See* Until.

To Long (*after another*). उकंढिजणु.

Long-cloth. बाफ्तो.

A Longing (*desire*). खाइश, इछा, सिक, लालिचि.

A Longing (*to meet a friend or lover*). उकंढ, उकीर, सिक.

One who Longs, or covets. सिकिणो.

A Look, Looking. नजर, निगाह, निहार.

Look (*appearance, q. v.*). ड्रेखु, ड्रे-खारो.

To Look at. निहारणु, ड्रिसणु, पसणु, निगाह करणु.

To Look or spy about. सूंझणु.

To Look for (*seek*). ग़ोलणु, खो-जणु, वउडणु, निहारणु, ढूंढणु.

Looking after. टहोड, निगाह. *See* Watching.

A Looking-glass. आर्सी, आहिरी, आईनो, टिक, दर्सनी.

A Loom. श्राड़णो.

A Loop. फाही, फांदो.

A Loop-hole. ग़िर्खी.

To Loose (*act.*). छोडणु, छड़णु.

To be, or get, Loose. छुटणु, छुडणु, छुट्कणु.

Loose (*not tight or firm*). ढिरो, ढरो, हिलिडो, फिल्हो, फिल्हिडो.

Loose (*as clothes*). वेकिरो. *See* Wide.

Loose (*from being too large*). विपिलो.

To Loosen, or make Loose. ढारणु. *See* To Loose.

Looseness. ढिराई, ढराई, हिलिडाई; of bowels, *See* Diarrhœa.

To Lop off (*branches*). छांगणु, मु-छणु.

Loquacious. कांविलो, घणग़ाल्हाओ. *See* A Chatterer.

Loquacity. कहत, कांविलाई.

A Lord. धणी, आग़ो, नाथु.

To Lose (*mislay*). विञाइणु, गुमु करणु.

To Lose (*opposed to win*). हारणु, हाराइणु.

A Loss. छीओ, जिआनु, टोटो, पउणी, घाटो, नुक्सानु, हर्जु, अञोछो, कसु *f.*

To suffer Loss. खाञाइजणु, छाओ, *&c.* पाइणु or खाइणु.

Lost. गुमु, अलूपु.

To be Lost. वञणु, गुमु, *&c.* थिअणु.

To be Lost, or ruined. उझिडणु.

Lot (*fate, q. v.*). नसिबु.

To cast Lots. कुणो-पुखो-विझणु.

A Lotus. पबुणि, पदमु, कंवलु.

The pod of the Lotus. पाञोडो, टिकी.

The fruit of the Lotus. ड्रोड्रो, पब्रि-णी; root or tubers eaten, बिहु.

Loud. वड्रो, ड्राढो.

Loudly. ड्राढ्यां, वड्रे सड्रि.

Love. नींहु, नेहु, सिक, भाउ, प्रीति, प्रेमु, पिआरु, इश्कु, हुब, मोहु.

To Love. नेहु *&c.* करणु, घणो घु-रणु.

To be in Love. आशिकु–छकनु–थिअणु.

Lovely. मोहिणो. *See* Charming, Beautiful..

A Lover, in Love. आशिक़ु. *See* Sweetheart.

A Louse. जूं *f*.; to pick out Lice, जूं कढणु, सीर ड़िभणु, ढूंगिडो हणणु.

Lousy. जूंइरू.

Low (*adj*.). नंढो, मंधिरो, बिंदिरो, हेठांभों.

Low (*price, sound*). थोरो.

Low (*adv*.). हेठि.

Somewhat Low, or Lower. हेठ्ते, हेठ्तांहों, हेठभरो.

To Low. रंभणु, ढिकणु.

To Lower (*neu*.). घटिजणु. *See* To Abate, To Lessen.

To Lower (*act*.). हेठि करणु, लाहणु.

Lower, Lowest (*of the lower part*). हेठ्यों, हेठांभों.

The Lowing of a cow. रंभ, रांबाह, ढिक.

Lowness (*in place*). हेठांई, हेठाणि.

Lucerne (*grass*). रिज्को, रिश्को, उस्तुपुस्तु.

Lucid. जोतिवारो. *See* Bright, Clear.

Luck. नसीबु, भागु. *See* Fortune.

Luckless. निभागो. *See* Unfortunate.

Lucky. वड़भागो. *See* Fortunate.

Lucrative. नफ़ाइतो, लाहाइतो, खट्याइतो.

Ludicrous. खिलिणो.

Lues venerea. पर्मेलु, गर्मी.

Luggage. मड़ी. *See* Baggage.

Lukewarm. नँहँसोसिडो.

A Lullaby. ओराणो, लोली.

Lumbago. चुक.

A Lump. ग़ोड्हो, पिनु, ग़ंढो, टेरो. *See* Clod.

A Lump (*of sugar candy, indigo, &c*.). ग़डी.

In the Lump (*taken together in the gross*). बिल्मुक्तो, दोम्सोमि, ब्रभों, उको.

Lunar. चंड्रणो, चांडु, क़मिरि.

A Lunch, Luncheon. मांझांदो.

The Lungs. फिफिड़ु.

To Lure. *See* To Allure.

To Lurk. छपिकरे विहणु.

Lust (*carnal*). अंगेजु, शह्वत, कामु. *See* Desire.

Lustiness. मताराई, पटाई, सघाराई.

Lustful. अंगेजो, कामी, जाहू, मस्तु.

Lusty. मतारो, पटो, सघारो, चोबुको, सटरवटो, चुपो. *See* Stout.

Lustre. चिम्को, जुल्वो, झल्को, झल्क, जोति. *See* Brightness.

Luxurious. ऐशी, भोगी.

Luxury. ऐशु, भोगु, विखइ.

Lying (*adj*.). कूडो, खोटो.

The Lying in of a woman after childbirth. सुभांजो, छिलो.

A Lynx. फेकारो.

M

Mace (*the spice*). जांइट्री, आंवत्री.

A Mace (*club*). छड्ही, लठि, चोबु, सोटो.

A Macebearer. छड्हीदारू, लठिड्यो, चोब्दारू.

A Machine, Machinery. कल.

Mad, a Madman. चर्यो, मस्तानो, बांविरो, सौदाई, चर्यदु, मतिवालो, मस्तु; mad, madly, चर्याइतो, मस्ताइतो.

Mad, (*from hydrophobia*). छितो, छिड्यो, छिड्क्यो, हड्क्यो.

To go Mad (*as a dog*). छिड्किजणु, हड्किजणु.

Madam. ज़ाई, बीबी.
Of a Madman. चर्यांणो, सौदाइको.
Madder. मञ्जुठ, मैंठ; different kinds, रिट, फरह, खखिरी.
To be Made. जुड़णु, ठहणु.
Madness. चर्याई, सौदाउ, मस्ताई.
A Magazine. कार्खानो; for powder, बारूद्खानो.
A Maggot. किंभौं.
Maggoty. किंभरो.
Magic (*sub.*). जादू. *See* Enchantment.
Magic, Magical. जादुभको.
A Magician. जादूगरु, जादूखोरु, भोपो, कामिण्गोरु.
A Magistrate. हाकिमु.
Magisterial, of a Magistrate. हाकिमाणो.
Magnanimity. वड़गुदाई, वड़जिगिराई.
Magnanimous. वड़गुदो, वड़जिगिरो.
A Magnet. *See* Loadstone.
Magnificence. सोंगारु, ठाटु, ठासु, ठाहु, शानु.
Magnificent. ठाटवारो, शान्दारु.
To Magnify. वधाइणु. *See* To Increase, Praise, Exaggerate.
Magnitude. वड़ाई.
A Maid, Maiden. कुंआरो, कन्या.
Maiden, of a Maid. कुआरिको.
To deflower a Maiden. मोंढी-भोंड़ो-छोड़णु.
Maidhood. कुंआराई.
A Maidservant. पोर्ह्यति, चाकियांणी, नफियांणी, दाई.
A coat of Mail. ज़िरिह.
Maimed. जड़ो, खेरो.
Main (*principal, q. v*). वड़ो.
Mainly. घणो करे.
To Maintain. रखणु, पालणु. *See* To Preserve, Bring up, Continue, Support.
A Maintenance (*supply of food*). जीविका, खर्चु, खर्चुपखो, तँवणि, तोंणि.
Maize. मकाई, मकाइणि, मकी.
Make (*sub.*). ढ़ौलु. *See* Form.
To Make (*form*). जोड़णु, ठाहणु. *See* To Create, Induce, Gain.
To Make up. *See* To Reconcile, Settle, Collect, Form, Reimburse.
A Maker. जोड़ोंदड़ु. *See* Creator.
Making (*sub.*). जोड़, जोड़िणी.
A Malady. रोगु. *See* Disease.
Male. नरु. *See* Man.
Malevolence. मठपुराई, मंद्खाहो, खौंस. *See* Malice.
Malevolent, Malicious. मठपुरो, मंट्खाहु, खुंड़ो.
Malice, Maliciousness. खुंड़, खुंड़ाई, खारु, भकसु, कीनो.
To bear Malice. खौंसणु.
To Malign. गिला करणु, निंदणु. *See* To Slander.
A Maligner. गिलाखोरु.
A Mallet. मेखमारु, मुड़िरो, ठोकिणो.
Mamma. अमा. *See* Mother.
A Man (*not a brute*). माण्हूं, माड्हुं, शक्सु, आदिमी, ज़णो, आसामो, मानुखु, मनुखु. *See* Mankind.
A Man (*not a woman*). मुसु, मर्दु, मुर्साडू, पुर्षु, पानउ.
Of a Man (*or male*). मुर्साणो; मर्दाणो. *See* Human.
Manacles. हथोड्यूं *plu.*
To Manage (*carry on*). निभाइणु, हलाइणु. *See* To Govern, Perform.
To be Managed (*carried on or*

through). निबड़णु, सरणु. *See* To be Accomplished.

Management. सर्बराई, सिजिलि. *See* Arrangement.

The Mane of a horse, &c. बुश्कूं *plu.* बुर.

The Mange. गरु *f.* किरांहिं. *See* Itch.

A Manger. आहुरो.

To Mangle (*in cutting*). चिथिड़णु.

A Mango. अंबु, आमी ; *small unripe*, अंबिड़ी, आमी.

The stone of the Mango. कोर, कोइरो.

The strings in the pulp of the Mango. ज़ारो.

Mangy. गरो.

Manhood. (*man's life*) मानिखो, (*virility*) मुर्साई, मुर्सपनो.

A Maniac. *See* Madman.

Manifest. पधिरो, जाहिरु, निशांबरु, रोशनु, अयां, चिटो.

A Manifestation. जाहिरी.

Manifold. घणे तरहं जो.

Mankind. आलमु, खलक, विशु *f.*

Manliness. मुर्सी, मड़दी, जांमड़दी.

Manly, Manful. मर्दानो, जांमड़द, हिमथो.

Manner. दस्तूरु, तरहं, ड़ौलु, ड़ांउ, ढंउं, रीति, तिर्कारु, वझु. *See* Custom, Sort.

Ill-Mannered, in bad Manner. अढंगो, कुढंगो, कुढबो.

Well-Mannered, Mannerly, in a good Manner. ढंगाइतो, ड़ौलाइतो, ढंबाइतो.

Manners. ढंगु, चालि, ललु, अफालु, रहति, रहणी, गति, अर्कानु, ढबु, ढंउं, वडु.

A Mansion. हबेली. *See* House.

A lunar Mansion. नखटु.

A Mantle. ओढिणी. *See* Cloak.

Manual (*done by the hand*). हथिरादी.

Manure (*dung used as*). ज़मु, भाणु.

Many. घणा *plu.* झझा *plu.* गचु, जाम, कईं. *See* Abundant.

As Many as. जेतिरो; so Many, तेतिरो, हेतिरो, एतिरो, ओतिरो.

How Many. केतिरो.

A Map. चादर.

To Mar. *See* To Injure, Spoil.

Marble. संग्मर्मरु.

A Marble. चिधो, चिणो, ठेड़ी.

A hole for Marble playing. सुचु.

March, and part of April. चेटु.

A March (*journey*). सफरु, मुसाफिरी, पंधु.

To March (*on a journey*). वञणु, लड़णु.

A Mare. घोड़ी.

Margin. हशो, किनारो. *See* Edge, Brink.

A Marigold. गेंटो.

Marine. दर्याहो.

A Mark. निशानु, निशानी, नीशानी, दागु.

A Mark in a book. संधो, संधि.

The Hindoo Mark on the forehead. तिलिकु, टोको.

To Mark. निशानु &c. करणु. *See* To Cauterize.

A Market. बजारि, बाजारि, बाजरि.

Of a Market. बाजारी.

The Market price. अघु, निर्खु, भाउ, पीठि.

A Marking-iron. ड़ंभिणो, दागु.

Marriage. विहांउ, परणो, शादी, निकाहु.

A Marriage feast. जुञु.

A Marriage procession (*accom-*

panying bridegroom). जुञ ; one of those forming the party, ज़ाञी.
A Marriage song. सिहिणी. *See* Hymeneal.
A Married man. सपिरो.
A Married woman. (*not a maid*) वराइतो, (*not a widow*) सुहागिणि.
Marrow. मिञ, मिखु *f*. मग्जु.
To Marry or to enter into the Marriage state. परणिजणु, विहांउ *&c.* करणु.
To Marry, or take in Marriage. परणणु, वरणु.
To Marry, or cause to Marry. परणाइणु.
Mars (*the planet*). मंगलु.
A Marsh. खुब्रणि, गपिणी.
A Martingal. लवंदु, तालीम.
A Martyr. शहीदु.
The Marvel of Peru. आवासो, गुलाबासी.
Marvellous. अजबु, अजब जिहडो, अचर्जजिहडो.
Masculine. मुसांणो, मड्दाणो, (*gender*) पुंल्लिंगु, मुजक्करु, नरनांउ.
To Mash. चिपणु.
A Mason. राजो.
A Mass. ढिगु. *See* Heap.
A Massacre. मारो, कोसु.
A Mast. खूहो, शीकिलो.
A Master. सांई, धणी, मालिकु, खाँवंदु, साहिबु, आगो, नाथु, वालो.
A Master (*in skill*). उस्तादु, भडु.
The Master of a vessel. नाखुंओ.
To Master. जीतणु.
Masterly. भडाणो, उस्तादाणो, उस्तादिको.
To Masticate. चञाडणु, चबणु.
Mastich. मस्तकी.
A Mat (*varieties.*) नुख, तड़ो, तोंरो, पटिछु, सदिरो.
A kind of Matting for roofs. पखो, टुओ.
A maker of Mats. नुखाई, तड़ाई, टुआई, पखाई.
A Match (*equal*). जोड़ु, शानी, मटु, जोसु, तुलि, थोडी, समानि.
The Match of a gun. जामकी, पलीतो, तोड़ो.
To Match (*neu.*). ठहणु, मिलणु.
Matchless. बेजोड़ो, बेजोसो.
A Matchlock. जामकीदार बंदूक.
Material. देहिधारी.
Materials. शइबइ, सामानु, सरंजामु.
Maternal (*of mother's family*). नानाणो.
Matrimony. विहांउ. *See* Marriage.
Matted hair. जटा, लिट, वुजु,
Matter (*substance*). जुसो, डेहि. *See* Body, Pus.
Matter (*thing or business*). गाल्हि, बाबति, बाबु. *See* Affair.
No Matter, it Matters not. भउ भोलो-कोन्हे, भईकान्हे.
What's the Matter. छा थिओ.
A Mattress. पथर्णी, तूलि.
Mature. पको.
Matureness, Maturity. पकाई.
A Maund (*the measure*). मणु.
May, a part of June. जेठु.
A Maw. भांडो. *See* Belly.
A Maze. अवझडु, ओझडु, कुझडु, माँझारो. *See* Perplexity.
A Mead, Meadow. रख, वीड.
Meal. अटो, (*of pulse grains*) बेसणु.
A Meal. खाइणु, खेणु.
Mean (*adj.*). नोचु, ओछो, हेठो. *See* Ignoble, Middle.

To Mean (*purpose*). दिलि, *&c.* करणु, दिलिमें हुअणु. *See* Intention.

Meantime, Meanwhile. एतिरे में.

Meaning. अर्थु, माना, मुदाउ, मत्लबु, हाशो.

Meanness. ओछाई, नीचाई.

Means (*power, income*). वसिअत, सगति, तोफ़ीक, पुजिण्याती, हूंदि.

By Means of. करे.

Measure, Measurement. काछो, कछ, मापु.

A dry Measure. मापु.

A long, or cloth, Measure. गजु, गजो.

A Measure for liquids. माणी, मुविरी, मुविरो.

A land Measure. ग्रंडो.

Measure (*limit*). अंदाजो.

To Measure (*act.*). कछणु, मइणु, मापणु, भरणु, मेचणु, (*land only*) जब्त करणु.

A Measurer of grain. भडुवाई.

A land Measurer. जाबितु, काछू, तनाबो.

A Measuring rope. तनाब

The Measuring of grain, &c. भडु.

Meat (*flesh, q v.*). माँसु, (*food, q. v.*). मानी.

A Mechanic. करबी.

To Meddle. हथु विझणु, दखलु करणु.

To Mediate (*neu.*). विचि अचणु or पवणु.

A Mediator. वेचुओ, विचवारो, शफी.

Medical. हकीमाणो, वेज़ाणो, तबीबाणो, वेज्ञिको.

Medicine. दवा, दारू. *See* Physic.

To Meditate. ग़णणु, ध्याइणु, विचारणु, चिनवणु. *See* To Consider.

Meditation. ध्यानु, चितवना.

Meditative. ध्यानी.

A Medium (*middle place*). विचु, राधावेधो. *See* Means.

Meek. गरीबु, निवंदडु, निउडतधारो. *See* Humble.

Meekness. निउडत, निंवति, गरीबी. *See* Humility.

Meet. *See* Fit, Becoming.

To Meet. गडिजणु, मिलणु, भिडणु.

A Meeting (*interview*). मुलाक़ाति, मुखमिलो, मुखामुखो. *See* Assembly.

Melancholy (*sub.*). उदास, उन्नाफिकाई, ज्ञताउ. *See* Dejected.

To grow Melancholy. ज्ञताइणु.

A musk Melon. गिदिरो, (*small*), पितो, (*unripe*), कटुं, कटीं.

A water Melon. हिंदाणो, छांहों.

A Melon field. भारउ, आरणु, छछु.

To Melt (*neu.*). ग़रणु, पघिरणु, रिजणु.

To Melt (*act.*) ग़ारणु, पघारणु, रिजाइणु, आउटणु.

Melting (*sub.*). ग़र्णी, ग़ार्णी, पघिर्णी.

A Member (*of body*). उज्ञिवो. *See* Limb, Part, Individual.

A Memorandum. यादास्त.

Memory. याद्दोरो, जाद्दोरी, संभार, सुर्ति, सार.

To commit to Memory. कंठि-बांजि बान-यादि-करणु.

A Menace. दड्को, ताबु, दबाउ, डखो.

To Menace. दड्को *&c.* डिअणु.

To Mend (*repair*). मरामत करणु, जोडणु. *See* To Correct, Improve.

To be Mended. जुडणु.

Mendacious, Mendacity. *See* Lying, Falsehood.

Mendicancy, Mendicity. गदाई. *See* Begging.

A Mendicant. विनिणो, फक़ीरु. *See* Beggar.

Mending. मरामत.

A religious Mendicant. फक़ीरु, (*different kinds*) कापिड़ो, जंगमु, सुथिरो. *See* Devotee.

The Menses. रुति, मथों, रतु, हैजु, फुलु.

To have the Menses. कपिड़ा-रुति &c. अचणु, with agent in the dative.

Having, or with, the Menses. गथेमेरी.

Mention. ज़ाहिरु, हक़ीक़त.

To Mention. चवणु, बुधाइणु. *See* To Name.

Mercantile. वापारिको, वछातिको.

Merchandize. वापारु, सौदो, वणिजु, वछातो. *See* Trade.

A Merchant. वापारी, वपारी, वणजारो, वछातु, सौदागरु.

Merciful. रहमी, बख़्शभर्यो, दयालु, रहमाइतो, सबाझो, सतारु.

Merciless. बेरहमो, बेबाझो. *See* Unmerciful.

Mercury (*the planet*). बुधु. *See* Quicksilver.

Mercy. रहमु, बख़्श, दया, मिहिर, इछा.

Mere, Merely. रुगो, निरो, निलो, निसोरो, छड़्हो, फक़तु.

The Meridian (*noon*). ब्रिपहरी.

To be past the Meridian (*sun, &c.*) लडणु.

Merit. गुणु; moral or religious Merit, पुञु, सवाबु.

To Merit. लाइकु-जागु-थिअणु.

Meritorious. गुणाइतो, पुञाइतो.

Merriment. खिलखुशी, रौंशो, रोझ, रंगु.

Merry. खुशीजिअड़ो, खिलमुंहो, खिलिणो. *See* Happy.

A Message. निआपो, सनेहो.

A Messenger. निआपाई, काशीदु.

A Mess. *See* Dish, Confusion.

Messing, Messing expenses. वीसो, खाधि, खाधो.

A Messmate. भातो.

Metal. धातु *f.*

A Method (*manner, q. v.*) ड़ोलु, ढबु, ढंऊं, ड़ाउ. *See* Order.

Methodical, Methodically. गिजिलाइतो, सिट़ाइतो.

To Mew (*as a cat*). म्याऊ करणु.

Miasm. उब्र, हुब्र.

Mica. अबिरक.

Midday. ब्रिपहरी.

Middle (*adj.*). विचों.

The Middle. विचु.

In the Middle or Midst. विचि.

Middling. विचोंवहु, पूरोपूनो, मिअनो.

Midnight. अधराति.

A Midwife. दाई.

Midwifery. दाइपो, दाइपाई.

Might. सघ, जोरु, बलु. *See* Strength.

Mighty. पुजिण्यातु. *See* Powerful.

To Migrate. लड़णु.

Milch. खाहर, खीरवारी, खीरेती, सुआ.

Mild. नर्मु, कुंभरो. *See* Gentle.

Mildew. रती.

Mildness. नर्माई, कुंभराई.

Military. सिपाहिको, सिपाह्याणो.

Milk. खीरु, ड़ोधि.

Giving milk (*adj.*). खीरेती. *See* Milch.

Milk and water. लसी.

Milk, sour, or coagulated. भौंरो, डुबु, ड़ड़ो.

A lump of thick Milk. दिगु, फुटु, चकों.

Camel's Milk coagulated. दोंगु.

A woman's Milk. थञु *f.*

To cause to give Milk, (*a cow, &c.*). विहुकणु.

To Milk. डुड़णु.

To be Milked. डुभणु.

A Milker. ड़ोहो.

A Milkseller. ड़ोधी, माह्यडु.

Of a Milkseller. ड़ोधिको.

Milk selling. माहिडो, ड़ोधिपो-पाई.

A Milkwoman. ड़ोध्याणो, ड़ोधिणि, माह्यडि.

A Mill. जांडुहि; a hand mill, जंडु, चकी.

Millet (*kinds of*). चीणो, किरिंगु; some grass seeds are, सांभों, नानोई, सांविडी, ग्रमु, मखिणी.

A Million. डह लख.

Ten Millions. किरोडि.

A thousand Millions. अर्बु.

A hundred thousand Millions. खर्बु

A Mill stone. चकिअ जो पुडु.

The Milt of fish. खोरी. *See* Spleen.

A Mimic. लातिरू, अहलो.

To Mimic. विचारणु, लाति–अहल-करणु.

A Minaret. मुनारो.

To Mince (*act.*). चिथणु, चिचिरणु.

Minced Meat. कोमो.

The Mind. दिलि, चितु, मनु, चेतो, हिंभों, हांउ, हिंभांउ, हिदों, घटु. *See* Inclination, Intention, Memory.

To Mind (*act.*). चेतणु. *See* To Attend to, Take Care.

Mindful. यादगीरिअवारो.

Mindless. बेसिभों, गाफिलु, गहेलो. *See* Forgetful, Regardless.

Mine (*of me*). मुंहुंजो, मुंहिंजो.

A Mine. खाणि.

A Mine (*in sapping*). सिरिंघ, सिणिघ. *See* Hole.

To Mingle (*act.*). गड़णु, मिलाइणु. *See* To Mix.

To Mingle (*neu.*). गड़िजणु, मिलणु.

Mingled. गाडुड़, गाडुओं. *See* Mixed.

A Minister of state. वजोरू, मुख्त्यार्कारू. *See* Agent.

To Minister. *See* To Serve.

Minor. नंढो.

Mint (*the plant.*). फूदिनो.

A Mint (*for coining*). जर्बखानो.

Minute (*adj.*). सन्हो.

A Minute. पलु, पलक, साइथ. *See* Moment.

A Miracle. करामत, सिधो.

Miraculous. करामती, सिधाणो.

Mire. गप, चिक, चिकडि, चिकणि, गरणि, चिकिराठो.

A Mirror. आर्सी, आहिरो, आईनो.

Mirth. खिलखुशी, रंगु. *See* Merriment.

Miry. गपारो, चिकारो, चिकिराठो.

Misbehaviour, Misconduct. कुढंगाई, अढंगाई.

To Force a Miscarriage (*in child-birth*). पेटु *&c.* केराइणु, कीसु करणु.

To Miscarry (*in child-birth*). पेटु -झारू-कचो-किरणु, (*used of cattle*) टुंबिजणु, टुइजणु.

To Miscarry (*fail*). गुसणु.

Miscellaneous. मुतफर्को.

Mischief. जिआनु, नुक्सानु. *See* Hurt, Damage.

A Mischief-maker. ब्रिचापिडेा, फिन्नती.

Mischief making (*sub.*). लाईचाई, ब्रिचापिडाई.

Mischievous (*harmful*). जिआन्खोरू. *See* Mischief-maker.

To Misconceive. उबतो समुझणु.

Misconduct. *See* Misbehaviour.

To Misdirect (*a person*). उबतो ज़ुसणु.

A Miser. शूमु, चूठु, मचूंठु, बखोलु, नंदु, मूज़ो. *See* Niggard.

Of a Miser, Miserly. शूमाणो, चूठाणो, मचूंठाणा.

Miserable. डुख्यो, डुख्यो, डुखो. *See* Wretched.

To be Miserable, or in Misery. डुलणु.

Misery. ड़ोलो, डुखु, ड़ोखिडो.

Misfortune. आफति, विपति, निभागु, घाणी, मुसीबत, आई, बला, वाकिओ, वैलु.

A stroke of Misfortune. धकु.

To talk over one's Misfortunes. ओरणु, डुखिडा ओरणु.

To Misinform. उबतो चवणु.

To Mislay. रखी भुलणु, विसारणु.

To Mislead. भुलाइणु, मुंझाइणु. *See* To Misdirect.

To be Misled. भुलणु, मुंझणु.

To Mismanage. खारणु. *See* To Spoil.

Mismanagement. वेसिजिलाई, अणढाहु.

To Misplace. कुहंभि रखणु. *See* To Mislay.

A Miss. भुल. *See* Mistake.

To Miss (*act. not to hit*). गुसाइणु

To Miss (*neu. fail to hit*). गुसणु.

Misshapen. कुढलो, कुड़ोलो, बेढंगो.

Missing (*adj.*). विभलु, वेयलु, विसियलु, भुल्यलु.

A Mist. लुडाटु, लुडु, धुंधु, माक, दूई.

A Mistake. भुल, भोलो, भोलि.

To Mistake. भुलणु, गुसणु. *See* To Misconceive.

A Mistress (*lady*). सांइणि, धणिआणी, धण्याणी, आगा.

Mistrust. वेवेसाही. *See* Distrust.

Misty. लुडाट्यो, धुंधारो.

To Misunderstand. *See* To Misconceive, Mistake.

A Mite. सोनो. *See* Insect.

To Mitigate. घटाइणु, हलको करणु, हपाइणु, झकाइणु.

To Mix (*act*). रड़णु, मिलाइणु, रलाइणु, भिडाइणु.

To Mix (*neu.*). गड़िजणु, मिलणु, रलणु.

Mixed. गाडुओं, गाडुडु, हिलु, हलु.

To Moan. कंझणु, चिंघणु.

A Moat. खाही.

A Mob. मेडाको. *See* Crowd.

To Mock. *See* To Mimic, Ridicule, Deride.

A Mockery, or Mocking. मश्किरी. *See* Derision.

Mode. तरहँ, दस्तूरु, ड़ांउ, ढँउं. *See* Manner.

A Model. नमूनो. *See* Mould.

To Model. घड़णु. *See* To Form.

Moderate, Moderately. पूरीपुनो. *See* Middling.

Moderation. पूरीपुनाई.

Modern. नँओं, हाणोकों.

Modest, Modestly. लज़ारो, लज़ाइतो, शर्माऊ, हयाइतो, लोहाइतो.

Modesty. लज़, हयाउ, मरमु, शरमु, मुहाबो, लोह, दीदु.

A Moiety. अधु.

Moist. आलो, आळोको, पाण्याटो, तरि.

To Moisten. पुसाइणु.

Moistness, Moisture. आलाणि, आळोकाई. *See* Damp.

Molasses. गुडु.

A Mole (*on the skin*). तिरू. *See* Dike.

To Molest. डुखोइणु, रंजाइणु, अंहंजाइणु. *See* To Trouble.

Molestation. डुखु, रंजु, अंहंजु.

Molten. पाल्टू.

A Moment (*of time*). पलु, दमु, साइथ, लहजो, पलक, खिण, लिख. *See* Importance.

Momentous. ग़ौरो, वड़ो.

A Monastery. आखाडो, मड़ही, दाइरिओ. *See* under Devotee.

Monday. सूमरु, सूमारु.

Money. पैसा *plu.* नाणो, टका *plu.* रूपया *plu.* ड़ोकड *plu.*

Ready Money. रोकडि, रोकु, रोकिडो, नगदु.

A Money changer. सराफु, शराफु.

Money-changing. सराफी, शराफी.

Moneyed. शाहूकारु, दुआदारु. *See* Rich.

A Mongoose. नोरु.

A Mongrel. गड़ो.

A Monkey. भोलो, भोलिडो, बांदरु.

A Monopoly. हिकहटी.

A Monster. आफात, बला.

A Month. महीनो, मांहु.

The half of the lunar Month. पखु, पछु.

Monthly, Month by Month. महीनेसिमहीने, महीनेमहीने.

Monthly wages. महीनो, दमांहो.

Mood. *See* Humor.

The Moon. चंडु.

The full Moon. पूनंइ, पूरणमासी, पूरणिमा, चोड़हिंअजो चंडु.

The new Moon. नंओं चंडु, बीज जो चंडु, उमास.

Of the new Moon. चंडूणो.

Moonlight (*adj.*). चांडोको.

Moonlight, Moonshine. चांडोको, चांडिणो.

A Moral. मुदाउ, हादंउ.

Moral, Morally. नीताइतो.

Morality, Morals. नीति.

A Morass. धुबणि. *See* Swamp.

More. वाधू, सर्सु, वधीक, वधिक, वधि.

A little More. ससेरो, घणेरो, घणेरिडो, सुंआलो, सुंआलेरो.

More or less. घटिवधि.

Moreover. ब्रिओ बि, अञा बि.

Morn, Morning. सुभू, फजुरु, सुभाणो, उथेणो.

Early Morning. वड़ो वेलो, सुभुअमदांनो, दको. *See* Dawn.

Morning (*adj.*). सुभूणिको, सुभूणो, सुभुअको.

Morose. खटो.

The Morrow, to Morrow. सुभाणे, सुबांहीं, सुभांई, सुभां, सुबंहं.

Of the Morrow. सुभाणिको, सुभांको, सुबंहंको.

A Morsel. ग़भो, चपो. *See* Mouthful.

Mortal (*subject to death*). मर्णो, फानो. *See* Human.

Mortal (*deadly*). मारू.

Mortality (*dying*). मरी, मारो, मर्णो.

A Mortar (*for pounding*). हमामु, उखिरी, कूंड़ो, खरलु

A Mortar (*gun*). गुबारो.

One who fires a Mortar. गुबाची.

Mortar (*cement*). गचु.

Plastered with Mortar. गचि.

A Mortgage. गाटु, गाटणो.
To Mortgage. गाटु रखणु.
To Mortify (*neu.*). गारणु, सडणु.
A Mortise. सलु.
A Mosque. मिहिति, मसीति.
Mostly. घणो, घणोकरे.
A Mote (*in the eye*). करड़, सटुं. *See* Particle.
A Moth. पतंगु, परवानो.
A Mother. माउ, माई, माता, अमा, अमो, जीजलि, आई, अमणि, अमडि, जीजी, जननी.
A Mother (*one who has borne a child*). गाभोरा ो.
One having a Mother. माइतो.
A Mother's family. नानाणा *plu.*
A Mother-in-law. समु.
The Mother-in-law of one's son or daughter. सेणि.
Mother of pearl. सिप.
Motion. हलिणी, हलहलि. *See* Agitation.
Motionless. अणहलु, अचलु, थिरि.
A Motive. वास्तो, कारणु, सबबु.
Motley. रंगारंगो.
A Move (*in chess, &c*). चालो.
To Move (*neu.*). हलणु, चुरणु, टुरणु, जुलणु, रिड़्हणु, सिरणु, सुरणु, सिर्कणु.
To Move (*act.*). हलाइणु, चोरणु, टोरणु, रेड़्हणु, सेरणु, सोरणु, सिर्काइणु.
To Move back. हटणु.
Moveable. खज़णजिहडो, खज़िणो.
A Mould (*matrice*). कालिबु, सांचो. *See* Form, Earth.
To Mould (*shape*). घडणु. *See* To Form.
To cast in a Mould. पल्टणु.
Cast in a Mould. पाल्टू.

Mould (*the concretion*). सेंवरू, सिंअरू.
To Mould, or become Mouldy. सिंआर्जणु, सेंवार्जणु.
To Moulder. सडणु, गारणु.
To Moult. कुरीज खाइणु or कढणु.
The Moulting of birds. कुरीज.
Mound. दडो, ड़िब, ड़िंड. *See* Hillock.
To Mount (*neu.*). चड़्हणु.
To Mount (*act.*). चाड़्हणु.
Mounted (*in riding*). सवारू. *See* Horseman.
A Mountain. जबलु, डूंगरु, टकरु, पर्बतु.
Mountainous, a Mountaineer, of the Mountains. जबली, डूंगरी, टाकिरू.
To Mourn. मातमु, &c. करणु. *See* To Lament.
Mournful, Mournfully. गमाइतो.
Mourning (*sub.*). मातमु, सूभ, स्यापो, उजिरु, गमी, हशरू. *See* Grief.
A Mouse. कूओ. *See* Rat.
The Mouth. वातु, थूथु, मुंहु, मुखु.
The Mouth of a gun-barrel. मुहुरी, बुंदी.
By word of Mouth. वातवेणी, जबानी.
To open the Mouth wide. वातु फाडणु.
A Mouth bag (*for feeding a horse*). तोबिरो, पाहोडो.
A Mouthful of meat. गिरहु, लुक्मो; of drink, ढुकु.
The Mouth piece of a hooka. टोटो.
Much. घणो, गाचु, झझो, ब्रहूं, मडू, जाम, गाइबो, गालु, सुन्हो. *See* Abundant.
Too Much, a little More. संभालो, संभालिरो, घणेरो, झझेरो.

As Much as. जेतिरो ; how much, केतिरो. *See* Many.

Mud. गप, चिक, चिकडि, चिकणि, गर्णि, चिकिराठो.

Mud plaster. गारो.

A Mud wall. गंब जी भिति.

A builder of Mud walls. मिद्यरू.

Muddiness. लुडाटु, लुडु, मेराणि.

Muddy. लुडाटो, लुडु, मेरो.

To Muddy. लुडाटणु.

To become Muddy. लुडाटिजणु.

To Muffle. ढकणु.

A Mug. गडूं, आब्खोरो.

A Mulberry. तूतु, (*varieties*) शहतूतु, शकिरीतूतु, सिंधीतूतु.

To Mulct. *See* To Fine.

A Mule. (*male*) खचरू, (*female*) खचरि.

Of, or like, a Mule. खचराणो.

The Multiplication table. खोड्हो.

Multiplicity. घणाई, झझाई.

To Multiply (*neu.*). वधणु.

A Multitude. दलु, घणि, मेडु, पोंढ. *See* Crowd.

To Munch (*in eating*). मिर्काइणु, चाझा *plu.* ड्रिभणु.

To Mumble. गुड्बुडि करणु.

The Mumps (*swelling of parotid glands*). मली, छाली.

Mundane. संसारी.

Munificence. शखा, डातारी. *See* Liberality.

Munificent. शखी, डातारू, दाता सवाई. *See* Liberal.

A Murder. खूनु, हचा, हत्या, कीसु.

To Murder खूनु *&c.* करणु.

A Murderer, Murderous. खूनी, हचारो, हत्यारो.

A Musalmán. मुसिल्मानु, मोमिनु, मुसिल्मीनु, वंझ्यरू, (*so called by Hindoos*), ज़टु, मुसिलो.

Musalman (*adj.*). मुसिल्मानिको, ज़ाटिको, ज़ट्को, ज़ाटो.

The Musalman faith. मुसिल्मानी.

A Muscle. रग, नस.

A Mushroom. खुंभी. *See* Toad-stool.

Music. गाइणु वज़ाइणु.

A Musical instrument. साज़ु, वाज़ो.

Musician. साजो, साजोंदडु.

Musk. खथूरी, खस्तूरी, मुश्कु.

A pod of Musk. ब्रोडो, नाफो.

Of Musk, Musky. मुश्की.

A Musket. बंदूक, दंबूक, तूफाक.

A Musketeer. बंदूकची.

A Musk melon. गिदिरो. *See* Melon.

Muslin (*varieties of fine cloth*). मल्मल, आभिओ, पंज़्तोलो, महमूदी, शब्नुम.

Striped Muslin. डोर्णो.

A Musquito. मंढों, मछरू ; a small kind of musquito, कुति.

Musquito curtains. महारी.

A Mussulman. *See* Musalman.

Must. *See* Necessary.

A Mustache. मुछ, शहपरू.

One with large Mustaches. मुछिरू.

Mustard seed. अहुरि, (*kinds of*) ज़ांभो, सह्रों.

Mustard (*used as a seasoning*). राई.

A Muster. हाज़ुरी.

To grow Musty. बुसिजणु. *See* Mouldy, Fusty.

Mute (*dung of birds*) निठि. *See* Silent.

A Mutiny. फ़शादु, खललु.

To Mutiny. फ़शादु, *&c.* करणु.

To Mutter. भुण्कणु, गुड्बुडि, *&c.* करणु.

Muttering. भुण्भुणि, गुड्बुडि.

Mutually. पाण में, हिकबिए में.

A Muzzle (*for the mouth*). छिकी.

The Muzzle of a gun. बुंदी, मुहुरी.

Myrolaban (*distinct kinds*). आंविरी, ब्रहेडो, इंजिडो, हरीड; the three myrolabans, ट्रिफला *plu.* ट्रिफुडा *plu.* ट्रिफुला *plu.*

Myrrh. मुर.

Mysterious. गुझो.

A Mystery. गुझु, गैबु.

N

A Nag. ड्रड़ो.

A Nail (*iron.*) किली, कोरी, (*of kinds*) कोरू, कोकी, मेख, गुल्मेख, नाँगफणी.

To Nail. जडणु, किली, *&c.* हणणु.

A Nail (*of finger or toe*). नँहुं.

A scratch with the Nails. नँहंडु, रहंडु, रुहुंडो, नुहुंडो. *See* Scratch.

To scratch with the Nails. नँहंडुणु, रहँडुणु.

An instrument for paring the Nails. नहेरणि.

Naked. उघाडो, नँगो, नँगु.

Nakedness. उघाडाई, नँगाई.

A Name. नालो, नांउं, नामु. *See* Reputation, Fame.

In or to the Name of, by Name, Named. नांइ, नाले.

Ill Name. गिला, बद्नामी.

One bearing an ill Name. गिलारो, बद्नामु. *See* Infamous.

To Name. (*give a name*) नांउं रखणु, (*mention by name*) नांउं *&c.* गिन्हणु-वठणु.

A Nap (*sleep*). ढोंको.

The Nap (*of cloth*). बुर.

The Nape. कंधु, ग़ाटो, गर्दनि.

A Napkin. रूमालु. *See* Towel.

To Narrate. *See* To Tell.

A Narration, Narrative. किसो. *See* Story.

Narrow. सोड्हो, तंगि, नंढबरो.

Narrowness. सोड्ह, सोड्हाई, सोड्हाणि, तंगी.

Nasty. मेरो, गंदो, गलीजु. *See* Dirty, Nauseous.

Native (*indigenous*). देसी, ड़ेसी, ड़ेही.

A Native. वतनी, रहाकू.

One's Native place. वतनु.

Nativity. ज़मु, जन्मु.

Natty. *See* Neat.

Natural (*innate*). असली.

Nature. जाति, सुभाउ. *See* Disposition, Good nature.

Naval (*adj.*). जहाजी.

The Nave of a wheel. नांहीं.

The Navel. दुनु.

The Navel string. नाड़ो.

Naughty. बुछिडो. *See* Bad.

Nauseous. उगिरो.

To Nauseate. बुछां भांइणु.

To be Nauseous. बुछां लग़णु.

Nauseousness. उगिराई.

Near. (*prep.*) वटि, (*prep. or adv.*) वेझो, वेझिडो, ओड़ो, ओड़िडो, ओरे.

The Near side, this side. ओरारि, हिन भरि.

Near, Nearer, (*adj.*). ओर्यों.

Somewhat Near, or Nearer. ओरांहों, ओरांहों.

Nearness. ओड़ाई, ओड़िडाई, वेझाई, वेझिडाई.

Neat, Neatly. सिजिलाईतो, सिट्राइतो,

सिजिलो, संजीलो, संजेतो, संजाइतो, संजट़ाइतो.

Neatness. सिजिलि, सिट़, सिजिलाई, संज, संजट़.

Necessarily. जाई, जरूरू, अबसि.

Necessary. जरूरी.

To be Necessary. घुर्जणु.

It is Necessary. घुर्जे.

A Necessary. पुई. *See* Privy.

A Necessity. जरूरू, घुर्ज. *See* Need.

The Neck. गिची, कंधु, ग़ाटो, गर्दनि.

A Necklace (*varieties*). हारू, माला, कंठो, जविडा *plu.* कठमाल, कंढो, कंढिलो, चंदनहारू, दुग्दुगी, संघर, चप्कली, दुरी, सपिडो, गल्पटो.

Nectar. अंब्रितु, अम्रितु.

Need (*want, lack of*). घुर्ज, लुगीज, ओखप, गर्ज, तांघ, जरूरू, लोड, गतो, खपु, खापो. *See* Poverty.

Needful. *See* Necessary.

A Needle. सुई, सिविणी, (*large*) सुओ.

Needlework. सिविणो.

Needless, Needlessly (*uncalled for*). अजायो, नाहकु. *See* Useless.

Needy. सखिणो, सुओ. *See* Poor.

Negative (*implying denial*). नाकार्यो.

Neglect, Negligence. ग़हेलाई, गाफिलाई, गाफिली.

Neglectful, Negligent. (*person*) ग़हेलो, ग़हिलो, गाफिलु, (*act*) ग़हेलाणो, ग़हिलाणो, गाफिलाई.

To be Negligent. ग़हिलाइणु, ग़हेलाइणु, गाफिलाइणु.

A Negro. शीदो.

A Neigh, Neighing. हिण्क, हिण्कार.

To Neigh. हिण्कणु, हिण्कारणु.

A Neighbour. पाडेसी, पाडेसिरी, पाडेचो, पाडेवारो, पाडोसी, पडोसी.

A next door Neighbour. सिआंई, सिआंइतो-ती.

The Neighbourhood. पाडो, ओडोपाडो, कंधीपासो; the next door in Neighbourhood in a town, सिआंदिरी.

Neighbouring. वेझो, वेझिडो, ओड़िडो, ओड़ो, पाडेचो, पाडेसिरी, पाडेसी.

Neither. (*pro.*) हिकिडो बिन, न ही न हू, (*conj.*) न.

A Nephew. (*brother's son*) भाइट्यो, (*sister's son*) भाणेजो, भाणिजु, (*husband's brother's son*) ड़ेरोटु, (*husband's sister's son*) नाणाटु, (*wife's brother's son*) सालाटु, सालाजु.

Nervous, having weak Nerves. खफ़कानी.

Nervousness. खफ़कानु.

A Nest. आखेडो.

A Net. ज़ारी, ज़ारू, (*varieties for fishing*) घाओ, भनु, रछु, (*for birds*) ज़ारी, दामु, ग़लो, लाखिकी, वालछट्टी, दुग्जो, (*for animals*) पंजोड़ु.

Netted, Net-worked. ज़ारोदारू.

Nettle-seed. उटंगणु.

Never. कड़हीं न, हड़ि न, पटिअ न, मूरि-मूरों-मूरां-न, मुंढों-मुंढाँ-न, बिनिह न.

Nevertheless. त बि, तड़हीं बि.

Neuter, Neutral. न हेड़हों न होड़हों. *See* Separate.

A Neuter verb. अकर्मक, लाजिमो.

New, Newly. नँओं, (*not ancient*) हाणोको.

Newness. नँवाई.

News. खबर, समाचारू, खबरचार, समाउ, सुधि; good news, खुशि खबर.

A News-writer. खाबिरू.

Next. भरिचारो, पासेचारो, ओयाँ, ब्रिओ.

The Next, or coming, month. ड्रिसँदो, अग्यों, महँद्यो.

The month after Next. उत्यो.

The Nib of a pen, &c. अणी, नोक, चुहुंब.

Nice (*pleasing*). मलूकु, सुटो, सफिरो, पोशीदो. *See* Accurate, Scrupulous, Fastidious, Fine.

Niceness, Nicety. मलूकाई, मलूकी, पोशीदाई, सफिराई.

A Niche. जारो, ताकु, ताको.

A Nick (*notch*). खपु, खपो.

To Nick (*cut a nick*). खपणु.

Niece. (*brother's daughter*) भाइटो, (*sister's daughter*) भाणेजो, (*husband's brother's daughter*) ड्रेराट्रि, (*husband's sister's daughter*) नाणाट्रि, (*wife's brother's daughter*) सालाट्रि, सालाजि.

A Niggard. मचूंठु, चूठु, शूमु, चोडालो, संखु, चिचोमारू. *See* Miser, Miserly.

Niggardliness. चूठाई, शूमाई, चिचमार्णी, मचूंठाई.

The Night. राति.

Of the Night, Nightly. रातूणो.

All Night, during the Night. रातोराति, रातोवाहि.

To-Night. अजु राति.

Last Night. काल्ह राति.

Of the past Night. रातोको, रातूणो.

A Night attack. राताहो.

A Nightingale. बुबुंल, बुबिलो, (*kinds of*) भोरो, खेदो; a young Nightingale, नवलु.

A Nightmare. ओथारो.

Night shade. पटपेरू, कांइल्पेरू, (*leaves*) कांवल.

Nimble. छुहो. *See* Active, Swift.

Nine. नवं.

The Nine at cards, dice, &c. नहलो.

Nine (*per cent*). नओतिरो.

Ninefold (*adj.*). नवँऊंणो, नांऊंणो.

The Ninefold. नवँऊंणि, नांऊंणि.

Nineteen. ऊणीह, उण्वीह.

Nineteenth. ऊणीहों.

Ninetieth. नवेओं.

Ninety. नवे.

Ninety-one. एकानवे.

Ninety-two. ब्रिआनवे.

Ninety-three. ट्रिआनवे.

Ninety-four. चोरानवे.

Ninety-five. पंजानवे.

Ninety-six. छहानवे.

Ninety-seven. सतानवे.

Ninety-eight. अठानवे.

Ninety-nine. नवानवे, वधानवे.

Ninth. नांओं.

The Ninth day of a lunar fortnight. नांई.

To Nip. छिनणु. *See* To Bite, Cut.

The Nipple of a dug. डुंड्री, ब्रिड्रो.

A Nit. लीख.

Nitre. शोरो.

Nitty, full of Nits. लीखिरू.

No. न.

Noble (*of high family*). सुजात्यो, जातीरो, आकाह्यो. *See* Family, Illustrious.

A Noble, Nobleman. भुडो, अमीरू, मीरू, उमिराहु.

Nocturnal. रातूणो.

To Nod. कंधु धूणणु.

To Nod from drowsiness. पिर्टुझूटो-खाइणु, ओझिरणु.

Noise. हुलु, गोडु, लुडु, आवाजु, बखेडो, गोगाऊ. *See* Outcry.

Noisome, (*hurtful q. v.*) जिआनो. *See* Injurious, Bad.
Noisy. लुडाई, गोगाई, गोडो, गोडाऊ.
Nolens volens. खामखाह, हरूभरू.
Nominally. नांव लेखे-भर.
Non (*prefixed to words*). न, म, अण, अ.
None. कोई न, को न.
Non-existent. अणहूंदो.
Nonsense (*silly talk*). फस्तो.
To talk Nonsense. जखणु, जख मारणु. *See* To Chatter.
Nonsensical, Nonsensically. अजायो.
The Noon, Noonday. ब्रिपहरी.
A Noose. फाही, फासी, सिर्किसाई.
Nor. न.
The North. उतरू.
Of the North. उतिराधो.
Northerly, Northern. ओतियों.
Northward. उतर ड़े-ड़ुँहँ-ड़्हों.
The Nose. नकु.
A bleading at the Nose. नकहीरो, नाकेरी, नकहीर.
To speak through the Nose. मिनाइणु, घुणाइणु.
One who speaks through his Nose. घुणो.
To blow the Nose. नकु सुण्कणु or सुंघणु.
A Nose bag for a horse's grain. तोबिरो, पाहोडो.
Flat-Nosed. मिनो.
Large-Nosed, Nosey. नकिरू.
A Nosegay. छुग़ो, दस्तो, तुरो.
Noseless. बुरो.
A Nose ring. नथ, बूलो.
The Nose string of a bullock. नथ; of a camel, चिमिरि.
The plug in a camel's Nose to which the leading string is tied. नाकेलो, नाकेलि, लांटी, नाको.
A Nostril. नास, नाकोट्टो, छोटो, छोटो.
To bore the Nostril. टोंपणु; नथणु.
Not. न, म, मतां.
Notable. See Notorious, Remarkable.
A Notch. खपु, खपो.
The Notch of an arrow. गोशो.
To Notch. खपणु.
A Note (*letter*). पुर्जो, रुको, चिठी. *See* Mark, Reputation, Consequence.
A Note (*in music*). सुरु.
To run over the Notes to catch the key, &c. आलापणु.
A Note of hand. अंगुडो.
To Note (*observe*). ड़िसणु, दिलि-ध्यानु-चितु-ड़िअणु.
Nothing (*nonentity*). आणहूदि.
Nothing (*not any thing*). को न.
Good for Nothing. को न जिहडो.
Notice (*observation*). नजर, ध्यानु, निगाह. *See* Information.
A Notice (*cried out*). होको, पड़्हो.
To Notice (*observe, q. v.*). ड़िसणु, (*mention*) चवणु. *See* To Tell.
A Notification. इश्तिहारु.
To Notify. ज़ाणाइणु, पधिरो, करणु. *See* To Inform.
Notion. गुमानु, खिआलु, समाउ. *See* Conception, Thought.
Notoriety. हाक, हाकार, सुणाणी, पधरि.
Notorious. नांइचड़्हो, नालेरो, हाकायों, नामकिढ्यो, नामकढो, पधिरो.
Notwithstanding (*although*). तोड़े, जे तोड़े or तोणे.
Novel. नँओं.
November, and part of December. नहरी, नाहरी.

A Novice. सेखिज्यातु, नँभौं, नविलो.
A Noun. नालो, नांउँ.
To Nourish. निपाइणु, पालणु, तातणु, सांढणु, सांभणु.
To be Nourished. निपज़णु.
A Nourisher. निपाइणहारू, पालणहारू.
Nourishing (*sub.*). पालना, पर्वरसी, निपाजु.
Nourishment (*food q. v.*). निपाजु, खाजु.
Now. हाणे, हिंअर, हेर, इझो.
Now and then. कड़हीं कड़हीं.
Just Now, a little while ago. अग़इडो, सवेरिडो.
No way, No wise. कहीं ग़ाल्हि मैंन.
No where. किथे न.
Noxious. जिआनो, जिआन्खोरू.
A Nuisance. बला, आफति, उपाधि.
Null. बेकमो. *See* Useless.
Numb. ठाल्यो, ठंभ्यो, साणो.
To Numb. ठालणु, ठंभणु.
Number (*quantity*). ग़णति, ग़ण्ती, अंदाजु.
A great Number. घणि, घणाई.
To Number (*count q. v.*). ग़णणु, (*affix a number*) अंगणु.
Numbering. ग़णति. *See* Counting.
Numberless. अणग़णति, बेशुमारू. *See* Innumerable.
A Numeral. अंगु.
Numerous. घणा *plu.* अनेक. *See* Many.
Nuptial. विहांइतो.
A Nurse. दाई; a man nurse, दायो.
Of a Nurse. दाइको.
To Nurse, (*tend*). निपाइणु, तातणु. *See* To Suckle.
Nurture, Nutriment. निपाजु, खाजु. *See* Food.
A Nutmeg. जाफरू.

O

O'! ए, ओ, अइ, (*addressing males only*) रे, डे, अडे, (*addressing females*) ई, अई, री, डी, अडी.
On oar. ग़नु, चपो, ओलो.
An Oath. सँहुँ, सौगंदु, कसमु, डुांही.
To take an Oath. सँहुँ &c. खणणु or खाइणु.
To administer an Oath. सँहुँ &c. खणाइणु–ड़िभणु.
Obdurate. कठोरू. *See* Unfeeling, Obstinate.
Obedience. मञ्जिता, मञाति.
Obedient. मात्रू, आग्यावानु, आग्याकारी, चएवारी.
An Obeisance. सलामु.
To Obey. मञणु, बुधणु.
An Object (*design*). मतलबु, वास्तो, मुदो, मुदाउ, अर्थु, मनोरथु, पिरोजनु, खिआलु.
The Object (*in grammar*). कर्मु, मफऊलु.
To Object. नाकारणु, आड़ो फिरणु. *See* To Oppose.
An Objection. रदु, नाकार, शकु, संका.
An Oblation. अखो, भेटा, निआजु, बहराणो, देगि. *See* Sacrifice.
An Obligation (*favor*). थोरो, गुनु, बारो. *See* Necessity.
One under Obligations. काण्यारो, कांयारो, ग़ह्यलु.
To Oblige (*compel*). हल्भरू-जोरु करे-कराइणु &c.
To Oblige (*confer favor*). थोरो लाइणु, गुनु &c. करणु.
Obliging, Obligingly. वडाइतो, गुणाइतो, उपकारी, थोराइतो. *See* Kind.

Oblique, Obliquely. उरेबी, टेढ़ो, ड़िंगो. *See* Crooked, Slanting.

The Oblique form of nouns. विभक्ति.

Obliqueness, Obliquity. ड़िंगाई. *See* Crookedness.

To Obliterate. ड़ाहणु, मेटणु. *See* To Erase.

Oblivion. वेसरि. *See* Forgetfulness.

Obloquy. गिला. *See* Defamation, Reproach.

Obnoxious, (*subject q. v.*). जोगु, लाइकु. *See* Disagreeable.

Obscene. गंदो, कमीणो. *See* Filthy.

Obscenity. गंदाई, कमीणाई.

Obscure. अणचिटो, ऊंधाभो. *See* Dark.

Obscurity (*indistinctness*). अणचिटाई. *See* Darkness.

Obsequies. क्रिआ, सिराधु, कर्मु, कर्णी.

Observance (*respect paid*). मञिता, मञणु. *See* Rite.

Observation (*seeing*). निहार, निगाह, नजर, ड़िसणु, वाइसणु.

To Observe (*watch q. v.*). निहारणु. *See* To See, Obey, Note, Say.

To Observe, (*keep religiously*). रखणु, करणु, मनाइणु.

An Obstacle. झल, रोक, अटिक, अट्काउ, विघिनु, भञ्किडी, भाञो, सोड.

Obstinacy. होड़, आटो, धोड़ि, गहु, ड़िठाई, निठराई, बहशु.

Obstinate. होड़ो, निठरू, अटरू, गुठो, गहगीरू, अणोठो, हठो, हठीलो, ड़िठो, बहशोलो.

To Obstruct. रोकणु, झलणु, अट्काइणु, सोडाइणु.

To be Obstructed. अट्कणु, सोडिजणु.

An Obstructer. अट्काऊ.

An Obstruction. झल, अटिक. *See* Obstacle.

To Obtain (*act.*). पाइणु, लहणु, पिराइणु, मखणु, सिझाइणु.

To Obtain (*neu.*). हलणु.

To be Obtained. मिलणु, लभणु, पिडिपणु, ढ़इजणु, सिझणु, all with agent in the dative case.

To Obtrude (*act.*). जोरू करे आणणु-विझणु (*neu.*) जोरू करे घिड़णु.

Obtuse. मुड़ो, लाभो. *See* Blunt.

To Obviate. टारणु, दूरि करणु. *See* To Prevent.

Obvious. पधिरो, जाहिरू. *See* Manifest.

An Occasion. *See* Occurrence, Opportunity, Cause, Time.

To Occasion. कराइणु. *See* To Cause, Produce.

Occasionally. कड़्हींकड़्हीं, कड़्हीकदाने-कड़्हीकजाने.

To be Occasioned. थिअणु, उथणु. *See* To be Produced.

The Occiput. किआडी.

An Occupation (*business q. v.*). कमु, किर्ति, कारि.

To be Occupied (*engaged*). रूंभणु, अट्कणु.

To Occupy (*possess q. v.*). रखणु, (*take up*) रूंभाइणु. *See* To Fill, Employ.

To Occur (*happen*). थिअणु, पवणु.

An Occurrence. गाल्हि, कमु.

The Ocean. समुडु.

Ocean, Oceanic, (*adj.*). सामुड्रो.

Ochre. गेडू, दाउ.

Cloth dyed with Ochre. भगुभों.

Ochreous. गेडुओं.

Octagon, Octangular. अठकुंड्यारो, अठकुंड़ो.

October-November. कती.

An Odd number. इकी.

Odd (*strange*). नँओं, अजबु.

Odds and ends. बखेड़ो, किचिरो, जरोपुर्जो. *See* Rubbish.

Odium (*invidiousness*). ड़ोहु. *See* Blame.

To cast the Odium (*upon another*). ड़ोहु, विझणु, ठिकरू भञणु.

Odoriferous. सुरहो.

Odour. बोइ, बास, भप, भमक. *See* Fragrance.

Of. जो, संदो, वारो.

Off (*down from*). तां, तों, उतां, उतों. *See* Distant.

Offal. छिछिड़ु, छिछिड़ो, छोछिड़ो.

An Offence (*crime q. v.*). ड़ोहु, गुनाहु, खता. *See* Trangression, Attack.

Offence (*anger q. v.*). चिड, रंजु. *See* Huff.

To Offend (*make angry*). रंजाइणु. *See* To Anger, Annoy.

To Offend (*transgress*). ड़ोहु &c. करणु.

To be Offended (*displeased q. v.*). मत्थां-बुछां-भांइणु, वटिजणु.

An Offender. ड़ुहारी, गुनहगारू. *See* Transgressor.

An Offer, Offering (*of a gift*). आछ, सलाह.

To Offer (*present for acceptance*). ड़िअणु, सलाह करणु, आछणु. *See* To Propose.

To Offer (*agree to give*). ड़िअणो करणु. *See* To Bid.

To Offer up (*in sacrifice*). वारणु, घोरणु, सदिके, &c. करणु.

To Offer (*neu.*). अचणु, सामुहो अचणु-थिअणु.

An Offering. घोर, सदिको, निआजु, भेटा, नजुरू, नजराणो, कुनी, उर्सु. *See* Oblation, Sacrifice.

A burnt Offering. होमु.

To offer a burnt Offering. होमणु.

An Office (*post*). हुदो, कमु.

A public Office. दफ्तरू.

An Officer. हुदेदारू, कामोरो, कामी.

Offspring. ओलाधु, वंसु *f.* अंसु *f.* वाड़ो.

Often. वरीवरी, घणा भेरा or घुमिरा. *See* Constantly.

As Often. जेतिरा भेरा; so often, तेतिरा-ओतिरा-भेरा; how often, केतिरा भेरा.

To Ogle. अखि हणणु or वनुड़ाइणु.

Oh! आह. See Ah.

Oil. तेलु.

To Oil. मखणु, तेलु लाइणु.

A leathern vessel for Oil. दबो, दबी, ताकु, ताकी, घोघारी.

A maker of leathern Oil vessels. दबारू, बब्बारू.

Dry from want of Oil. अणभो.

Oil cake. खड़ु.

Oiliness. सणभाई, सणिभु, सणभाणि.

An Oilmaker. चाकी, तेली.

An Oilman, Oilseller. बदिली.

An Oilpress. घाणो.

Oily. सणभो.

Ointment (*salve*). मलमु. *See* Oiliness.

Old (*not young*). बुढो, पर्यो, पोड़हो, कुराड़ो, झूरू.

How Old. केतिरे वर्ह्यनि जो, केतिरिअ उमिरि जो.

Old (*not new*). पुराणो, कुहुनो, झूनो, झूरू. *See* Ancient, Original.

Old age. बुढाई, बुढेपो, बुढेपाई, पर्यांई, पोड्हाई, पीरी, कुराडाई.

Oldness (*antiquity*). पुराणाई, कुहुनाई, झूनाई, आग़ाट्राई.

An Oleander. जंगीगुलु.

Olibanum (*the perfume*). लोबानु, कुंदिरू.

An Omen. सौंणु, सुग़िणु, सगुणु, फार, फाल, ओसहि.

A bad Omen. अपसुग़िणु, बदि सौंणु.

Of, or with, good Omen. सौंणाइतो, सगुणाइतो.

An Omission. भुल, वेसरि.

To Omit. छड़णु, विसारणु. *See* To Pass over, Neglect.

Omnipotent. सर्वसग्नि.

Omnipresent. सर्वव्यापी, सभ जाइ मौजूदु.

Omniscient. सर्वगु.

On (*prep*). ते, उते, परि, भर.

On (*forward*). अग़े, महँदि.

Once. हेकर, हिकड़ांहो, हिकिडे भेरो. *See* Formerly.

At Once (*promptly*). उन्हे–उनिह–महल. *See* Quickly, Together.

At Once. (*together, in a lump*) हेकांदो.

One. हेकिडो, हिकिडो, हिकु, एकु, बखु. बखत. *See* Alike.

The figure, or number One. एको.

One and a half. ड़ेढु.

Consisting of One and a half. ड़ेढो, ड़ेढुओं.

The One and a half. ड़ेढूंणि. *See* Half, Quarter.

One (*per cent*). एकोतिरो.

One and a half (*per cent*). ड़ेढोतिरो.

One hundred and one. एकोसउ, एकोतर्सउ, सउहिकु.

One by one. हिकुहिकु, हिकिडो हिकिडो.

Of One mind. हिकदिल्यो.

One-eyed. काणो.

Oneness. हिकिडाई, हेकिडाई, एकाई.

Onerous. ग़ौरो, ग़रो, औखो.

An Onion. बसरु; the bulb, ग़ांढि.

A fresh Onion with top. पनिरु.

A dried Onion. वाढुउ.

Only. रुग़ो, छड्हो, निरो, निलो, निसोरो, फकतु.

An Onset. काह, उलर, लूह, बछ. *See* Attack.

Onward. अग़े, महँदि.

Ooze (*mud q. v*). गप, चिक.

To Ooze. सिमणु, टि्मणु, चुअणु.

Oozing, (*sub.*). सिम, टि्मटि्मि.

Oozy. गपारो. *See* Slimy.

Open (*not shut*). पट्यो, उपट्यलु, खुल्यो. *See* Public, Roomy.

To Open (*act.*). पटणु, उपटणु, खोलणु. *See* To Expand.

To Open (*neu.*). खुलणु, पटिजणु.

To be Opened or laid bare. उघिड़णु.

An Opening. वाट, मुँहुं.

Openly. दलेबादले, दीनादास्तो, पधिरो.

Openness. पधिराई.

To Operate (*produce effect*). असरु करणु, लग़णु.

An Operation (*action*). असरु, कसु.

To have Ophthalmia. अखि उथणु.

An Opinion. मतु, समुझ, पखु.

Opium. अमलु, आफीमु, कसुंबो.

An Opium-eater. अमलो, आफीमो, मवालो.

An Opponent. *See* Enemy.

Opportune, Opportunely. वेलाइतो, वखताइतो, महल्लाइतो.

Opportunity. दाउ, वझु, सझु, ग़ाणु, वखतु, सांगो, सठो.

At a convenient Opportunity. वझाइतो, सझाइतो.
To Oppose. आड़ो फिरणु, सामुहों थिअणु, झलणु.
Opposite (*fronting*). सामुहों, आमोसामुहों, आंभारो सांभारो. *See* In Front, Adverse.
The Opposite side. पर्यों पासो, परारि.
Opposition. सामुहाई, सामुहूणाई. *See* Hinderance.
To Oppress. पीड़णु, दुखोइणु, जुलिमु &c. करणु.
Oppression. जुलिमु, अंधेरु, गजबु, बग्दादु, अलटु, कलूरु.
Oppressive. जुलिमी, अंधेरी, गजबी.
An Oppressor. जालिमु, बग्दांदी.
Opprobrium. गिला, निंदा. *See* Reproach, Blame.
Option. वसु, इख्त्यारु.
Optional, in one's Option. वसाइतो, वसि, इख्त्यारि.
Opulence. वँझाँई, शाहूकारी. *See* Wealth.
Opulent. वँझों, शाहूकारु, दुआदारु, भाग्यों. *See* Rich.
Or. जां, कि, तोडे.
Oral, Orally. जबानी, वातूणो, वातवेणी.
An Orange. संग्तिडो.
An Orb. चकिरी, मंड़लु.
An Orchard. बागु.
To Ordain (*establish*). काइदो-नेमु -केतु ब्धणु.
An Ordeal. आज्मुदो, परीछा; trial taken by lifting a red hot iron, मेली; trial by water, टुबिअ जो सँहुं; by fire, चर जो सँहुं.
Order (*method*). सिजिलि, सिट, ठाहु, संजट, संज.
In Order, or what is in Order. सिजिलाइतो, ठाहाइतो, सिटाइतो, संजाइतो, संजटाइतो.
An Order, (*command*). हुकुमु, आग्या.
A written Order. पर्वानो.
An Order (*society*). पंथु, मजहबु. *See* Sect, Rank.
To Order (*arrange q. v.*). ठाहणु.
To Order (*command*). हुकुमु &c. ड़िअणु, फर्माइणु.
Orderly. ठाहाइतो, ड़ौलाइतो. *See* In Order.
An Ordinance. कानूनु, काइदो, नेमु.
Ordinary (*usual*). आम, रीताइतो. *See* Middling.
Ore. धातु *f.*
An Organ of sense. इंद्री, हवासु.
To Organize. ठाहणु.
Oriental (*adj.*). उभिरंदो.
An Orifice. मुँहुं.
Origin. मुंढु, आदि, बिनाह, असुलु, मूलु, धुरु, बुनिआदु. *See* Source, Root.
An Original (*first writing*). असुलु.
Original, Originally. असुली, असुलाइतो, असुलिओं, मुंढाइतो, धुराइतो, आदऊ.
To Originate (*act.*). कढणु, पैदा करणु.
To Originate (*neu.*). निकिरणु, उथणु, थिअणु.
An Ornament. सींगारु.
An Ornament for the person. गहु, गहणो, मण्यो, जेवरु, थोकु. For different kinds of Ornaments. *See under* Arm, Neck, &c.
A set of personal Ornaments. साहि.
To Ornament. सींगारणु, सँवारणु.
Ornamental. ड़ेखाइतो, सींगाराइतो
An Orphan. छोरो, छोरोछिनो, यतीमु.
Of an Orphan. छोराणो.

Orpiment. हर्तालु, जर्नी.
To Oscillate. लुड़णु, झूलणु.
Oscillation. लोड़ो, झूलो.
Ostensible, Ostensibly. जाहिरी, ब्रहयाँ, ड़ेखाइतो.
Ostentation. ठाटु, ठाहु, ड़ौलु. *See* Pomp.
Ostentatious (*fond of display*). ठाटी, ठासी, तूमानी.
An Ostrich. शुतिर्मुर्गु.
Other. ब्रिओ; every other day, ड़िंहु विचि पाए-विझो.
Each Other. हिकब्रिए खे, पाण में.
Other's (*belonging to another*). धार्यो, पराओ, वेग्यो.
On the Other side. पर्यें-हुन पासे, परारि.
Otherwise (*in another manner*). ब्रिअ तरैंहं.
Otherwise (*else*). नत, नात.
An Otter. लुधिड़ो.
An Oven. तनूरु.
Over (*above the top*). मथां, मथों, मथैंउं, उतां, उतों, उतैंउं. *See* Across, Above.
Over, Overplus. वधीक, वाधू, वधिक.
To be Over, give Over. *See* To be Ended, to Stop.
To Overcome. जीतणु, फतिह करणु. *See* To Subject, Surmount.
To Overflow, or Overflood, as the river, (*neu.*). लेटणु, उथिलणु.
To Overflow, Overwhelm (*act.*). ब्रोड़णु, ब्रोड्ब्रोड़ा करणु.
Overmuch. वधीक, वाधू, घणो.
To Overpower. केराइणु, जोइणु, दसणु, ड्राहणु, जीतणु.
An Overseer. दरोग़ो, लाकुडी.
An Oversight (*mistake q. v.*). भोलो.
To Overspread. छोइणु.

To Overstep. ओरांघणु, लंघे हलणु.
To Overtake. अची पहुचणु-गड़िजणु.
To Overthrow, Overturn. केराइणु. *See* To Overpower, Upset.
Our. असां जो; our own, संदुऊं, संदूं.
Ourselves. असीं पाण.
To Oust. तड़णु, कढणु.
Out (*not in*). ब्राहरि, ब्रहरि. *See* Loudly, Publicly.
Out of. मों, मैंउं, मां, ओं, अंउं, आं, मझों-झैंउं-झां, अंदिरों-रैंउं-रां.
To put Out, be Out. *See* To Extinguish, be Expended.
Out-bidding. चड्हति.
An Outcast. बेज़ात्यो.
An Outcry. कूकिड़ो, ब्राकार, ब्राकरकुटो, रड़ि, हुलु, दांह, वाको. *See* Uproar.
To Outdo, Outgo. *See* To Outstrip.
Outer, Outward, Outermost. ब्रहयाँ, ब्राहियाँ.
Outlay. खर्चु. *See* Expenditure.
An Outlet. वाट. *See* Road.
To Outlive. वधि-वाधू जिअणु.
Outparts. ब्रहराड़ो.
An Outrage. अंधेरु. *See* Tyranny.
Outright (*at once, on the spot*). उफटु. *See* At Once, Plainly.
Outside, Outward. ब्रहरि, ब्राहरि.
The Outside. ब्रहरु, ब्राहरु.
Outstanding debts. ओधरि, ओधरिपाधरि.
To Outstrip. वधी वञणु, पोइ ते करणु. *See* To Surpass.
To be Owed. ड़िअणो थिअणु.
Owing (*due*). ड़िअणो.
An Owl. चिब्रिरो, चिब्र, मुबारो, बूमु, शाहबूमु.

Own. पंहंजो, पिंड्जो; my own, संदुमि; thy own, संदुइ; his own, संदुसि, &c.

To Own (*admit*). आँकारणु, अँहिकारणु, हाम भरणु, कबूलु करणु. *See* To Confess.

An Owner. धणी, मालिकु, सांईं.

Ownerless. निधण्को, बेवारिसो, गेवाणो.

Ownership. मालिकी.

An Ox. ड्ढांदु. *See* Bull, Bullock.

An Oyster shell. सिप.

P

A Pace. विख, कदमु.

Pace (*gait q. v.*). टोर, चालि.

To Pace. विखूं भरणु.

Pacific, Pacificatory. सुलिहाइतो. *See* Gentle.

To be Pacified. ठरणु, पर्चणु, सांति थिअणु.

To Pacify. ठारणु, पर्चाइणु. *See* To Appease.

A Pack of cards. गंजिफो.

A Pack of cloth. बुङ्को. *See* Bundle.

A Pack of dogs. लोध.

A Package, Packet. बिद. *See* Bundle.

A small Package. बिदिड़ी.

A Pack cloth. वेठणु, बार्दानो.

A Pack needle. सुओ.

A Pack saddle, (*camel's*). पलाणु, (*horse's, bullock's, &c.*) आधरु.

To put on a Pack saddle. पलाणणु.

Pack thread. धागो, सगो.

A Pad (*foot path*). चारो, पेचिरो.

A Pad (*put under saddle*). थडो, थही. *See* Cushion.

A Paddock. वाडो.

A Pad-horse. राहदारु घोडा.

A Padlock. कुफु. *See* Lock.

The Page of a book. पासो, सुफो.

A Pagoda. मंदरु, ठाकुद्वारो.

To be Paid (*as a debt*). पोचणु.

Pain. सूरु, दर्दु, डुखु, डेखिडो, पीड, (*distress*) अँहंजु, अँहँजाउ, औखु, औखो.

To Pain (*neu.*). डुखणु, लुछणु, सूर &c. करणु.

To Pain (*act.*). डुखाइणु, डुखोइणु, पीडणु, साडणु, लुछाइणु.

To suffer Pain, be Pained. सूराटिजणु, डुखो थिअणु, कुड्हणु.

Painful, Painfully. डुख्यो, डुखाइतो, सूराइतो, सूरेतो.

Painless. अणसूरो, अणसूराइतो, अणसूरेतो.

Paint. रङु.

To Paint (*color*). रङणु, (*in variegated colors*) चिट्रणु.

Painted (*in various colors*). चिट्कमिरो.

A Painter. कमांगरु.

Painting (*the art*). चिट्रिकारी, कमांगरी, चिट्रिणो.

A Painting. चिटु.

A Pair. जोडो, जोड़ी.

In Pairs. ब्रिट, ब्रिन्हहिड, ब्रेन्ह, सन्हडु, ब्रेलास. *See* In Couples.

Paired (*coupled*). ब्रिटो.

A Palace. महलातु, महलु.

A Palanquin. पाल्की, (*varieties*) ड़ोलो, लोड़ी, चोबानु, चौड़ोलु, (*borne on mules*) माफो.

A Palanquin-bearer. कहारु.

The Palate. तारूं.

Pale (*adj.*). साओ, जर्दो, पीलो, (*as colors*) फिको, झको.

To grow Pale. सावकाइजणु.

Paleness. सावाई, सावकि, सावकाई, जदांई, पीलाई.

A Paling, Palisade. कटहडो.

A Pall (*over a corpse*). छाउ.

To be Palled. जोग़ीर्जणु, खटो थिअणु, थकणु.

A Palm-tree. खजी. *See* Date.

The leaves of the hill Palm, used for making mats, &c. फडह, पीसि.

The Palm of the hand. तरी, तिरी.

The Palm contracted to hold any thing, a Palmfull. लप, चुरू, बुकी ; both Palms joined, बुकु.

A Palm (*measure*). चपो.

Palpable. *See* Manifest.

To Palpitate. ड़कणु, धड़्कणु.

Palpitation. धक्धकि.

The Palsy. लकुओ ; hemiplegia, अर्धांगु.

Paltriness. ओछाई, नीचाई.

Paltry. ओछो, नीचु.

To Pamper. मचुलाइणु, दादुलो-मचुलो-चचुलो करणु.

A Pan (*varieties*). कडाहो, तओ, तई, दांगो, ब्राटो, लुहांड़िडो.

To flash in the Pan. लबु चटणु-खणणु.

The Pan of a gunlock. कनु.

The Pan of the knee. टकिणो.

A Pane of glass. शीशो, कायो. काओ.

A Panegyric. साराह, तारीफ. *See* Praise.

A Pang. सूट, चिणिग.

A Panic. हूक, ड़हकारू, ट्राकोडो, ड़ोलाओ. *See* Fright.

A Pannier (*for camels*). पाल्णो, कजाओ.

To Pant. सहकणु, हुफिजणु.

A pair of Pantaloons (*of different kinds*). सुथण, कांच, चर्नो.

A Panther. चोनो.

Panting (*subs.*). सहकी.

A Pap (*nipple*). डुंडो, बिंड़ो. *See* Breast.

Pap for infants. पेज़ी.

Papa. बाबो, अबो. *See* Father.

Paper. कागजु, काग़रू, पनो.

Paper, made of Paper. कागिजी, काग़िरी.

A Paper-maker. काग़रकुटो, कागिजी, काग़िरी.

A Paper-seller. काग़राई, पनाई.

Pappy. फेफो. *See* Soft.

A Parade, Parading (*of troops*). कवाद. *See* Pomp.

Paradise. बिस्तु, सर्गु, सुर्गु.

A Paragraph. कलमु, ग़ालिह.

Paralytic. अर्धांगी. *See* Palsy.

Paramount. मुंहु, मुखि, सिरे, अवलु. *See* First, Chief.

A Paramour. चघु, यारू.

A woman who has a Paramour. चघोटी.

A Paraquet, Parasol. *See* Parrot, Umbrella.

A Parcel. ग़ंढिडी, हड, ग़ंढि. *See* Packet.

A Parcel (*of groceries, physic, &c.*). पुडो, पुडी.

To Parcel. वंड़णु. *See* To Divide.

To Parch (*grain*). भुञणु. *See* To Scorch.

To be Parched with thirst. ट्रिहाइजणु.

Parched *chana*. भुग़िड़ा *plu.*

Parched (*a crop*). तई, सोकडि.

A Parcher of grain. भोंग़िड़ी, वांहें, बठारी.

The cost of Parching. भुञाणी.

Pardon. माफी, बक्श, खिमा.

To Pardon. बक्शणु, माफु-खिमा करणु, छड़णु.

Pardonable. माफ जिहड़ो.

A Pardoner. बक्शींदड़ु, माफु कँदड़ु.

To Pare. छिलणु, तराशणु.

A Parent. *See* Father, Mother.

Parentage. घराणो. *See* Lineage.

A Paring. छिल.

A Park (*for deer, &c.*). शिकार-गांहु.

A Paroxysm. झूटो, लहरि, लहरो. *See* Fit.

A Parrot. तोतो, चतूं.

To Parry. टारणु.

Parsimonious. सर्फाई. *See* Frugal, Stingy.

Parsimony. सर्फो, सांगुसर्फो. *See* Frugality, Stinginess.

A Part. टुकिरु, भाङो. *See* Piece, Share, Side.

On the Part of. पारां, पारों, पारँडं.

To Part (*act.*). जुदा करणु. *See* To Separate, Divide, Quit.

To Partake, Participate (*neu.*). भाङो &c. वठणु, भाईवारु &c. थिअणु.

Partial (*favouring one side*). रिआई, रवाजी, पख्याती, पछी.

Partiality. पासि, वटिप, पछु, रिआउ, पखु, पख्यातु, पछपातु, पारखातरि, बदरि, बदिलो, रवाजु.

A Particle. रती, जरो, की.

Particular, Particularly. निजो, धार, निआरो.

To Particularize. विचूरणु, निर्वारु करे ड़ेखारणु.

Partition (*dividing*). विछं, वंड़. *See* Division, Compartment.

Partly. की.

A Partner. भाईवारु, पतिआरु, हिसेभाई, शरीकु, हिसेदारु, भाङेरो, हिसेरो, हामो, भाईंठो, भायोठो.

Partnership. भाईवारी, पतिआरी, भाइपो, शराकती, भायपो-पाई, शराकती, भाएठो, भायोठो.

A Partridge. तितिरु.

A black Partridge. (*male*) कारिड़ो, (*female*) कग़हरी, कग़ी.

A Party. दफो, धुरि. *See* Side, Band.

A Party wall. वोरी.

A Pass (*in mountains*). लकु, दरो, घाटी. *See* Road, Passport.

To Pass, or Pass away (*neu.*). वञणु.

To Pass, or Pass current. हलणु.

To come to Pass. थिअणु.

To Pass by, or over. लंघणु, वटाइणु, गुदिरणु, (*over water, through pain, &c.*) तरणु.

To Pass over (*omit*). छड़णु, वांजणु, रेटणु.

To Pass away (*time, neu.*). गुजिरणु, विहामणु.

To Pass away (*time, act.*). गुजारणु, विहाँइणु, निबाहणु, काटणु, घारणु.

Passable (*indifferent q. v.*). हालूचालू.

A Passage (*journey q. v.*). अचणु, वञणु. *See* Road, Paragraph.

Passage money. भाडो, (*across a river*) पतणु.

A Passenger. चाङ्हू.

Passion (*anger q. v.*). कावड़ि, ड़मरु, कोपु. *See* Rage, Zeal, Eagerness, Love.

Passionate, Passionately. निखो, कड़ों, खहुरो, गर्मु, जहलो, चिड़िणो, ड़्मराइतो क्रोधो.

A Passport. पर्वानो, राहदारिअ जो पर्वानो.

The Past tense of a verb. भुनू, माजी.

Paste. लेई, लेटी.

To Paste. ज़पुडाइणु, चंबुडाइणु, गंढणु.

Paste-board. दफ्तरी, (*varieties*) कुटो, मुकवा.

The Pastern of a horse. फोजु.

Pastime. रंगु, खिलखुशी, रौंशो, *See* Amusement.

A Pastor (*spiritual guide*). मुर्शिदु, मुर्शिदु, गुरू.

Pasturage, Pasture. चरहो, चारो.

Pasture ground. बीड, बीअ, कोछो, छन.

A Pat, Patting. टपुड, टपुर.

To Pat. टपुडणु.

To Pat, or flatten by patting (*as a cake*). थपणु.

A Patch. अगिडो, चती, पेवंदु.

To Patch. अगिडो *&c.* विझणु.

Patched. अगिड्यांओं.

The Pate. कोपिरी, केपिराटी. *See* Head.

Patent. *See* Open, Plain.

Paternal. अबाणो, ड़ाड़ाणो.

A Path. वाट, रस्तो, गसु, रंदु, दगु, राह. *See* Footpath.

Pathless. बेवाटो, अणवाटो, रेवाटो.

Pathetic, Pathetical. ब्राझारो, ब्राझाइतो.

Patience. सबुरु, खांदि, थांहर, समाई, धीर, धीर्जु, तहमुल, तहमुर, थामुर, ठहर, थँहर.

Patient, Patiently (*adj.*). खांदीरो, खांदाइतो, सबुराइतो, धीरो, धीराइतो, ठहराइतो, सहिणो.

Patrimony. वर्सो.

A Patron. मुरबी, वसीलो. *See* Protector.

Patronless. बेवसीलो, बेवाहु.

A pair of Pattens. चाखिडी.

To Patter. ठड्कणु, खड्कणु, भड्कणु, खुड्कणु, ठुड्कणु.

A Pattering or Patting noise. ठड्को, खड्को, धड्को, खुड्को, ठुड्को, खुड्खुडि.

A Pattern. नमूनो, भड़ो. *See* Sample.

A Pavilion. तंबू. *See* Tent.

The Paunch. भांड़ो. *See* Belly.

A Pauper. पिनिणो. *See* Beggar, Poor.

A Pause (*for rest*). बेसांई, साही, बिसिरामु. *See* Rest.

To Pause. तर्सणु, विहणु. *See* To Rest, Hesitate.

A Paw (*foot*). पेरु, चंबो.

To Paw (*as a horse*). दड़हो हणणु.

A Pawn (*pledge*). गहु, गहणो.

To Pawn. गहु, *&c.* रखणु.

To redeem a thing Pawned. मोखणु.

A Pawn (*in chess*). पिआदो.

Pay. मवाजिबु, वजिहु.

Daily Pay. रोजीनो, रोजु.

Monthly Pay. महीनो, दर्माहो.

Pay given every six months. छमाही; at spring and autumn harverts, फसुलाणो.

Yearly Pay. सालिआनो, बारँहँमाँहो.

Pay, or fixed fee, to a fukeer, &c. ड़नु, ठुक.

A Pay-abstract. वजिह जो चिठो.

To Pay. ड़िअणु, पिआरणु, भरणु. *See* To Discharge, Repay.

Payable. ड़िअणो.

Peace (*not war*). सुलिहु. *See* Quiet, Rest.
Peaceable, Peaceful. सुलही; or peacefully, सुलिहाइतो.
A Peace maker. पर्चाऊ, ठाहू.
A Peach. शफ्तालू.
To Peach (*inform*). सलणु, चुगिली करणु.
A Peacock. मोरू.
A Peahen. ढ़ेल.
Peagreen. सूफांओ.
A Peak. चोटी, चुहुंब.
To Peal. कड्कणु.
A Peal, or Pealing noise. कड्काउ, कड्काटु.
A Pear. नास्पातो.
The prickly Pear. नागफणो थूहरू.
A Pearl. मोतो.
Small Pearls. पुति, खाको.
Mother of Pearl. सिप.
Of Pearls, adorned with Pearls. मोतिअांओं.
A Peasant. हारो. *See* Husbandman.
Peasantry. रैअत, राजु.
A Pebble. पहणी, ककिरो
To Peck. चुहुंब हणणु; up, चुग़णु.
To Peculate. खाई-गि़हो वञणु, फ़ब़ाइणु.
Peculation. खाज़ो, खुर्दिबुर्दि.
Peculiar, Peculiarly. निजु, निजो, निआरो, धार.
Pedigree, (*lineage q. v.*). बुणु, पीडो, वंसु, (*genealogical list*) वंसावलि, सुजिरो.
A Pedlar. घोड्यों, घोरारो.
Peel. छिलु *f.* *See* Skin.
To Peel. छिलणु.
Peeled, devoid of Peel. छेलुओं.
A Peep, Peeping. झातो, लिओ.
To Peep. लिओ &c. पाइणु.
A Peeper. झात्यरू, झातिरू, लिअरू.
Peevish. खिजिणो.
To be Peevish. खिजणु, खपणु.
A Peg. किलो, किलो, कोरो, कोरी, मेख.
A Pellet. गुलेलो, ग़ोड्हो.
A Pellet bow. गुलेलि.
Pellitory. आकड्करहो.
To Pelt. हणणु *See* To Cast.
The Pelvis. निहांई.
A Pen. लेखणि, किलिक, कलमु, कानो.
To make, or mend, a Pen. घड़णु.
A cattle Pen. वाड़ो, वथाणु, भाणो, भाणु, (*for camels*) झोक.
A Penalty. ड़ंडु. *See* Punishment.
Penance. पुनश्चरणु, कफ़ारत.
A Pen case. कलम्दानु, नड़ो.
Penetrable, Penetrative. पिहणवारो, घिड़णवारो.
To Penetrate (*neu.*). पिहणु, घिड़णु. *See* To Pierce.
Penis. लनु, लौडो, टटो, खाझो, इंड़ो, लुंगु, काडु, वाडु.
Penitence. तोबह, पछुताउ, पिशेमानी.
Penitent. तोबह &c. कँदडु, पिशेमानु.
A Penknife. चाकूं, कपु.
Penniless. सुञो, सखिणो. *See* Poor.
Pentagon, Pentangular. पंजकुंड़ो.
Penurious, Penuriousness. *See* Niggardly, Niggardliness.
Penury. सखिणाई, बुख, अणउपति.
A Peon (*belted attendant*). पटेवालु.
People. माण्हूं *plu.* आलमु, खलक.
To People. वसाइणु.
A grain of Pepper. मिर्चु, मिरो, मिर्च, मिर्चो; the plurals of these are general terms for pepper.
The long Pepper. पिपिरो.

Red Pepper. लाहोरी-ग़ाड़हा-गोगाई मिर्चं *plu.*

To Pepper (*sprinkle with pepper*). मिर्चं बुर्कणु-उबूरणु.

Cooked with Pepper. मिर्चाई.

Per annum. वर्ह्य वर्ह्य में, वर्ह्यों वर्हि, वर्ह्यसिवर्हि.

Per cent. सव ते, सैकिडे, (*affixed to numbers*) ओतिरो सउ.

To Perceive. ड़िसणु, सहो करणु, समुझणु, ज़ाणणु.

To be Perceived. भासणु, सुझणु.

Perception. समुझ, सोझ. *See* Notion.

To Percolate (*neu.*). सिमणु, टि़मणु. *See* To Strain.

Peremptory. पक्को, पुख़्तो, खुतो.

Perfect, Perfectly. पूरो, सज़ो, पक्को. *See* Proficient.

Perfection. पूराई, काबिली.

Perfidious. बेईमानु, निमकहरामु, कुलालु, कुपत्यो. *See* False.

Perfidy. बेईमानी, निमकहरामी, कुपति, वेसाहघाती.

To Perforate. टुंगु करणु, सलणु. *See* To Bore.

Perforce. ज़ोर सां, ज़ोरू करे. *See* Violently.

To Perform. करणु, पूरो करणु, बजाइ आणणु, पुज़ाइणु, निबाहणु, निभाइणु, पाडणु, साधणु.

A Perfume. सुरहाणि, सुरहाई, सुगंधु, खुश्बोइ, (*for burning*) धूपु, वासु.

To Perfume. सुरहो करणु. *See* To Incense.

A Perfumer. फुलेली.

Perfumery. सुरहाणि.

Perhaps. जेकुसि, मतां, अलाजे, निआणा, कदाचिति, शाइत.

Peril. जोखो. *See* Danger.

Perilous. जोखाइतो. *See* Dangerous.

A Period of time. मुदत, ड़िंहं *plu.*

To Perish. मरणु, नासु थिअणु.

Perishable. फानी, नासवंतु.

A Perjurer. कुसाख्यो, कूडो.

Perjury. कुसाख, कूडो सँहुं.

To commit Perjury. कूडो सँहुं खणणु.

Permanence. टिकाउ, जटाउ, विहक. *See* Stability.

Permanent. जटाऊ. *See* Durable.

Permission. मोकल, रुख़सत.

A Permit. चिठी, दाखिला.

To Permit. मोकल ड़िअणु, ड़िअणु.

Pernicious. ज़िआनी, ज़िआनुकंदडु, बुछिडो. *See* Bad, Hurtful.

Perpendicular, Perpendicularly. सँओं.

Perpetually. सदाईं. *See* Always, Unintermittingly.

In Perpetuity. सदा ताईं.

To Perplex. मुँझाइणु

Perplexed. मूझहो, मुझडो, हैरानु.

Perplexity. मोंझि, मोंझारो, जंजलु, रोलो, पेचु.

A Perquisite, Perquisites. लागा, लागो, लापो, बाबु, बाट, वर्सो, वसुर.

To allow Perquisites. वर्साइणु, वसुराइणु.

To Persecute. डुखोइणु, पोडणु. *See* To Annoy.

Perseverance. उज़मु, अविचाई.

To Persevere. लगो रहणु.

Persevering (*adj.*). उज़मी, अविचुं, अटरू. *See* Resolute.

Persia. ईरानु.

Persian, a Persian. ईरानी.

A Person (*individual*). माण्हू, ज़णो, शख़्सु, आदिमी, बांह, (*one, a body*) पहर, वांगी.

In Person, Personally, (*in propriâ personâ*). भुरि, पाण.
Personal (*individual, peculiar*), is expressed by using संदुसि *his wn*, संदऊं or संदू *our own*, संदुनि *their own*, &c.
To Personate. वेसु करणु or ठाहणु.
Personation. वेसु, सांगु.
Perspicuous. चिटो, सफा. *See* Plain.
Perspiration. पघरु.
To Perspire. पघिर्जणु.
To Persuade. मञाइणु, समुझाइणु. *See* To Prevail upon.
To Pertain. हुअणु with जो, साणु लग्गणु. *See* To Appertain.
Pertinacity. होड़. *See* Obstinacy.
Perturbation. विग़ोड़ु, खोभु. *See* Agitation, Disquiet.
Perverse. होड़ी, अणांगो, ऐथिरो. *See* Stubborn.
Perverseness. होड़, वहशु. *See* Stubbornness.
To Pervert. फेरणु, उबताइणु. *See* To Corrupt.
To Pester. अकाइणु. *See* To Annoy, Tease.
A Pest, Pesterer. मथे-जिभ खाऊ or खपाऊ.
A Pestilence. मरी, ओथिड़ि.
A Pestle (*varieties*). दस्तो, मुहुरी, ड़ंडो, मुहुलिडो, मुहुरो, मुतहरो.
A Pet (*darling q. v.*). लाडुलो, दाडुलो, चचुलो. *See* The Sulks.
To Pet. मचुलाइणु, लाडुलो &c. करणु.
A Petition. अरीजी, अर्जु, अर्जी.
To Petition. अर्जु करणु.
A Petitioner. सुआलो, अर्जी.
A Petticoat. पडो.
Pettish, Petulant. खिजिणो.

Pewter. जिस्तु.
A Phial. शीशो.
The Philosopher's stone. पारसु.
A Philter. मोहिनी.
To Phlebotomize. सीर-फस्त-छोडणु.
Phlegm. खांघारो, गिग, कफ.
To Physic. दवा ड़िअणु.
The art or practice of Physic. हकीमी, तबीबी, हकीमाई, तबीबाई. *See* Medicine.
A Physician. हकीमु, तबेबु, बोजु, वैदु.
Physiognomy. मुहांड़ो. *See* Countenance.
A Pice (*coin*). ड़ोकडु, पैसो.
To Pick. (*select*) चूंड़णु, धुणणु, (*gather*) चूंड़णु.
To Pick (*the teeth, a hole, &c.*). खोटणु.
To Pick up. खणणु.
A Pickaxe (*or rather crowbar*). चंजूरु.
A Pick-pocket. गंढिछोड़ु.
Pickles. आचारु, आथाणो, सांधाणो.
To Pickle. संधणु.
A Picture. चिटु, तस्वीर.
Piebald. अब्लखु, सिंजाफु.
A Piece. टुकरु, टुकिरो, पुर्जो.
A Piece of bread. ग़चु, पारिचो, खनु, ग़भो, कनी, कनो, (*large*) ग़पलु.
A Piece at chess. मुहुरो; at tables, सारी.
A Piece of cloth (*rag q. v.*). चोवट, चोउट, (*web*) थानु, ताको, जोडी.
A Piece of fish, or meat. तिको, ब्रेरो, कोरो, कतिरो, (*of meat only*) बूटी, सुधी, सुंदी.
In Pieces, Piecemeal. टुकर टुकर, पुर्जापुर्जा.

To Pierce (*act.*). टुंबणु, टुंगु करणु, सल्णु. *See* To Perforate, Stab.

To Pierce, as a thorn does. चुभणु.

Piety. धर्मु, दीनु, दीन्दारी.

A Pig. सुअरु, (*female*) सुअरि, भूंडिणि.

A Pigeon. कबूतरु, पारेलो.

One who keeps Pigeons. कबूतडाई.

A tumbler Pigeon. तिखो, लेटणु; other kinds, and of different colors, are शीराजो, लुको, जागु, कागजी, मोजपरु, मोहनो, बीनिरु, आहू, हारपानु, संगारु, चेल्टो, खोल्सरु, रठो, होरो.

A Pile. (*stack*) दनि, खोडु, (*of things piled up*) थहो, थही. *See* Heap, Post.

A funeral Pile. चिख्या.

The Piles. बवासीरु, मोका *plu.*

To Pilfer. हथछुहाई करणु.

A Pilferer. हथछुहो.

A Pilgrim. जारती, जाटो; to Mecca, हाजी.

A Pilgrimage. जारत, जाट़ा; to Mecca, हजु.

A body of Pilgrims. जाट़.

A Pill. गोरी, हबु.

To Pillage. फुरणु, लुटणु.

Pillage. फुरि, लुटि.

A Pillar. थंभु, थूणो, पोल्पाओ.

A Pillow. विहाणो, तकिओ, सिराणो.

A Pilot. सूंहों.

Pilotage. सूंहांई, सूंहप.

A Pimp. भडुओ, धूतो, विचकुटो, भकुओ, भाडो, भाड्यो.

The wages of a Pimp. भाडि.

Pimping (*subs.*). भडुवाई, धूताई.

A Pimple on the face. मोहोडो.

Pimples. बुडिबुडि.

A Pin. कंड़ो, कोको. *See* Peg.

The Pin at the end of a yoke. ड़ोरिणो.

A pair of Pincers. अंबूरु, चूथ.

A Pinch. चुहुंडी, चुहुंड़िडो, चमोटो; the quantity taken in a Pinch, चपुटी.

To Pinch. चुहुंडो, *&c.* पाइणु.

To Pine. ग़रणु, सुसणु, पघिरणु.

A Pine-apple. अनानासु.

Pine-wood. दियारु.

A Pinion. खंभ्डाटो. *See* A Wing.

To Pinion. पछोड़की-चोखंभो बंधणु.

Pink (*color*). गुलाबी, गिभाजो.

A Pinnacle (*spiral ornament*). नील, कलिसु. *See* Peak.

Pious. धर्मी, दोन्दारु, दीनो, संतु, धर्मात्मा, धर्मिष्ठु; or Piously, दीनाइतो, धर्माइतो.

A Pipe (*tube*). नडो, नडी. *See* Hooka.

A musical Pipe. शर्नाई, मुर्ली, बैंसुरी, बांसुरी, नडु, तूतारी, तूतूरी.

A Piper. शर्नायो.

To Pique (*anger q. v.*). चेडाइणु.

The sign Pisces. मीनु.

Piss. पेशाबु, मुट्ठु.

To Piss. मुट़णु, सन्हो-पेशाबु-नाडा-छोडु, करणु.

A Pistachio-nut. पिस्तो.

A Pistol. तमाचो, तपाचो.

A Pit. खड़, चुढो. *See* Hole, Quarry.

A Pit dug for a water wheel. पडुहो, पड़हूड़ो, पड़हाड़ो, खुहाड़ो.

A Pit or Pitfall for trapping animals. पडणु.

To Pitch a tent. हणणु, खोडणु, अड़णु. *See* To Throw.

Pitch-dark (*a night*). अघोर उंदाही.

A Pitcher. कूलो. *See* Jar.

Piteous, Piteously. बाझारो, बाझाइतो, डुखाइतो.

Pith. गभु, बचो.

Pitiful, Pitifully (*compassionate, piteous q. v.*). बाझाइतो. *See* Mean.

Pity. रहमु, बाझ, दया, मया, इछा, रहमत, करूणा.

To Pity, take Pity. रहमु, *&c.* आणणु or करणु.

To feel Pity. रहमु, *&c.* अचणु.

Placable. कुंभरो. *See* Gentle.

A Place. जाइ, जगह, जागह, हंधु, थांउ, मागु, थहु, थाणो, आस्थानो.

In the proper Place. हंधाइतो, मागाइतो.

To take Place. थिअणु.

To Place. रखणु, धरणु.

Placid. सांतीको. *See* Gentle.

A Plague. *See* Pestilence, Pest.

To Plague. खपाइणु, अकाइणु. *See* To Tease.

A Plain. पधिरो, पीठो, मैदानु, पटु, पधरू, पिडु, चौगानु.

Plain (*level q. v.*). सैंओं, सूधो.

Plain, Plainly (*distinct*). चिटो, सफा, पधिरो, जाहिरू.

Plain. (*simple, void of ornament*) सादो, (*fare, person, &c.*) रूखो. *See* Artless, Frank.

Plainness (*levelness q. v*). सैंवाई. *See* Distinctness, Simplicity.

A Plaintiff. दांही, मुदई, छेकू, छिकींदडु.

Plaintiff and Defendant. दई मुदई.

To Plait or Plat. वटणु, गुंधणु, गुतणु.

A Plait in clothes. चुणु.

To Plait clothes. चुणणु.

Plaited hair. मनहडो, मींढो, मींढो-

A Plan. ढंढ, ठाहु, तद्बीज. *See* Contrivance, Design.

To Plan. ठाहणु, कढणु, रचणु.

A Plan (*sketch, plot*). चादर.

A Plane. रंदो ; (*kinds for moulding*). पेशिरो, माहीचो, झरीरंदो, दराजो, तब्‌ली रंदो.

To Plane. रंदो हणणु.

A Planet. ग्रहु, गिरहु.

A Plank. तख़्तो, फरहो.

Ceiled or floored with Planks. तख्तापोशु.

A Plant (*sprouting up*). सलो, अंगूरू.

A small Plant or shrub. बूटो.

A Plant taken up for transplanting. चकी.

To Plant. हणणु, विहारणु, लगाइणु, रूंबणु, विहरणु. *See* Transplant, Fix.

The Plantain tree. केविडो.

The Plantain fruit. केविडे, जी फरी.

The seed of the Plantain or fleawort. इस्पंगरू.

Plaster for building. (*of mud*) गारो, (*of lime*) गचु.

Plaster (*salve*). मलमु.

To Plaster. लिंबणु, लेपो, *&c.* डिअणु, लेपणु पाइणु. *See* To Besmear.

Plastering. (*with mud*) कहगील, (*with mortar*) गच्कारी.

To Plat. वटणु. *See* To Plait.

A Plate, Platter. रिकेबी, थालो, थारी, ठांठि, (*of leaves*) पतलि. *See* Dish.

A thin Plate of metal. चादर, पडिछु.

To Plate. मुलिमो करणु.

Plated. मुलिमी.

A Platform (*raised, of earth*). थ-लो, थडी.

Plating. मुलिमी.

Plausible. मथों मिठॊ, मुहों मिठॊ.

Play. रांदि, खेल, खेड़, बाजी.

To Play. रांदि, &c. करणु-रहणु-कुड़णु, खेलणु, खेड़णु.

A Play (*comedy*). नाटकु.

To Play (*on an instrument*). वज़ाइणु.

A good Player. खेड़ारी, रांदीकड़ु.

Playful, Playsome. खुशीजिभॾो, रौंशाइतो, रौंशाई. *See* Merry.

Playfulness. खिलखुशी, तमाशो, रंगु, रौंशो.

A Plaything. रांदीको, घोॾोपटहलो.

Pleasant, Pleasantly. सुहाइंदो. *See* Merry.

Pleasantry. खिलखुशी. *See* Merriment, Playfulness.

To Please (*give pleasure*). रीझाइणु, तुसाइणु, खुशि, &c. करणु सरदाइणु.

To Please, or suit, (*with object as nom.*). वणणु, सुहाइणु, सेबाइणु, भाइ पवणु, रुचणु, आखुरणु, आडडणु, उज़हणु.

To Please or satisfy, (*a wayward child, &c.*). पर्भाइणु, पर्चाइणु.

Please God. खुदा करे.

Pleased. खुशि, सरहो, निहालु, राजी.

To be Pleased. खुशि थिभणु, रीझणु, सरहिजणु, तुसणु.

Pleasing (*adj.*). सुहाइंदो, वसजिहडो. *See* Amiable.

Pleasure (*delight q. v.*). खुशी, रीझ, जौंकु, जशनु, ऐशु, बिलासु, खुश्दिली.

Pleasure (*will*). मर्जी, खुशी, पहति, रजा.

A Pledge. जामिनु. *See* Bail, Promise, Pawn.

The Pleiades. कत्यूं.

Plentiful. घणो, झझो, जालारो, जाम, मुक्तो, अकीचारु, मड़, जाल, जाग, अमूंगिडो, बहूं. *See* Abundant.

Plenty. झझाई, घणि, घणाई, वाधि.

Pliable, Pliant. कुंभरो, मुडिणो, (*in disposition easily led*) परमतिड्यो.

To Plod along. हज़ी-खणी टोरणु.

To Plot. ढ़ोलु &c. बंधणु. *See* Contrivance.

A Plough. हरु.

A drill Plough. हरी; the tube in it through which the grain falls, नाडी.

The body and tail of a Plough. हरोथो.

The handle of a Plough. मुठी.

The front pole of a Plough. हर्ख, हल.

The cord that fastens the yoke to the Plough. नाडो.

To Plough. खेडणु; to Plough over a second time, बेलणु.

A Plough bullock. हारी-हरवहू ढ़ांढु.

Ploughing (*subs.*). खेड; a second ploughing, बेल.

A Ploughman. हारी.

A Plough share. फारु, (*temporary, of wood*) घोत्रो.

That part of a Plough to which the share is fixed. चूनी.

To Pluck, or snatch. खसणु, झपोछिको-झटु-पाइणु.

To Pluck up, or out. पटणु, खोहणु.

To Pluck (*a flower, &c.*). छिनणु, टोडणु, पटणु.

A Pluck. छिको, छिक.

A Plug. डटो, बुंजो.

To Plug. डटणु.
A damascene Plum. अलूबुखारो.
Plumage. खंभ *plu.* पर *plu.* *See* Feather.
To Plumb (*sound*). तांघणु.
A Plume. तुरो, कलंगी.
A Plummet (*mason's*). शाल, शाहलु.
Plump (*adj.*). मतारो, थटो. *See* Fat.
Plumply. साफु, मफा.
Plumpness. मताराई, थटाई.
Plunder. फुरि, लुटि, फुर्दी.
To Plunder. फुरणु, लुटणु.
A Plunderer. फोरू.
To Plunge (*act.*). घेडणु, टुब्राइणु.
To Plunge (*neu.*). घिडणु, टुब्रो ड्रिअणु.
Plural. जमा, ब्रहुवचनु.
A Ply. तहु.
A Pocket. खीसो.
A Pockmark. सिंअरो.
Pockmarked. सिंअरनि चुघ्यलु.
A Pod. फरो, फरही.
A Pod of the cotton tree, &c. ड्रेनो, ड्रेड़ो, गोगिडू; after bursting, with the cotton in it, फुटो.
Podded. फर्यांभी.
A Poet. शाइरू, कवी, कवीसरू.
Poetry. शाइरी, कविता.
Poignant. तिखो, ड्राढो.
A Point. चुहुंब, नोक.
The Point of death. अंतिकालु, सकिरात.
A Point of the compass. ड्रिसा, ड्रिसि.
To Point (*sharpen*). चुहुंब घडणु.
To Point out. ड्रसणु, ड्रेखारणु, निर्वारू करणु, लखाइणु.
Pointed. चुहुंबिरू, चुहुंबारो.
Poison. विहु *f.* विखु *f.* जहरू.
To Poison. विहु *&c.* ड्रिअणु.
Poisonous. विहुवारो, जहरी, विखिरू, विहिरू.
To Poise. सँभों बिहारणु.
A Poke (*thrust*). चुंग, चोंक.
To Poke (*thrust*). चोंकणु, चुंगणु.
A Poker, one who Pokes. चोंकिरू.
A Pole. छडू, लडू; for carrying a burden on, &c. लठि.
A Pole with a crook to pull down fruit. अंगुडो.
A boat Pole. वंझु.
A tent Pole. सुखुं, चोब.
One Poled (*a tent*). यकूचोबो.
Two Poled (*a tent*). ब्रिसुखों;
A Police office. चबूतिड़ो.
The chief officer of Police in a town. कोट्वालु, कोटारू.
Polish. ओजरू. *See* Gloss, Brightness.
To Polish. मलणु, माञणु, उजारणु, ओजारणु. *See* To Brighten.
A Polisher of jewels. वोंझरू.
Polite, Politely. भावभर्यो, भावाइतो.
Politeness. भाउ, आउ, आउभाउ.
A Poll tax. मथगी, पेश्कशी.
To Pollute. पलीतु-नापाकु-असुधि-अपविटु करणु. *See* To Defile, Dirty.
Pollution. नापाकी, अपविटाई.
A Poltroon. कांइरू. *See* Coward.
A Pomegranate. ड्राडू.
The rind of a Pomegranate. छोड़ो, छिलु *f.*
The Pommel of a saddle. कोचु, भिरिणो. *See* Knob.
Pomp. ठठु, ठाहु, ठासु, तूमानु, तूलानु, शानु.
Pompous. ठासो, तूमानी, ठाठी.

A Pond. डुबो, ढोरो, तलाउ, कुंभु, छन, पलु, पल्हरू, चहब्रिचो.

To Ponder. ग़णणु, विचारणु, पढ़णु, रिथणु, कथणु, तकणु, जाचणु, हंड़ाइणु, चितवणु, ध्यांइणु.

A Pony. टुड़ो, टटूं, याबू.

Pooh. हुं.

A Pool. डुब्रो. *See* Pond.

The Poop of a vessel. पाछलि, पाछेलि.

Poor. गरीबु, कंगालु, फकोरू, मिस्कोनु, सुत्रो, ठल्हो, सखिणो, विल्हो, ड़ालड़ो, ड़ोनु, दीनु.

The Poor. गरीबावादि.

Of a Poor man. गरीबाणो, गारीबो.

A Pop. फह.

A Poppy. पुस्त.

The Poppy head, or capsule. पोस्तु, पुस्त.

Poppy seeds. खस्खसि, कणि.

Population (*inhabitants*). माण्हूं, माड़्हूं.

Populous. आबादु, वस्यो.

A Porch. ड़ेढी, ड़ेउढी.

A Porcupine. सेड़ह ; male, सेड़्हो.

Pork. सुभर जो मासु.

Porous. सिमिणो.

A Porpoise. बुल्हणि, ब्रिरू.

A Port (*harbour*). बंदरू.

Portable. खड़िणो.

To Portend. ज़ाणाइणु, ड़ेखारणु, लखाइणु.

A Portent (*ill omen*). अपसुगिणु, बदि सोंणु.

A Porter (*at a gate*). ड़ेढीवानु, दर्वानु.

A Porter for bearing burdens. भर्यतु, हमालु. *See* Labourer.

Porterage. खणाणी, मजूरी.

A Portion. भाड़ो, पतो, हिसो, तकु, वखिरो, वंड़. *See* Share.

Portly. मयो, मतारो. *See* Stout.

A Portrait. सूरत, मूरति, तस्वीर.

To Pose. मुँझाइणु.

Position (*situation q. v.*). जाइ. *See* Manner, Condition.

Positive (*certain q. v.*). पको, खुलो, तक्रारू.

Positively. जाई, जरूरू, अवसि, निहिचे. *See* Certainly.

To Possess. रखणु, हुअणु with जो, खे, वटि, governing the possessor.

To be Possessed with a devil. भर्जणु.

Possession. मालिकी, हथु.

A Possessor. धणी. *See* Owner.

Possible. थिअणो.

To be Possible. थी सघणु.

A Post of wood. थंभु, थूणो, मुनो, बुंदु. *See* Situation.

A military Post. चौंकी.

The letter Post. टपाल.

Postage. चिठ्याणो.

A Post bag. थेलो.

Posterior. पोयो.

Posterity. ओलाधु.

A Postern. दरी.

To Postpone. रखणु.

Posture of body. विहणु, विहणो, आसणु.

A Pot (*varieties for cooking*). देगि, देगिड़ो, चरू, ट्रामिड़ो, कुनो, हड़ी, तापेलो, खुमिरो, तसिलो, तासिरो. *See* Vessel.

A small Pot or jar. कुपिड़ो, टिभो, छल.

The round body of a Pot. ढढरू.

Potash. खारू.

A sweet Potato. लाहोरी गजर.
Pot bellied. ढिढिरू, भभिरू, पेटिरू, चढरि.
A Pot-belly. भभु, भिभु, टुटी, ढिढु, चढरि.
Potency. *See* Strength.
Potent. पुज़िण्यातु, सग़तो. *See* Powerful.
A Potion. सुनो.
A Pot-sherd. ठिकरू, ठिकिरी; small pieces, ठिकिराठो.
A Potter. कुंभारू, कुंभरू.
Of a Potter. कुंभार्को, कुंभराणो.
Potter's earth. चीकी मिटी, फोडु, सिक.
A Potter's kiln. निहाँई.
A Potter's wheel. चकु.
A Pouch (*for cartridges, &c.*). किस्बत.
Poverty. गरीबाई, गरीबो, कंगालाई, अणहूं, दिउल्हाई, विल्हाई, सखिणाई, ड़ालड़ि.
A Poultice. लुपिडो.
Poultry. कुकिड *plu.*
One who rears Poultry. कोंकिडी.
A Pounce. चंबो, झटु, झपो.
To Pounce. ओलारी-चंबो *&c.* पाइणु.
To Pound. कुटणु, गुड़णु, चिथणु, चिल्हणु.
To Pound rice and other grains in cleaning them. छड़्हणु.
A Pound (*for cattle*). ढक.
To Pound (*cattle*). ढकणु.
To Pour (*act.*). विझणु, पाइणु, ओतणु.
To Pour out. हारणु, ओतणु, ढारणु.
Pouring (*subs.*). ओत.
To Pout the lips. चप कढणु *or* डूला करणु.

A Powder (*any thing pulverized*). बूरो, चूरो, मेदो.
A Powder (*medicine so formed*). फकी, बुको.
Powder (*gunpowder*). दारू, बारूदु, बारूतु.
A Powder-horn. हंबाचो; for priming powder, रंजक.
A Powder-manufacture. खिडाई.
Power. सघ, वसु, ब्रलु, पहुच, पुज़ंदो, पुज़िण्याती, सग़ति, कुंभत, कुदिरत, वितु, मजाल, वसिभत, तोफीक, विचु, वजूद. *See* Strength.
In one's Power. हथवसीको, वसि, वसाइतो, हथि, हथिरादो.
Powerful. सघारो, सघाइतो, पुज़िण्यातु, पुज़ंदिअवारो, पहुचवानु, जोराइतो, सग़तो, ब्रलो, वसाइतो.
Of a Powerful person, or one in power. सग़राणो, सग़ताणो.
Powerless. बेसघो, बेज़ोरो, बेवसि, बेवसो. *See* Weak.
Powerlessness. बेवसी, बेसग़ताई-ग़तो. *See* Helplessness.
The Pox (*venereal*). बादफिरंगु, टाको.
The small Pox. सीतला, माई, माता. *See* Smallpox.
Practice (*habit q. v.*). हेर, आदत.
Practice (*custom q. v.*). चालि, रीति, दस्तूरू, मुहाविरो.
Practice (*experience, use*). इस्तमाली, अभ्यासु.
To Practise oneself in any thing. हेरणु.
Praise. सारह, वखाण, तारीफ, साख, सलाह, उस्तुति.
To Praise. साराहणु, वखाणणु, सलाहणु, वधाइणु.
Praiseworthy. वखाणजिहडो, जसाइतो.

A Prance. छालु.
To Prance. छाल, डि़भणु or मारणु.
Prate (*much and idle talk*). फस्तों. *See* Chattering.
To Prate, Prattle. बकणु, बड्बडाइणु, झकणु. *See* To Chatter.
A Prater. बकवादी, पणग़ाल्हाभो, बड्बड्यो, वातिरू. *See* Chatterer.
A Prawn. गांगटु, झकमु.
To Pray, say Prayers. निमाज करणु, जपणु.
A Prayer. दुआ, निमाज.
Precarious (*uncertain q. v.*). बेकाथो.
Precaution. अगाणी, अगविचारू.
To Precede. अगे वञणु.
Preceding (*adj.*). अग्यों, महँद्यों, अगूणिको, अगूणो, महँदूणो, महँदूणिको.
A Precept. नसिअत, उपदेसु, हुकुमु
A Preceptor. उस्तादु, वाझो, आखुंदु, गुरू. *See* Teacher.
Precious. कोमती, अमुलु.
Precipitation. हूडाई, हबॆरि. *See* Haste.
Precise, Precisely. ठीकु, सही. *See* Exact.
To Predict. अगमें चवणु.
A Prediction. अगकथी, कलामु.
Predominance. सर्साई, सर्सी, वाधि.
Predominant. सर्सु, वाधू.
A Preface. देबाचो.
To Prefer (*regard more*). चडो-वधीक-सर्सु भांइणु. *See* Exalt.
Preferable. सर्सु, सुहाइंदो, वणंदो.
Pregnancy. दुक्याई, दुकलाई.
Pregnant. दुकी, दुकलि, गर्भिणो, गौरहारी, गारखुडो, ग़भिणि, पेटसां, ब्रिनि जिअनि सां.
To be Pregnant. दुकिजणु.
Pregnant for the first time (*a woman*). पन्झाति, पेह्याति.
A Prelude to music. आलाप.
A Premium (*gift q. v.*). इनामु.
The Premium on a bill of exchange. हुंड्याणो.
Preparation. तयारी, सांबाहो, सायो.
To Prepare (*neu.*). संबहणु, संभिरणु, तयारी करणु. *See* To Gird the loins.
To Prepare (*act.*). तयारू करणु, ठाहणु, जोडणु, साहणु.
Prepared. तयारू, रासि.
To be Prepared. तयारू, *&c.* थिअणु, ठहणु, जुडणु.
To Preponderate. वधीक, *&c.* थिअणु. *See* More.
The Prepuce. खोलो.
A medical Prescription. नुस्खो.
Presence. हाजुरी.
In Presence of. रूबरू, मांहो, आडो.
Present (*adj.*). हाजुरू.
Of the Present. हाणोको.
The Present tense. हालु, वर्तमानु.
A Present. बक्शीस, इनामु, डानु, दानु; or offering of fruit, &c. डोइणो. *See* Offering.
To Present (*give*). डि़अणु. *See* To Shew.
A Presentiment. ज़ागु, भास, भासु, बास.
Presently (*now q. v.*). हाणे, (*shortly*) थोरिडे में, पोअ भरो. *See* Soon.
Preservation. रख्या, रख, सांढ, सांभ, जतनु, बचाउ. *See* Protection.
A Preserve (*of fruit*). मुर्बो.
To Preserve. रखणु, रख्या *&c.* करणु, बचाइणु, तारणु. *See* To take Care of.

To be Preserved. बचणु, तरणु.

A Preserver. रछकु, बचाइंदडु, तारणहारू, छुटाऊ, बचाइणहारू, रखणहारू.

A Press (*for pressing*). शिकंजो. *See* Oilpress, Sugarcane press.

A President. पर्यो मुसु. *See* Principal, Chief.

To Press (*compress*). दबणु, पीडणु, निपूडणु.

To Press (*into service*). बेगरि करणु.

To Press down (*in filling any thing*). थन्हणु, सथणु, सिथणु.

A Pressed workman. बेगारी, छेडो; a body of such, छेड.

Pressing (*for labor*). बेगरि.

Pressing (*urgent*). जरूरी.

Pressure. दब.

Presumption. गुस्ताकी, मचुलाई, ढ़िठाई.

Presumptuous. गुस्ताकु, मचुलो.

A Pretence. मिंहु, बहानो.

A Pretence, or sham (*as of being hurt*). गेगु, छहर, तीतालु, सांगु, मकरू.

To Pretend. बहानो &c, करणु, मिंहाइणु. *See* To Sham.

A Pretender. बहानाई, सांगी. *See* a Shammer.

Pretension (*claim q. v.*). दावा.

Pretext. मिंहु. *See* Pretence.

Prettiness. सुंहुणाईं, पोशीदाई. *See* Beauty, Niceness.

Pretty (*adj.*). सुंहुणो. *See* Beautiful, Nice.

Pretty (*adv.*) is expressed by putting the word with which it is used in its diminutive form, as चङो; good, चङेरो, चङेरिडो, Pretty good.

To Prevail (*be in force*). हलणु.

To Prevail, or Prevail over. जीतणु, गालिबु थिअणु. *See* Predominant.

To Prevail upon (*induce*). कुच्कुचि करे कराइणु. *See* To Persuade.

Prevalence. घणाई, वधीकाई. *See* Predominance.

To Prevent. झलणु, टारणु, रोकणु. *See* To Stop.

Prevention. झल, रोक.

Previous. अग्यों, मढ़ँदों. *See* Preceding, Before.

Prey (*seized for food*). शिकारू. *See* Plunder.

Price. मुल्हु, कीमत, गथुं, अघु. *See* Market price.

The Price of labour, or work. पोर्हो, कमिअत, मिह्नताणो, मिह्नत, मजूरी.

At or for a Price, Priced. मुल्हाइतो.

To Prick. टुंबणु, चुभाइणु, चूंगणु, चोकणु.

A Prick (*puncture*). चूंग, चोक.

The Pricker of a gun. सूजनु.

Pricking (*subs.*). चुभिचुभि, टुंबिटुंबि.

A Prickle. कंड़िडो, कंडो.

Prickly. कंड्यारो, कंड़िरू. *See* Thorny.

A postute from Prickly heat. आरांई; the plural of this, आरांयूं, is the name for the eruption.

Pride. हठु, मग्रूरी, आकडि, अहंकारु, हठीलाई, अंधु, मदु, ओजु, भानु, अभिमानु.

A Priest (*Musulman*). मुलो.

A family Priest (*Hindoo*). प्रोहितु.

Primary. पेह्रों, अवलु. *See* First, Original.

To Prime. लबणु.

At Prime cost. मूरिग़ो. *See* First, Original.

A Prime minister. वज़ीरु, मुख्त्यारु.

Priming power. लबु.

To burn Priming. लबु चटणु-खणणु.

Primitive. मुंढाइतो, असुलाइतो, असुलिओं. *See* Original.

A Prince. शहजादो, साहिब्ज़ादो.

Princely. बाद्शाहो, राजाणो.

A Princess. शहज़ादी, शाहिब्ज़ादी.

Principal (*adj.*). वड़ो, मुंढु, सिरे, मुखि.

A Principal person. पर्यो मुसुं, चड़ो-मुसुं, धुडो. *See* Chief.

Principal (*capital sum*). मूरु, मूड़ो, रासि.

Principally. घणो.

A Principle (*original cause*). असुलु, मुंढु. *See* Element, Motive, Rule.

A Print (*mark q. v.*). छाप, छापो.

To Print. छापणु, छुरणु, ठपणु.

Printing (*on cloth*). छुर्णी.

Prior (*adj.*). अग़्यों, अग़ूणो, महँद्यों. *See* Preceding.

A Prison. बंदीखानो, कैद्खानो.

A Prisoner. बंदी, कैदी, बंदीवानु.

Pristine. मुंढाइतो. *See* Original.

Privacy. हेकलाई, निवेकिलाई, एकांति.

Private, Privately (*solitary*). खुलासो, निवेकिलो. *See* Personal.

A Privilege. हकु. *See* Immunity.

Privity. सोझ. *See* Knowledge.

Privy (*having knowledge of*). सोझू, सहो, वाकुफ़ु. *See* Acquainted, Secret.

A Privy. पुई, सिँहत्खानो, जाइजरूरु.

A Prize. *See* Spoil, Reward.

A Probability. ड़ौलु, वझु, आकारु.

To think it Probable. भांइणु.

Probity. नेकी, पनि. *See* Honesty.

A Proboscis. सूंढि.

A Procedure. हलति, गति, कसु.

To Proceed (*move on*). हलणु, वञणु.

To Proceed (*issue or spring from*). निकिरणु.

The Proceeds. उपति, आवति.

The going round of a Procession. सर्गसि.

To Proclaim. ज़ाणाइणु, हुलाइणु, पधिरो, करणु, पड्हो घुमाइणु.

A Proclamation. (*written*) इश्तिहारु, (*cried out*) पड्हो, होको.

To Procrastinate. रखणु, सीडाइणु.

Procrastination. रखुरखां, अज़ुसुभाँ. *See* Evasion.

To Procreate. उपज़ाइणु, उपाइणु.

Procurable. लभिणो.

To Procure. लहणु. *See* To Obtain.

To be Procured. लभणु, मिळणु. *See* To be Obtained.

A Procuress. धूती, धुतिणि, भड़ुई.

Prodigal. लोटू, लुटाऊ, उड़ाऊ.

Prodigality. लुटि.

Prodigious. *See* Wonderful, Vast.

A Prodigy. अजबु, आफ़ात, धुरि.

Produce, Production. उपति, उपाजु, पैदाश, हासुलाति.

To Produce (*yield*). उपाइणु, करणु, ड़िअणु. *See* To Bring forth.

Produced. पैदा.

To be Produced. उपज़णु, थिअणु.

Productive. उपतिवारो, नफाइतो, उपाऊ, नफाऊ. *See* Profitable.

Profane, To Profane. *See* Impious. To Pollute.

To Profess. मुहों-मथों चवणु.

A Profession. (*trade q. v.*). क्रिति.

Proficiency. भडाई, काबिलो.

Proficient. भडु, काबिलु.

Profit. खट्यो, खट, खटी, लाहो, नफो, फाइदो, सूदु, लाभु, वाधो, वाधारी, प्रापति, फैजु.

To Profit. खटणु. *See* To Gain.

Profit and Loss. उधीखुटी.

Profitable, Profitably. नफाइतो, लाहाइतो, लाभाइतो, सफलु, सजायो, सच्यार्थो, खट्याइतो, नफाऊ, खटाऊ. *See* Useful, Beneficial.

Profitless. बेसूदो, बेफाइदो, बेफैजो. *See* Fruitless.

Profligacy. लंड़ाई, लांगछोटाई.

Profligate. लंड़ो, लांगछोटो, लंगोताजो, लांबडु.

Profound. ऊन्हो, ग़रो, गंभीरु.

Profoundness, Profundity. ऊन्हाई, ग़राई.

Profuse. उड़ाऊ. *See* Extravagant.

Progeny. ओलाधु. *See* Offspring.

Progress. हलिणी.

To Progress. वधणु, हलणु.

To Prohibit. मनिह करणु, झलणु. *See* To Forbid.

A Prohibition. मनिह, झल.

A Project. ठाहु, ढँउं. *See* Contrivance.

To Project (*contrive*). ढँउं, *&c.* कढणु or ठाहणु.

To Project (*jut out*). निकिरणु.

The Prolapsed gut from Prolapsus ani. पछो.

Prolific. विआटू. *See* Productive.

Prolix, (*long, tedious q. v.*). तूलांओं, लांढ, घणअखरो.

Prolixity. तूलु, कढ, काढ, काढारो, वधाउ, काढो, फैलाउ, मंड़ाणु, तूलानु.

To Prolong. ड्रिघेडणु.

A Promise. बोलु, वचनु, जाइजु, वाइदो, करारु, कौलु, सुखुनु, पिणु.

To Promise. जाइजु, *&c.* करणु, बोलणु.

Promising (*hopeful*). थिअणवारो.

A Promissory note. अंगुडो, कबजु.

To Promote. वधाइणु. *See* To Exalt.

Promotion (*exaltation*). सर्फिराजी.

Prompt, Promptly. जल्दु. *See* Quick.

To Prompt. कन में चवणु.

To Promulgate. हुलाइणु. *See* To Publish.

Prone (*with face downwards*). मुँह भर, ऊंधो.

To Pronounce. चवणु.

Proof (*evidence*). शाहिदी, पिर्माणु. *See* Trial.

To Prop. पुस्तो, *&c.* ड्रिअणु.

A Prop. टेक, पुस्तो, आधर, आधारु, आसिरो.

A Propensity. खफ्तु, लाग़. *See* Inclination.

Proper, Properly. लाइकु, मुनासिबु, दुरुस्तु, जुग़ाइतो, जोगु, वडाइतो, ठाहूको, सुबतो, (*used only adverbially*) सुबतडि, सँयाँ.

At the Proper time. वेलाइतो, महलाइतो, वखताइतो.

In the Proper place. हंधाइतो, माग़ाइतो.

Property (*quality*). खस्लत, गुणु, धर्मु. *See* Nature.

Property (*goods q. v.*). मिल्क, मालु, धनु, सामानु, रासि, माल्यात, भिटाओ, किमासु.

A Prophecy. कलामु, सिधवाकु.

To Prophesy. अगु में चवणु.

A Prophet. पैगंबरू, नबी, रसूलु, सिधु.
To Propitiate. रीझाइणु, राजी करणु.
Propitious (*auspicious*). सगोरो, सभागो, सणाओ, सणोलो.
Propitiousness. सगोराई, सभागाई.
In Proportion to. सारू, आहिर.
Proportionably, Proportionally. सरासरो करे, भाङेरो, भाङाइतो, हिसेरो. *See* In Shares.
To Propose. चवणु.
A Proprietor. धणी, मालिकु.
Propriety (*fitness*). लाइकी, वडु, जोगिता.
With Propriety, or one so acting. सुवाटो.
Prose. नसर, वार्ता.
A Prosecutor. मुदई.
A Prospect (*place affording such*). निजारो. *See* Hope, View.
To Prosper, be Prosperous. साओ, &c. थिअणु, वधणु, विझणु.
Prosperity. बर्कत, आबादानी, सावाई, सरहाई, सुभु, चढ़हिती, विर्धी.
Prosperous. साओ, हयों, सरहो, सुरहो.
A Prostitute. कस्ब्याणी, खोन्निली, रंगोली, कुर्‍याणी.
Prostitution. कसबु, हरामु.
The hire of Prostitution. जहाणो, (*eaten by another*) भाङि; one who lives on such, भाडी, भाड्यो.
To Prostrate. केराइणु. *See* To Throw down.
To fall Prostrate. डुियो थी पवणु.
Prostration (*in adoration*). सिज्दो, ढंडोति.
To Protect. रख्या, &c. करणु, बचाइणु, तारणु.
Protection. रख, रख्या, रछा, रिछा, बचाउ, आसिरो, अझो, पनाह, ओट, अड, छांव, वाहर, वाह, हिमाइत, वसीलो, सहाइ.
Protector. राखो, रछकु, रख्यकु, बचाइंदडु, पालकु, वसीलो, वाहरू.
Protectorless. बेवारिसु, निधण्को, बेवाहु-हो-हर-हुरू, गैबाणो.
To Protract. डिघेरणु, वधाइणु.
To Protrude (*act.*). ब्राहरि कढणु, (*neu.*) ब्राहरि निकिरणु.
Proud. हठो, मग्रूरू, अहंकारी, अभिमानी; *or* proudly, हठोलो, हठाइतो.
To become Proud. आकिड्जणु, हठ्याइणु, अहंकार्जणु.
To Prove (*establish by proof*). बजाइणु, इस्बातु &c. करणु.
To Prove (*try q. v.*). कसणु, परखणु.
To Prove (*be found eventually*). थिअणु, निकिरणु.
Proved (*established*). इस्बातु, साबितु.
A Proverb. पहाको.
To Provide (*procure*). तयारु-मौजूदु करणु. *See* To Prepare.
Providence (*foresight*). अग्र जी ग्रणती.
Provident. ग्राणू.
A Province. सूबो.
Proving (*establishing by proof*). साबिती, इस्बाती.
Provision (*measures taken*). बिलो. *See* Arrangement.
Provision for a journey. समरू, तोशो.
Provisions (*food q. v.*). खाधो, खाजु, सीधोपाधो.
Undressed Provisions. सीधो.
A Provocation. चेड, छेड.
To Provoke. चेडणु, छेडणु.
The Prow of a ship. मुहुरी.

Prowess. सूरिहाई पहिल्वानी. *See* Bravery.

Proximity. वेझिडाई, वेझाई, ओड़िड़ाई, ओड़ाई.

Prudence. साञाह, साञाह, ग़ण्ती.

Prudent. ग़ाणू, साञाहू; *or* prudently, साञाहितो.

Prudish (*a woman affectedly modest*). मथलज़ी.

To Prune. छांगणु.

To Pry. तकणु.

Pshaw. हुं, छी, छि.

Puberty. बालगी; the season of the first signs of approaching puberty, बोराकी.

Pubescent, one at the age of Puberty. बालगु; at the age when the first signs of its approach appear, बोराकु.

Public. पधिरो, जाहिरू, निशांबरू.

A Publican. कलालु.

Publicity. पधिराई, जाहिरी, पध्रर.

Publicly. दलेबादले, दीनादास्तो.

To Publish. पधिरो, *&c.* करणु, पखेडणु, हुलाइणु.

To be Published, become Public. हुलणु.

A Pucker. घुंजु.

To Pucker. घुंजाइणु.

A Puddle. दुबो.

Pudendum feminæ. चुडु, पीकु, चूति, तीती, गांड़ि, भिगु, भगु, टणो.

Puerile. छोकिराणो.

A Puff. फूक. *See* Blast.

To Puff (*blow with the mouth*). फूखणु. *See* To Pant.

To Puff up (*wares, &c.*). पड़ाइणु.

To be Puffed (*swollen with air*). वाव भर्जणु, फूकिजणु.

To be Puffed up (*as with pride, &c.*). फूंड़िजणु, आभामणु, आफिजणु, बम्जणु, फूकिजणु.

Puffy. फेफो.

Pugnacious. झेडाई. *See* Quarrelsome.

To Puke. ओकणु. *See* To Vomit.

A Pull. छिक, ताण.

To Pull. छिकणु, ताणणु, विचणु.

To Pull (*a flower, &c.*). छिनणु. *See* To Pluck.

To Pull (*or shake*) about. गींदाडणु, धुंधाडणु, धांधोलणु.

To Pull down (*demolish*). डाहणु.

To Pull off (*as clothes*). लाहणु.

To Pull on (*as clothes*). पाइणु. *See* To Put on.

To Pull out. कढणु.

To Pull tight. कसणु, कशणु, साहणु.

To Pull up (*as a bush*). पटणु.

The Pulla-fish. पलो, (*male*) खोरो, (*female*) आन्यारो.

A pair of Pulla fish. हारो.

A Pulla-fisherman. माल्परू; his pot, माटो; pole and net, संभुई, संबुही.

A Pulley. कपी.

Pulling and Pushing. घीचो.

The Pulp of a fruit. ग़रू *f.*

A Pulpit. मुंबरू.

Pulpous, Pulpy. ग़रूदारू.

The Pulse. नब्ज, नाडि, नाडी.

To feel the Pulse. नब्ज, *&c.* ड़िसणु.

Pulse (*grain*). दालि, (*varieties*) मुङ *plu.* चणा *plu.* मटर *plu.* महुरी, मोठ, मांहि, कुल्डी.

Split Pulse. ड़ारि.

Bits and powder among split Pulse. सूड्ही.

The flour or meal of Pulse. बेसणु.

A dish of two or three kinds of Pulse. केवटो.
Pulverable. भुरिणो, भोरू.
To Pulverize. चूरू-मैदो करणु, भोरणु.
To be Pulverized. भुरणु.
Pumice stone. कुरिंडु.
A Pumpion, Pumpkin. कदू.
An iron Punch. सुंबो
Punctual. महल जो पूरो.
Punctually. महलाइतो.
A Puncture. चुपु.
To Puncture, Punctulate. चुपणु.
Pungency. चहराई.
Pungent. चहरो.
To Punish. सजा, &c. ड़िभणु.
Punishable, deserving of Punishment. सजा जिहडो, सजाइतो.
Punishment. सजा, सेखति, डंडु, जुठि.
The Pupil of the eye. तारो. *See* A Scholar.
A Pup. *See* Puppy.
A Puppet. पुतिली.
To set off a Puppet show. पुतिल्यूं विझणु or पाइणु.
A Puppet show-man. पुतिल्युनिवारो.
A Puppy. गुलिरू.
Purblind (*dim sighted*). चुंझो, चूचो.
To Purchase. ग़िन्हणु, मुल्हि वठणु, खरीदणु, विहाइणु, वण्जणु.
Purchased. खरीदी, मुल्हाइतो.
A Purchaser. खरीदारू, ग़िन्हँदडु, ग्राकु.
Purchasing, or the thing Purchased. खरीद.
Pure (*undefiled*). सुठो, पाकु, अछुतो, अछुतु, निर्मलु, लालु सुचि, पवित्रु, जुग़तो. *See* Clear.
Pure (*unadulterated*). निजातु, निजु, निलो, निरो, (*as gold*) तिखो, सचो.
Pureness. *See* Purity.
A Purge, Purgative. जुलाबु.
To Purge (*by stool*). दस्त आणणु or करणु.
To be Purged. पेटु छुडणु, दस्त अचणु or थिभणु.
To Purify. सुठाइणु, सुठो &c. करणु.
Purity. सुठाई, अछुताई, जुग़िति, पाकाई, पवित्राई, निर्मलाई.
Purple. वाड़िणो, वाड़िणाई.
Purport. मत्लबु, भाउ, हार्दउ.
Purpose. दिलि, इरादो. *See* Intention.
Purposely. ज़ाणीवाणी, ज़ाणोवेणी, ज़ाणीबुझी, ड़िसीदाइसी, दीनादास्ती.
To Purr. गुड्कणु, गुर्कणु.
A Purse. थैलो, हम्याणी, डोरी, वासिणी, सग़िडो, गोलक.
Purslane. लूणक; its seed, कुल्फो.
To Pursue (*follow*). पुठ्यों-पुठ्यों लग़णु.
A Pursuer. पुअलगु.
Pursuit. पुअलग़ो.
Pus. पूंइ, रेगु.
A Push. धिको, थेल्हो.
To Push. थेल्हणु, धिकणु.
To Push in. विहारणु.
Pusillanimity. कांइराई, कुचिराणी. *See* Cowardice.
Pusillanimous, (*action*). कांइराणो, गांडुआणों, नामर्दाणो.
A Pustule. दाणो.
To Put (*lay*). रखणु, धरणु.
To Put in. विझणु, पाइणु.
To Put in mind. यादि ड़िभणु or ड़िआरणु.
To Put off (*postpone*). रखणु,

(*evade q. v.*) रखुरखां करणु, नटाइणु.
To Put on (*as clothes*). पाइणु, पहरणु, करणु, ढकणु, ओढणु.
To Put out (*a light*). विसांइणु, उझांइणु. *See* To Extinguish, Expel, Repress, Stretch out.
To Put to rights. ठाहणु, सँवारणु.
Putting off (*evading*). गोथ्नाथ, गोही, टालो, नटाउ.
Putrid. क्रिनो.
Putridness. क्रिनाई.
A Puzzle. गोरखधंधो. *See* Enigma.
To Puzzle. मुँझाइणु.
A Pyre (*funeral pile*). चिख्या.

Q

A Quadrangle. चौंकु.
Quadrangular. चौकुंड़ो, चौंकुंड्यारो.
A Quadruped. चौपिरो; quadrupeds, चौपाई.
Quadruple (*adj.*). चऊंणो.
The Quadruple. चऊंणि.
To Quadruple. चऊंणाइणु.
Quadruplication. चऊंणाई.
A Quag-mire. गपिणि, गरणि, धुब्रणि.
A Quail. बुडेरो, (*fem.*) हूंगरि.
To Quake. ड़कणु, कंबणु. *See* To Tremble.
A Qualification. गुणु, फनु.
To be Qualified. किडणु.
To Qualify (*make fit*). लाइकु करणु, केडणु, केडाइणु.
Quality. गुणु, सुभाउ. *See* Property, Disposition, Kind.
Qualmish. *See* Squeamish.
Quantity. अंदाजु, पिर्माणु.
A Quarrel, Quarreling. करहि, किल्फिटि, किट्किटि, गहपिह, खर्पति, झेडो, झगिडो, बखेडो, रगिडो, किलोसु, खललु, चटाभेटो, फितूरू, कुरसो. *See* Fight, Squabble.
To Quarrel. विड्हणु, झगिडणु.
A Quarreler, Quarrelsome. झेडाई, झेडाकु, झगिडाई, वेड्डू, खलली, बखेडाई, रगिडाई, जंगी, फितूरो, फिन्नाई. *See* Squabbler.
To Quarry. टुकणु, टाकणु.
A Quarry. खाणि.
The Quartan ague. ट्रिभडु.
A Quarter. चोथाई, चोथि, चोथो.
The Quarter of a rupee. पाइलो, पारूपो, पाइणि; of a guj, पाइडो; of a seer, पाउ.
Less by a Quarter. (*with a unit*) मुनो, (*with two, three, &c.*) पँउंणा.
With a Quarter more. सवा.
One and a Quarter (*adj.*). सवाऊंणो, सवायो.
Any whole sum with a Quarter added. सवाऊंणि, सवाई.
Three Quarters (*per cent*). ट्रिंपाण्यो.
Quarter (*in war*). जिअदानु.
A Quarter (*in a town*). पाडो, वेड्हो, महलो.
To Quash. दन्ने छड़णु.
A Quay. दम्दमो.
A Queen. राणी, पटराणी, बादशाहिणि.
Queer. अजबु. *See* Strange.
To Quell. टारणु, विसांइणु. *See* To Subdue.
To Quench (*thirst*). लाहणु. *See* To Extinguish.
Querulous. कुकुंयों, रूगिणो, कुंकिणो, विकिविक्यो.
Querulousness. कुकुंरि, विकिविकि.

Quest. गोल. *See* Search.

A Question, Questioning. सुआलु, पुछा.. *See* Inquiry.

Questionable. शको, शकाइतो, शकांभों.

Quick, Quickly. सिघो, तिखो, वहँदिडो-डे, वहँदो-दे, सुनतु, जल्दु, तुर्तु, चट्पटि, ठहफह, तहतलबि, झट्पटि. *See* Smart.

To Quicken (*make alive*). जिआरणु.

Quickness. सिघाई, सेघु, तिख, तिखाई, फुड़्ती, जल्दी, छडछोति, छूटि.

Quicksand. लस.

A Quickset. चको.

Quicksilver. पारो.

Quiet (*subs.*). माठि, ठहर, सांति, थांहर, थँहर.

Quiet (*adj.*). माठोणो, सांतीको, सांति.

To Quiet. माठि, *&c.* कराइणु.

To become Quiet. ठहरणु, थमणु.

Quietness. माठोणाई, सांतीकाई. *See* Quiet, Stillness.

Quietly. आराम सां, धीरे, आरास्तो-स्ते, होरे, होर्यं, हरेंहरें.

A Quill. खंभु, परु; a porcupine's Quill, सुभो, कानो.

A Quilt (*varieties*). सवडि, रलो, रजाई, गोदिडी, गूदडु

To Quilt. दोग़णु.

Fine Quilting. तेब्चो.

Quince-seed. बेहोदाणो.

The Quintan ague. चोथडु.

Quintuple. पंजूंणो.

The Quintuple. पंजूंणि

A Quire of paper. दस्तो.

To Quit (*abandon q. v.*). छड्णु.

Quite. तमामु, बिल्कुलु. *See* Entirely, Wholly.

To be Quits. पडणु, अडणुपडणु.

A Quiver (*for arrows*). वथो.

To Quiver. ड्कणु, कंबणु, थड्कणु. *See* Shiver, Tremble.

A Quotidian fever. हिकमहलो तपु.

R

A Rabbit. सहो, सह्युडु.

A Rabble. मेडाको. *See* Crowd.

Rabid (*as a mad dog*). छितो, छिड्यो. *See* Mad.

A Race (*family q. v.*). आकहि, ओलाधु, वंसु *f.* *See* Lineage, Tribe.

A Race (*run*). डुक, डोक, डुडु.

To Rack the brains. मथो हणणु.

A Racket (*noise q. v.*). गोगाड.

Radiance. चिम्को, जुल्वो, जोति. *See* Lustre.

Radiant. चिम्किणो. *See* Bright.

Radically. मुंढाई, मुंढोंई, मूराई, मूरोंई.

A Radish. मूरो.

A Raft. (*of floating wood*) टलो, (*made with pots*) तरि, (*of reeds &c.*) तुरहो.

A Rafter. पटि, पजरु, कायो.

A Rag. अगिडो, थिगिडो, चिडट, चीडट.

In Rags. लोडुंलीडुं.

Rage. कहरु, कोपु. *See* Anger.

A Railing. कटहडो, कंधी.

Raillery. घबो, ठठोलो, चर्चो, ठशो.

Raiment. कपिडा *plu.* See Clothes.

Rain. मींहु, बर्साति, वस.

Drizzling Rain. फुहार.

A fall of Rain. ओठि.

Want or deficiency of Rain. अणोठि, अवसरु.

Signs of Rain. ढोड.

To Rain. वसणु, मींहु पवणु.

A Rainbow. इंडुल्ठि.

It has Rained. उठो आहे.

Rainy, of Rain. मींहांओ, बसांतो.

Rainy weather. मींहोगो, झुडोफुडो.

The Rains, Rainy season. साविणो, बसांति.

To Raise. (*lift*) खणणु, चाड्णु, (*elevate*) चाड्हणु, मथे करणु. *See* To Levy.

To Raise in price. चाड्हणु.

To Raise the voice. ड़ाढ्यां–वड़े सड़ि गाल्हाइणु.

Raisins (*generic term*). ड्राख; small, without pips, किस्मिस; a raisin, ड्राख &c. जो दाणो-जी गड़ो.

A Rake (*debauchee q. v.*). लंड़ो, लांड़ारो.

A Rake (*for raking*). ड़ंदारो, ड़ांदारी, ड़ांदारू.

To Rally (*troops*). ठाहणु.

A Ram. घटो.

To Ram down or in. धोंकणु, दबणु. *See* To Stuff.

To Ramble. घुमणु. *See* To Wander.

A Rambler. घोमू.

Rambling (*subs.*). घोमि. *See* Wandering.

A Ramrod. शीख, गजु.

Rancid. खटो.

Rancorous, Rancor. *See* Malicious, Malice.

At Random. तवाई.

To Range (*dispose*). ठाहणु. *See* To Wander.

The Range of an arrow, &c. तीर &c. जी मार.

A Rank (*row*). कतार, सिफ, सिफा, संबीर.

Rank (*degree*). दर्जो, मरातिबो.

Of high Rank. शानाइतो.

To Rankle (*in the mind*). चुभणु. *See* To Fester.

To Ransack (*search*). फोल्हणु. *See* To Plunder.

A Rap (*as with a knuckle*). ठोंगो. *See* Blow.

Rapacious. फोरू.

Rapid, Rapidly. तिखो. *See* Quick.

Rapine. फुर्मार, फुर्कार.

Rare. विरिलो, अणलभु, अलभु, नापैदु. *See* Scarce.

Rarely. कँहिंकदाने-कजाने, कड़हीं-कड़हीं, कड़हीं कदाने–कजाने.

Rareness. विरिलाई. *See* Scarcity.

A Rascal. लेडपिड, लुचु, लुचो, हरामज़ादो, ड्रांड़ो, लोंबड़ु, हरामी, शाही.

Rascality. लेड्पिभाई, लुचाई, लुचपणो.

Rascally. लेड्पिभाणो, लुचाणो, लुचिको.

Rash. हूडु, अणगाणू. *See* Unadvised.

Of a Rash person. हूडाणो.

A Rash on the skin. बुर्बुरि, बुभारि, बुरूडि.

Rashness. हूडाई.

A Rasp. रवात, सूहणु.

To Rasp. रवातणु.

A Rat. कुओ, चूहो, घरभणी.

Ratably. सरासरी करे, भाङाइतो. *See* Proportionally.

A Ratan. नेटु.

Rate, fixed Rate or scale. शरह.

Rate (*a scale*). अघु, निर्खु, नुर्खु, भाउ, पोठि.

To Rate (*fix the value*). अघु, &c. ब्भणु.

A list of Rates. अघोतिरी.

Rather (*somewhat q. v.*). की, जे

की सो, or by putting the adjective with which it is used in its diminutive form, as नंढो small; नंढेरो, नंढेरिडो, rather small.

To have, or desire, Rather. चङो भाइणु.

To Ratify. बहालु करणु.

Rational, Rationally. अकुलाइतो.

Rations, or fixed allowance of provisions. विरउ, विर्छ, (*to animals*) रातबु.

A child's Rattle. झिंझिणु, झिंझिणो, छिण्किणो, छिर्किणो.

To Rattle. खुड्कणु, खड्कणु, छिण्कणु.

A Rattling noise. झिण्झिणि, खुड्को, खड्को, खड्खडि, खड्काउ, ठड्काउ, छिण्काटु.

To Ravage. फुरणु फारणु.

To Rave. वाउलजणु.

Ravenous. हब्छी, बुखमुभो. *See* Gluttonous.

Ravenousness. हब्छ, उलो, बाठि, बांउठि.

A Ravine. घारो.

To Ravish. (*construpate by force*) जोरु करे जहणु, (*take by force*) खसणु.

A Ravisher (*of one's property*). खोसु.

Raw. कचो.

Rawness. कचाई, कचाणि.

A Ray. किरिणि, कनो.

To Raze. ड्राहणु, पटु करणु.

A Razor. पाकी *m.* & *f.*

Reach. पहुच.

To Reach (*arrive at*). पहुचणु.

To Reach out (*extend*). ड्रिघो करणु, ड्रिघेडणु, वधाइणु.

To Read. पड्हणु, वाचणु.

To Read out. पधिरो पड्हणु.

Reading (*subs.*). पढ़िहणो.

Reading and writing. लिखणु पड्हणु, लिख पड्ह, लिखा पड्ही, लिखति पड्हति.

Readiness (*the being ready*). तयारो. *See* Quickness.

Ready. तयारु, हाजुरु; for Ready money, *See* Money.

To be Ready. तयारु थिअणु, जुडणु, ठहणु.

To make Ready. तयारु करणु, जोडणु, ठाहणु.

To get Ready or equipped (*as for a journey*). संबहणु, संभिरणु.

Real. सचु, सति. *See* True.

Reality. सचाई. *See* Truth.

Really. सचु, ठीकु, तहकीकु. *See* Certainly.

To Reap. लुणणु.

To be Reaped. लुबणु, लाबार्जणु.

A Reaper. लाहायो, लोबो.

Reaping (*subs.*). लाबारो, लोबु.

The cost or wages of Reaping. लुणाणो, लाई.

A Reaping hook. ड्रांटो.

The Rear. पुठि, पोउ.

To Rear (*bring up*). निपाइणु, पालणु, धारणु.

To Rear up on the hind legs. नरा खणणु, शीख थिअणु.

To be Reared, or brought up. निपजणु.

Reason (*reasoning faculty*). अकुलु, बुधि, ग्यानु. *See* Understanding.

A Reason (*cause*). सबबु, वास्तो, कारणु, सांगो.

By Reason of. सांगे, विधे. *See* On Account of.

To Reason. (*exercise the reason*) ग़णणु, जाचणु, (*argue q. v.*) बह-सु करणु.

Reasonable. *See* Rational, Moderate.

To Reassure. दिलासो ड़िअणु, सत्या मंड़ाइणु. *See* To Encourage.

A Rebel, Rebellious. याक़ी, फिर्यलु.

To Rebel. फिरणु

A Rebellion. फ़ितिनो, फ़साादु.

A Rebound. उथिडाणि, उथड़.

To Rebound. उथिडणु.

A Rebuff (*sharp repulse by word or look*). हुड़ो, घुर्की, छिड़िब, झिण्क, झिण्कार.

A Rebuke. छींभ.

To Rebuke. छींभणु.

To Recall. (*call back*) वराए सड़णु, (*revoke, retract*) फेरणु, मोंडणु, भञणु.

To Recede. हटणु, मोटणु, वरणु, लडणु.

A Receipt (*written acknowledgement*). रसीद, पहुच.

A Receipt, or Recipe. नुस्ख़ो, टोटिको.

Receipts (*income*). आवति.

To Receive. वठणु.

A Receiver of stolen property. चोरिअ जो गिराकु-छेकू-गोन्हू-लेऊ.

Recent. नँओं, ताज़ो, हाणोको.

Recently. हाणे.

Reciprocal, Reciprocally. हिक ब़िए सां.

To Recite. पड़्हणु.

Reckless. बेफिकिरो. *See* Regardless, Impetuous.

To Reckon. ग़णणु, लेखणु. *See* To Count.

To Reclaim. सँभारणु, सुधारणु.

To Recline. अहलणु, लेटणु.

A written Recognisance. मुचिल्को, इक़्रार्नामो.

To Recognise. सुञाणणु.

To Recoil. पोइ ते हटणु.

To Recollect. यादि करणु, सारणु, संभालणु, संभारणु, संभिरणु.

Recollection. याद्गोरी, जाद्गोरी, सुर्ति, सार, संभार, सांभरि.

To Recomend to one's charge. सुपारणु.

A Recommendation. सुपारस, सुपारत, पारत.

To Recompense. बदिरो-एवज़ि ड़िअणु.

To Reconcile. (*persons differing*) पर्चाइणु, सर्चाइणु, (*or things*) ठाहणु.

To be Reconciled. पर्चणु, सर्चणु, ठहणु.

Reconciliation. पर्चांउ, सर्चांउ, सुलिहु, सूलु, पहति, पइ, ठाहु.

To Record. लिखी रखणु.

Written Records. दफ़्तरू.

To Recover (*a thing lost*). लहणु. *See* To Find.

To Recover (*from sickness*). संभालणु, सखर-चङोभलो-निमिरो ताज़ो थिअणु. *See* Well.

To Recover one's senses. सँभालणु, चेतणु, सुधि में बोदि अचणु.

Recovery (*from sickness*). सखराई, निमिराई, निरोआई, सिंहत.

Recreation. वेसाहि. *See* Amusement, Rest.

To Rectify. सही करणु, सोधणु.

Rectitude. सँवति. *See* Uprightness.

To Recur (*happen again*). वरो थिअणु.

Red. ग़ाड़्हो, लालु, रतो, सुर्खु; deep red, रतोलु.

Reddish, somewhat Red. ग़ाड़्हेरो, ग़ाड़्हेरिड़ो.

To be Reddish, have a tendency to Red. ग़ाड़्हाइणु, लालाइणु.

To Redeem. छड़ाइणु, मोखणु.

Redemption. छोट्कारो. *See* Deliverance.

Redness. ग़ाड़्हाणि, ग़ाड़्हाइणि, ग़ाड़्हाई, सुर्ख़ी, सुर्ख़ाई, लालाई-णि.

To Redouble. ड़ुंबारणु.

Redress. दादु, बिलो, उपाउ.

To Redress. दादु *&c.* करणु.

To Reduce (*make less*). घटाइणु, सुसाइणु, हपाइणु, झकाइणु.

To Reduce to obedience. नाति मञाइणु. *See* To Subdue, Subject.

To become Reduced (*in circumstances, from sickness, &c.*). पडणो पवणु, खिसणु, धकाणो थिअणु.

Reduction. सोसि.

Redundance. वधिक, सर्साई, वाधि.

Redundant. वधीक, वाधू.

A Reed. कानो,

A Reed, used for pens. वास्तीन, कांहु.

A frame work of Reeds. छिपिरी.

Made of Reed frame work. छिपिर्यांओं, छिपिर्यांणो.

The Reef of a sail. बंदरू.

A Reel (*for yarn*). ओबिरो.

To Reel (*yarn*). ओबणु.

To Reel (*stagger*). घिड़णु.

To Refer (*send to another*). मोकिलणु.

To Refer (*bear reference to*). लगणु.

To Refine (*purify*). सोधणु.

To Reflect (*consider*). सोचणु, विचारणु, ग़णणु, चितवणु. *See* To Ponder.

To Reflect (*throw back*). ड़ेखारणु.

Reflection (*thought*). विचारु, ग़ण्तो, ध्यानु.

Reflection (*shadow*). पाछो, पछांओं, पाछुओं.

The Reflection, of the sun thrown off water, &c. ओलिड़ो.

To Reform, (*neu.*). सँविरणु, सँभारणु, चेतणु.

To Reform (*act*). सँवारणु.

Refractory. *See* Obstinate.

To Refrain. परे रहणु. *See* To Cease, Stop.

To Refresh. ताज़ो करणु.

A Refrigerant medicine. थाधलि.

Refrigeratory. थधो, ठारू.

Refuge. अझो, पनाह, आसिरो. *See* Protection, Shelter.

For Refuge or protection. साम, शाम, सरनि.

Refulgence. चिम्को, जुल्वो, जोति. *See* Brightness.

Refulgent. चिम्किणो, चिल्किणो.

To Refund. मोटाए-वराए ड़िअणु.

Refusal. नाकार.

To Refuse. नाकारणु, नाकार करणु.

Refuse. फोगु, किचिरो. *See* Leavings, Trash.

Refutation. रदु, रंदु.

To Refute. कूडो करणु, रंड़णु, रंदणु.

To Regain. लहणु. *See* To Find.

Regal. बादशाही, राजाणो, राजसी.

Regard (*respect, reverence, q. v.*). लिहाजु, रखिणो, सांगो, खातरि.

Regard (*heed q. v.*). संग, गूंदरू, साड़ाह, सांगो, दर्दु.

To Regard (*value*). भांइणु, ग़णणु, लेखणु.

Regardful. ग़ाणू, ग़णू, साड़ाहू, सांगाइतो. *See* Thoughtful.

Regardless, Regardlessly. बेपर्वाहु, बेगर्जो, अलगर्जो, अलबेलो, बेगूंदिरो, बेफिकिरो, बेदर्दो, बेसंगो. *See* Thoughtless.

Regimen. क्रिरी, पथु.

A Regiment. पल्टणि.

A Region. मुल्कु, डेहु. *See* Country.

A Register. दाखिला. *See* Records.

To Register. दाखिलि करणु.

Regret. पछुताउ, पिशेमाणो. *See* Sorrow.

To Regret. पछुताइणु.

Regular, Regularly. केताइतो, नेमाइतो.

Regularity (*observance of rule*). कैतु, काइदो, नेमु.

To Regulate. सँवारणु, सुधारणु, ठाहणु, सिजिल्राइणु.

Regulation (*arranging*). सँवार, सुधार, ठाहठूह, सिज़िलि, ठाहुसिट्.

A Regulation (*rule*). काइदो, कानूनु, नेमु.

To Reject. मोटाइणु, वराइणु.

Rejected. रदि, नापसंदि.

Rejection. नापसंदो.

A Reign, Reigning. बादशाही, बाछाई, पात्शाही, राजु, साहिबी.

To Reign. बादशाही &c. करणु.

To Reimburse. भरे डिभणु.

The Rein of a bridle. वाग़ ; for a camel, महार.

The Reins (*loins*). कुखि.

To Reinstate. वराए विहारणु.

To Rejoice (*neu.*). सरहिजणु, रीझणु, विहसणु, खुशि, &c. थिभणु. *See* Glad.

To Rejoice (*act.*). सरहाइणु, रीझाइणु.

Rejoicing. सरहाई-णि. *See* Joy.

To Relapse. वरी-मोटी पवणु-किरणु.

To Relate (*tell q.v.*). चवणु, बुंधाइणु, वराइणु, (*refer*) लग़णु.

Related by blood. हिकरतु.

Relation (*connection of things*). सन्बंधु, मेलु. *See* Narration.

A Relation (*relative q. v.*). माइटु.

Relationless. बेकुड़भो.

Relations. बिरादरी, भाईचारो, राजु, मारिको, मिट्माइट् *plu.*

Of one's Relations. राज़ूणो, माइटाणो, शरीकाणो.

The customs, or habits of one's Relations, or family. राज़ूणी-णाई.

Relationship. माइटो, मिट़ो, नातो, सड़ु, सकाई, सक़ावत, शरीको, भाइपो-पी, भाईचारो-री.

A Relative. माइटु, मिटु, सको, शरीकु, छिलेरहमु.

To Relax (*act.*). ढारणु, ढिरो करणु.

Relaxation. आरामु, वेसांहों, राहत, ड़ाओ. *See* Rest, Ease.

Release, Releasing. छोट्को, छोट्कारो, छुट्कारो, खलासी, मोखु.

A deed of Release. फार्कतो.

To Release (*let go*). छड़णु.

To Release (*act. a thing pawned*). मोखणु, छड़ाइणु.

To be Released. छुटणु.

To Relent. रहमु करणु.

Relentless. बेरहमो, बेक्राझो. *See* Unmerciful.

Reliance. वेसहु. *See* Trust.

Relief. छोट्को. *See* Release, Ease, Assistance.

To Relieve (*ease*). आरामु, &c. करणु-डिभणु. *See* To Mitigate, Assist.

Religion. दीनु, ईमानु, धर्मु.

Religious (*of persons*). दीन्दारु,

दीनो, धर्मी, साधु; *or* of religion, religiously, दीनाइतो, धर्माइतो. *See* Pious.
To Relinquish. छड़णु.
Relinquishment. तर्कु, त्यागु.
A Relish (*taste q. v.*). सवादु, लजत, चूश.
Reluctance. बेदिली, नाखुशी.
Reluctant, Reluctantly. बेदिलि-लो, नाराजो.
To Rely. वेसाहु *&c.* करणु-आणणु--रखणु, विसहणु. *See* To Trust.
To Remain (*continue*). रहणु, टिकणु.
To Remain (*be left*). बचणु, बाकी *&c.* रहणु, उबिरणु, पाछी पवणु.
The Remainder. बाकी, छाणो. *See* Leavings.
To Remark (*note*). ड़िसणु. *See* To Observe.
Remarkable. ड़िसण जिहड़ो, अजबु.
Remediless. बेबिलो, बेइलाजो.
A Remedy. बिलो, दारू, उपाउ, एलाजु.
To Remember. यादि-जादि करणु, or रखणु, संभालणु, संभारणु, सारणु.
Remembrance. याद्गोरी, सार. *See* Recollection.
To Remind. यादि ड़िआरणु.
Remiss. ग़हेलो, ग़हिलो, गाफिलु, ढिरो.
Remission (*abatement*). छड़ति, छूटि, छड़, रिआइत, मरूअत.
Remissness. ग़हेलाई, ग़हिलाई, गाफिली-लाई, ढिराई.
To Remit (*let off, pardon q. v.*). माफु-छुटि-रिआइत करणु. *See* To Send, Relax.
A Remnant. *See* Remainder.
Remorse. पछुताउ.
Remote. डूर्रो परे, डूरि. *See* Distant.
Remoteness. परांहीं, डूरांहीं, डूराई.
To Remove (*neu.*). लड़णु.
To Remove (*act.*). खणी, रखणु, रेड़्हणु, सेरणु, सोरणु.
Removing, Removal (*flitting*). लाद्गि, लाड़ाणो, लड़.
To Rend. चीरणु, फाड़णु.
To Render. *See* To Return, Give, Make.
To Renew. नंओं करणु, वराए करणु.
To Renounce. *See* To Deny, Give up.
Renown. नाँउँ, नामूसु, नाम्दारी, नामाचारू, नाम्वरी, जसु, हाक. *See* Fame.
Renowned. नाम्दारू, जसाइतो, नालेरो, जसो. *See* Famous.
A Rent (*break*). फोड़, चीर, ड़ार. *See* Tear.
Rent (*of land*). हल, राजरू, महसूलु; taken at a fixed rate, contracted for, मुटो; fixed in kind on the water wheel, or per beegah, कासिगो; assessed on the standing crop, दानवंदी; the dividing produce after harvest in paying rent, बटई.
Rent (*of houses*). मस्वाड, भाड़ो, किराओ.
A Rent roll. खसिरो.
To Repair. जोड़णु, मरामत *&c.* करणु.
Repair, Repairing. दाग्दोजी, मरामत, जोड़जक.
To Repay. भरे ड़िअणु, भोचाइणु, पीचाइणु, (*requite*) मोखणु, लाहणु.
To Repeal. मोड़णु, भञणु.
To Repeat. वराए चवणु-करणु, *&c.* टुंवारणु.

Repeatedly. भेरेभेरे, वरीवरी, हरहर, घड़िअ घड़िअ, पलिपलि.
To Repel. टारणु, हटाइणु.
Repelled. दफे, रदि.
To Repent. तोबह, &c. करणु, पछु-ताइणु, पिशेमानिजणु.
Repentance. तोबह, पछुताउ, पिशे-मानो.
To Repine. गमु-डुखु करणु.
To Replace. वराए रखणु.
To Replenish. वराए भरणु.
Replete. पुरि, गिडि. *See* Full.
Repletion (*of food*). गोराई, गिरा-नो, जोगोरू.
A Reply. वरंदो, वराणी, जवाबु.
To Reply. वरंदो, &c. डिभणु.
Report (*account received*). खबर, समाउ, चितार. *See* Intelligence.
Report (*rumour, q. v.*). उफवाई, (*repute*) नांउं. *See* Reputation.
By mere Report. कूडे कनें.
The Report of a gun, &c. धकाउ, धधको, ठकाउ.
To Report (*a matter*). ज़ाणाइणु, चिताइणु, जताइणु.
A Reporter. खाबिरू.
Repose. आरामु, रांहत, साही. *See* Rest, Quiet.
To Repose. *See* To Rest, Sleep.
To Reprehend. छींभणु, सूटणु, झि-ण्कणु.
Reprehension. छींभ, झिण्क, सूट.
To Represent (*tell, q. v.*). ड़ेखारणु, अर्जु करणु, चवणु, वरनाइणु. *See* To Personate.
A Representation (*by words*). अर्जु, गालिह. *See* Image.
A Representative. एवजु-जो, बदरू.
To Repress. दबणु, मिटाइणु, लाहणु. *See* To Stop, Restrain, Subdue.

To Reprimand, Reprove. छींभणु, झिण्कणु, सूटणु.
A Reprimand, Reproof. छींभ, झिण्क, सूट.
A Reproach, Reproaching. ड़ोरापो, उभालो, ओलांभो, पारांभो, मिहिणो, इताबु.
To Reproach. ड़ोरापणु, ड़ोरापो, &c. करणु-डिभणु.
To suffer Reproaches. ड़ोरापिजणु.
Reproachful, Reproachfully. ड़ोरा-पाइतो, मिहिणाइतो.
A Reprobate. लोच्चो, खर्यलु, लुंड़ो.
Reproof, To Reprove. *See* Reprimand.
A Reptile. किंओं, जीतु.
Repugnant. *See* Contrary, Unwilling.
To Repulse. टारणु, दफे करणु, हटा-इणु.
Reputation, Repute. नांउं, आबु, साख, आबिरूइ, नामाचारू, कीरति. *See* Fame.
A Request. सुआलु.
To Request. घुरणु, सुआलु करणु.
To Require. घुरणु.
It is Requisite. घुर्जे.
To Requite. मोखणु, पाउणु.
To Rescind. भञणु, मोडणु.
To Rescue. छड़ाइणु, बचाइणु.
Research. सोझ्न, गोल. *See* Search, Inquiry.
Resemblance. हिकजिहड़ाई, मुशाबत, बरोबरी.
To Resemble. बांगे-वांगिआं-जिहड़ो-आचारि हुअणु.
To Resent. मठ्यां-बुछां भांइणु, डुमां-इणु. *See* To be Offended.
Resentful. खुंड़ो, खुंड़िरू, खुंड़ाइतो. *See* Spiteful.

Resentment. खुंडु, खौंस, खारु. *See* Malice, Spite.

To Reserve. रखणु.

A Reservoir for water. हौदु, तलाउ, (*round a tree*) ग्वारो, ग्वारो, चब्हो.

To Reside. विहणु, टिकणु, रहणु, सहउणु.

Residence, Residing. रहाश, रहाशत; place of residence, जाइ, घरु, हंधु, मागु.

A Resident. रहाकू, रहाशी, वेठलु, रहाऊ, रहू.

Residue. *See* Remainder.

To Resign. छड़णु.

Resignation (*to the will of God*). सबुरु.

Resigned (*submissive*). राज़ी, सबुराइतो.

Resin. धूपु, रिआल, राल.

To Resist (*act.*). आड़ो फिरणु-थिअणु. *See* To Oppose.

Resistance. सामुहाई, सामुहुणाई.

Resistless. अणग्रार्यो, अझलु.

To Resolve (*determine*). ठाहणु, ठहराइणु, पक &c. करणु. *See* To Melt, Explain.

Resolute. खाहोडो, हिकमत्यो-तो, हिकग़ाल्ह्यो, हिकसुखुनो.

Resoluteness. खाहोडाई, पक, हिकसुखुनाई, ड्डिढ़ता.

Resolution (*determination*). ठहराउ, पक, निहिचो.

Resolution (*boldness q. v.*). सत्या, हिमथ.

To Resound (*neu.*). पड़लाउ पवणु.

Resource. उपाउ, एलाजु. *See* Remedy, Expedient.

Resourceless. वेवसो, वेवाह-हु-हो.

Respect. (*regard*) आदरु, मानु, आबु, आउभाउ, सहजु, कुर्भु, कुबुं, (*reverence*) मञ्ता, अदबु.

Respect (*particular*). ग़ाल्हि.

To Respect (*reverence*). मञणु, ग़ाणणु, लेखणु.

Respectability. मातिबरी-राई, पति, साख, आबु, मानु.

Respectable. मातिबरु; *or* Respectably, आबाइतो, मानाइतो, साखाइतो, पत्याइतो, कुबांइतो, हशीको, बिलाइतो.

A Respectable person. अश्राफु, चङो मुसुं.

Respected. मानाइतो. *See* Respectable.

Respectful, Respectfully. भावाइतो, भाभर्यो, मानाइतो.

Respecting. ग़ाल्हि में, बाबति.

A Respite. मुहलत. *See* Rest.

To be Responsible. फलाणे ते जवाबु हुअणु, जवाबु करणु-ड्डिअणु.

To make Responsible. फलाणे खों जवाबु वटणु.

Rest (*ease q. v.*). आरामु, सुखु, (*cessation of labor*) वेसांहिं, साहो, विसिरामु, ड्डाश्रो. *See* Quiet.

The Rest (*remainder*). बाकी.

A Rest (*support q. v.*). टेक, आधर.

To Rest, or take Rest. वेसांहिं &c. करणु, थकु-चोकिडो लाहणु-भञणु.

To Rest (*to lay, as on a support*). रखणु.

To Rest upon (*lean*). टेक ड्डिअणु, अहलणु.

Restiff, Restive. *See* Obstinate.

Restless. (*uneasy*) बेसुखो, बेआरामु, (*fidgety*) चल्रिलो, चंचलु, खेचिरो.

Restlessness. बेसुखाई, बेआरामी, खेचिराई, फथिकिणी, चल्रिलाई, चुर्पुरि, तिर्तिरि. *See* Disquiet, Uneasiness.

To Restore. वराए-मोटाए ड़िभणु.
To Restrain. झलणु, पलणु.
Restraint. झल, पल, बंदु.
To Restrict. संधो &c. करणु.
A Restriction. संधो, झल, नेमु. *See* Limit.
To Result (*rise, issue*). निकिरणु, थिअणु. *See* To End.
A Result. पीछो, फलु.
To Resume (*take back*). वराए-मोटाए वठणु. *See* To Begin.
The day of Resurrection. क़िआमत, हशरु.
To Retail. रेजिकी विकिणणु.
To Retain. रखणु
To Retaliate. बदिलो वठणु, पाडणु.
To Retard. सीडाइणु. *See* To Hinder; Stop.
To Retch. ओकारो *&c.* ड़िभणु.
A Retching. ओकारो, उब्रिड़ाकु, उब्रिड्को.
Reticulated. ज़ारीदारु.
Retinue. लश्करु, हम्लो, अम्लो.
To Retire (*go back*). हटणु, मोटणु, लडणु. *See* To Withdraw.
Retired (*private*). निवेकिलो, खुलासो.
Retirement (*privacy*). निवेकिलाई, हेकलाई, एकांति.
To Retort, (*act.*). उथिलाए-उटिलाए-वराए-विझणु.
To Retract. फिरणु.
To Retreat. हटणु, मोटणु.
To Retrench. घटाइणु, कटणु.
A Retrenchment. कट.
Retribution. पाडोझाडो, एवजु, बदिलो.
To suffer just Retribution. किओ-कीतो लोडणु-पाइणु.
To Retrograde. पुठि ते अचणु-वञणु.
To Return. (*come back*) मोटी-वरी अचणु-वञणु, (*turn back*) मो. टणु.
To Return (*give back*). वराए-मोटाए ड़िभणु, मोटाइणु. *See* To Repay.
To Reveal. पधिरो, करणु खोलणु. *See* To Disclose.
Revelry. ऐशु, जशनु, विलासु.
Revenge. पाडोझाडो, पाडझाड, बदिलो.
To take Revenge. बदिलो-पाडोझाडो-वेरु वठणु, गुसिरु कढणु.
Revengeful. खुंडो, खारी, वेरवठू, वेरू.
See Spiteful.
Revenue. उपति, हासुलाति, पैदाश, आवति.
Reverberation of sound. पर्लाउ.
To Revere, Reverence. रुञणु.
Reverence. भक्तिता. *See* Respect.
To Reverse. उबतो *&c.* करणु, उथिलाइणु.
The Reverse. उबति-ताई.
Reverse, Reversed. उबतो, ऊंधो.
To Revert. वरी-मोटी अचणु.
To Review (*look back on or into*). वराए ड़िसणु. *See* To Look at, Examine.
To Revile. गारि-ड़ेरापो *&c.* ड़िभणु, फिट्कारणु, निंदणु.
A Reviler. गिलाखोरु, निंदकु.
Reviling (*subs.*) गिला, निंदा. *See* Reproach.
To Revise. *See* To Review.
To Revive (*regain vigour*). संभालणु, चेतणु. *See* To Quicken.
To Revoke. फेरणु, भञणु.
To Revolt. फिरणु.
To Revolve (*neu.*). फिरणु, घुमणु.
A Revolution (*turn q. v.*). फेरी, फेरो.
A Reward. इनामु.

Rheumatism. वाई.
A Rhinoceros. गेंड़ो.
Rhubarb. रेवंद्चीनी.
Rhyme. अंबिओ, तुकांतु, काफिओ.
The Rib of a boat. पसुं.
The Ribs of the body. पासिरी, पि-
ञिरी.
Ribaldry. गंदु, कमीणाई.
A Riband, Ribbon. फँहीं, कोर.
Rice (*a grain of*) growing, or in the husk. सारो; its plu. सार्यूं is the generic name for the grain. Some kinds are, सिंधी, सुग्दासी, नेण्वासो, रतिड्या *plu.* कामोल, कांबिरू, गंजा *plu.* मोतीआ *plu.* सडिड्या *plu.* कन्ंघो, अछिडो.
Rice (*a grain of*) cleared of the husk. चांवरु, चांउरु, (*plu.* चांवर, चांउर).
Of cleaned Rice. चांउरो.
Boiled Rice. खुश्को, भतु, चोखा *plu.*
Rice cooked with pulse grain. खिचिणी, अंब्रितपाकु.
Rice cooked with sugar. तहरो; with milk, खीर्नी, तस्मई.
A plant or tuft of Rice in transplanting. मराई; a bundle of such, गुराडो.
The first sowing of Rice afterwards transplanted. ब्रिजारणु, ब्रेजारो, बेजो.
The transplanting Rice or Rice transplanted. विहराजु.
Rice sprung up from old scattered seeds. कोरडि.
Rice straw. परारु, पलालु.
Rice water. पेज़ो, पेज़, पिछ, पिछो.
Rich (*wealthy q. v.*). वँहीं, साऊ, साओ, शाहूकारु, दुत्रादारु, भाग्यो, धनवानु, साज़ो, सधरु, तुजारु, धनपात्रु.
Rich (*abounding in, having plentifully*). गिडि, पुरि.
Rich (*as a dish*). झिबु.
Riches. दुत्रा, दौलत, धनु, जरि, रिजिकु, माया, लछिमी. *See* Wealth.
Richness. वँह्याँई, शाहूकारी.
Rickety. ढिरी, धुड़िणी.
To be Rickety. उलिडणु.
A Riddle. पिरोली, गुझारत, बुझारत.
To Ride. चड़्हो-सवारिअ हलणु.
A Ride. चड़्हो, सवारी. *See* Riding.
A Rider. सुआरु, सवारु, हस्वारु, स्वारु.
A Ridge of earth. ब्रनो.
The Ridge round a flat roof. ब्रनोडो, ब्रोडबनोडो, बोडबनो, ब्रजिरो.
A Ridge pole. करंघो, कण्घो, लाटणि.
Ridicule. घब्रो, चथर, चर्चो, ठठोली, खिल, ठ्ठो.
Ridiculous, Ridiculously. घब्राइतो, चथराइतो, खिलारो, खिलाइतो.
Riding (*subs.*). सुआरी, सवारी, हस्वारी, स्वारी.
Rife. ग्राढो.
To Rifle. फुरणु, लुटणु.
Right (*not left*). सज़ो, साज़ो.
Right, Rightly. ठीकु, सही, दुरुस्तु, बहालु, रइ, रासि, सुबति. *See* Proper.
A Right. हकु. *See* Justice.
The Right side (*as of cloth*). सुबताई, सुबति.
A Right and wrong side. उबताई-सुबताई, उबतिसुबति.
To be Right or Rightful. रिहणु, रिहाइणु.
Right-handed. साज़ुडु.
Righteous. दीन्दारु, धर्मी. *See* Pious.

Righteousness. दिन्दारी. *See* Piety, Justice.

Rightful. हक्वारी, हकी; or Rightfully, हकाइतो, रिहँदो.

Rightness. सुवताई, सुवति, सँवाई, सचाई.

Rigid, Rigidly. ड़ाढो. *See* Hard, Stiff.

Rigidity. ड़ाढाई. *See* Stiffness.

Rigorous, Rigorousness. *See* Severe, Severity.

A Rim. कनो. *See* Edge.

The Rim plank of a boat. पातारी, अड़ो.

The Rind. खल, छिल.

A Ring (*circle q. v.*). पिङु.

A metal Ring used as a fastening, &c. कड़ो.

A finger Ring. (*plain*) छलो, (*with stone*) मुंड़ो; some other kinds of finger rings are, वेढ़ु, सुस्तु, नहिड्यो, आंङूठी, खीरमुंड़ो, वींढो, वींटी, विछुंभडो. *See* Ear ring, Nose ring.

A toe Ring (*of kinds*). अणिवटु, किचिंडो, बंदिडो, विछुंभडो.

To Ring (*neu.*). घिण्कणु, घण्कणु, घड्कणु.

To Ring (*act.*). घिण्काइणु, वज़ाइणु.

A Ring-dove. गेरो.

Ringing (*subs.*). घिण्कार, घण्कार.

A Ringlet. वरू, घुंड़ी.

A Ring-worm. ड़द्रु *f.*

To Rinse. (*a vessel*) आघारणु, आछुलाइणु, (*the mouth*) गुर्डी करणु.

A Riot. बखेडो, लुडु, हुलु. *See* Tumult.

A Rioter, Riotous. लुडाई, झेडाई.

To Rip (*neu.*). उड़िडणु, उखिलणु.

To Rip (*act.*). उड़ोडणु, उखेलणु, उखोलणु.

Ripe. पको.

To Ripen. पचणु.

Ripeness. पकाई.

A Ripple. छोली.

To Ripple. छुलणु.

Rippling. छोलिरू.

A Rise (*increase, elevation*). चड्हु, चाड्हु.

A Rise in price. आकिराई, चड्हति, सझाई.

To Rise. (*get up*) उथणु, (*ascend, increase*) चड्हणु.

To Rise (*as the sun*). उभिरणु.

To cause to Rise, or get up. उथारणु.

Risibility. खिलिणाई.

Risible. खिलिणो.

A Risk. जोखो, जोखमु, खतिरो.

A Rite. कर्मु, क्रिआ.

Rival (*adj.*), A Rival. रीसिरू, रीसारी.

To Rival. रीसाइणु.

Rivalry. रीस.

A River. दरिआहु, दरिआउ.

Of the River. दर्याही.

The deity of the River. खाजो खिदिरि *m.* वरूणु; an angel, or attendant of the deity, ब्रह्रू.

A hymn in honor of the River. पंजिडो.

A Rivet. किली, मेख.

A Rivulet. नँईं.

A Road. वाट, रस्तो, राह, राहु, दगु, गसु, रंदु.

In the right Road. सुवाटो.

In the wrong Road. कुवाटो.

To Roam. घुमणु, फिरणु. *See* To Wander.

A Roar, Roaring. रडि, राडि, राडो, गड्कार. *See* Shout.
To Roar. रडणु, गजणु.
To Roast. पचाइणु.
Roasted meat. कबाबु.
To Rob. चोरी करणु, फुरणु, लुटणु.
A Robber. चारू, फोरू.
A highway Robber. वाटमारू.
A band of Robbers. घलि, धाड; one of such, घल्लिरू, धाडेलु.
A Robbery. चोरी, फुरि, फुर्मार.
A gang Robbery. धाडो, घलि.
Robust. सघारो. *See* Strong, Stout.
Robustness. सघाराई. *See* Strength, Stoutness.
A Rock. छिप.
To Rock (*act.*). लोड़णु, झूलाइणु.
To Rock (*neu.*). लुड़णु, झूलणु.
A Rocket. हवाई.
Rock-salt. संधोलूणु.
A Rod. चहो.
The Roe of a fish. आनो, गुरू.
A Rogue. ठगु, दल्वाई, छहल्बाजु, हर्ालो. *See* Cheat, Knave, Vagabond.
Roguery. ठगी, दल्बो, छहल. *See* Cheating, Deceit.
A Roll, (*thing rolled up*). वेड़्हो.
A Roll, Rolling (*on the ground*). लेथिडी, लेटिडो.
A Roll, or list. चिठो, यादास्त.
To Roll or Roll over (*neu.*). लेटणु, लेथिडणु, लेटिडी &c. पाइणु; to roll round or revolve on its axis, फिरणु.
To Roll or Roll over (*act.*). लेटाइणु, लेथिडाइणु; to roll round or cause to revolve, फेरणु.
To Roll out paste with a rolling pin. वेलणु.
To Roll up. वेड़्हणु, वल्हेटणु.
A Rolling pin. वेलणु.
A Roof. छिति, छति; the outside of a flat roof, खुडु, कोठो.
To Roof. छाँइणु.
A Room. कोठो.
To take up Room. जाइ मलणु-वालारणु.
Room, Roominess. जाइ, हंधु, वेकिराई-राणि, मोकिराई-णि.
Roomy. वेकिरो, मोकिरो, कुशादो.
A Roost. वाहेरो, आहेरो.
A Root. पाड, मूलु, वेख, ज़ड्ह. *See* Origin.
A Rope. नोड़ो, रसो, रसो, नोड़ु, वार्कशु, वाझु, वाढि, लज़; of leather, वर्त, माहो, वढो, वाढो; of goat's hair, तैलु, संल्ही.
A piece of Rope. टोब्रूहो.
A Rosary. तस्बो, माल्हा, सुमर्णी.
A Rose tree. गुलाबु; a species of rose tree, सदागुलाबु.
Rose-colored, Rosy. गुलाबो.
Rose water. गुलाबु.
A bottle for sprinkling Rose water. गुलाबासी, गुलाब्दानी.
A conserve of Roses. गुल्कंदु.
To Rot (*act.*). ग़ारणु, साडणु.
To Rot (*neu.*). ग़रणु, सडणु.
Rotation, (*wheeling motion*). फेरो. *See* Turn, Succession.
Rotatory. फेराइतो.
By Rote. वर्जिवान, कंठि, जवानी.
Rotten. किनो.
Rottenness. किनाई.
To Rove. घुमणु. *See* To Wander.
A Rover. घोमू. *See* Wanderer.
Rough, Roughly. खहुरो, (*in manners*) रूखो. *See* Uneven.
Rough or rugged ground. खड्बडि.

A Rough copy. मुसौदो.
To Roughhew. तरणु.
Roughness. खहुराई-णि.
Round (*adj.*). गोलु, चकिरांओं.
Round (*around q. v.*). चौगिर्दि, चौधारी.
The Round of a ladder. ड़ाको, ड़ाउको.
A Round (*revolution*). फेरी. *See* Circle, Turn.
To Round. गोलु करणु.
To go Round, turn Round. फिरणु.
Round-about (*adj.*). फेराइतो.
Slightly Rounded. बादामी.
Roundnesss. गोलाई-णि.
The Round of a guard. फेरो, घुमिरो.
To Rouse. जाग़ाइणु, उथारणु.
Roused. सुजागु, सुजींतु.
A Rout (*defeat and dispersion*). भाज़ड़ि. *See* Flight.
Route *See* Road.
A Row (*line*). कतार, सिफ, पंगति, सिफा, संवीर, सिंबीर.
A Row (*tumult q. v.*). मोड़ु, हुलु.
To Row. ग़नु मोडणु.
Royal. बाद्शाही, पाछाई-ही, पात्शाही. *See* Kingly.
Royalty. बाद्शाही, पाछाई-ही, पात्शाही.
A Rub. गहको घर्जो.
To Rub (*neu.*). गसणु.
To Rub (*act.*). गहणु, महटणु, मलणु. *See* To Scour.
To Rub out. मेसारणु, मेटणु.
To Rub over with oil, &c. मखणु.
A Rubber (*cloth*). रूमालु.
Rubbing (*subs.*). मलिणी, गहणी.
A mark or sore from Rubbing. गाठि, गीसो.
A gentle Rubbing of the limbs. थ-थिडो.
Rubbish (*trash*). गंडुगोडु, किचिरो, अंडुगंडु
A Ruby. लाल, याकूदु, माणिकु, चूनी.
A Rudder. सुखानु.
Ruddy. ग़ाड्हेरो.
Rude (*uncivil*). गुस्ताकु, बेअदबु, ड़ीठु, (*coarsely executed*) कचो.
Rudeness. गुस्ताकी, बेअदबी, ड़ीठाई.
To Rue. पछुताइणु, पस्ताइणु. *See* To Regret.
Rue (*the plant*). सुदाबु.
A Ruffian. चंडालु, हरामी. *See* Rascal.
To Ruffle (*rumple*). घुंजाइणु.
A Rug. गालोचो, गिआली.
Rugged. खहुरो. *See* Uneven, Rough.
Ruggedness. खहुराई-णि. *See* Unevenness.
Ruin (*destruction*). नासु, खराबी, खड़.
In Ruins. ड़ुठो, ड़ुठलु.
To Ruin. फिटाइणु, विञाइणु, बिगाड़णु, मुसणु, मुसाइणु.
To go to Ruin. रूलणु, फिटणु, मुसणु,
Ruined. फिटो, उजड़ु, खराबु, दुफु, भुटु, खड़. *See* Destroyed.
A Ruiner, Ruinous. फिटाऊ, फेटाऊ.
Rule (*government*). अमलु, राजु, साहिबी, हुकुमु, हुकूमत, हाकिमी.
A Rule (*canon*). कानूनु, काइदो, नेमु. *See* Standard.
A Rule, or Ruler. मस्तर, फतील.
To Rule (*govern*). अमलु &c. करणु.
To Rule a line. लीक &c. कढणु.
A Ruler (*governor*). हाकिमु.
To Rumble. गुड्कणु, गुर्कणु, गुड़गुड़ि, &c. करणु.

The Rumbling of the bowels. गु-ड्गुडि, गुड्को, गोड.

To Ruminate (*chew the end*). ओ-ग़ारणु, उग़ारणु. *See* To Ponder.

To Rummage. फोल्हणु. *See* To Search.

Rumour. उफवाई, अफवाई.

The Rump. चुतड *plu.* बुंड्ड *plu.* ग़ुई, चुति.

A Rumple. घुंज़ु.

To Rumple (*act.*). घुंजाइणु.

Rumpled. घुंजिरू.

A Run, Running. डुक, डोक, डोड.

To Run. डुकणु, डोकणु, डोडणु, दउ-डणु, डुक &c. पाइणु.

To Run (*a sore or as water*). व-हणु.

To Run after. पुभां-पुठ्यां डुकणु.

To Run away or off. भज़णु.

To Run away with, or off with. खणी भज़णु.

To Run through (*expend*). निवा-हणु, निभाइणु. *See* To Squander.

To Run through (*pierce*). टुंबणु. *See* To Stab.

A Runaway. भज़िणो.

The Rundle of a ladder. ड़ाको, ड़ाउको.

A Runner (*courier*). कासिदु, रैबारी. रहबरू.

Running (*flowing as water or a sore, adj.*). वहँदडु.

A Rupee. रूपयो; some different coinages of rupees are, कल्दारू, कोरी, मशहदी, अखेशाही, काशानी, ढोल्क्यो, गोबिंदी, नानकशाही.

A half Rupee. भाविओ, अधेलो; a quarter rupee, पाइणि, पाइली, पा-रूपो; three quarters of a rupee, टेपाण्यूं.

A Rupee with a flaw in it. कैड़ी; the flaw itself, कैड़ु.

A Rupture (*breach*). फोटि.

A Rupture (*hernia*). छिको.

Rural. ब्रहरतू. *See* Rustic.

To Rush. तिखो हलणु, काहणु.

To Rush at or on. उल्लरणु. *See* To Spring at.

A Rush, Rushing, (*attack q. v.*). काह, वछ, लूह, उल्लर.

A Rush (*the plant*). कलु.

Rust. कटु *f.* मुर्चो; जंगु: green rust, कसु *f.* जंगालु.

To Rust (*act.*). कटणु, (*as copper*) कसणु.

To Rust (*neu.*). कटिजणु, (*as copper*) कसिजणु, जंगालिजणु.

Rustic (*adj.*), a Rustic. वहणाई. *See* Rural.

To Rustle. खड्खडि करणु.

Rusty (*affected by rust*). कटु खाधो.

A Rut (*in a road*). चरो.

The Rut, or desire for the male, of cows, buffaloes, and goats. वहुर, मुहारि; of mares, वडु, छाणो; of camels, मिहिर.

To be in Rut. (*cows, buffaloes, goats*) वहुर्जणु, मुहार्जणु, (*mares*) वड्जणु, (*camels or mares*) मिहि-र्जणु, मिहिर आणणु, To be in Heat.

S

A Sable-skin. समूरू.

A Sabre. तरारि, खनो.

A Sack (*various kinds*). बोरी, बो-रो, पलो, तुआलु.

A double Sack for animals. खाही, हर्तोरू; one side of such, खुथो.

Sackcloth, Sacking. टपडु, गूणि.

Sacred. पाकु, पवित्रु, (*of the Deity*) खुदाई, ईसुरी.

Sacredness. पाकाई, पवित्राई.

A Sacrifice. ब्रलि, सदिको, कुर्बानु, घोर, फिदा, ब्रलिहारु.

To Sacrifice. ब्रलि, &c. डिअणु -करणु.

Sad, Sadly, (*sorrowful q. v.*). उञाणिको, बेदिलि, उदासु, अनमन्यो, दिल्गीरु.

A riding Saddle. हनो. *See* Pack-saddle.

The wooden frame of a Saddle. काठोडो.

A camel's Saddle. पाखिडो.

The pad under a Saddle. थडो, (*camel's*) थडी.

The cloth covering a Saddle. गाशो.

The cloth below the Saddle. तलु, टपुड.

To Saddle. पलाणणु.

A pair of Saddle bags. खुर्जीन.

Sadness. ऊञाणिकाई, उदासो, बेदिली, दिल्गीराई-री.

Safe, Safely. (*free from danger*) बेजोखो, सोघो, हथीको, बिलाइतो, (*free from hurt*) बेजोखो, सलामत, सहोसलामत.

A Safe convoy. बोराओ, बदिको.

Safety. सलामती, सोघाई, हथीकाई, अमुन.

Safflower. खुहुंबो.

The seed of the Safflower. पवाडो.

Colored with Saflower. खुहुंबो.

Saffron. केसरि.

Colored with Saffron. केसरी.

Sagacious. स्याणो, सिआणो, खांदो, सुतो, सुज़ाणु. *See* Wise.

Sagacity. स्याणप, सोझो, सुर्ति.

Sage. ड़ाहो. *See* Wise.

The sign Sagittarius. धनु.

A Sail (*large*). सिड्हु; other varieties are, कल्मी, पालु, बदिबानु.

To Sail. सिड्हु ते हलणु.

A Sailor. मुहाणो, नाखुँओ, मोबेहरु.

A Saint. पीरु, औलिआउ, सिधु साधु.

Of a Saint, Saintly. पीराणो, साधिको.

Saintiness. पीराई, साधाई.

For the Sake of. सांगे, खातरि, कारणि, लाइ, लइ, लग़ि, अथि. *See* On Account of.

Sal-Ammoniac. नोशादरु.

A Salary (*monthly*). महीनो, दर्माहो. *See* Pay.

A Sale (*selling*). विकिरो, हलाउ. *See* Auction.

The government Sale of grain. मुंबई; the bill of Sale of grain, साटो.

For Sale. वेकाऊ, वेकू.

A ready Sale. खापो. *See* Demand.

To have a ready Sale. खपणु.

Salep. सालिबु.

Saline, Salinous. खारो. *See* Salt.

Saliva. थुकु, पिकु, फीणो, लब.

To be Salivated. वातु अचणु.

Sallow. विअरो, जर्दो.

A Sally. ढूहु, काह. *See* Attack.

A Sally port. दरो.

Salt (*subs.*). लूणु, निमकु.

Salt (*adj.*). खारो.

A seasoning of Salt in food. सलूणाई.

Seasoned with Salt. सलूणो.

Salt earth. कलरु; a shallow surface of Salt earth, ढुंगो.

Impregnated with Salt (*the soil*). कलराठो.

To Salt. लूणणु.

Black Salt. सोंचरलूणु.

Rock Salt. संधोलूणु.
To taste Salt, or Saltish. खाराइणु.
Saltless. अलूणो.
Saltlessness. अलूणाई.
Saltness. खाराई.
A Salt manufacturer. नूनारी.
A Salt pan or pit. नूनारू, नूनरू.
Saltpetre. शोरो; purified, कलमी शोरो.
A manufacturer of Saltpetre. चिडाई, शोराई.
Salvation. छोट्को, छुट्कारो, गति, मुक्ति, मोखु. *See* Deliverance, Preservation.
Salubrious. चङो, निरोयो.
A Salve. मलमु, लेपु.
Salutary. नफाइतो, गुणाकारी, गुणकारी. *See* Beneficial, Salubrious.
A Salutation. सलामु, रामराम, नमस्कारु.
To go through the complete forms of Salutation. खोंकारणु.
To Salute. सलामु, &c. करणु–चवणु.
A Salute of cannon. सलामी.
Same (*identical*). साग्यो, सागूंणो, उहोई.
Sameness (*identity*). साग्याई.
A Sample. वनिक, नमूनो.
Sanctified. पाकु, पवित्रु. *See* Pure.
To Sanction. कबूलु–बहालु करणु.
Sanctity. पाकाई, पवित्राई. *See* Purity.
A Sanctuary, (*asylum q. v.*). अझो, ओट.
Sand. वारी; gravelly sand, राओ.
To be filled or choked with Sand. थर्जणु.
A pair of Sandals. खकंणु.
Sandal wood. चंदनु, सिखंडु, (*red*) रक्तचंदनु, रतानणु.
Sandarach, (*the resin*). चंद्रसु.
A Sandback, (*in water*). लस.
A Sand board for writing on. पटी. फरही.
A Sand-hill. भिट, ड़िहु.
Sandy. वार्यासो; sandy and dusty, डुसड़.
Sane. सँभो, सँभो सँवाटो.
Sanity. सँवाई.
Sap, (*in plants*). रसु. *See* Mine.
Sapless. बेरसो.
A Sapling. गूहो.
Sappan wood. बकमु.
A Sapphire. नीलमु.
Sappy. रसाइतो, घणरसो.
A Sarcasm. टोकबाजो, तानो, मिहिणो, टोक. *See* Taunt.
Sarcastic, Sarcastically. तानाइतो, टोकाइतो.
Sarcocalla. गूणि.
A Sash. चेल्हिबंदु, पट्को, लुंगी, बोछणु.
Satan, Satanic. *See* Devil, Devilish.
A Satchel. खलीथो, पोटिडी.
To Sate, Satiate. ट्रइणु, रज़णु.
Sated. रजु. ट्रिपिति.
To be Sated. ढ़ापणु, ढ़ाइजणु, धाइ करणु, ड़ल्हिजणु.
Satiety. ढ़उ, रजु, ट्रिपिति.
Satin. अतिलसु.
Satirical. *See* Sarcastic.
Satisfaction. खुशी, खुश्दिली, रीझ, सरहाई.
Satisfied. राजी, सरहो, खुशि.
To Satisfy. राजी, &c. करणु, मञाइणु, पर्चाइणु, सरहाइणु.
To Saturate. भरणु, लोइणु.
Saturday. छंछरु, शनिश्चरु.
The planet Saturn. शनिश्चरु.
Savage. झंग्ली. *See* Cruel.

Sauce. चटिणी. *See* Seasoning.

A Saucepan. कण्छी, कण्छु, कड्छु, लड़लग़ो.

A Saucer. रिकेबी, रिकाबी.

Sauciness. गुस्ताकी, मचुलाई, चचुलाई. *See* Insolence.

Saucy. गुस्ताकु, मचुलो, चचुलो. *See* Insolent.

To Save (*preserve*). बचाइणु, तारणु, रखणु.

To Save (*lay by*). कौए-बचाए रखणु, मेडणु.

To Save (*hinder from being spent*). कोइणु, सर्फो, &c. करणु.

To be Saved (*preserved*). बचणु, तरणु.

A Saving. सर्फो, किफात, कसर, कोअ, कसकोअ.

Saving (*frugal q. v.*). सर्फाई; or with Saving or economy, सर्फाइतो, कसराइतो.

A Saviour. बचाइणहारू, तारणहरू। *See* Preserver.

To Saunter. घुमणु. *See* To Wander.

Savour. सवादु, लजत, साउ. *See* Taste.

Savoury. सवादी, चसाइतो, लजती, लजताइतो. *See* Tasteful.

A Saw. काराई, जवानो ; a sawyer's saw, कट्टुं.

To Saw. चीरणु

Sawdust. बूरो.

A Sawyer. चोरो.

Sawyer's hire. चोराणी.

To Say. चवणु, ग़ाल्हाइणु, उतणु, कहणु, (*repeat as prayers, a lesson, &c.*) पड्हणु.

A Saying. चविणी. *See* Proverb.

A Scab. कडी, खरंडु.

A Scabbard. खिप, मिआनु.

The mounting at the bottom of a Scabbard. तहनालु ; at the top, मुहनालु.

A Scaffold, Scaffolding. कवाजो, छिको.

To Scald. साडणु.

Scaldhead (*the disease*). गंजि.

Scaldheaded. गंजो.

The Scale of a balance. पुडु.

A pair of Scales (*a balance*). साहिमी,ताराजी, टकिडी, (*small*) कंड़ो, मरारी, तुरी.

The Scale of a fish. छिलुरू.

To Scale (*act. peel off*). छिलणु.

Scaled, Scaly. छेलुओं, छेलुरो.

Scammony. महमूंदी.

To Scan (*scrutinize*). सोझणु, जाचणु, छाणणु.

Scandal. बदूनामी, गिला.

Scandalous. गिलारो.

Scantiness. थोराई, कोताही.

Scanty, Scantity. घटि, थोरो, कोतहु. *See* Deficient.

A Scar. .चिटो, दागु.

Scarce (*rare q. v.*). विरिलो, अणलभो.

Scarcely, (*as regards time*). अञा, (*with difficulty*) मसां, मसें, मसमस.

A Scarcity. थोराई, थोरिडाई, अणलभाई, विरिलाई, ऊणाई, ऊणि, कमी.

A Scarf. चुनी, चादर.

A Scarification. ड़ंगु, पछिडो, पछु.

To Scarify. पछणु, ड़ंग &c. हणणु.

Scarlet. रतोलु.

Scatheless. बेजिआनो.

To Scatter. छट्टणु, खिंड़ारणु, खिंड़ेरणु, खिंड़ाइणु, विखेडणु, (*and lose*) वीटणु, हारणु.

To Scatter about. हारणु वीरणु.
Scattered. कणोकणो, कुणोकुणो, तवाई.
To be Scattered. खिंड़िरणु, खिंड़णु.
A Scavenger. चुहुडो, हलालखोरु.
Scent. बोइ, बुंइ, बास, धप, धमक.
To Scent (*perfume*). बोइ &c. ड़िअणु, सुरहाइणु. *See* To Smell.
To search for by Scent. नूसणु.
Scented. बुंआइतो, बासारो.
Scentless. बेबासो, बेबोयो.
A Sceptic. *See* Skeptic.
A Schedule. यादास्त. *See* List.
A Scheme. ठाहु. *See* Contrivance.
A Schism. डुफेडु.
A Scholar. खुताबी, शागिरदु, सिखु, सेखिड्यातु, सेखिड़ाऊ.
A School. खुताबु, मख्तबु.
A School-fellow. खुताब भाई.
A Schoolmaster. उस्तादु, वाझो, ओझो, आखुंदु, मुलो.
Science. इल्मु, विद्या, विद्या.
Scientific. इल्मी, इल्माइतो, विद्याइतो.
A pair of Scissors. कैंची, कतर.
To Scoff. निंदणु, गिला, &c. करणु.
A Scoff, Scoffing. गिला, निंदा.
A Scoffer. निंदकु, गिलाखोरु.
A Scold. छोंभिरु, रनोड.
To Scold. छोंभणु, सूटणु, विड्हणु.
A Scolding. छोंभ, सूट.
To Scoop. कोरणु.
Scope. *See* Meaning, Room.
A Scorch. लहस, लूसाट, झराट.
To Scorch (*act.*). लहसाइणु, लहसणु, झराटणु, लूसाइणु, लूसणु, लूहणु.
To Scorch (*neu.*). लहसिजणु, झराटिजणु.
A Score (*twenty*). कोडी, वी. *See* Line.
To Score with a line. लीक कढणु.
To Score out (*cancel*). वारणु.
Scorn, Scorning. ठुठि, फिट्कार, खुआरी. *See* Contempt.
To Scorn. धिकारु &c. करणु, फिट्कारणु. *See* To Spurn.
The Sign Scorpio. वृश्चीकु.
A Scorpion. विछूं, भटूं, (*small*) भटूंअडो, विछुंअडी.
The game Scotch-hop. तीजो, चोदो, चीकिले रांदि.
A Scoundrel. लुचो, लुचु, शाही. *See* Rascal.
To Scour. मलणु, मांजणु.
A Scourge. चहबुकु, कम्ची.
To Scourge. चहबुकु, &c. हणणु-मारणु.
A Scout. चारो, जासूसु.
A Scowl. सूंडु, छोडु, घुंडु. *See* Frown.
To Scowl. सूंडु, &c. पाइणु-विझणु. *See* To Frown.
To Scramble for any thing. लेटी-पई-किरी झटु विझणु.
To Scramble up. कुरूंड़िडो थी हथ विझी चढ़हणु.
A Scrap. टुकिरु, टुकिरिडो, पुर्जो, रेजो, (*of paper*) चुट्को. *See* Piece, Morsel.
To Scrape. खुर्डणु, खर्डणु.
To Scrape up. खुर्डे कढणु.
A Scrape (*difficulty q. v.*). औखु, डुखु. *See* Perplexity.
A Scraper. खुर्पो, (*for scraping up grass*) रंबो, खुर्यो.
Scrapings. खुर्डि.
Scraps. रेजिकी.
A Scratch. रहड, चोर, रूहुंड़ो, नुहुंड़ो, नंहंड़ो. *See* Scratching.
To Scratch (*for itching*). खनहणु, (*lacerate*) रहडणु, (*with the nails*) नंहंड़णु, नुहुंड़णु, रहंड़णु, रूहुंड़णु.
To Scratch out (*erase*). खुर्डे छड़णु.

Scratching (*for itching*). खन्खनि, (*and clawing*) नँहँड़ु, रहँड़, रुहुंड़. See A Scratch.

To Scrawl in writing. रहड़णु.

A Scream, Screech. वाकों, रढि, दांह, खबिरी, कीक, कूक, कीह, रीह, रीहार.

To Scream, Screech. रडणु, फाटणु, ब्राकारणु, कूकणु, कूकारणु, वाकों, &c. करणु.

A Screecher. वाकिरु, रड्यो, कीकिरु, दांहिरु.

A Screen. पड्दो, पल्वेडो.

To Screen. ढकणु. *See* To Protest.

A Screw. पेचु.

To Scribble. रहडणु.

A Scroll. *See* Roll.

To Scrub. माञणु, मलणु, गहणु.

A Scrub for scrubbing with. मुई, मुओ.

A Scruple. शकु. *See* Doubt.

Scrupulous. विस्वासी, शकाइतो.

To Scrutinize. जाचणु, सोझणु, चकासणु, चाकासणु.

Scrutiny. जाच, सोझ, चकास.

A Scuffle. थिकमुठि.

To Sculk away. खिस्कणु, गुसाइणु, कंधीपासों करणु. *See* To Hide.

The Scull. *See* Skull.

Scum. छटी. *See* Foam.

The foul Scum formed on standing water. छटु, छटो, ज़ारी, सेंवरु, सिंअरु.

Scurf. ब्रफो.

Scurfy. ब्रफारो, ब्रफिरु.

Scurrilous. कमीणो. *See* Abusive.

The Sea. समुंडु, दरिआउ, बहरु.

Of the Sea. सामुंड्रो, दर्याही, बहरी.

A Seal (*stamp*). मुहुर; affixed in sealing up goods, &c. ठपो, मुंड़.

To Seal. मुहुर हणणु.

To Seal up. ठपणु, मुंड्रणु.

Sealing wax. ज़ज *f*.

A Seam. सेबो.

A Searce. मैदाबेगु.

To Searce. छाणणु.

A Search, Searching. ग़ोल, ग़ोला, ग़ोलाओ, गोलप, खोज, ढूंढ, ड़ोर, वउड, परो, परखुर, सोझ, निहार, फोल्ह, घोर.

To Search (*act.*). फोल्हणु.

To Search for. ग़ोलणु, खोजणु, ढूंढणु, ड़ोरणु, निहारणु, वउडणु, सोझणु, घोरणु.

To Search into (*investigate q. v.*). सोझणु, छाणणु.

To Search out. ग़ोले, &c. कढणु.

A Searcher. ग़ोलाऊ, ग़ोलो, घोरी.

A Season. मुंद, मइसुम, तुडि, फसुलु, रुति.

At the proper Season. मुंदाइतो.

Produced out of Season. कुमुंदाइतो, कुमुंदो.

To Season (*food*). मसालो, &c. ड़िअणु.

Seasonable, Seasonably. महलाइतो, वेलाइतो, वख्ताइतो. *See* Opportune.

A Seasoning. मसालो, (*eaten with rice or bread*) ड्रेडु, तीवणु, गुंभणु, (*put into food in cooking*) दागु, राई.

To Seat. विहारणु.

To Secede. धार–ब्राहरि थिअणु.

To Seclude. धार रखणु.

Second (*adj.*). ब्रिओ, ब्रोजो.

The Second day of the lunar fortnight. ब्रीज.

A Second of time. पलु, दमु. *See* Moment.

A Second time. ब्रिहर, ब्रिहार.

To Second. पुठि भरणु.

Seconding. खादारी.

Secrecy. गुझाई.

A Secret. गुझु, मँझु, भेतु, विचु, अंतु, मेदु.

Secret, Secretly. गुझो, गुप्तो, गुझाइतो, मँझाइतो.

The knower of one's Secrets. भेती, मांझिरू.

A Secretary. मुन्शी.

To Secrete. लिकाइणु, लुकाइणु, छपाइणु.

A Sect. धुंओं, बारी, मतु, पंथु, वेखु, मजहबु, परू, जाति.

A Section (*division q. v.*). वंड़, भाङो.

Secular. संसारी.

Secure, Securely. सोघो, हथोको, पुख्तो, काबू.

To Secure. सोघो, &c. करणु.

Security (*safety*). सोघाई, हथोकाई, पुख्ताई.

Security (*pledge*). जामिनि, जामिन्गीरी, खोलांदिरी.

A Sedan. ड़ोली, लोड़ो. *See* Palanquin.

Sedate. धीरो, ग़ौरो, ग़रो, गंभीरू.

Sedateness. ग़ौराई, ग़राई. *See* Staidness.

Sediment (*dregs*). किटो, तरो.

The Sediment or deposit from the river. नँउं, रउ.

Sedition. फशादु, फितिनो, खललु, फितूरू.

To excite Sedition. फशादु, &c. मचाइणु.

Seditious. फशादी, खलली, फितूरी.

To Seduce. भुलाइणु, धुतारणु, रेबणु, धुतणु, चतिराइणु.

A Seducer. धुतारू, रेबी. *See* Enticer.

Seducement, Seduction. धुतार, रेबु धुत. *See* Wheedling.

Sedulous, Sedulously. सायाइतो. *See* Diligent.

To See (*perceive*). ड़िसणु, पसणु.

To See (*direct the sight*). निहारणु.

Seed. ब़िजु, ब़ीहणु.

For Seed, kept for Seed. ब़ेजो, ब़िजाइतो.

Seedless. बेब़िजो.

Seedy. पर्णब़िज़ो, ब़िजेरो, ब़िजाइतो, ब़ेजो.

Seeing (*sub.*). ड़िसणु. *See* Sight.

To Seek. ग़ोल्णु, ढूंढणु, वडडणु. *See* To Search for.

To Seem, be Seen. ड़िसिजणु, सुझणु, भासणु.

Seeming (*sub.*). ड़िसिणी. *See* Appearance.

Seemingly. ड़िसण में, ड़िसिणिअ.

Seemliness. लाइकी, वडु.

Seemly. (*comely*) ड़िसिणो, (*becoming q. v.*) लाइकु, जुग़ाइतो, वडाइतो.

A Seesaw, Seesawing. लोड़ालोड़ी, लोडझूल.

To Seeth, (*act.*). सिझाइणु. *See* To Boil.

To Seeth (*neu.*). सिझणु. *See* To Boil.

To Seize. झलणु, वठणु.

A Seizing, Seizure. झल, वठु *f.*

Seldom. कँहिं-कँहीं-कड़हीं कदाने *or* कजाने, कड़्हींकड़्हीं, थोरो, विरिलो, विरिले.

To Select. चूंड़णु, धुणणु, (*fix upon, mark off*) वारणु, वालारणु.

Selection. चूंड़.

Self. पाण, पिंड़, धुरि.

Self-conceit. टिंड़ि.

Self-denial. किरो, संजमु.
Self-denying. कियांइतो, संजमी.
Self-dependence. पाणभराई.
Self-dependent. पाणभरो.
A Selfish person. पाणघुरो, पाण-भरू.
Selfishness. पाणघुराई.
Self-same. सायो. *See* Same.
To Sell (*act.*). विकिणणु.
To Sell, or be Sold. विकामणु.
A Seller. विकिणँदडु.
A Semblance. जिहडाई.
Semen virile. धातु *f.* मद्दी, बिंदु *f.*
To Send. मोकिलणु, मुंजणु, पठणु.
To Send for. सड़ाइणु, कोठाइणु, घु-राइणु.
Senile. बुढाणो, बुढाइतो, पर्याणो, पर्या-इतो, कुराडाणो, कुराडाइतो.
Senility. *See* Old age.
Senior. वड़ो, पर्यो.
Seniority. वड़ाई.
Senna. सना, सनामकाई.
Sensation, Sense. ग्यानु, सुधि.
Sense (*intellect*). अकुलु, बुधि, हो-शु, वकूफु, होसिलो, चेतो, औसानु, ग्यानु. *See* Understanding.
Senseless. बेहोशु, अचेतु, बेसुधि, गेरो. *See* Unmeaning.
Senselessness. बेहोशी. *See* Insensibility, Folly.
The Senses. हवासु.
To come to one's Senses. बोदि अ-चणु. *See* To Recover.
Sensible (*having consciousness*). सुचेतु, होशाइतो, चेताइतो, सुध्याइतो, (*wise q. v.*) डाहो, स्याणो, दानाहु, होसिलाइतो, सुर्त्याइतो, सुर्त्यो, ग्यानी.
Sensitive. कुंभरो. *See* Tender.
Sensual, a Sensualist. शहूती, विख-ई, ऐशी, अयाशी.

A Sentence (*paragraph.*). वाक्यु, गाल्हि.
A judicial Sentence. हुकुमु, फत्वा.
To Sentence. सजा जो हुकुमु डिअणु.
Sentient. *See* Sensible.
Sentimental. ब्रह्म–भाव भर्यो, भावाइतो.
A Sentinel, Sentry. जागो, चौकी-दारू, पहरो, पहरेदारू. *See* Watchman.
To Separate (*act.*). धार *&c.* करणु, विछोडणु, वखिराइणु.
To Separate (*neu.*). विछुडणु, धार, *&c.* थिअणु.
Separate, Separately. धार, जुदा, अलगु, वखिरो, निधारो, संधाइतो, आरादो.
Separation. जुदाई, आरादाई, वखि-राई, (*from a loved object*) वि-रिहु, विछोडो, फोडाओ, फिराकु.
Septangular. सतकुंडो.
September-October. असू.
Septuple. सतूंणो.
A Sepulchre. *See* Tomb.
The Sequel. पोयों भाङो. *See* Conclusion.
To Sequester, Sequestrate. जब्त -खाल्से करणु.
A Seraglio. *See* Harem.
Serene. सांतीको, माठीणो, सांति.
Sereneness, Serenity. ठहर, थांहर, थँहर, सांति, सांतोकाइ, माठीणाई.
A Series. सिफ, कतार, वहीर, संबोर. *See* Row.
Serious, Seriously. गौरो, गरो.
Seriousness. गौराई, गराई.
A Serpent. सपु, नांगु. *See* Snake.
A Serpent-charmer. जोगी, मांड़ो.
Serpentine (*winding*). वरारो, वरा-इतो.
Serrated. डंदिरू, डंदाइतो.

A Servant. नोकरू, चाकरू, ब़ेलो, खिज़्मत्गारू, पोह्रंतु, नफरू, टहल्यो.

A Servant-maid. पोह्रंति, चाकरि, नफियांणी.

Servants. अमूलो.

To Serve. नोकिरी &c. करणु, सेवणु.

To Serve out. *See* To Distribute.

Service. नोकिरी, चाकिरी, ब़ेलीपणो, ब़ेलिपो, खिज़्मत, नफिरी, कमाई, टहल, बंदगी, सेवा.

Serviceable. कमाइतो, काराइतो. *See* Profitable, Useful.

Servile. गोलाणो.

A grain of Sesame. तिरू; its plural, तिर, is the generic name for the grain.

To Set (*place, lay*). रखणु, धरणु, (*fix, plant q. v.*), विहारणु.

To Set (*a razor, &c.*). लाइणु.

To Set a going (*commence working*). जोड़णु.

To Set on (*as in the chase*). बछणु.

To Set out or off. निकिरणु, रवानो थिअणु.

To Set up (*erect*). बिहारणु, खड़ो –उभो करणु.

To Set (*as the sun*). लहणु, उलहणु.

To Set jewels. जड़णु.

Set with jewels. जड़ाऊ, जड़ितू.

A Set (*batch*). दफो.

The Setting jewels. जड़िणी, जड़िति.

Settings of jewels. जड़ाउ, जड़ितु.

To Settle (*determine, establish*). ठहराइणु, विहारणु.

To Settle (*as water*). आठिरणु, आछिरणु, ठहरणु, थथिरणु.

To Settle an account, &c. निबेरणु. लाहणु, चुकाइणु, उकिलाइणु, निछोड़णु, उकारणु.

To Settle down, (*become fixed after fluctuation*). विहणु, विहणु. *See* To become Quiet.

To be Settled (*adjusted*). निबिरणु, लहणु, चुकणु, उकिलणु, निछुड़णु.

A Settled custom, or continuous engagement. नेमु, ठुक, कैतु.

A Settlement, Settling. निबेरो, निबेर, निछेड़, निछोड़ु, निछेड़ो, ठहराउ, (*of price*) चुकति.

Seven. सत.

Name of the number Seven. सतो.

Seven (*per cent*). सतोतिरो.

And or with Seven (*prefixed to hundreds, &c.*). सत्यो, सतोतरू.

Sevenfold (*adj.*). सतूणो.

The Sevenfold. सतूणि

Seventeen. सत्रँहें.

Seventeenth. सत्रँहों.

Seventh. सतों.

The Seventh day of the lunar fortnight. सतँहिँ.

Seventieth. सतर्यों.

Seventy. सतरि.

Seventy-one. एकहतरि.

Seventy-two. ब़ाहतरि.

Seventy-three. ट्रेहतरि.

Seventy-four. चोहतरि.

Seventy-five. पंजहतरि.

Seventy-six. छाहतरि.

Seventy-seven. सतहतरि.

Seventy-eight. अठहतरि.

Seventy-nine. उणासी.

To Sever. धार करणु. *See* To Separate.

Several (*many*). कँईं *plu.* केतिरा *plu.* घणा *plu.* *See* Distinct, Single.

Severally. धार धार, हिकिड़ो हिकिड़ो.

Severe. ड़ाढो, सख़्तु, कड़ो, कठोरू.

Severity. ड़ाढाई, सख़्ताई, सख़्तो, कड़ाई.

To Sew. सिबणु.
Sewing (*sub.*). सिविणो, सेबो, सेवणि; various kinds of Sewing, टॉपो, खीर, ओंटो, बख्यो, कंड़िजो, ओलिंमो, तेबुचो
Charge for Sewing. सिबाणी.
Sex (*gender*). निशानो.
Sextuple. छहूंणो.
Shabby. लाओ. *See* Old, Mean.
To Shackle a beast. ड़ाइणु, ड़ावणु &c. विझणु.
Shackles for shacking beasts, &c. ड़ावणु, ड़ाणु, इश्केलु, इश्कोलु, नेलु, निभरू, नेरू, जंजोरू. *See* Fetters.
The Shade. छांव, छां, पाछो, ओलो. *See* Shadow.
A Shade for lamps. फानूसु.
To Shade. ढकणु, छांव &c. करणु.
Shadiness. छांवेलाई, छांवेराई.
A Shadow. पाछो, दहो, पाछांओ, पाछुओ, पाछूलो, दओ. *See* Shade.
Shady. छांइरू, छांविलो-वेरो.
A Shaft of wood, &c. सराई
Shag (*woolly hair*). बज.
Shaggy. बजिरू.
Shagreen. कोमुखतु.
To Shake (*act.*). लोड़णु, धोड़णु, धूणणु, धुड़काइणु; or pull about with force, धूंधाडणु, धांधोलणु, गींदाडणु, (*water*) छोलणु.
To Shake (*neu.*). लुड़णु, धुड़णु, भुड़कणु, खिड़कणु, चुरणु, टुल्कणु, लिच्कणु, ड़कणु, कंबणु, (*as the ground in an earthquake*) धुन्नणु. *See* To Tremble.
A Shake, Shaking. लोड़ो, धोड़ो, लोड़, धुड़ूको, ड़किणी. *See* Trembling.
To be Shaky or loose. ढलिडणु,
Shallow (*as water*). तांघो, लांघो, तांघिडो, (*as a dish*) तराखिडो, तांघिडो. *See* Flat.
Shallowness. तांघाई, लांघाई.
A Sham. मिंहु, गेगु, मिखिरू, तोतालु. *See* Pretence.
To Sham. मिंहाइणु, गेगाइणु, मिखिराइणु.
The Shambles. कमेलो.
Shame. लज़, शरमु, हया, हयाउ, नकु, मरमु, लोह, आरू, भरमु.
To Shame. लज़ाइणु, शर्माइणु, नकु वढणु.
To feel Shame. लज़णु, लज़िजणु, शर्माइणु.
Shameful, Shamefully. लज़ारो, लज़ाइतो, शर्माइतो.
Shameless, Shamefaced. बेलज़ो, बेहया-याउ, बेनंगो, निर्जो, बेदोदो, उघाडो.
Shamelessness. बेलज़ाई, बेहयाई, निजाई.
A Shammer. गेगो, मिखिरेलो, तोतालो.
To Shampoo. मनणु, भीड़ूं ड़िअणु.
Shape. ड़ौलु, ढंउं, ढबु, सूरत, घाटु, आचारू.
To Shape. घड़णु. *See* To Form.
Shapeless. बेड़ौलो, कुढबो, बेढबो, बेढंओ.
Shapelessness. बेड़ौलाई, बेढंवाई.
Shapely, well-Shaped. ड़ौलाइतो, सुड़ौलो.
A Share. भाङो, पतो, हिसो, बखिरो, वखिरो, वाटो, विर्छ, विहांङो, वंड़, वंड़ो, फांड़, फांड़िणी, तकु, छांदो, तपो.
The Share of a plough. फारू.
To Share (*distribute q. v.*). विराइणु, वंड़णु, विर्छणु.
To Share (*participate*). भाङो &c. वठणु, भाङेरो, &c. हुअणु.
A Sharer. पतिआरू, हिसेदारू, हिसेभाई, भाङेरो, हिसेरो. *See* Partner.

A half Sharer. अधोभाधि *m.*
In or by Shares. हिसाइतो, हिसेरो, भाङाइतो, भाङेरो, भाईठों, भायोठों, भायाठो.
A Shark. वेसाणु.
Sharp, Sharply. तिखो, तेजु.
Sharp-witted. खांदो, सुज्ञाणु.
To Sharpen. तिखो करणु, लाइणु.
Sharpness. तिखाई, वहुक, वहु, रउ.
To Shatter. टुकिर टुकिर करे विझणु.
To Shave. कूडणु, हजामत करणु.
To Shave the privities. पाकी खणणु-कमाइणु.
A Shaveling, one with head shaven. रोड़ो, ठोड्हो.
Shaving (*sub.*). हजामत, संवारत.
A Shawl. शाल; a double shawl, दुशालो.
She. हिअ, हुअ, हो, हू; indicating or distinguishing, इहा, उहा.
A Sheaf. बंदु, गड़ो, लड़.
To Shear. कतिरणु.
A pair of Shears. कतरिं, (*for cutting betlenut*) सुभडो.
A Sheath. खिप. *See* Scabbard.
To Sheath. थेकणु.
To Shed. *See* To Spill, Drop.
To Shed tears. ग़ोड्हा, &c. ग़ाडणु, हंजूं हारणु.
A Shed. मनहु, छनो, छाजो.
A Sheep. रिढ; a species of sheep with fat tail, दुंबो.
Of a Sheep. रेढो.
Sheer. स्गो, निरो, निसोरो. *See* Mere.
A Sheet (*cloth*). चादर.
A Sheet of paper. पनो.
A Shelf. पछटी, पेढी, तकु; a kind of hanging shelf, छिको.
The Shell of an egg, nut, &c. खल, खोपो, छिल.
The Shell of the seed of siliquous plants. फरी.
A Sea-Shell or species of such. सुती, सुतो, सुतिभडो. *See* Conch, Oyster.
To Shell (*take out of the shell*). फोडणु.
Shelter. अझो, अड, ओट, आसिरो, ओलो, ढक. *See* Protection.
Shelving. लाडुओं. *See* Sloping.
A Shepherd. रेढारू, रेढरू.
Sherbet. शर्बतु.
A Sherd. *See* Potsherd.
To Shield. रखणु. *See* To Protect.
A Shield. ढाल, सिपर, खेडो,
A Shift (*expedient, q. v.*). वझु, वाझु, सझु.
A woman's Shift. पपो, पपिरो.
To Shift (*act. change, q. v.*). मटणु. *See* To Veer.
The Shin. बुकिअ जी नरी.
To Shine. झल्कणु, चिल्कणु, चिम्कणु, बृहकणु.
Shine, Shining. चिल्को, झल्को. *See* Brightness.
Shining, Shiny. चिल्किणो, चिम्किणो.
A Ship. गोराबु, जहाजु.
Of a Ship. जहाजी.
To Shirk. गुसाइणु, नटाइणु. *See* To Evade.
A Shirker. गोह्यारू, गुसाऊ. *See* Evader.
Shirking (*sub.*). गोह्री, नटाउ. *See* Evasion.
A Shirt. पहिराणु, अंगरखो, जामो.
To Shiver (*tremble q. v.*). डकणु, फड्कणु, थड्कणु, हड्कणु. *See* To Shatter.

A Shivering. ड़किणी, फड़को, फड़्किणी, थड़्किणी, सिआंदो.

A Shoal (*bank*). चिकणि, ब्रेटु, रेट.

Shoal (*adj.*). तांघो. *See* Shallow.

A Shock. धकु.

A Shoe. पादरू, मोचिडो, (*old*) छितरू, (*wooden*) चाखिडो.

A pair of Shoes. जुती, पेतिलो, जोडो.

A horse-Shoe. नालु.

To beat with a Shoe. खलो–मोचिडो &c. हणणु.

To Shoe (*a horse*). नाल बंधणु.

The Shoeing horses. नालबंदी.

A Shoe-maker. मोचो, सोचो, मेघिवाडु, ढेढु.

Of a Shoe-maker. मोचिको, मोच्याणो, सोचिको, सोच्याणो.

A seller of Shoes. जुत्यरू.

To Shoot. (*discharge*) हणणु, छोडणु, (*kill*) मारणु.

To Shoot up (*as plants*). उग़णु, ज़मणु, ज़ापणु. *See* To Spring up.

To Shoot out (*as leaves or foliage*). मोर्जणु, अंगूर्जणु.

A Shoot (*sprout q. v.*). गौंचु, अंगूरू, कख्यो.

A Shop. हटी, हटु, दुकानु.

Of a Shop. हाटेलो, हटेलो.

A Shop-board, or platform for goods. पिडो, दिको.

To open a Shop. हटु पटणु–कढणु.

To close a Shop. हटु पूरणु–सरहणु–पर्चाइणु–खणणु.

A general shutting of Shops. हटताड.

A Shopkeeper. हटवारो, हटवाण्यो, हटाई, दुकान्दारू, दुकानी, किराडु.

The Shore. कपु, कंधी, किनारो, भरि, ड़नी, कंठो, तोरू.

Short. (*in size*) नंढो, लाठो, (*in height only*) मँझिरो, बिंदिरो, (*deficient*) लाभो, घटि, कसो, कोतडु, (*in time*) थोरो.

A little Short or deficient. उँभालो, उँभालेरो, घटेरो, घटेरिडो.

To fall Short. खुटणु.

A falling Short. ऊणाई, ऊणि. *See* Deficiency.

To Shorten. नंढो–घटि &c. करणु, घटाइणु.

Shortly. थोरिडे मैं, पोभभरो. *See* Soon.

Shortness. (*in size*) नंढाई, लाठाई, (*in time*) थोरिडाई. *See* Deficiency.

A Shot, or grain of Shot. छरो, छिरो. *See* Ball, Bullet.

Shot (*the affix, as in bowshot, musketshot*). पंधु.

A Shove. धिको, थेल्हो.

To Shove. धिकणु, थेल्हणु.

The Shoulder. कुल्हो.

The Shoulder blade. फणि, हंझो.

A Shout, Shouting. वाको, दांह, रडि, कूक, ब्राकार, खबिरो.

To Shout. वाको, *&c.* करणु, ब्राकणु, ब्राकारणु. *See* To Bawl.

Show (*false appearance*). ड़ेखु, ठाटु, ठाहु.

A Show. तमाशो, बाजी, मजो.

To Show. ड़ेखारणु, पसाइणु, लखाइणु.

A Showman. तमाश्गरू, तमाशी.

A Shower. ओहिडो, छल्को, झट्को, छुलिंगी, छुहो.

To Shower (*neu.*). वसणु.

Showy. ड़ेखाइतो, ड़ेखिरू.

A Shred. अग़िडो, चिडट, लीड; in shreds, लीडूं लीडूं.

A Shrew. रनोड.

Shrewd. स्याणो, सुघड़ु. *See* Wise, Cunning.

Shrewdness. स्याणप, सुघड़ाई.

A Shriek. कीक, कीह. *See* Scream.

Shrill. सन्हो.

A Shrimp. गांगटु.

A Shrine. दर्गाहु, दर्गहु.

To Shrink. सुसणु, घटणु.

To Shrivel (*neu.*). घुंजिजणु, गुञाइजणु.

A Shroff. शराफु, सराफु.

A Shroud. खफणु.

A Shrub. बूझो, बूटो, बूटी.

To Shudder. कंबणु. *See* To Tremble.

To Shun. परे-अलगु रहणु.

To Shut (*act.*). पूरणु, बंदि करणु, लग़ाइणु, वारणु, वराए छडणु, पाइणु, बूटणु, ब्रेकिडणु, भीडणु. *See* To Close.

To Shut (*neu.*). पूर्जणु, बंदि थिअणु, वरणु.

A Shutter (*for a window*). दरो.

A Shuttle. नडो.

Shy. ट़हिणो, ट़ाहडु, ट़हडु.

To Shy. छिर्कणु. *See* To Start.

Sick. नाचङो, अणचङो, लडो, बेमजे, नाचाकु, रोगी, रोग़ाइतो, मर्जीलु, मरीज़, डुभारी.

To Sicken, get Sick. नाचङो, &c. थिअणु.

A Sickle. ड़ांटो, लस.

Sickly. मर्जीलु, आजारी, रोगी, डुभारी.

Sickness. नाचङाई, अणचङाई, लडाई, बेमजाई, नाचाकी, रोगु, मर्जु, डुभारि, आजारु, जहमत.

A Side. पासो, पहलू, (*direction*) तर्फु, पारु, ड़िसा, ड़िसि. *See* Party.

The Side of a boat. कछो.

The near Side. ओरारु.

The further, or opposite, Side. परारु.

On this Side. हिन पासे, हिन भरि, ओरारि, ओरिंअ भरि.

On that Side. हुन पासे, हुन भरि. पारि, परारि, परिंअ भरि.

From all Sides, on all Sides. चौधारी.

Side (*adj.*). पासीरो.

To Side (*lean to a party*). पासि &c. करणु. *See* Partiality.

To Sidle. पासोरो हलणु.

A Side-lock of hairs. चूणो, कलमु, बटूरु.

Sideways, on one's Side, to one Side. पासारो, पासोरो.

A Siege. घेरो, वेड्हु.

A Sieve. परणु, मैदाबेगु, गेचणु.

To Sift. छाणणु, (*clean by shaking in a fan*) छंड़णु, उपिणणु.

The act of Sifting. छाणिणी.

The cost of Sifting. छाणाणी.

The Siftings. छाणु, छाणो.

A Sigh. थधो साहु, शूकारो.

To Sigh. साहु भरणु, शूकारणु.

Sight. निर्ति, निगाह, नजर, निहार.

A Sight (*spectacle*). तमाशो, मजो.

The Sight of a gun. मखि.

Payable at Sight (*a bill*). दर्सनी.

To be in Sight. ड़िसिजणु.

Sightly. दर्सनी, ड़िसण जिहडो.

A Sign. निशानी, पारु, चिह्नु. *See* Indication, Token.

To Sign (*affix signature*). सही, &c. विझणु–करणु.

A Signal. इशारो. *See* Sign.

To Signalize oneself. मशहाइणु, मर्काइणु.

A Signature. सही, हथ अखर *plu.*

A Signet. मुहुर.

Signification. माना. *See* Meaning.

To Signify (*make known*). ज़ाणाइणु. *See* To Inform.

It does not Signify. भउ-भोलो कोन्हे, भई कान्हे.

Silence (*sub.*). माठि, चुपु *f.* सुंन, गुंगशोडि, गुपुचुपु *f.* माठोणाई.

Silence (*interjec*). माठि, चुपु, चिहु, बसिकरि.

To Silence. माठि कराइणु.

Silent, Silently. माठोणो.

To be Silent. माठि थिअणु.

Silk. पटु, रेशमु; some varieties of silk stuffs are, मशिरू ताखतो, खारो, एलाचो, अतिलसु, गुल्दोजु, तसरि, गुलूबदनु, खुदिबाफु, तहमूरो, हीराकणी, दर्याही, सिण्यो.

Silken. रेशमी.

The Sill of a door. चाउठि.

Sillily. जला.

Silliness. भोरिडाई, भोराई.

Silly. भोरिडो, भोरो, भोलू. *See* A Fool.

Silver. चांदी, रुपो.

Of Silver. रोपो.

Similar. जिहडो, समानि, हिकवांगुरु, तुलि, हिकसँभों, सखों. *See* Alike.

Similarity, Similitude. जिहडाई, हिकजिहडाई, मुशाबत, बरोबरी.

A Simile. मिसालु, बयानो, द्रिष्टांतु.

Simple (*uncompounded*). निजातु, निरो, निखालिसु. *See* Pure.

Simple (*easy*). सँहँजो. *See* Easy, Plain.

Simple (*artless*). भोरिडो, आलो भोलो, भोरो, आलोभोलो, साधू. *See* Artless, Guileless.

Simplicity. भोरिडाई, भोराई. *See* Artlessness.

Simply (*merely q. v.*). रुगो.

To Simulate. *See* To Pretend.

Simultaneous, Simultaneously. गडु, भेडो.

Sin. गुनाहु, गुनहु, डोहु, पापु, अपिराधु, पिराछतु, पातकु.

To Sin. गुनाहु &c. करणु.

Since (*after, from the time that*). खां पोइ, लाकू, आकुरू; from such time as, जड्हाकुरू-हाको-हींको-हूणो-हूणिको; from that time, तड्हाकुरू-हाको-हींको-हूणो-हूणिको; since how long, कड्हाकुरू-हाको-हींको-हूणो-हूणिको.

Since (*because that*). तँहिं करे. *See* On Account of.

Sincere. सचो, सचारू, सलों, सिदिकी, असोलु, सचाइतो. *See* Honest.

Sincerity. सचाई, सचाराई, सचारो, सिदिकु.

A Sinew. नस, रग.

Sinewy. नसिरू, रगिरू.

Sinful. डुशरी, गुनाही, गुनहो, पापी, पिराछती, पातकी; or sinfully, पापाइतो, डोहाइतो, गुनाहितो. *See.* Wicked.

Sinfulness. पापीपणो. *See* Sin.

To Sing. गाइणु, (*as a bird*) बोलणु.

To Singe. लहसाइणु, ज़राटणु, लूहणु, लूसणु, लूसाटणु.

To be Singed. लहसजणु, लासजणु.

A Singer. गाईंदडु, गाइणू, कलावंतु, रागी, गाइकु, रागींदडु.

Single, Singly, (*sole, alone*). हेकलो, हेको, हिको, हेकिडो, छड्हो, जको, यको. *See* One, Alone.

Single (*not double*). हेकूणो, हेकूटो.

The Single. हेकूणि, हेकूणाई.

Singleness. एकाई, हिकिडाई, हेकिडाई, हिकाई, हेकाई.

Singular. *See* Single, Unusual.
The Singular number. हिकुवचनु, वाहिदु.
A Sink. मोरी.
To Sink (*neu.*). बुड़णु. *See* To Decrease, be Lost.
To Sink (*act.*). ब्रोडणु.
To rise and Sink, as a drowning person. गोता खाइणु.
Sinless. बेड़ोहो, बेगुनाहो.
A Sinner. डुहारी, ड़ोहो, गुनहगारु, पापी, गुनाही, गुनही. *See* Sinful.
Sinuous. वरारो, वराइतो.
A Sip. सुर्की.
To Sip. सुर्की भरणु.
Sir. जीउ, सांई.
Sirup. चाश्नी, चाशि, पति.
A Sister. भेणु *f.* भेण, अदी, दादी.
Of a Sister. भेणिको.
Sisterhood (*office of a sister*). भेण्पो, भेण्पाई.
Sister-in-law. (*wife's sister*) साली, (*husband's sister*) निणुन, महंदी, (*brother's wife*) भाज़ाई, भाभी, (*husband's brother's wife*) ड़ेराणी.
To Sit. विहणु; on the heels, ओकिड़ू विहणु; cross-legged, पल्थी मारणु; on knees and heels, गोड़ा-जोड़ा भञी विहणु; down low, झुकी विहणु; resting on one thigh and knees, ऊंधा जोड़ा करे विहणु.
Site. *See* Situation.
Sitting (*sub.*). विहक.
A Situation. जाइ, जगह, हंधु. *See* Place, Station.
Six. छ.
The name of the number Six. छको.
Six (*per cent*). छहोतिरो.
Sixfold (*adj.*). छहूणो.
The Sixfold. छहूणि.
Sixteen. सोरहं.
Sixteenth. सोरहों.
Sixth. छहों.
The Sixth day of a lunar fortnight. छठि.
Sixtieth. सठ्यों.
Sixty. सठि.
About Sixty. साठीको.
Sixty-one. एकहठि.
Sixty-two. ब्राहठि.
Sixty-three. टेहठि.
Sixty-four. चोहठि.
Sixty-five. पंजहठि.
Sixty-six. छाहठि.
Sixty-seven. सतहठि.
Sixty-eight. अठहठि.
Sixty-nine. उणहतरि.
Size. काछो, कछ, अंदाजु.
A Skain, Skein. फोरो.
A Skeleton. ढूंढु, ठूंठु.
A Skeptic. शकी, भिर्मी, भणवेसाहो.
To Sketch. अंगारणु, लीकणु.
A Skewer. शीख.
A Skiff. ड़ूंडी.
A Skilful person. भडु, कारीगरु, सुघडु, हुनिरेली, हुनिरी, गुणवंतु, बहुगुणो-णु, उस्तादु, गुणी.
Of a Skilful person. भडाणो, कारीगराणो, उस्तादाणो-दिको.
Skilful, Skilfully. हुनिराइतो.
Skill, Skilfulness. भडाई, कारीगरी-राई, सुघडाई, उस्तादाई.
A Skillet. कण्छु, कढुछु. *See* Saucepan.
To Skim (*act.*). छटो लाहणु.
The Skin. खल, खलिडी, चमु, छिलु *f.* छिल.
An untanned Skin or hide. छोडो.
A cow's or buffalo's Skin tanned. अधोड.

A dealer in Skins. छीडाई.
To Skin. खलणु, खल लाहणु.
To Skip (*neu.*). ट्पणु. *See* To Leap, Frisk.
To Skip over (*in writing or reading*). तर्क हणणु, छड्गु. *See* To Pass over.
A Skirt. दाँवणि, पलउ, पलादु, पांदु. *See* Border.
The Skull. कोपिरो, केपिराटी.
The Sky. उभु, आस्मानु, आकासु.
Of the Sky, Sky-blue. आस्मानी.
A Sky rocket. हवाई.
A Slab (*stone*). तख्ती.
To Slabber. गिग वहाइणु-गाडणु.
A Slabberer. गिगिहू.
Slack, Slackly. ढिरो, ढरो.
To Slacken (*act.*). ढिरो करणु, ढारणु.
To Slacken (*neu.*). ढिरणु, ढरणु.
Slackness. ढिराई, ढिराणि, ढराई-णि.
Slander. लेउ, लीभ, तूफानु.
To Slander. लेउ &c. लाइणु, निंदणु.
A Slanderer. लेभरू, लीभरू, तूफानी.
Slanderous. तूफानी; *or* slanderously, लीभाइतो.
Slanting, Slantingly. लामारो, लाडुओं, टेड़ो, आड़ोटेड़ो. *See* Sloping.
A Slap. चमाट, लपाट, चपाट, थपड, तमाचो, चंबो, बुजो.
The sound from a Slap. फहको, फहकारो, फहकाउ, फहकाटु.
To Slap. चमाट *&c.* हणणु.
To Slash (*act.*). वाढोडणु.
A Slate or board for writing on. पटी, फरही.
A Slattern. अगलो. *See* Sloven.
A Slave. ब्रान्हो, गोलो, गुलामु, दासु.
Of a Slave. गोलाणो.
The offspring of a Slave. गोलाडो.

Slaver. गिग.
Slavery. ब्रान्हिपो-पाई-पणु, गोलपणु, गुलामी.
Slaughter. कोसु, माहो, मारो.
For Slaughter. कोसडु.
To Slaughter. (*animals for food*) कुहणु, विझणु, निडो-हलालु करणु, पाइणु, कमाइणु, तकबीर करणु or वहाइणु; with a sword, झट्को करणु.
To be Slaughtered. कुसणु.
To Slay. मारणु. *See* To Slaughter.
A Sledge-hammer. वड़ाणु, वटोहडु.
Sleek. लसो.
Sleekness. लसाई.
Sleep. निंड, ऊंघ, ऊंग.
To Sleep or fall asleep. सुम्हणु.
To put to Sleep. सुम्हारणु.
To talk in Sleep. उफिड्कणु.
A Sleeper. निंड्राकु, निंड्रिरू.
Sleepiness. ऊंघाई.
Sleeplessly. बेनिंड्रो.
Sleeplessness. बेनिंड्राई, ओजागो, जागु.
Sleepy, Sleepily. निंड्राखिडो, निंड्राखो, निंड्राइतो, निंड्रारो.
To be Sleepy. निंड्राइजणु.
A Sleeve. बांह, आस्तीन.
Slight of hand. हथ्नटु, फेराटो, चलतो, चलटु.
Slender. सन्हो.
Slenderness. सन्हाई.
A Slice of a fruit, &c. फार.
To Slide. तिर्कणु. *See* To Slip.
Slight (*inconsiderable*). थोरो. *See* Small, Slender.
To Slight. को न लेखणु.
Slightly, Slight, (*lightly*). उछातिरो, मथाछिरो.

Slim, Slimness. *See* Slender, Slenderness.

Slime. गप, चिक. *See* Mire.

Slimy. गपारो, चिकारो, चिकिराठो.

Sliness. छंदाई, फंदाई.

A Sling for throwing. खांभाणी, घुब्रणि.

To Sling (*throw by a sling*). खांभाणी &c. हणणु.

The stone or pellet used with a Sling. गुड्हो, गुलेलो.

To Slink. *See* To Sneak off, Miscarry.

To Slip (*slide*). तिर्कणु, फिस्कणु; down, घिर्कणु.

To Slip, Slip away, (*glide or pass out, or away*). खिस्कणु.

A Slip, of wood, &c. फतोल, पूटो; of cloth, &c. पटी, पटो.

A Slip (*cutting let to grow*). कलमु.

A Slip, Slipping. तिर्किणी, फिस्किणी.

A pair of Slippers. जुनो. *See* Shoe.

Slipperiness. तिर्किणाई, तिर्कणी.

Slippery, Slippy. तिर्किणो.

A Slippery place. तिर्कणि.

Slipshod. पेलांघो.

To Slit (*act.*). चीरणु. *See* To Split.

A Slit. चीरु, चीर, चिहिकु, टुको; in clothes, चाकु.

To Slobber. गिग वहाइणु or गाडणु.

A Slope. लाड, लेट, लाहु, सलामी.

To Slope (*act.*). लाडणु, लेटाइणु.

To Slope (*neu.*). लडणु, लेटणु.

Sloping (*adj.*) लाडुओं, लेटाओं, लामारो, गल्तां, लाडूकडु.

Sloping, Slopewise. *See* Obliquely.

Sloppy. चिकिराठो. *See* Miry.

Sloth, Slothfulness. आरिसु, आलिसु, सुस्ताई, टोटिअणो-टिपाई. *See* Laziness, Sluggishness.

Slothful. आरिसी, आलिसी, सुस्तु, रोगी, विसाणो, टिकू; *or* Slothfully, आरिसाइतो, आलिसाइतो. *See* Lazy.

To be Slothful. आर्साइणु, आलिसाइणु.

A Sloven, Slovenly. अगलो, गदिलो, अल्लुजल्लु, छेगिरो, बेसिजिलो, अतावो, खिर्विखिरो.

Slovenliness. अगलाई, गदिलाई, खिर्विखिराई, छेगिराई.

Slow. ढिरो, ढिराइतो. *See* Dilatory.

To be Slow. ढिराइणु, ढिकणु.

Slowly. ढिरो, होयां, होरे, हरेहरे, ढिराइतो.

Slowness. ढिराई, ढिर.

To Slubber over hastily. रहडणु. *See* To Slur over.

A Sluggard, Sluggish. सूंमतो *See* Slothful.

Sluggishness. सूंमत, नेस्ती. *See* Sloth.

A Sluice. मोरी.

To Slumber. *See* To Sleep.

A Slur. लोंघो, कलंकु, दागु, टिको. *See* Blemish.

To cast a Slur. लोंघो &c. लाइणु.

To Slur over lightly. मथाछिरो करणु. *See* To Slubber over.

A Slut. अगलो. *See* Sloven.

Sly. छंदो, फंदो; *or* Slily, छंदाइतो, फंदाइतो.

A Smack (*crack*). ठकाउ.

To Smack. ठकाउ कढणु.

Small (*in size*). नंढो, लाठो, विंदिरो, (*in amount*) थोरो, थोरिडो.

Too Small, Smaller. नंढेरो, नंढेरिडो, लाठेरो, लाठेरिड़ो.

Very Small. नंढिडो.

Smallness (*in size*). नंढाई, लाठाई, (*in amount*) थोराई.

The Small pox. सोतळा, माई, माता, सिभरि, सिथरी; some kinds of small pox or varieties in the eruption are, चेट्टी, पंजिडी, सतिडी.

A spot or pustule in Small pox. दाणो.

The freckle or pit left by Small pox. सिभरो.

Smallness. नंढाई, (*in amount*) थोराई, थोरिडाई.

To Smart. कुरणु, पोसिरणु.

Smart (*brisk*). झांझिरो, तिखो, तखडु, फुड्तु, फुड्तो, चालाकु, चर्बटु चंचलु. *See* Active, Sharp.

A Smart, Smarting. पोसिणी, पोसरि, पोसिराटु.

Smartness. झांझिराई, फुड्ती, तिखाई, चालाकी.

To Smash. भञी भोरणु, टुकिर टुकिर-पुर्जा पुर्जा करे भञणु or विझणु.

To Smear. मखणु, लाइणु. *See* To Besmear.

A Smearing of cowdung. चौंको. *See* Besmearing.

To Smell (*act.*). सिंघणु, सुंघणु.

To Smell (*neu.*). बोइ, &c. डिभणु.

Smell. बोइ, बूंइ, बास, भप, मुश्क, धमक.

To Smile. मुर्कणु, मुश्कणु, पाक्षोहणु.

A Smile, Smiling. मुर्क, पाक्षोह, पाबूइ.

A Smiler, Smiling. मुर्किणो.

To Smite. मारणु. *See* To Strike.

A Smith. *See* Blacksmith, Goldsmith, &c.

Smitten (*enamoured q. v.*). मुस्ताकु.

Smoke. दूंहों.

To Smoke (*fill or affect with smoke*). दूंहांटणु.

To Smoke (*emit smoke*). दूंहांइणु, दूंहों करणु.

To Smoke (*a pipe*). छिकणु, पिभणु.

To be Smoked (*affected by smoke*). दूंहांटिजणु, दूंहाइजणु.

A Smoker. छकाऊ, छेकू, हुकाई, पिआकु.

Smoky. दूंहारो, दूंहेरो.

Smooth. लसो, लासुड.

To Smooth, make Smooth. लसाइणु.

To feel Smooth. लसाइणु.

Smooth-faced (*wanting hair*). खुसिरो, खुसु.

A Smooth-faced boy. गल्पटु.

Smoothness. लसाई, लसाणि, लस.

To Smother (*act.*). बूसाटणु.

To Smuggle. इजारे जो चोरी करे आणणु.

Smut in corn. अड़ारी, काणी.

Smutty (*as corn*). काणो. *See* Obscene.

A Snaffle. लसो लगामु.

A Snail. किंभों.

A Snake (*different species*). सपु, नांगु, बला, संग्चूरु, खपुरु, घोडालि, भरडि, अरोड, लुंडो, वासींगु, डुमणि, पदमु, कोरकिंडु, कोराड.

To Snap (*break at once; act.*). छिनणु.

To Snap or Snatch. खसणु.

To Snap as a rope, (*neu.*). छिजणु.

To Snap at one angrily. चहड पाइणु, छिडिब्र डिभणु, ड़ाड्हणु, झिण्कणु.

A Snap of the fingers. चपुटी.

Snappish. चहडी-डोलु, छिडिब्रो; *or* Snappishly, चहडाइतो, छिडिब्राइतो.

A Snare. कोड्को, फासो, फाही, फांदी, फांधो, गारी.

To Snare. फासाइणु.

To Snarl. गोंरणु, गिरणु.

To Snatch (*act.*). खसणु.

A Snatch. झपो, झटु, छिकी.

A Sneak (*shirk*). गोझरू, गुसाऊ, गोसिरू, गोसिडू, नटाऊ.

To Sneak off. खिस्कणु, गुमाए -नटाए वञणु.

To Sneer. नकु मोड़णु, टोक, &c. हणणु.

A Sneer, Sneering. टोक, तानो, तुन्को.

A Sneerer. तानिरू, टोकिरू.

Sneering, Sneeringly. टोकाइतो, तानाइतो.

A Sneeze. छिक, निछ.

To Sneeze. छिक &c. ड़िअणु.

To Sniff. सुण्कणु.

To Snivel. सिंघ, &c. वहणु. *See* Snot.

A Sniveller. सिंघिरू, गोबिरू.

A Snore. घोंघिरो, खोंघिरो.

To Snore. घोंघिरो ड़िअणु or हणणु.

A Snorer. घोंघिराई.

A Snort. फूकारो.

To Snort. फूकारो हणणु *or* ड़िअणु, फूकारणु.

Snot. सिंघ, गोबो, बोगो, बोड़ो.

Snotty-nosed, Snotty. सिंघिरू, गोबिरू, बोड़िरू.

Snow. बर्फ.

To Snub. दब्राइणु, झिण्कणु.

Snuff (*tobacco*). नास.

The Snuff of a candle. फुलो.

To Snuff a candle. फुलो लाहणु.

To Snuff up, Snuffle. सुण्कणु, सिण्कणु.

Snuffing, Snuffling. सुण्कि सुण्कि, सुण्कार.

So. (*in this manner*) हिंअ, इएँ, (*in that manner*) हुंअ, उएँ, तिंअं, तिहड़ो.

So (*for that reason*). तँहिं करे.

So, Such like. (*proximate*) इहड़ो, हिअड़ो, (*remote*) उहड़ो, हुअड़ो.

So much, So many. एतिरो, हेतिरो, ओतिरो, होतिरो, तेतिरो ; so ever much, हेतिरोसारो.

So large, So great. एड़ो, हेड़ो, ओड़ो, होड़ो, तेड़ो ; so very large, हेड़ोसारो.

So Small. एड़िड़ो, हेड़िड़ो, ओड़िड़ो, होड़िड़ो, तेड़िड़ो.

So long (*in time*), So far. एसों - हेसों-ओसों -होसों- तेसों- ते with तोणी-ताईं, &c. affixed. *See* Till.

To Soak (*steep*). पुसाइणु, (*grain, &c. in hot water*) आड़ारणु.

To Soak up (*absorb*). चुहणु.

To Soak (*lie steeped*). पुसणु.

Soap. साबुणु.

To Soap. साबुणु लाइणु *or* मलणु.

A Soapnut. आरोठो.

Soapy (*smeared with soap*). साबुणहाणो.

To Soar. शोख थिअणु.

A Sob. सुड़िकु, सुड़िको, सुड़िको.

To Sob. सुड़िकणु, सुड़िक, &c. भरणु.

Sober. Soberly (*not drunk*). सँभों, सुध्याइतो, सुर्त्यो, सुर्त्याइतो. *See* Temperate.

To Sober, become Sober. सँभों, &c. थिअणु.

Sobriety. *See* Temperance.

Sociable. मिलिणो, मुहबती, मेली, मेलापी, मेळाइतो, संगती.

Sociableness, Sociability. मिलिणाई, मेलु.

Social. सुहुबताणो. *See* Sociable.

Society. सुहुबत, संगु, संगति, मेलु.

A religious Society. पंगति. *See* Sect.

A Sock. जुराबु.
A Socket. घरु, खड़.
A Sodomite. चुतू. *See* Catamite.
To commit Sodomy. गुई चोदणु.
Soft, Softly. (*not hard*) कुंभरो, नर्मु, कूमलु. (*gentle q. v.*) झीणो.
To Soften (*act.*). कुंभरो करणु.
To Soften (*neu.*). कुंभराइणु.
Softness. कुंभराई, कुंभराणि, नर्माई.
To Soil (*act.*). मेरो करणु, फिटाइणु, विञाइणु. *See* To Dirty.
Soil (*earth q. v.*). भुंइ, धर्तो; different kinds of soils, कलराठो, ड़ुंगेवारो, वार्यासो, ड़सड, खरिड़ो, अड़ारी, चीको, रववारो, कचो, ड़ाभो.
Soiled, हाणो affixed in composition, as धूड़िहाणो 'Soiled with dust.'
Slightly Soiled. मेरांझिड़ो.
To Sojourn. टिकणु, रहणु, दिहणु, सहउणु.
To Solace. तसलाई ड़िभणु.
Solar. शम्शो, सौरू.
To be Sold. विकामणु, विकिजणु, अघणु, अघामणु.
Solder. पनो, रेहु, धकिड़ि.
To Solder. रेहणु.
A Soldier. सिपाही.
Of a Soldier, Soldier-like, Soldierly. सिपाह्याणो, सिपाहिको.
Soldiering, Soldiership. सिपाह्गरी, सिपाह्गीरी.
The Soldiery. सिपाहु.
The Sole of the foot. तरो, तिरो
The Sole of a shoe. तरो.
A Sole (*the fish*). थेली.
Sole (*adj*). *See* Single, Only, Alone.
Solely. रुगो, निलो. *See* Only.
Solemn. ग़ोरो.
To Solemnise. *See* To Celebrate.
To Solicit. (*ask*) पुरणु, सुआलु करणु, मङणु, (*implore*) लीलाइणु.
Solicitation. सुआलु, लीलिडाटी, लोल्डी.
Solicitous. फिकिरवारो, फिकिराइतो, उलिकाइतो, ओनाइतो.
Solicitude. फिकिरु, विस्वासु, चिंता, अर्मानु, चौरोखौरो. *See* Anxiety.
Solid. (*not liquid*) ड़ाढो, (*not hollow*) निहुरो. *See* Thick.
Solidity. (*thickness, density*) घाटु, घाटाई-टाणि, गहराई, गूढ़ाई, (*not hollowness*) निहुराई.
Solitary (*adj.*). हेकलो, निवेकिलो. *See* Single.
Solitude. हेकलाई, निवेकिलाई.
A Solstice. अयनु.
The summer Solstice. उतराइणु.
The winter Solstice. ड़खिणाइणु.
Soluble. गारुओ.
To Solve. *See* To Explain, To Melt.
Solvent (*able to pay*). शाहू.
Some. को, कोको, केके *plu.* (*a small quantity*) कीं.
Some body, Some one. को, कोइ.
A Somerset. बाजी.
Something. का शइ, कीं.
Sometime. कड़्हो, कड़िहिं.
Sometimes. कड़्हीं कड़्हीं.
Somewhat. कीं, थोरो, जरो, जेको सो. *See* Rather.
Somewhere. किथे. काथे, केड़े, काड़े.
A Son. पुटु.
Of a Son. पुटाणो.
One having a Son. पुटेतो.
A Son-in-law. नाठो, निआणो, ज़ाटो; the brother of one's son-in-law, सेणोटु.
A Song. रागु, गीतु, साखी, छन्दु.
Sonless. निपुटो.

Soon. (*shortly*) पुइंओं, पोइताहें, पोअभरो, थोरे में, (*early q. v.*) सवेलो.

Sooner (*earlier*). अगेरो, अगेरिडो.

Soot. ज़ारो.

To Soothe. (*coax*) पर्चाइणु, मनाइणु, (*mitigate q. v.*) हपाइणु.

Soporiferous. निंड्राइतो, निंड्रारो.

A Sorcerer. जादूगरु, कामिण्गोरु -रो, इस्रारी.

Sorcery. जादू, कामिणु, जादूगरी, इस्रारु, इस्रालु, सिहिरु, शिहिरु.

A Sordid person (*miser q. v.*). चूठु, नंदु, चीड़ालो-रो, कुजटु.

Sordid, of a Sordid person. चूठाणो. *See* Miserly.

A Sore. फटु, चाकु.

Sore (*adj*). सूराइतो, सूरेतो, डुखाइतो.

Soreness. सूरु, डुखु, डोखिडो.

Sorrel. चूकों.

Sorrow. वेधन, गमु, सोगु, सोसु, सोजु, डुखु. *See* Mourning, Repentance.

To Sorrow, be Sorrowful. अर्माणिजणु, सूराटिजणु.

Sorrowful, Sorry. डुखी, सोग़ी, दिल्गीरु; *or* Sorrowfully, डुखाइतो, डुखोरो, डुखेरो, सोजाइतो

Sorrowless. वेगमु-मों, अणसूरो, अणसूराइतो, अणसूरेतो.

Sort. वझु, वाझु वहु, तरँहँ, दस्तूरु, जिनिस, क़िसिमु, भाँति, भति. *See* Manner, Kind.

The Soul. जीउ, रूहु, अर्वाहु, आतिमा. *See* Essence.

A Sound. आवाजु, पलांउ, तदार, धुनि, नादु, शब्दु.

Sound. (*without blemish*) बेऐबो, (*in health*) निरोगो. *See* Well, Just, Valid, Deep.

To Sound (*neu. make a noise*). वग़णु, वज़णु.

To Sound (*cause to make a sound*). वग़ाइणु, वज़ाइणु.

To Sound (*plumb*). तांघणु.

Soup. शुर्वो, रहो, रसु.

Sour. खटो, ट्रिडु.

To become Sour, taste Sour. खटाइजणु.

Source. मुँहु, मुइगु, मुहडु, मुंढु. *See* Origin.

Sourness. खटाई, खटाणि, खटिखटि.

A Souterrain. बुड्डुरो.

The South. ड़खिणु.

A Sovereign. *See* King.

Southerly, Southern. ड़ाखिणो.

The South-west wind. भड्रूकणि.

A Sow. सुअरि, भूंड़िणि.

To Sow. पोखणु, ब्रिजु विझणु *or* छट़णु. *See* To Plant.

Sowing (*sub.*). पोख, पोखी.

The first Sowing made for after-transplanting. ब्रेज़ो, ब्रेजारो, ब्रिजारणु.

To be Sown. पुखणु.

Space. (*room q. v.*) जाइ, (*interval q. v.*) विथि. *See* Distance, Period.

Spacious. वेकिरो. *See* Wide, Extensive.

A Spade. कोड़रि.

One who works with a Spade. कोड़रिओ.

A Spadeful of earth, &c. लपो.

A Span. (*between thumb and fore finger*) ब्राचू, वालू, गोकूं, (*between thumb and little finger*) गिराठि, ब्राडी, वजब. *See* Girth.

A Spar of wood. शहतीरु.

Spare (*overplus*). वधीक, फाल्तू. *See* Scan, Scanty.

Spare time. वांदाई. *See* Leisure.
To Spare. जतनु-बचाउ करणु, बचाइणु. *See* To Save.
A Spark. चिणिग, उलो, चिण्गारी.
To Sparkle (*emit sparks*). चिणिगूं *plu.* छड्णु. *See* To Glitter.
A Sparrow. (*cock*) झिर्कु, चिडो, (*hen or the species*) झिर्की, चिडी.
A Spasm. ग़िढी, ग़िढ.
A Spavin. सुटो, बादिभो.
To Speak. ग़ाल्हाइणु, कुछणु, अलाइणु, चवणु. *See* To Say.
A Speaker. ग़ाल्हाईंदडु.
Speaking, way of Speaking. चविणी.
A Spear. भालो, बर्छी, नेजो, ढुकी, (*fisherman's*) छनि.
A Spear-head. फरू.
Special. धार. *See* Particular.
A Species. वह, जाति. *See* Kind.
Specific (*a medicine*). अणगुसु, अगुसु.
To Specify. विचूरणु, निर्वारू करे ड़ेखारणु.
A Specimen. नमूनो. *See* Sample.
Specious. ड़ेखाइतो, ड़ेखिरू.
A Speck, Speckle. चिट्टिडो. *See* Spot.
To Speckle. चिट्णु.
A Spectacle (*show*). तमाशो, मजो.
A pair of Spectacles. ऐनक, चश्मो.
A Spectator. ड़िसँदडु, तमाश्गीरू, तमाश्बीनु.
A Spectre. भूतु, प्रेतु. *See* Ghost.
To Speculate. *See* To Consider.
Speech. ग़ाल्हि, बोली, वाई, बाति, बाणी. *See* Language.
Speechless. *See* Dumb, Silent.
Speed. तिख, तिखाई, सेघु, सिघाई, सट, छूटि. *See* Quickness, Swiftness.

Speedy, Speedily. तिखो, तेजु, झांझिरो, छोहो, छुहो, हलिणो, डोकिणो. *See* Swift.
A Spell. मंडु, मंटु, मंत्र. *See* Charm.
To Spell. हिजे करणु, अखर-लाकना-ग़ंढे चवणु.
To become Spellbound. मुंढिजणु.
A Spencer (*kind of*). गिड़िलो, पुठो.
To Spend (*expend*). खपाइणु, खचंणु. *See* To waste.
To Spend (*to pass q. v.*) गुजारणु, विहाइणु, काटणु.
A Spendthrift. उड़ाऊ, लोटू, लुटाऊ.
To Spew. ओकणु, कइ-मुहखालकरणु. *See* To Vomit.
Spice. मसालो, वेगरू.
Spiced. मसालेदारू.
A Spider. कोरिभडो.
A Spider's web. ज़ारो.
A Spike of corn. संगु. *See* Ear.
The Spike of a top कुंदु.
A Spike (*nail q. v.*). कोरू.
To Spill (*act.*). हारणु, वीरणु, ओतणु.
To Spill (*neu.*). हार्जणु.
To Spill about (*act.*). हारणु, वीरणु.
To Spin. कतणु; to Spin a top, वज़ाइणु, फेराइणु.
A Spindle. ट्कु *f.*
The Spine. करँघो, कण्घो, पुठि जो कंड़ो.
A Spinning-wheel. एंटु, चर्खो.
A Spinster. कुंआरी.
A Spire (*pinnacle q. v.*). बुर्जु, चोटी.
Spirit (*breath*). साहु, जीउ, रूहु, *See* Soul.
Spirit (*courage*). हिमथ, हुसेनी, सत्या, ज़ुरिअत, मर्दान्गी.

Spirit (*distilled*). अर्कु. *See* Liquor.

An evil Spirit. भूतु, इस्तारू, इस्तालु, साँईवालो. *See* Demon.

Spirited (*bold q. v.*). हिएँड़ाडो, हिमथी.

Spiritless. *See* Dejected, Weak, Vapid.

Spiritual (*immaterial*). असरीरू-रो.

A Spiritual guide. मुर्शीदु, गुरू.

A Spit (*spittle q. v.*). थुकु.

A Spit (*of iron*). शीकु.

To Spit. थुकणु.

Spite, Spitefulness. खौंस, चावति, अकसु, वेरू, खुंडु, खुंड़ाई कीनो, ड़ोहु, चक्मको, खुसूमत, खारू.

To bear Spite. उत्ताइणु, खौंसणु, खहणु.

Spiteful. चावती, खुंडो, खुंड़िरू, खारी; *or* Spitefully, खुंड़इतो, खौंसाइतो, खौंसिरू.

Spitting (*sub.*). थूथू, थुकिथुकि.

A Spitting-pot. पिक्दानी, चिलिम्चो, ओग़ादानी,

Spittle. थुक, पिक, फोणी, लब.

To Splash. छंडा *plu.* विझणु.

The Spleen. तिरी, तिलो.

A disease of the Spleen. बड़ाँलि, बड़ँलि.

Splendid. उजारो, शानाइतो, शान्दारू, सोभ्यावानु, तेजवानु, उम्दो, आबाइतो. *See* Bright.

To make Splendid. उजारणु.

Splendour (*brightness q. v.*). चिम्को, जुल्वो, झल्क, झल्को, जोति, चटिको.

Splendour (*magnificence q. v.*). शानु, सोभ्या.

To Splice. गंढणु, गोपणु.

The Splicing a rope, &c. गोप.

To throw out a Splint (*as a horse*). हड़ी कढणु.

A Split. चीर, सीर, ड़ार, फोटि, फोड़. *See* Crack, Slit, Tear.

To Split (*act.*). चीरणु, ड़ारणु, फोड़णु, भञणु.

To Split (*neu.*). ड़रणु, फुटणु, भज़णु. *See* To Crack.

A Splinter (*chip*). छेति.

To Splinter into pieces (*neu.*). छेत्यूं थिअणु. *See* To Split, Shiver.

Spoil. फुरि, लुटि. *See* Plunder.

To Spoil (*plunder*). फुरणु, लुटणु.

To Spoil or injure (*act.*). खारणु, विञाइणु, फिटाइणु, विगाड़णु. *See* To Injure.

To Spoil, become Spoiled. खरणु, फिटणु, विगिड़णु.

A Spoiled child. लाड़गिदूरो, मचुलो.

The Spoke of a wheel. ओभारो, अरो.

A Spokesman. ग़ाल्हाईंदडु, ग़ाल्हाइणवारो.

Spontaneously. पाण्हेई, पाणहीं.

A Spool (*weaver's*). नाणाड़ो, नाड़ांड़ो.

A Spoon. चम्चो. *See* Ladle.

Sport. रांदि, खेल, रौंशो. *See* Merriment, Play.

Sport (*mockery q. v.*). ठशो.

Sport (*diversion of the field*). शिकारू, आहिड़ो.

To Sport. *See* To Play, Jest.

A Sportsman. शिकारी.

Sportive, Sportful. रौंशाइतो, रौंशाओं. *See* Playful, Merry.

A Spot. (*stain, mark*) चिटो, दागु, कलंकु, टिको, (*in a jewel*) ड़ोधकु.

To Spot. दागणु, चिटणु. *See* Dot, Place.

Spotless. बेदागो, बेदागो, बेऐबो. *See* Pure.

Spotlessness. बेदागाई, बेऐबाई.

Spotted, Spotty. निट्कमिरो, दागो.

A Spouse. *See* Husband, Wife.

A Spout (*for water; from a roof*). नेसारो, नारो, (*to a pot, &c.*) तुनि.

To Spout up. उछिलणु.

To Sprain. मोडणु.

To be Sprained. मुडणु.

To Sprawl. हथ पेर ड्रिघेडे (*or* पखेडे) पत्रणु.

The Spray of the sea. फुहार, फुहारो.

To Spread (*act.*). पखेडणु, विछांइणु, पसारणु. *See* To Scatter.

To Spread (*neu.*). पखिडणु, पसिरणु.

Spread, Spreading. पखेड. *See* Expansion.

A Sprig (*branch q. v.*). टारो. *See* Shoot.

A Sprig in embroidery. बूटो, फुलो.

Sprightly. रौंशाइतो. *See* Playful, Merry.

The Spring. (*season*) बसंतु, बहारु, (*or crop*) चेटु, रबो.

Spring, of the Spring. बसंतो, बहारो.

A Spring (*elastic body*). कमानि, कलि.

A Spring (*bound*). छालु, ठेंगु, ट्पो, कुडु.

A Spring (*upon or at; as to catch*). लूह, झटु, झपो, झट्को.

A Spring (*fountain*). सेमो, नारु, झर्गो. *See* Origin.

To Spring (*out of the ground*). उग़णु, उभिरणु, ज़मणु, ज़ापणु, उसिरणु.

To Spring from (*issue, proceed*). निकिरणु.

To Spring up or out; suddenly. उछिलो- ट्पो- कुड़ो- छालु &c. ड्रेई - उथणु or निकिरणु. *See* To Leap.

To Spring (*upon or at; as to catch*). झटु, &c. हणणु-विझणु-पाइणु.

A Springe. कोडूकी, सिर्किणो, फाहो. *See* Snare.

To Sprinkle (*act.*). छिण्कणु, छिट़णु, छिण्कारणु, छाटारणु.

To Sprinkle (*salt, sugar, or any powder*). बुर्कणु, बुर्काइणु.

A Sprinkle. छंड़ो.

The act of Sprinkling. छाटार, छिण्कारु, छट्ट, ट्रेह, वट़, छंड़, छंड़्कार.

To damp (*clothes, &c.*) by Sprinkling. ट्रेहणु, वट़णु, छंडणु.

To Sprout (*germinate*). मोर्जणु, अंगूर्जणु. *See* To Spring up.

A Sprout. सलो, गुहो, अंगूरु, गोशु, गौंचु, कुओ.

Spruce. *See* Neat.

A Spur. कंड़ो; the prick of a Spur, चूंग, चोक.

To Spur. चूंग ड्रिभणु, चोकणु, चूंगणु, (*strike with the heels*) अड़ो -अंगुडो हणणु.

Spurious. खोटो, कूडो, जुडितू.

To Spurn (*scorn*). धिकारु करणु, नालत विझणु, बाहि ड्रिभणु.

To Spurt. *See* To Squirt.

A Spy. चारो, जासूसु.

The business or pay of a Spy, Spying. चारिपो-प-पाई, चारिअपो.

To Spy (*explore*). चाकासणु, तकणु, सुधि लहणु, (*about*) सूंझणु. *See* To See.

A Squabble, Squabbling. खपति, किल्किलि, किट्पिटि, खिड्फिटि, खटिखटि, किर्किरि, खिट्फिटि, किल्फिटि. *See* Quarrelling.

To Squabble. किल्किलि, &c. करणु.

A Squabbler. किल्किल्यो, किट्पित्यो, किर्कियो, खिट्फित्यो.

Squalid. गदिलो. *See* Filthy.

To Squall. रडणु, खबिरा भरणु. *See* To Cry, Scream.

A Squall of wind. छोहो, छुहो, खहो. *See* Blast, Scream.

Squamous. छेलुरो, छेलुओं.

To Squander. उड़ाइणु, लुटाइणु.

A Squanderer. उड़ाऊ, लुटाऊ, लोटू.

Square (*adj.*). चौरासि, चौकुंड्यारो, चौकुंडो.

A Square (*in shape*). चौंकु.

A Square (*carpenter's tool*). गूनी, गूनीआ.

To Squash. फेहणु. *See* to Crush.

To be Squashed. फिसणु.

To Squat. ओंकिडू विहणु. *See under* To Sit.

A Squeak, Squeal. कोक, रोड़, कूक, कोह.

To Squeak, Squeal. कोकणु, कोकाइणु, कूकणु.

To feel Squeamish. हिंओं रेहिजणु, दिलि, &c. बुछिडो-कची थिअणु, दिलि, &c. लुड़णु.

A Squeeze. दब्र.

To Squeeze. दब्रणु, पीडणु, निपुडणु. *See* To Press, Crush, Squash.

A Squib (*of powder*). फटाको. *See* Fireworks.

A Squint. टाणो, टेड़ाई.

To Squint. टेड़ाहणु.

A Squinter, Squint-eyed. टेड़ो, टब्रर में टाणो.

A Squirrel. नोरिअडो, गालहडि.

A Squirt (*syringe*). पिचकारी.

A Squirt (*stream, spurt*). पिचकार, पिचिक.

To Squirt. पिचिक, &c. हणणु.

A Stab, Stabbing. चुंगणु, चोकणु.

To Stab. चुंग, चोक, घुत.

Stability, Stableness. काइमी, टिकाउ, नेबाही, बिहक, डिड्हता. *See* Durability.

Stable (*adj.*). काइमु, नेबहु, नेभउ, डूहु. *See* Firm, Durable.

A Stable. कुडहि, तबेलो.

A Stack. दनि, खोडु. *See* Heap.

To Stack. दनि, &c. करणु.

A Staff. लकुणु, लठि, छड्ही; a flag Staff, छड्ह.

A Stag. हरणु.

A Stage in a journey. मेंजल, मंज़ल. *See* Platform.

To Stagger (*neu.*). थिड़णु, लुड़णु, झूलणु.

To Stagger (*act.*). लोड़णु, थिड़्काइणु.

Stagnant. ब्रथो, ब्रथलु.

To Stagnate. ब्रझणु.

Staid. ग़ौरो, ग़रो, गंभीरू.

Staidness. ग़राई, ग़ौराई, गंभीराई, ठहर, थांहर, थँहर.

A Stain. चिटो, दागु, टिको.

To Stain. दागणु.

Stained. दागी.

Stainless. बेदागो, बेदागी, बेऐबो. *See* Pure, Unblemished.

A Staircase. डाकणि, चर्णी, पौडो.

A Stake (*wooden*). मंघो, मुनो, थूणी.

A Stake (*wager q. v.*). दाउ.

Stale. पारूथो, ओसिनो, बासी.

Staleness. पारूथाई, ओसिनाई.

The Stalk of grain plants. कानों, कानो; or straw of leguminous plants, किटो. *See* Straw.

The Stalk of a flower, fruit, &c. ड़ांड़ो, ड़ुंड़ि, बूंड़ि.

To Stalk (*walk stately*). आकिड्यो -सोत्यो हलणु.

A Stall in a stable. थानु, थाणु, ठाणु.

A vender's Stall. पिड़ो, दिकी.

A Stallion. सानु.

To Stammer. हकड्जणु, हकडाइणु, हब्कणु, हब्काइणु.

A Stammer, Stammering. हकड, हकडाई, हब्क.

A Stammerer. हकडु.

A Stamp (*the instrument or impression*). छाप, ठपो.

The Stamp made on coins. जर्ब, छिको.

The Stamp with which coins are struck. बालो.

A Stamp used in dying, &c. पोरू.

To Stamp (*impress q. v*). छापणु, छुरणु, जर्बणु, हणणु.

A Stamp of the foot. दड़हो.

To Stamp the foot. दड़हो हणणु.

Stanch. *See* Constant, Firm.

To Stanch. झलणु. *See* To Stop.

To Stand (*become erect, stop*). बिहणु, उबिहणु, उभणु, बीहणु, उभो थिअणु. *See* To Endure, Continue.

To Stand stiff or on end (*the hair of the body.*) कांड़ार्जणु.

A Stand. *See* Station, Stop, Halt; for water vessels, घडाम्जो.

Standard (*rule, measure*). नमूनो.

A Standard measure, weight, &c. kept as a sample. मलु.

A Standard (*ensign.*). झंड़ो, नीशानु, बैरक. *See* Flag.

A Standard-bearer. झंड़ाई.

Standing (*sub.*). बिहक. *See* Endurance, Continuance.

Standing (*motionless, as water*). ब्रभलु, ब्रधो. *See* Erect.

A Stanza. बैतु, शिलोकु, शिलोको, छंदु.

A Staple (*loop of iron*). कुंधो.

A Star. तारो; the North Star, ड्रूहु, कुतिबु.

A Star on the forehead of a horse, cow, &c. also the animal so marked. ब्रोलाहो.

Starch. कलफु, आहरु, (*weaver's*) पेणु, (*wheaten, used in sweetmeats*) निशास्तो.

To Starch. कलफणु, आहरणु.

To Stare. तकणु, निहारणु.

A Stare, Staring. तक, निहार, हिकटिक.

Stark. रुग़ो, निसोरो. *See* Entirely, Purely.

A Start, Starting. छिकुं, ट्राहु, छिकिणी.

To Start, Startle, (*neu.*). छिकणु, ट्रहणु, छिकुं खाइणु-मारणु.

To Start, Startle (*act.*). छिकाइणु, ट्राहणु.

To Start (*on a journey*). निकिरणु.

Starvation. बुख.

To Starve from hunger (*neu.*). बुख-लंघणि-फाके मरणु.

State (*condition*). हालु, हवालु, ड़सा, रुड, रुइदादि.

State (*pomp q. v.*) शानु, ठाडु.

The State (*governing power*). सर्कारि.

State, of the State (*adj*). सर्कारी, सर्कारिको.

To State. चवणु. *See* To Tell.

A Stated or fixed rate. नेमु, ठुक, बृधलु अघु. *See* Rate.

Stately. शानाइतो, आबाइतो. *See* Magnificent.

A Statement (*representation*). इज़हारु, ग़ाल्हि.

A Station. जाइ, हंधु, थडु, थाणो, आस्थानो, जूइ. *See* Place.

To Station. बिहारणु.

Stationary. काइमु, (*motionless*) अचलु, थिरि, (*having a fixed residence*) हंधाइतो, माग़ाइतो, थहाइतो, थानीको, थांईको, हिकथांईको, हिकथाणोको.

Stationless, (*not having a fixed station*). बेथहो, बेहंधो, बेथांईको, बेथाणोको, बेमाग़ो.

A Statue. मूरति, पुतिली.

Stature. कदु.

To Stay (*neu.*). टिकणु, रहणु, विहणु, सहडणु.

To Stay (*act.*). रहाइणु. *See* To Stop, Support.

A Stay, Staying. रहणु, रहणी. *See* Support.

Stead. जाइ. *See* Lieu.

Steadfast. नछुडु, अछुडु, पको, ड़ाढो. *See* Constant, Firm.

Steadiness, Steady. (*firmness*) ड़ाढाई, पुख़्ताई, (*sobriety, calmness*) थांहर, थँहर, ठहर.

Steady. थिरि, अचलु, पुख़्तो, (*resolute*) हिकमत्यो-तो. *See* Firm.

To Steady. बिहारणु, झलणु.

To Steal. चोराइणु, चोरी करणु.

Stealth, Stealing. चोरी.

Stealthily, by Stealth. चोरिअ.

Steam. ब़ाफ, उब़, दूंहों.

To Steam (*act.*). ब़ाफणु, सेइणु.

A Steamer, Steamboat. बूंबु, दूंहे जो जहाजु.

Steel. रूकु, फोलादु; a kind of Steel, पारिचो.

Of Steel. रूकांओं, फोलादी.

Steep (*adj.*). चाढ़हिअवारो, औखो.

To Steep. पुसाइणु, (*grain*) आड़ारणु.

A Steer. वहुडो.

To Steer (*neu.*). सुखानु हलाइणु -फेरणु.

A Steersman. सुखानी.

The Stem of a tree. थुडु. *See* Stalk.

Stench. बास, छट्. *See* Stink.

A Step. विख, कदमु.

The Step of a ladder, stair, &c. ड़ाको, ड़ाउको.

To Step (*take steps*). पेरु खणणु -रखणु, विख खणणु-भरणु.

To Step on or upon. पेरु रखणु -ड़िअणु, लताडणु.

To Step over. ओरांघणु.

To Step out. वधी हलणु.

A Step-brother. लग़ो भाउ, (*having the same mother*) माइतो भाउ, (*having the same father*) पेइतो-माटे जो-माटेयो भाउ.

A Step-daughter. लग़ो धिउ, (*a woman's*) माटे जो-माटेई धिउ, मुंसं जी अग़ज़ाई- अगुआई, (*a man's*) जालजो अग़ज़ाई-अगुआई.

A Step-father. लग़ो पिउ.

A Step-mother. लग़ो माउ, माटे जी -माटेई माउ.

A Step-sister. लग़ो भेण, (*having same mother*) माइतो भेण, (*having same father*) पेइतो-माटे जो -माटेई भेण.

A Step-son. लग़ो पुटु, (*a woman's*) माट़े जो-माट़ेयो पुटु, मुस जो अग़ज़ा-ओ-अगुआओ, (*a man's*) जाल जो अग़ज़ाओ-अगुआओ.

Sterile. ढिलो. *See* Barren.

Sterile land. खजडि.

Stern (*adj.*). खहुरो, रूखो.

The Stern of a vessel. पाछिलि.

Sternness. खहुराई, रूखाई.

To Stew. रँधणु.

A Steward. मुख्त्यारू.

To Stick (*fasten, make adhere*). ग़ंढणु, ज़पुडाइणु, चहुटाइणु, ज़माइणु.

To Stick (*adhere*). ज़पुडणु, चहुटणु, चंबुडणु, वचुडणु, लग़णु.

To Stick (*as in mud*). गपणु, गरणु, फासणु, फसणु.

To Stick. (*pierce*) टुंबणु, (*stab*) चोकणु, चूंगणु.

To Stick out (*be prominent*). ब्राहरि निकिरणु.

Stick (*generic term*). काठो. *See* Wood, Fuel.

A large thick Stick. काठु. *See* Beam.

A walking Stick. लठि, लकुणु. *See* Staff.

A Stick (*stab*). चोक चूंग.

Stickiness. चीड़्हालाई, चोड़्हु, लिग़िलिग़ि. *See* Viscosity.

The Stickings. लग़ार.

Sticky. चोड़्हालो, लिग़िलिग़ि-ग़्यो, लेसिरू.

Stiff. सोटु. *See* Hard.

To Stiffen (*act.*). सीटणु, सोटु करणु.

To Stiffen (*neu.*). सोटिजणु.

Stiffness. सोटाई, सोटाणि.

To Stifle. घुटणु, ब्रूसाटणु.

A Stigma. लोंघो. *See* Blemish.

To Still. माठि, &c. कराइणु, थमाइणु.

Still (*adj.*). सांति, माठि. *See* Quick, Motionless, Stagnant.

Still (*adv. till now*). अञा, एसीं, हेसीं, अञा-एसीं-हेसीं with तांई-तोणी, &c. attached (*See Till*). *See* Nevertheless, Yet.

A Still. कर्णफुलु.

To be Still-born. कुहाई थिअणु.

Stillness. निवाई, माठार, माठरि, माठोणाई. *See* Quiet.

To Stimulate. मचाइणु, चोरणु, उथारणु.

A Sting. ड़ंगु, ड़ंगिणी.

To Sting. ड़ंगणु, खाइणु.

A Stinger, Stinging. ड़ंगिरू.

Stinginess. सोसु, शूमाई, बखोली, मचूंठाई, चूठाई.

A Stingy person. चिचमारू, शूमु, मचूंठु. *See* Miser.

Stingy, Stingily. सोसाइतो. *See* Miserly.

To be Stingy. चिच मारणु.

A Stink. बास, बदि बोइ, गंदु, छट़.

To Stink. बास, &c. करणु, किनो थिअणु, टकिजणु.

Stinking (*adj.*). छट़ारो, किनो, गंदो.

Stint. संधो, झल. *See* Limit, Restriction.

A Stipend. *See* Pay.

To Stipulate. ग़ोलु, &c. करणु.

A Stipulation. ग़ोलु, जाइज़ु. *See* Agreement.

Given, or made under a Stipulation. शर्ताऊ.

To Stir (*act.*). हलाइणु, चोरणु. *See* To Move.

To Stir (*neu*). हलणु, चुरणु. *See* To Move.

To Stir up. छाछोलणु, झोंगणु, झुगणु.
A Stir (*bustle*). हल्चलि.
Stirring up. झोंग.
A Stirrup. रिकेबु.
A Stirrup-leather. दुआलु.
A Stitch. टांको, टोपो.
To Stitch (*sew slightly*). तागणु, टांको ड़िभणु, टांकणु.
Stitching (*a kind of sewing*). बख्यो.
A Stoccade, Stockade. मुहाडो.
The Stock of grain plants. कानो, कानी; of flowers, fruit, &c. ड़ांडो. *See* Stalk, Stem, Trunk, Handle.
The Stock of a gun. कुंदाकु.
Stock (*capital*). मूड़ी. मूरु.
A Stock (*store q. v.*). सथो, (*of cattle*) मालु.
Stock (*race, breed*). बुणु, असुलु, बुनिआदु. *See* Root, Origin.
Of good Stock or lineage. बुणाइतो, बुनिआदी. *See* Noble.
Of a bad Stock. बेबुणो.
The Stocks (*for the feet*). काठु, फलकु.
A Stocking. जुराबु.
Stolen. चोराणो, चोराऊ, चोरालो.
The Stomach (*the ventricle*). ओझिरी. *See* Belly.
A Stone. पहणु, पथरु. *See* Grindstone, Whetstone, Philosopher's stone, &c.
The Stone or pebble in a ring. टिक.
The Stone of fruit. खखी, खखिड़ो, ककिड़ो, (*of the mangoe*) कोर, कोईरो.
The Stone (*disease*). पहणी, पथिरी, राओं, ककिरो.
Stone, of Stone (*adj.*). पहणेरो.

To Stone. संगसारु करणु.
A Stone-cutter. संगतराशु.
Stone-cutting. संगतराशी.
Stony. पहणनिवारो, पहण्यारु, पहणेरो.
A Stool (*seat without back*). मंज़ो, चौंकी, संदलो. *See* Footstool.
A Stool (*evacuation*). दस्तु, खर्चू, झाड़ो.
To Stool, have a Stool. हँगणु, झाड़ो-करारु-मैदानु, &c. करणु, टोरो फिरणु.
To have a thin Stool. तीकणु, (*spoken of cattle*) तीरणु.
To Stoop. निंवणु, नंवंणु, निउडणु, झुकणु, कुबिड़ो-ब्रावंजिरो थिअणु.
One with a Stooped back. कुबिड़ो.
To Stop (*make stand, hinder*). बिहारणु, थमाइणु, थाथिराइणु, रंड़णु, झलणु, अट्काइणु, रोकणु, ठहराइणु, तर्साइणु, बंदि करणु, ब्रझाइणु, सोडाइणु. *See* To Delay.
To Stop an aperture. पूरणु, बंदि-करणु, भरणु.
To Stop (*stand still, pause*). बिहणु, थमणु, थथिरणु, उबिहणु, उभणु, रहणु, ठहरणु, तर्सणु, ब्रझणु, बंदि थिअणु, सोडिजणु. *See* To wait.
To Stop (*leave off*). छड़णु, झलणु, बसि करणु, रखणु.
To Stop at (*alight, stay*). रहणु, टिकणु, लहणु.
A Stoppage, Stopping. झल, रंड, अट्काउ, रोक, सोड, भाओ.
A Stopper, Stopple. ड़टो, बुंजो.
Without Stopping. हिकसारि, हिकलस, हिकलूइ.
Storax. सिलाजीतु, सलारसि.
A Store (*stock*). सथो, अंबारु.
To Store. सथणु, गडु करणु.

Stored. सथु.

A Store-house, Store-room. भांड़ो, वखार, खोठी, पाइलो, अंबाखांनो.

A Government Store-house keeper. अंबादारू.

A yard for Storing grain in. खरी.

A Storm of wind. वाच, तूफानु, टूफानु, झक.

A dust Storm. धूड्यो.

To Storm (*a fort*). काह करे वठणु. *See* To Rage.

Stormy. वाचिरू.

A Story (*tale*). आखाणी, गाल्हि, किसो, कहात, कहत, कथा, साखो, नकुल, किहाणी.

The Story of a house. तबकु; ground floor, घरू; upper rooms, माडी; third floor, त्रिमाडि, त्रितब-की माडी.

To relate a Story. आखाणी, &c. खणणु.

To tell idle Stories. लब्राड-पड्ब्राट-टिबु-ब्राक-फटाक हणणु.

A teller of idle or lying Stories. लब्राडी, पड्ब्राटी, टिब्रो, ब्राको, फ-टाकी.

A Story-teller. किसिरू, किसाईं, नकुली.

Stout. सधरू, मतारो, यटो, दौंसो, डुड्टिो, ड्टोमुटो, चौबुको, सटरवटो, चुर्यो.

Stoutness. सधराई, मताराई, यटाई, दौंसाई.

To Stow. ठाहे सथणु-रखणु.

The Straddle or dorsal pad of a pack saddle. बिंड़ी, बिनो.

To Straddle. ज़ंघूं फाड़े हलणु *or* बि-हणु.

To Straggle. रूलणु, खिंड़िरो वञणु.

Straight. सैंधों, सिधो, सूधो, सवलो.

To Straighten (*act*). सैंधों, &c. करणु, वर लाहणु.

To Straighten (*neu*). सैंधों, &c. थिअणु.

Straightness. सैंवति, सैंवाई, सिधाई, सुधाई.

To Strain through a strainer (*act*). छाणणु (*neu.*) छणणु.

To Strain (*sprain*). मोड़णु.

To Strain (*draw tense*). छिकणु.

A Strain (*pull*). छिक.

A Strainer. परणु, साफो, छाणो, छाणी, अचिलो.

Straining (*filtering*). छाणिणो.

Strainings. फोगु, पिनो, (*of bhang*) जोगु.

Strait (*narrow*). सोड्हो, तंगि. *See* Strict, Severe.

A Strait (*pass q. v.*) दरो. *See* Distress, Difficulty.

Straitness. सोड़ह, तंगी.

A Strand (*beach*). कंधी. *See* Shore.

A Strand of a rope. गुरू, तंदो.

Strange (*alien, of another*). ओ-पिरो, धार्यो, पराओ, बेर्यो, बेगाणो, सतधार्यो. *See* Foreign.

Strange (*odd, queer*). नैंओं, अजबु, अजबजिहड़ो. *See* Wonderful.

A Stranger. परू, धार्यो, ओपटू. *See* Strange, Uninformed.

To Strangle. घोघो ड़िअणु, घुटणु.

A Strap of leather. कशु, कसिणो.

A Stratagem. ढंगु, वझु, दाझु. *See* Artifice, Contrivance, Wile.

A Stratum. *See* Layer.

A Straw of *Juwarí* or *Bajuri*. का-नो,; Straw (*generally*), काना *plu.* कड्ब,; chopped Straw, कुतिरि, (*done coarsely*) ड़ाकरि.

A Straw of wheat or barley. तीलो, कांगिडो, कानी ; broken Straw बुड़.
Rice Straw. पराल़, पलालु.
The Straw or stalks of legumes. किटी.
A Straw, bit of Straw. कखु.
To Stray. रुलणु, भट्कणु, भिट्कणु, भर्मणु, भँवणु. *See* To Wander.
Stray (*adj.*). रोलु, रोलाकु, रोलू, रोलाकड़ु, लोटिको, फिरोई. *See* Wandering.
A Streak. लीक.
To Streak. लीकणु.
Streaked. लीकाँओं.
A Stream (*continuous flow*). धार, रेलो, वहु, वहक, वहुकुड़ो, (*as through a small hole*) ठीढी. *See* Rivulet, River, Current.
Against the Stream. ओभारो.
With the Stream. लाव्हारो.
A rapid Stream or current. तिख, छड़ह.
That part where the Stream is weak. माठो.
The deep Stream. सीर.
A Street. घटी, ग़ली, घिटी
Strength. सघ, जोरु, सतु, सघाई, सघाराई, सग़ति, ब़लु, कुंभत. *See* Power.
Strength of liquors. तल्खाई, तल्खाणि, तिखाई, तिखाणि.
Strength (*endurance in cloth, &c.*). चोड़ु, सतु.
To Strengthen (*act.*). जोरु &c. ड़िअणु, ड़ाढो &c. करणु.
To Strengthen (*neu.*) सघाइजणु.
Strengthening (*adj.*). जोराइतो, कुंभतो, खोराकी.
Strenuous. गोरशी, उज़मी. *See* Zealous.

Stress (*strain*). छिक. *See* Force, Pressure..
To Stretch by pulling. छिके वधाइणु, पखेड़णु. *See* To Spread.
To Stretch out (*extend the hand, &c.*). ड्रिघेड़णु, वधाइणु, सड़णु. *See* To Extend.
To Stretch (*open out in wear*). इंघणु.
To Stretch one's limbs, (*through laziness, and strain them*). कर मोड़णु, लिङ ग़ामोड़णु, ग़ामोल्ड़जणु.
To Strew. पखेड़णु. *See* To Spread, Scatter.
Strict, Strictly. पूरो, सचो, ठोकु. *See* Severe.
A Stride. विरांघ, व्रिरांघ.
To Stride. विरांघ पाइणु.
Strife. झग़िड़ो, झेड़ो. *See* Quarrelling.
To Strike (*with anything*). मारणु, कुटणु, हणणु, ठोकणु.
To Strike (*against anything*). लग़णु.
To Strike (*hit a mark*). चुटणु.
To Strike (*as the sun, hot wind, &c.*). झड़पणु.
To Strike out or off. वारणु. *See* To Erase.
To make a motion as if to Strike. ओलारणु, उलारणु.
A String. सुट्टु, नाड़ो. *See* Cord, Twine, Series.
The String of a bow. जिहु, नारु ; of a garment, कँहों; of a kite, ड़ोरि, ड़ोरो ; of a musical instrument, तार ; round a spinning wheel, ड़ोरि ; for drawing water, ड़ोरो.
A piece of String for tying anything with. अटहु.

To String (*file on a string*). पुअणु.

A Strip. पटो, पटी, फतोल; a torn Strip of cloth. लोड.

To Strip (*deprive of covering*). उघाड़ो करणु.

To Strip off (*clothes*). लाहणु.

A Stripe (*line q. v.*). लीक, लोको.

A Stripe (*stroke*). चहबुकु. *See* Lash.

A Stripe (*weal*). ड़नो.

Striped, in Stripes. लीकांओं.

A Stripling. लाय्यारू, ग़भिरू, ग़भरू.

To Strive (*contend q. v.*) विड़हणु.

To Strive (*make great efforts*). सायो-वसु-उज़मु करणु, मथो हणणु. *See* To Labor.

A Stroke (*blow q. v.*). धकु, ठोक. *See* Stripe, Thump, Slap, Line.

A Stroke of the wind, sun, &c. झडप.

To Stroke. हथु फेरणु.

To Stroll. घुमणु. *See* To Wander.

Strong (*powerful q. v.*). ड़ाढो, सघो, सघारो, करारो, जोरभर्यो, जोरारो, जोराइतो, जोराणो, सघाइतो, सतो, सतारो, सताइतो, सत्रू, सग़ती, ब्रली, कुंअती.

Strong, Strongly (*firm q. v.*). ड़ाढो, पुख्तो, हथीको, सुब्रंधु.

Strong (*rapid; as a stream, wind, &c.*). तिखो.

Strong (*as cloth*). चोडाऊ. Strong (*as smell*). ड़ाढो, घणो. Strong (*potent; as liquor, medicine, &c.*). तलख, तिखो, ग़ूड्हो, घाटो.

To Struggle. *See* To Strive, Labor, Contend.

A Strumpet. कुत्थाणी. *See* Prostitute.

To Strut. आकिड्जी-सीटिजो हलणु. *See* To Swagger.

A Stub, Stubble. सुंढो, खुती, नाडो.

A Stubble-field. कांगड़ु, नाड़ु.

Stubborn. होड़ी, ड़िठो, निठरू, अटरू, अणटरू, गहगोरु, गुठो, हठोलो, हठो, बहसीलो, कदी; *or* Stubbornly, होड़ाइतो, गहाइतो, हठाइतो.

Stubbornness. होड़, ड़िठाई, निटराई, बहशु, होड़याई, हठोलाई, कदु.

To Stud with ornaments. जडणु.

Studded with ornaments. जडाऊ, जडितू.

A Student. सिखंदडु. *See* Scholar.

Studious. पड्हण जो खपो, मिन्हतो, उज़मी, अभ्यासी.

Study. पड्हणु, अभ्यासु.

To Study (*apply the mind to learn*). पड्हणु, सिखणु, अभ्यासु करणु. *See* To Consider.

Stuff (*material*). जिनिस, वथु *f.* शइ.

To Stuff (*act.*). थन्हणु, दब्रे भरणु, ड़ल्हणु.

To be Stuffed (*the nose in a cold*). बुटिजणु.

To Stumble. थाब्रो *&c.* खाइणु, आथुडणु, थाब्रिड्जणु, थिड्कणु, थिडणु.

A Stumble. थाब्रो, थुड़ो.

A Stumbler. थाब्रिरू.

The Stump of a tree, &c. बुंड़ो, लाहु.

To Stun. विसाइणु, निहोडणु.

To be Stunned. विसामी वञणु.

A Stunted youth. कुकुंटु.

Stupefaction. बेहोशो, मोग़ाई.

To get Stupified. मोग़ो-वाइडो-विसो थिअणु.

Stupid. भौंदू, बेवकूफु, बेसमुझु, बेशहूरु, जडु, अब्रोझो, ग़हेलो. *See* A Blockhead.

Stupidity. बेवकूफी, मूर्खाई, भौंदुआई.
Stupor. मोंग़ाई, विसाई, ग़ाहेलाई.
Sturdiness. सधराई. *See* Stoutness.
Sturdy, सधरू. *See* Stout.
To Stutter. हकड्जणु, हकडाइणु, हब्र्काइणु.
A Stutterer. हकडु.
Stuttering. हकड, हकडाई, हब्रक.
A Sty in the eyelid. आनिडो.
Style (*manner q. v.*). ढ़ौलु, ढँउँ.
A Style for writing with. पूरिणो, इंड़ो.
Suavity. मिठाई, कुंभराई.
To Subdue. खटणु, तातिं-आण मञा-इणु.
To Subject (*subdue q. v.*). मोथाजु *&c.* करणु.
Subject (*placed under*). मोथाजु, ताबेदारू, अधीनु, तल्हेरू, वहीणो.
A Subject (*one owing allegiance*). रैअत, पिर्जा.
Subject (*matter*). ग़ाल्हि.
Subjected. तालजोरू, तातो.
Subjection (*conquering*). जीत, फतिह.
In Subjection or subordination to. ताबे, ताबाने आहर, हथिरादो-दी. *See* Subject.
Sublime. ऊचो.
Submissive. हुकुमीबंदो. *See* Obedient.
To Submit. तातिं-आण-हुकुमु मञणु, हुकुम में अचणु *or* रहणु.
To Subscribe (*sign*). सही-हथअ-खर विझणु or पाइणु. *See* To Agree.
A Subscription (*contribution*). चंदो, चिठो, चीरो, फोड, फोडी, फांड़.
Subsequent. पोंयों.
Subsequently. पोइ.
To Subside (*be quiet or still*). थमणु, विहणु, ठहरणु. *See* To Abate, Lessen, Settle.
To Subside (*as a flood*). छिजणु, लहणु, झपणु, झपिजणु, झपामणु. *See* To Lessen.
The Subsiding of a flood. छेनहडो, लाहु.
To Subsist (*neu.*). जिअणु, निभाइणु, निबाहणु, टोरणु. *See* To Get on, Maintain.
Subsistence, (*living, livelihood*). तँत्रणि, तौणि, गुजिरानु, कूतु. *See* Maintenance.
A Subsistence (*allowance*). विरउ.
A Substance (*real being*). वथु *f.* *See* Thing, Wealth.
Substance (*essence q. v*). मग्जु, सारू, (*body, material*) माओ.
Substantial (*having substance*). वथुवारो, माएदारू, पुर्कारू, निहुरो, भर्यलु. *See* Stout, Thick, Rich.
To Substantiate. वर्जाइणु, इस्वातु करणु.
A Substantive. नालो, नांउँ.
To Substitute. बदिरें ड़िअणु.
A Substitute. बदरू, एवजु, एवजी सारो.
A Subterfuge. *See* Evasion.
Subtile. सन्हो.
Subtle. पको. *See* Cunning, Knowing.
To Subtract. लाहणु, कढणु, कटणु. *See* To Deduct.
Subtraction. कट. *See* Deduction.
To Subvert. केराइणु, विञाइणु.
The Suburbs of a city. परिगराई.
To Succeed. (*follow in order*) पोइ उतां अचणु *or* थिअणु, (*take the*

place of) जाइ ते अचणु-विहणु -थिभणु.

To Succeed, be Successful. मुराद पुज़ाइणु *or* पाइणु, फञणु, अघणु, अघामणु.

Successful. समुरादो.

A Succession (*series*). कतार, बहीर.

In Succession (*one after another*). वाराइतो, वारेवतो.

In Succession to. उतां, उतूं, उतों, उतैंउं, मथां-थूं-थों-थैंउं, पोइ.

Successive, Successively. सिफाइतो.

Succint, Succinctly. थोरअखिरो -अछिरो.

Succory. कासिनी.

To Succour. पुठि भरणु. *See* To Assist.

Succulent. रसीलो, रसाइतो, घणरसो.

To Succumb. *See* To Submit.

Such. (*of this kind*) इहड़ो, हिअड़ो, अहिड़ो, (*of that kind*) उहड़ो, हुअड़ो.

Such a one. फलाणो.

To Suck (*draw with the mouth*). चूपणु.

To Suck the breast. धाइणु.

To Suck up (*absorb*). चुहणु.

A Suck. चूपो.

A Sucking-stick (*for infants*). चूपिणी.

To Suckle. धाराइणु, बुबो ड़िभणु.

A Suckling. खीरपिआकु.

Sudden. ओचितो.

Suddenly. अचानक, अचाचेति, ओचितो, उछतु, उमालक. *See* Unexpectedly.

Suddenness. ओचिताई.

Suds. गजो, झग.

To Sue (*prosecute*). दांह करणु -ड़िभणु with ते governing the object. *See* To Entreat.

Suet. वह. *See* Fat.

To Suffer. (*bear*) सहणु, जारणु, (*undergo*) भोगणु, झोगणु, (*loss*) खाइणु, पाइणु. *See* To Permit.

Sufferable. सहिणी, सहू.

Sufferance, Suffering (*enduring q. v.*). सहणी. *See* Patience, Pain.

To Suffice. पुज़णु, पूरो, &c. थिअणु. *See* To Satisfy.

Sufficient, Sufficiently. पूरो, जोगो, बसि. *See* Enough.

To Suffocate. घुटणु, ब़ूसाटणु. *See* To Choke.

To Suffuse. भरणु. *See* To Overspread.

Sugar. खंडु, (*varieties*) ब़ूरो, कनासिरो, शकर; made up into balls or shapes, ओलो, पताशो, निबात, खूंजो.

Raw Sugar, or the juice inspissated. गुड़, (*varieties*) भिंड़, मुस्तो.

Sugar candy. मिसिरी.

Sugarcane. कमंदु, कमांदु.

The leaves of the Sugarcane. पूटो, पांडुड़.

A Sugarcane press. चीचिड़ो, कोलू.

To Suggest. ज़ाणाइणु. *See* To Hint.

To commit Suicide. पाणु मारणु.

A Suit of clothes. वगो, पोशाख, (*woman's apparel*) जोरो. *See* Set, Suite.

A Suit of cards. रंगु, खेल.

A Suit at law. मामिलो.

To Suit (*agree*). टहणु, जुड़णु, जुग़ाइणु. *See* To Become, Please.

Suitable. जोगु, जोगो, जोड़ु, लाइकु, बाबु, ठाहू; *or* Suitably, ठहँदो, व-णँदो, ठाहूको, ठहाइतो, जुडाइँदो, जो-डाइतो, जुगाइतो, सुहाइँदो, सूळाइतो, सुहाइतो. *See* Proper.

Suitableness. लाइकी, जोगिता.

A Suite. अम्लो. *See* Retinue.

A Suitor (*petitioner q. v.*). दांही, फर्यादो.

To Sulk. रूसणु.

Sulkiness, the Sulks. रोसामो, रो-सु, रोसो, आरू, आरो, तोसो.

Sulky, a Sulker. रोसू, रोसामे &c. खाधो, तोसिरू.

Sullied. लीघाइतो.

To Sully. दागु-लीघो, &c. लाइणु. *See* To Slur.

Sulphur. गोगिड़ू, गंध्रकु, गोगिडींडु, आव्लासारू.

Sultriness. काड्हो, गर्बिरो, रुघ, रुं-भ, रुंभो, रुंभणु, बुट, घुट, आडंगु.

Sultry. काड्हाइतो, रुघाइतो, रुघारो, घुटाइतो, घुटारो.

Sum (*total*). जुम्लो. *See* Amount.

Summer. ऊन्हारो, आड्हडु, हाडु.

A Summer-set. बाजी.

A Summit. चोटी.

To Summon. सड़णु, कोठणु.

A Summons (*written*). पर्वानो. *See* Call.

Sumptuous, Sumptuously. घणख-र्चो, उम्दो. *See* Splendid.

The Sun. सिजु, सूंजु.

A stroke of the Sun. सिज जो झडप.

A Sunbeam. कनी, किरिणि, सिज-जी लाट.

To be Sunburnt (*the face, &c.*). टामिडो हणणु.

Sunday. आचरू, आर्तरू, आड़ितवारू, आइतवारू, आर्तवारू.

A Sunflower. सूंजु, सूंज मुखी *m.*

At Sunrise. सिज सँभों, सिज उभिर्ये.
See Morning.

At Sunset. सिज लथे. *See* Evening.

The Sunshine. उस, धुप.

To Sunder. *See* To Separate.

Sundry. घणा *plu.* जातोरो. *See* Several, Miscellaneous, Various.

A Sup. सुर्की, सुर्को, ढुकु.

To Sup. सुर्की &c. भरणु.

Superabundance, Superfluity. व-धोकी-काई, वाधि.

Superabundant, Superfluous. वधोकू. *See* More.

Superb, Superbly. शानाइतो. *See* Splendid.

A Supercargo. किर्याणी, दरोगो.

Supercilious. दिमागी. *See* Proud.

Superficial, Superficially. मथाछि-रो, मथछिरो, उछातिरो.

Superfluous. *See* Superabundant.

To Superintend. दरोगो थी ड़िसणु.

A Superintendent. दरोगो, लाकुडो.

Superior (*in place*). मथे. *See* Upper.

Superior, of Superior quality. ऊ-चो, उम्दो, सर्सु, जातोरो, अगिरो.

Superiority. ऊचाई, ऊचाणि, उ-म्दाई.

Supernumerary. वधोकू. *See* More.

Supine, Supinely (*with face downward*). पुठिअ भर, सँभों. *See* Indifferent.

Supineness (*carelessness q. v.*) अलगर्जाई, अलबेलाई. *See* Indifference, Indolence.

Supple. कुंभरो, मुडिणो.

A Supplement, Supplementary account, &c. वृन्नो.

A Suppliant, Supplicant, Supplicator. वेनतिअवारो, लीलिडाटू. *See* Petitioner.

To Supplicate. वेनती &c. करणु, लोलाइणु, लीलिडाइणु.

Supplication. वेनती, विनती, मिनथ, लीलिडाटी, लोल्डी, नीजारी, निआजु, अर्दास.

To Supply. पुज़ाइणु, पहुचाइणु, रसाइणु, ड़िअणु.

Support (*prop, help*). झल, टेक, आधर, आधरु, आधारु, आसिरो, ड़कु, तकिओ, पुस्ती.

Support (*maintenance q. v*). तवणि, तोंणि, जीविका.

To Support (*bear up*). झलणु, थंभणु. *See* To Endure.

To Support (*maintain, nourish q. v.*). निपाइणु, पालणु. *See* To Assist.

A Supporter. वसीलो, आधारू. *See* Support.

To Suppose. अट्कलणु, अट्कल &c. करणु, भांइणु, तकणु.

A Supposition. अट्कल, तक, उन्मानु.

To Suppress. दबाइणु. *See* To Overpower, Crush, Conceal.

To Suppurate. पुंइ करणु.

Supremacy. वड़ाई, मुखिपाई.

Supreme. वड़ो, सभिनो खां मथे-सिरे, सरि, मुखि, मुंढु. *See* Principal.

A Surcingle. बालातंगु.

Sure (*certain q. v.*). बेशको, पको, ठोकु. *See* Safe.

Sure, Surely. बेशकि, जाई, तहदिलि, ठोकु, खामखाह. *See* Certainly.

Sureness. बेशकाई, पक, पकाई, चिटाई, निहिचो. *See* Certainty.

Suretiship. जामिनो, जामिन्गोरा, खोलांदरो.

A Surety (*bailsman*). जामिनु, जमानु, खोलांदरू.

Surf, Surge. लहरि. *See* A Wave.

The Surface. मथो, मथु, तरू.

A Surfeit. जोग़ोरू. *See* Satiety.

To be Surfeited, or distended from overeating. जोग़ोजणु.

A Surgeon. जराहु.

Surgery. जराही.

Surgical, of a Surgeon. जराहिको.

Surly. रुखो, खहुरो, कौडो.

To Surmise. *See* To Suppose, Suspect.

To Surmount. तरो वञणु, टपणु.

To Surpass. सर्साई-सर्सो करणु *or* ड्रुखारणु, सर्सु - कांढ़ो-वधि करणु. *See* To Outstrip.

Surplus. वधीक, वाधू.

Surprise. See Suddenness, Astonishment.

To Surprise. (*take unawares*) ओचितो वठणु, (*astonish*) हैरत-अचुरज में विझणु.

Surprising, Surprisingly. अजबु, अजाइबु, अजीबु, अजब &c. जिहडो, अजबाइतो.

To Surrender (*act.*). छड़णु, छड़े ड़िअणु.

To Surround. वेढ्हणु, घेरणु, वराइणु, वकोडणु.

To Survey (*land*). जब्त करणु. *See* To Measure, Examine.

A Surveyor (*land measurer*). जाबितु. *See* Measurer.

To Survive. (*outlive*) वधि-वाधू-जिअणु, (*continue to live*) बचणु, जिअणु.

To Suspect, have a Suspicion. शकिजणु, गुमानिजणु. *See* To Imagine.

To Suspend (*hang*). टंगणु, लट्का-इणु, लड़्काइणु, टेड़णु. *See* To Stop.

Suspense. विस्वासु, उल्को. *See* Anxiety, Uncertainty.

Suspicion. गुमानु, शकु, भिमु, भमुं, संदेहु, सिस्सि. *See* Doubt.

Suspicious. गुमानी, शकी, भिर्मी, संसाई, विस्वासी, अणविसहू; *or* Suspiciously, शकाइतो, शकांओं, विस्स्यो, सिस्सिपो, बेवेसाहो.

To make Suspicious. शकाइणु.

To Sustain. *See* To Support.

Sustenance. खाधो, निपाजु, जीविका. *See* Subsistence, Food.

To Swaddle. तंजणु.

Swaddling-clothes. तंजणु, तंजिणी.

To Swagger (*in walking*). टिलणु. *See* To Boast.

A Swaggerer. टिलणु, टिलिणी.

A Swallow (*the bird*). अबाबीलु.

To Swallow. गिहणु, गिर्काइणु, गिर्कणु; in gulps, घुट्कणु.

A Swallow, Swallowing. गीत, गित, गिहणी.

A Swamp. धुबणि, गपिणि, गरणि.

A Sward (*green, grassy, land.*) रेल.

A Swarm of flies or bees. मखि. *See* Multitude.

To Swarm. *See* To Throng.

Swarthy. सांविरो.

To Swathe. वेड़्हणु.

To Sway. *See* To Influence, Wield, Govern.

To Swear. संहुं *&c.* खणणु.

Sweat. पघरु.

To Sweat, (*neu.*). पघिर्जणु.

To Sweep. मेडणु, बुहारणु.

A Sweeper (*scavenger*). बुहारीदारु, हलालखोरु, चुहड़ो, ड़फेरु, ग्रालेशाही, शिकारी.

Sweeping (*sub*). मेडसेड, बुहारिणी, बुहरू.

Sweepings. बुहारू, मेडो, किचिरो.

Sweet, Sweetly. मिठो, शीरी.

A Sweet (*endearing term*). मिठू, मिठिड़ो, मिठणु.

To taste Sweet or Sweetish. मिठाइणु.

The Sweetbread. शोदानु.

To Sweeten (*act*). मिठो &c. करणु.

Sweetish, slightly Sweet. मिठेरो, मिठेरिड़ो.

A Sweet-heart. ढोलणु, ढोलो, ढोल्यो, ढोलु, लालनु, साजनु, सज़णु, जानिबु, पपनु, जानी, पिरी, पीउ, बालमु, सुगिरी, सूंहणु, दिलदारु, दिलबरु, माशूकु, मुहुबु, महबूबु, प्रीतमु, प्रियु.

A Sweetmeat. मिठाई, शीर्णी; some kinds of Sweetmeats are, हल्वो, मेसूपाकु, लड़ूं, तलेबूषी, साटो, अकुभरी, जिलेबी, बर्फी, पेड़ो, खोरपेड़ो, टिकी, तोशो, बूंदी, गुबितु, कुर्सु, रेविड़ो, मोरिंडो, बोड़ींड़ो, खंडुभुगिड़ो, गिहुरु, पिस्तकंदी, नकुलु, गुल्कंदु, नानुखताई, पंजीरी, लाडुओ, मुटो, गाठो.

A maker of Sweetmeats. हल्वाई.

Sweetness. मेठु, मिठाई, मिठाणि, शीरी.

A Sweet smell. खश्बूंइ, खश्बोइ, हुबिगारु, हुबिकारु, सुगंधु-धाई. *See* Fragrance.

Sweet smelling. सुरहो, खश्बोयो, सुगंध्यो, हुबिगारी, हुबिकारी.

Sweet-toothed, fond of Sweets. चटो.

To Swell (*neu*). सुज़णु, आमासिजणु, थोथिजणु, फुंड़णु, फूलणु, (*as grain does in cooking*) ट्रिड़णु.

To Swell, or be Swollen, out (*as the belly, or with pride*). आ-

भामणु, भाफिर्जणु, फूंड़िंजणु, फूकिजणु, बमजणु.

A Swelling. सोज़ि, भामास, थोथरि.

To Swerve (*deviate*). लडणु, मुडणु.

Swift, Swiftly. तिखो, छुहो, छोहो, तेजु, तकिडो, हलिणो, डोकू, डोकिणो, छूटु, हथछूटु.

Swiftness. तिख, तिखाई, छुहाई, तेजु, तेजी.

To Swim. तरणु.

A Swimmer. तारू.

To Swindle. धुतणु, ठगणु. *See* To Cheat.

To Swing (*act*). लोंड़णु, झूलाइणु.

To Swing (*neu*). लुड़णु, झूलणु.

A Swing (*oscillation*). लोड़ो, झूलो,

A Swing for swinging in. पींघ; Swinging cot, or cradle, हिंदोरो. पींघो.

A Switch. चहो, छम्को.

To Switch. चहो हणणु.

A Swivel (*moveable ring*). भौंकेली.

A Swoon, Swooning. ढकरू, गशी, गश.

To Swoon. ढकिर्जणु.

The Swoop of a bird. लामारो.

A Sword. तरारि, खनो, (*varieties*) गोर्ख्यो, शकेलो, बनू, नीम्चो, मिसिरी, फड्केल, सर्वांही.

To draw a Sword. तरारि कढणु.

To sheathe a Sword. तरारि थेकणुविझणु.

The Sword-exercise. चकर.

A Swordsman. चाकिरी.

A Sycophant. *See* Flatterer.

A Syllable. अखरू, अछरू.

A Symbol. निशानी.

A Sympathiser. दर्दवंदु.

Sympathy. दर्दवंदी.

A Symptom. निशानी, पारू, लछणु.

A Syringe. पिचकारी.

A System. ठाहु, सिज़िलि, सिट.

Systematical. ठाहाइतो, सिज़िलाइतो.

To Systemize. ठाहणु, सिज़िलाइणु.

T

A Table. मेज़ु.

A Table cloth. दस्तर्खानो.

A Tabor. *See* Tamborine, Drum.

Taciturn. माठोणो.

Taciturnity. माठोणाई.

A Tack (*small nail*). रेंजा मेख, गुल्मेख.

A Tack, Tacking (*in sewing*). कोक.

To Tack (*stitch together*). कोकणु, कोक हणणु.

To Tack a boat. चापणु.

Tact. ढँउँ, चतुराई. *See* Skill.

A Tadpole. ढ़िड़िरी.

A Tail. पुछु, दुंबु; of a fish, snake, &c. पुछो, पुछिडो, पुछिडु.

Tail-cropped, Tailless. लुंडो.

Tailed, having a Tail. पुछिरू.

A Tailor. दर्जी.

A Taint (*stain q. v.*). टिको, कारँईं. *See* Blemish.

To Taint, (*corrupt q. v.*) खारणु. *See* To Stain.

To Take. (*accept*) वठणु, (*seize*) झलणु.

To Take away. निभणु, खणी वञणु.

To Take by force. खसणु.

To Take down. लाहणु.

To Take off. लाहणु, खणणु.

To Take out. कढणु.

To Take up. (*lift*) खणणु, (*occupy*) संभाइणु.

To Take up room or place. मलणु, वालारणु.

Taking up on tick. खणति.

Talc. अबिरक.

A Tale. आखाणी, किहाणी, ग़ाल्हि. *See* Story.

A Tale-bearer. चुगिलु.

A Talent (*faculty*). गुणु. *See* Intellect.

Talented. गुणाइतो, ब्रहुगुणु-णो, दानाहु, बुधिमानु. *See* Wise.

A Talisman. *See* Amulet.

To Talk. ग़ाल्हाइणु. *See* To Speak, Prate.

To Talk of one's own affairs or condition. ग़रहणु.

To Talk in sleep. उफिड्कणु.

Talk. ग़ाल्हिबोलि, ग़ाल्हिमुहाडि, तालि, ग़ाल्हाउ, ग़ाल्हु, चउवटु, बोल्णो, गोया, गुत्फार, पचर. *See* Conversation.

Much Talk. ग़ाल्होडो, कहत.

Talkative. घणग़ाल्हाओ, ग़ाल्हिरूल्हारू, वातड़ारो, वातिराधो, कावेलो, तातो. *See* Loquacious,

Talkativeness. कावेलाई. *See* Chattering.

Tall. डिघो, टोंगो, टोंगु, ठुठु.

Tallish, somewhat Tall or Taller. डिघेरो, डिघेरिडो.

Tallness. डिघाई, डेघु, टोंगाई.

Tallow. वह, चर्बी.

To Tally. ठहणु, जुडणु.

A Talon. चंबो, नँहुँ.

A Tamarind tree. आमिडो.

The fruit of the Tamarind tree. गिदामिडो.

The Tamarisk tree. लओ ; a small species, लई, टारो ; another variety, आतिरो *m*.

Tamarisk trees in general. लाउ ; shrubs, लाइ.

The flower of the Tamarisk. कुंगुअटारो.

The galls of the Tarmarisk. साकुडु, साकुणु.

Tamarisk, of the Tamarisk tree. लाओ.

A Tamborine. दफु, खंजिरी. *See* Drum.

A Tamborine-player. दफाई.

Tame. हियों, हेराकडु, हेराकु.

To Tame (*act.*). हेरणु.

To become Tame. हिरणु.

Tameness. हेर.

To Tan (*leather*). रङणु.

A Tangle. मोंझि, मोंझारो, गंडु.

To Tangle (*act.*). गंडणु, मुँझाइणु.

To Tangle (*neu.*). मुँझणु.

A Tangled lump. गोगोडो, बोलांड़ो, बोडो.

A Tank. तलाउ, दुतो, वाहो, चहबिचो, हौदु, कोलावु, सरु, सरोवरु.

A Tanner. चमारु.

To Tantalize. सिखाइणु.

To Tap. टपुडणु.

To Tap in fomenting a sore. टकोरणु, टाकोरणु.

A Tap, Tapping. टपुड.

Tape. कोर, कँहों, (*coarse kinds*) अग़ठु, नवाड, नव्हार.

Tapering (*adj.*). ड़ांदपुछो.

Tar. ड़ामरु.

Tardiness. ढिराई, ढिर, गिसिरि, गेसिरि.

Tardy. ढिरो, गेस्रिओ.

Tare (*in commerce*). बादानो.

A Target (*butt*). निशानु. *See* Shield.

A Tariff. अघोलिरो.

To Tarnish, become Tarnished. झकाइजणु, झकिजणु.

To Tarnish (*to stain*). दागणु. *See* To Sully.

To Tarry. रहणु, टिकणु, सहड़णु.

Tart. *See* Sour.

To Task, fix a Task. कमु बंधो ड़िभणु.

A Tassel. फुंदिणु, टोंरु, झाबो.

To Taste (*act.*). चखणु.

To Taste (*neu.*). लगणु, चसाइणु.

Taste (*flavor*). लजत, सुआउ, साउ, सवादु-डु, रसु, चस, रस्रा, (*liking*) चस, चसी, चस्को, चूश.

Taste (*nice discernment*). सिजिलि, सिट्, संजट्, शहूट्.

To get a Taste or liking for any thing. मिठाइजणु, चस्कणु.

To have a pleasant Taste. लजताइणु.

Tasteful (*savoury*). लजती, लजताइतो, सवादी, रसभर्यो, चसाइतो.

Tasteful, Tastefully, shewing Taste. सिजिलाइतो, सिजिलो, संजट्टाइतो, शहूट्टो-ट्टाइतो.

Tasteless. बेलजतो, बेसवादो-दी, बेरसो, फिक्रो, अलूणो, लिसो.

Tastelessness. बेलजताई-ती, फिकाई.

Tattered, in Tatters. लोडिरु, लोढुंलोडूं.

To Tattle. बकणु. *See* To Prate.

To Tattoo. तिरोखिडी &c. हणणु.

Tattooing. तिरोखिडी, सुइडी.

A Taunt. तानो, चाणक, तुन्को, टोक, तर्क, मिहिणो. *See* Reproach.

To Taunt. तानो *&c.* हणणु, मिहिणो ड़िभणु, टोकणु.

A Taunter. टोकिरु, तानिरु, मिहिणागोरु.

Taunting, Tauntingly. टोकाइतो, तानाइतो, मिहिणाइतो.

The sign Taurus. विरिखु, वृषु.

Tawny. कको.

A Tax. महसूलु; land Tax, हल, राउरु, खिराजु; fixed in kind on water wheel or per beegah, कासिगी; assessed on the standing crop, दानबंदो; the division of produce in assessment, बटई.

Taxable (*subject to assessment*). हलाइतो, राउरो, खिराजो.

Tax-free. बेराउरो, बेहलो, माफी.

A Tax gatherer. तहसील्दारु.

Tea. चाहि.

To Teach. सेखारणु, सिखाइणु, पड़हाइणु, पाड़हणु.

A Teacher. सेखारणवारो, उस्तादु, उस्तो. *See* Schoolmaster.

Teaching. सिख, सिख्या, तालीम.

Teak wood. सागु.

A Teal. चीकिलो.

A Tear (*in weeping*). लुड़कु, लुड़को, हंज, गोड़हो.

To shed Tears. गोड़हा गाडणु, हंजूं हारणु, लुड़क &c. वाहणु.

A Tear (*rent*). चोर, चिहिक, चाकु, अंगु *f.*

To Tear (*act.*). फाडणु, चीरणु.

To Tear (*neu.*). फाटणु.

To Tear to pieces. फाडे टुकिर टुकिर करणु.

To Tear up (*pull up*). पटणु.

To Tease (*cotton or wool*). तुंबणु, तुंबाइणु. *See* To Card.

To Tease (*annoy q. v.*). संदाइणु, हलाखु करणु, उहणु, खिजाइणु, ताइणु, तपाइणु.

The Teat of a beast. थणु.

With two Teats giving milk (*a cow, &c.*). ब्रिल्ह, with three do. ट्रिल्ह; having five Teats, पंजणि.

Tedious (*tiresome q. v.*). थकाऊ, डुख्यो, (*prolix*) तूलांभें.

To Teem. *See* To Bring forth Abound.

To Teeth. ड़ंदाइजणु, ड़ंद कढणु.

Teething (*adj.*). ड़ंदाइतो.

A Telescope. दूर्बीनी.

To Tell (*act.*). चवणु, बुंधाइणु, सुणाइणु, उतणु, आखणु, चिताइणु. *See* To Inform.

To Tell (*take effect*). लगणु.

A Tell-tale. चुगिलु.

Temper, Temperament. सुभाउ, मिजाजु, तबह.

Temper of metals. पाणी *m.*

Temperance. किरी, संजमु, जुगिति.

Temperate, Temperately. कियाइतो, संजमी, जुगितो.

A Tempest. वाच, तूफानु. *See* Storm.

Tempestuous. वाचिरू.

A Temple (*for idols*). ठाकुरदुआरो, दुआरो, मंदरू.

A Temple of the head. लौंदिडी, लौंणो.

Temporal. *See* Worldly.

To Tempt. भुतणु, भुतारणु, रेबणु. *See* To Allure.

Temptation. रेबु, बाँवली, लोभु. *See* Enticement.

A Tempter. रेबी, भुतिरू, भुतारू, चटिरू.

Tempting, Temptingly. रेबाइतो.

Ten. ड़ह.

The name of the number Ten. ड़हों.

The aggregate of Ten. ड़हाको.

The Ten at cards. दहलो.

About Ten. ड़हाको.

Ten (*per cent*). ड़होतिरो.

And Ten, or with Ten, (*prefixed to hundreds, &c.*). ड़होतर, ड़हों.

Tenacity. लगाति. *See* Stickiness.

To be Tenacious. लगो रहणु. *See* Sticky.

A Tenant (*of land*). रैअती.

Tenantry. रैअत.

To Tend (*guard, watch*). रखणु, तातणु, टहोडणु, सांढणु. *See* To Nurse.

To Tend (*lean towards*). लेटणु, अहलणु.

A Tendency. लेट, अहल.

Tender. कुंअरो, नर्मु, कूमलु, नाजुकु, (*as a sore*) कहरो, कहलो, कांहिरो, कांहिलो.

Tender-hearted. नर्मु दिलि. *See* Pitiful.

Tenderness. कुंअराई, नर्माई, नर्मी.

A Tendon. नस, रग.

The Tendon Achilles. खुच.

A Tenet. मतु.

Tenfold (*adj*). ड़हूंणो.

The Tenfold. ड़हूंणि.

The Tenon in joiner's work. चूड; having a tenon (*adj*). चूडांभों.

Tenor. वहु.

A Tense (*in grammar*). कालु, जमानो.

Tense, Tenseness. *See* Tight, Tightness.

A Tent. तंबू, (*varieties*) यकचोबो, बिसुर्खो, टंगोटी, पालु.

A Tent-maker. खीमादोजु.

A Tent-pole. चोब, सुर्खु.

A Tent-rope. तनाब.

A Tent-wall. कनात.

Tenth. ड़हों.

The Tenth day of lunar fortnight. ड़संईं.

Tepid. नँहँसोसिडो.

Tepidness. नँहँसोसिडाई.

Term (*limit q. v.*). संधो, खुणु, मिआदु. *See* Name, Period, Agreement.

For a specified Term or time. खुणाइतो.

A Termagant. रनोड.

To Terminate (*act.*). निबेरणु, निछेडणु, निछोडणु, पूरो करणु.

To Terminate (*neu.*). निबिरणु निछुडणु.

Termination. ओडकु, अंतु, छेडु, निछोडो, निछोडु, पारु, पारावारु, छेडो.

A Terrace. थलो, थडो, दुखाणो, (*small*) थली, थडो, दिकी; on the top of a house, खुडु, कोठो.

Terrestrial (*earthly*). दुआई, संसारी.

Terrible, Terrific. ड़ाढो, अघोरु, आफात, कडों.

To Terrify. डुजारणु, संगाइणु.

Territory. *See* Kingdom, Country.

Terror. डिजु, डपु, भउ, खोफु, डरु, डुजो, डाउ, ड़इकारु, हैबत, हौलु.

A Tertian fever. त्रिभडु, ब्रेंभों.

A Test. पर्खं. *See* Trial.

To Test. पर्खणु. *See* To Try; to test the precious metals by piercing into and heating them. रंदणु.

A Testicle. पेलो, आनूरो, नरो.

One with swelled Testicles. पेलिरु, टटिरु.

To Testify. साख &c. ड़िअणु.

Testimony. साख, शाहिदी, ओग़ाही, गुहाई.

Testy. चिड़िणो, चेडाकु.

A Tether. वाढि. *See* Rope.

To Tether. वाढणु, ड़िघरस करे बंधणु.

Tetter, the disease. ड़हु *f.*

The Text (*opposed to comment*). मूलु, मतनु.

Texture. ओज़, उणप, उणाति, उणति, उणावत.

Than. खां, खों, खूं, खँउं, भ़ग़ां -ग़ों-ग़ूं-ग़ँउं, आं, ओं, ऊं, अँऊं, गनां -नों-नूं-नँउं.

To Thank. शुकिरु &c. गुज़ारणु करणु.

Thankful. कदुराइतो, कदुर्दानु, गुणाइतो, थोराइतो.

To be Thankful. थोरो-गुणु मञणु.

Thankless. बेगुणो. *See* Ungrateful.

Thanks. शुकिरु, शुकिराणो.

That (*pron*). हू, हो, *correlative to* जो) सो; that one (*with indication*) उझो, (*before referred to*) उहो.

That like. हुअडो, उहडो.

That (*conj.*). त, कि, चे, जो.

To Thatch. छाँइणु.

A Thatched roof. छपरु, किड़ु.

The, The definite article is only expressed when used for "this" or "that" (*q. v.*). In other cases it is inherent in the noun.

A Theft. चोरी, चोराकारी, फुरि.

Their. हुननि जो, उन्हनि जो, हिननि जो, इन्हनि जो.

Their own. संदुनि.

Then. (*at that time*) तड़हीं, तड़िहिं, त, (*in that case*) त, तकरे, (*afterwards*) पोइ, वरी.

Of Then, or that time. तड़हुंणो, तड़हूंणिको.

Thence. हु-उ-ति-ता with the affixes तां-तों-तूं -तँउं- तांहीं- तांहों- तांहूं-तांहँउं-तहीं-तहों-तहूं-तहँउं- थां

-थों-थूं-थँउं-थांहीं-थांहों-थांहूं-थांहँउं -थहों-थहों-थहूं-थहँउं, attached to them तिहां.

Thenceforward (*from that time*). तड्हाकुरू, तड्हाको, तड्हूंणो, तड्हूंणिको.

A Theory. तक्र, अट्कल.

There. उते, उथे, हुते, तिते, तिथे, तिति, ताति, ताथे, तते, तति, तथे, तिहां, उ-हु-ति-ता with the affixes तहीं -तइं-तांहीं-ताइं-थहीं-थइं-थांहीं-थांइं, attached to them (*in that direction*) ओ-हेंते-ता with the affixes ड्डे-ड्डँहँ-ड्डां-डहीं-ड्डहूं-ड्डहँउं -ड्डांहीं-ड्डांहूं, ड्डांहँउं-डांहीं-ड्डहीं, (*in this direction, indicating*) ए with ड्डे-ड्डँहँ &c. as above.

A little way There. एड्ते, एड्तांहीं, एड्भरो.

Therefore. हुन-हिन-तँहिँ with करे -वास्ते-खां following them.

They. हू, हो, ही, ए, हे, (*with indication*) उहे, इहे.

Thick. (*not slender*) थुल्हो, (*approaching solidity, dense*) घाटो, गहरो, गूड्हो.

Thickish, somewhat Thick. थुल्हिडो, थुल्हेरिडो, थुल्हेरो.

To Thicken (*act.*). घाटो &c. करणु.

To Thicken (*neu.*). घाटो &c. थिअणु.

A Thicket. जुहो, झुमु, झुमटु.

Thickness. थोल्हि, थुल्हाई, थुल्हाणि, (*density*) घाटाई, घाटाणि, गहराई -णि-गूड्हाई-णि, घाटु.

A Thief. चोरू. *See* Robber.

Of a Thief or Thieves. चोराणो, चोरिको, चोरालो.

To Thieve. चोरी करणु.

Thievery. चोराकारी. *See* Theft.

The Thigh. सथर, रान.

The inside of the Thigh. चड्रो ; upper or front part of Thigh, जोट्.

A Thimble. अंगुस्तानो.

Thin (*slender*). सन्हो, पतिलो, पतिरो. *See* Lean.

Thin, Thinly (*not dense or close*). छिड्रो, छिड्रिडो, छिट्रो, छिट्रिडो.

Thin (*as a liquid*). पट्रिडो.

Thine. तुँहुंजो, तुँहिंजो.

Thine own. संदुइ.

A Thing (*substance*). शइ, वथु *f.* चीजु *f.* थोकु, टोलु, वस्तु *f.* पदारथु, (*matter*) ग़ाल्हि.

Things (*goods q. v.*). शइबइ, शइटोलु, वथुसिथु *f.*

To Think (*ponder q. v.*). ग़णणु, सोचणु.

To Think (*imagine*). भांइणु, समुझणु, पल्हडणु.

Thinness (*slenderness*). सन्हाई -णि, पतिराई-णि, पतिलाई-णि.

Thinness (*wanting density or closeness*). छिड्राई-णि, छिड्रिडाई-णि, छिट्राई-णि, छिट्रिडाई-णि, छिड्रु.

Thinness (*of liquids*). पट्रिडाई-णि.

Third (*adj.*). ट्रिओ, टोजो.

A Third, the Third part. ट्रिहाई, ट्रिओ भाङो ; of a rupee, लारी.

The Third day of the lunar fortnight. टीज.

Thirst. उञ, ट्रिह, तौंस, तास, पिआस, (*excessive*) उसाट, उसिराट.

To Thirst, be Thirsty. उञाइजणु, ट्रिहाइजणु, तासिजणु, पिआसिजणु, (*exceedingly*) उसाटिजणु, उसिराटिजणु.

To quench Thirst. उञ &c. लाहणु.

Thirsty. उञारो, उञायेा, उञ्यो.
Thirteen. तेरँहँ.
Thirteenth. तेहाँ.
The Thirteenth day of the lunar fortnight. तेरिसि.
Thirtieth. ट्रीहाँ.
Thirty. ट्रीह.
About Thirty. ट्रीहारो.
Thirty-one. एकट्रीह.
Thirty-two. ब्रट्रीह.
Thirty-three. टेट्रीह.
Thirty-four. चेाट्रीह.
Thirty-five. पंजट्रीह.
Thirty-six. छट्रीह.
Thirty-seven. सतट्रीह.
Thirty-eight. अठट्रीह.
Thirty-nine. उणेतालीह.
This. हिउ, ही, हे, ए, (*in distinguishing*) इहो.
This like. इहड़ो, हिअड़ो.
This very one present (*with indication*). इझो.
A Species of Thistle. कांड़ेरी, आड़ेरी.
Thither. उते. *See* There.
A Thong. वढी, कशु.
A Thorn. कंड़ो, सेल्हु.
A Thorn bush or branch, cut down. ढंगरू, (*small*) ढंगिरी.
The camel Thorn. कांड़ेरो.
The Thorn apple. धातूरो.
Thornless. बेकंड़ो, लासुड़.
Thorny. कांड़ेा, कंड़्यारो, कंड़िरू.
Thorough, Thoroughly. असहु, तमामु, अतंति, निपटु. *See* Completely, Wholly.
Thou. तूं.
Though. तोडे.
Thought. विचारू, वीचारू, ग़ण्तीग़णति, खिभालु, ध्यानु, कथ, क़िआसु, तपास. *See* Consideration, Care, Idea.
Thoughtful. वचारी, ग़ाणू, ग़णू, क़िआसी, संगाइतेा. *See* Meditative.
Thoughtless, Thoughtlessly. बेग़ण्यो, बेक़िआसु–सेा, बेखिआलो, अवेाचारी, बेध्यानु, अलगर्जो, अलबेलो, बेसंगेा.
Thoughtlessness. बेग़ण्ती, अवीचारू, अचेताई.
A Thousand. हजारू, सहसु.
By Thousands. हजारें. सहसें.
To Thrash. कुटणु, सटणु, गुड़णु, (*beat severely*) ड़ुडणु, ड़ाड़ेारणु.
To lay the Thrashing floor, or place for treading out corn. हलरि बंधणु.
Thread. सग़ो, धाग़ो, तंदु.
Raw Thread. सुटु, तंदु.
The sacred Bráhminical Thread. जण्यो.
To Thread. पुअणु.
A Threat. दड़्को, ताबु, दब्राउ, दाबु, ड़खेा.
To Threaten. दड़्को &c. ड़िअणु.
Three. ट्रे.
The figure or number Three. ट्रिको.
And, or with, Three (*prefixed to hundreds, &c.*). ट्रिरोतर्, ट्रिड़ो.
Three (*per cent*). ट्रिरोतिरो.
Three quarters. (*of a rupee*) ट्रेपाण्यूं, (*of a seer*) ट्रे पा ; one quarter less than one, मुनो.
Three quarters (*per cent*). ट्रिपाण्येा.
Three cornered. ट्रिकुंड़ो, ट्रिकुंड़्यारो.
Threefold (*adj.*). ट्रीणेा.
The Threefold. ट्रीणि.
Threefooted. ट्रिपेरो.
To Thresh. *See* To Thrash.
A Threshhold. चांउठि.

Thrice. ट्रिहर, ट्रिहार.

Thrift. सर्फो, किनाइत, कोञ. *See* Frugality.

To Thrive. साओ थिअणु, वधणु, वीझणु.

The Throat. निडी, निर्घटु, ग़ाट्टु, गलो.

To Throb. ड़कणु, फड़कणु, ट्पणु, धड़कणु, दहकणु.

Throbbing (*sub.*). ड़कड़कि, दकदकि, धकधकि.

A Throne. गादी, तख्तु, टोलो.

A Throng. *See* Crowd.

To Throng. मिडणु, मेडु करे अचणु.

To Throttle. घुटणु, घोघो ड़िअणु.

Through (*from one end to the other*). पारि, आरोपारि, मझां-झों -झू-झँउं.

Through (*by means of*). हथां-थों -थूं-थँउं, करे, मार्फत.

A Throw (*cast*). उछल, छाडप

To Throw. उछिलणु, उछिलाइणु, हणणु.

To Throw away. फिटी करणु.

To Throw down. केराइणु, केरणु, ड़ाहणु, (*in wrestling*) दसणु.

A Thrum. ड़ही.

A Thrust (*stab*). चोक, चूंग, पुत.

To Thrust (*shove*). धिकणु, थेल्हणु.

To Thrust (*stab*). चोकणु, चूंगणु, टुंबणु.

A Thumb. आङूठो.

A Thump (*with the fist*). मुक.

To Thump. मुकूं हणणु. *See* To Beat, Thrash.

To Thunder. गजणु, गुडणु.

Thunder. गोड, गाजि.

A Thunder-bolt. विजु *f.*

Thursday. खमीस, जुमेराति, विस्पति, विरस्पति.

Thus. हिंअ, हूएं.

Thus far. हेसों-एसों with तांईं-वोणो &c. *See* Till.

To Thwart. रंड़णु, रंड़ाइणु, झलणु, अट्काइणु.

Thy. तुंहुंजो, तुंहिंजो.

On Tick. उधारो.

To allow Tick. खणति-ओधरि-उधारो खणाइणु.

To Tick (*as a watch*). टिक्टिकि करणु.

A Tick (*louse of dogs*). चिचिड़ु.

A Ticket. चिठी.

To Tickle. किंतिकिताइणु, किंतिकिताई &c. करणु.

Tickling (*sub.*). किंतिकिताई, किंतिकिति, किंतिकाई.

The Tide. वीरि, जुहारू.

Tidiness. सिजिलि, सिट्, संजट्, ठाहु, संज, शहूट्.

Tidings. सुधि, खबर. *See* News.

Tidy, Tidily. सिजिलाइतो, सिट्राइतो, संजाइतो, संजेतो, संजीलो, संजट्राइतो, शहूटो-टाइतो.

A Tie (*fastening*). ग़ंदि.

The Tie or string of a garment. कँही.

To Tie. ब़ंधणु.

To be Tied. ब़झणु.

A Tier (*row q. v.*). सिफ, संबीर, सिंबोर.

A Tiffin. मांझांदो.

A Tiger. शेरू, वाघु.

Tight (*tense, firm*). ड़ाढो, पुख्तो, सुब़ंधु.

Tight (*as a garment*). सोड़्हो, तंगि, कोतड़ु.

To Tighten, or pull Tight. छिकणु, कशणु, कसणु, साहणु, सोटणु.

Tightly, Tight. ड़ाढां, महकुमु, काबू.

Tightness (*tenseness, firmness*). ड़ाढाई, पुख्ताई.

Tightness (*as of a garment*). सोड्हाई-णि, कोताही, तंगी.

A Tile. नरो.

A Till, Tiller. अगरू.

Till (*until*). ताईं, तोंईं, तोणो, तोडों, सूधो-धां सीभ, सों, लाकूं.

Till now. हेसीं-एसीं with ताईं &c. affixed.

Till then. तेसीं-ओसीं-होसीं with ताईं &c. affixed.

To Till. पोखणु. *See* To Cultivate.

Tillage. पोख, व्रनीव्रारो.

A boat's Tiller. वोणो.

Timber. काठोड़ि, काठु.

Time (*duration*). महल, वखतु, वेलो, वेरो, वेल, वेर, जमानो, समो, टाणो.

Time, turns or successions of Time. भेरो, भिर्को, घुमिरो, ड़ाईं, ड़ाहीं, दफो, लिङो, वेरो, वेरि, वारो.

A length of Time. मुदत, जमानो.

Time (*delay q. v.*). मुहलत, फुर्जो. *See* Term.

Timely, at a proper Time. महलाइतो, वख्ताइतो, वेलाइतो.

At an improper Time. कुमहलो, कुवख्तो, कुवेलो.

Timid, Timerous. ड़िजिणो, टहिणो, ट़हडु, ट़ाहडु, संगाइतो, (*scrupulous*) विस्विस्यो, विस्वासी, सिस्सिस्यो, (*nervous*) खफ्कानी.

To be Timid. ड़िजणु, ट़हणु, संगणु.

Timidity, Timorousness. ड़िजु, ट़ाहु, ट़हडाई, संग.

Tin (*the metal*). कलो, कलई.

Calx of Tin. बंग.

To Tin. कलो &c. करणु-लाइणु.

A Tincture. चट.

Tinder. पुड्दु.

A Tinge. चट.

To Tinge. चट ड़िअणु.

To Tinkle. छिण्कणु, छिम्कणु.

A Tinkle, Tinkling. छिण्को, छिम्को, छिण्काटु, छिम्काटु.

A Tinner. कलोगरू, कलईगरू.

A Tint. *See* Color, Tinge.

Tiny. नंढिडो.

The Tip. चुहुंब.

On Tiptoe. उभखुडो.

The Tire of a wheel. फोथे जो पटु.

To Tire (*act.*). थकाइणु, विर्चाइणु, खुहाइणु, कुड़ाइणु.

To Tire, be Tired. थकणु, कुडणु, हार्जणु, खुहिजणु, विर्चणु.

Tiresome. थकाऊ, विर्चाऊ, थकाइतो.

Tissue (*brocade q. v.*) कीम्खाबु.

A Titbit. लुक्मो, खूर्मो, खोर्मो, ग़फो.

An honorary Title. लकबु, खिताबु. *See* Name, Right.

A Title deed. सनत, सनद, कबालो.

To Titter. खिलिखिलि लाइणु.

To (*the sign of the dative case*). खे.

To (*denoting motion toward*). ड़े, ड़ंहें. *See* Towards.

A Toad. ड़ेड़रू.

A Toadstool. सपिडो, शैतान जो पेलो.

To Toast. सेकणु.

Toasted. सोकु.

Tobacco. तमाकु.

A second crop of Tobacco from the same plants. बजरि.

A ball of Tobacco for putting into hooka. ग़ोटी.

A load of raw Tobacco made up in five maunds. पोथ्यो.

A Tobacconist. तमाकी.
To day. अजु.
Of To day. अज़ोको, अज़ूणो.
A Toe. आङुरि.
The big Toe. आङुठो.
The little Toe. चीच.
A Toe-ring. बंदिडो. *See* Ring.
Together. गडु, हेकांदो, भेडो, (*among themselves*) हिक ब्रिए में.
Together with. सूधां, सूधो. *See* With.
To Toil. ग़हणु, हज़णु, वहणु, खपणु, कहणु.
Toil. कशालो, पतोड, कह, मिहनत, पोर्ह्यो.
Toiling (*sub.*). ग़ाहिणी, हज़िणी.
Toilsome. मिह्नताइतो, मिह्नती, मिह्नताणो.
A Token (*sign*). उहुञाणु, निशानी, नीशानी, ड़सु.
Tolerable (*endurable*). सहिणो, सहू. *See* Middling.
To Tolerate. *See* To Suffer.
Toll. महसूलु, सुंगु.
A Tomb. (*Musulman*) कबर, तुर्बत, बुठो, लोड्हु. (*Hindoo*) समाधि.
To morrow. सुभाणे-णा, सुबांहीं, सुभांईं, सुबहणे-णा. *See* Morrow.
Of To morrow. सुभाणिको, सुभांको.
A Tone. सुरु, सरोज़ु. *See* Sound.
A pair of Tongs. चिम्टो, सण्ज़ु.
A Tongue. ज़िभ, जबान.
The Tongue, of a buckle. जबानो; of a bell, लार.
Large Tongued. ज़िभिरु.
Double or forky Tongued. ब्रिज़िभो.
Tongueless. बेज़िभो.
A Tongue scraper. ज़िभी.
To night. अजुराति.

Tonsure. हजामत, सँवारत.
The first Tonsure of a child. मुनणु, झंड़ि, अकीको.
Too much. घणो, वधीक, वाधू, सर्सु; a little too much, सुंभालो, सुंभालेरो, ससेंरो.
Too (*also*). बि, पि, पिणि, पुणि, बी.
A Tool. ओजारु, हथ्यारु.
A Tooth. ड़ंदु.
A double Tooth. ड़ाठ, हौड.
The Tooth of an instrument. डंदो.
A Tooth brush. ड़ंदणु, पिर्भांतो; to brush or clean the teeth, ड़ंद मलणु.
Toothed, having large teeth. ड़ंदिरु.
Toothless. बेड़ंदो, पत्रो, भुड़ो, फदो, खंड़ो.
A Toothpick. ड़ंदखोट़िणी, ड़ंदेरी, ड़ंदोरी, छिंघ; to pick the teeth, ड़ंद खोट़णु.
The Top. (*upper part*) मथो, मथु, (*highest point*) चोटी.
A spinning Top. लाटूं, लाटिमो.
A humming Top. वांगोलाटूं.
The spike of a Top. कुंदु.
The string of a Top. ड़ोरि.
A Topknot. वांगूडो, चोटो.
Topmost. मथ्यों.
A Topaz. पुखिराजु.
A Topic. ग़ाल्हि.
Topsy turvy. उबतो सुबतो, उबतडि सुबतडि. *See* Upside down.
A Torch. मशालु, (*varieties*) ड़िआटी, खड्गो.
A Torchbearer. मशाल्ची.
To Torment. (*torture*) पीडणु, ड़ाढो डुखाइणु, (*tease q. v.*) संदाइणु, ड़हणु.
Torment (*anguish*). लोछि, सूरु.

A Tormentor. मथे खाऊ -खपाऊ, जिभ खाऊ-खपाऊ.

To be Torn. फाटणु.

Torpid. साणो, सुतो. *See* Numb.

Torpor, Torpidness. साणाई, सुंन.

A Torrent. नैईं.

A Tortoise. कछुँउँ, कछूं, कुमो.

Tortuous. वरारो, वराइतो.

To Torture. पीडणु, ड़ाढो डुखु ड़िअणु, ड़ंभणु.

Torture. ड़ाढी पीड. *See* Torment.

To Toss (*cast q. v.*). उछिलाइणु.

To Toss about (*act.*). पतोडणु, छोलणु, गोंदाडणु, झोंगणु.

To Toss up & down. टपाइणु, कुड़ाइणु.

Tossing about (*sub.*). पतोड, झोंग.

The Total. जोड़ु, जुम्लो.

Totally. सज़ोई, सभोई, सारोई, बिल्कुलु. *See* Wholly.

To Totter. लुड़णु, धुड़णु. *See* To Shake.

To Touch. छुहणु, छुभणु, हथु लाइणु.

A Touch, Touching. छुहिणी.

An impure Touch. छोप, छोति.

To be Touched by anything impure. छुपणु.

A Touchstone. कसटी, कसोटी.

Touchwood. पुड़दु.

Touchy (*irritable*). चिडाकु, चेडाकु, चिड़िणो, रोसू, रुसिणो.

Tough. चीड़हालो, चीड़हारो, ड़ाढो.

Toughness. चीड़हालाई, चीड़हाराई, ड़ाढाई.

A Tour (*journey in a circuit*). फेरी.

A Tour (*turn of duty, &c*). वारो, वारी, वार.

By Tours or turns. वारेवती, वाराइतो, हिसाइतो.

To Tow. छिकणु.

Toward, Towards. ड़े, ड़ेहं, ड़ांह, ड़हां, ड़हों, ड़ांहों, ड़ाहूं, ड़ांहों, ड़ाहेंउं, ड़हो, ड़हूं, ड़हों, ड़हंउं, पासे, पारि.

A Towel. रूमालु, अंगोछो.

A Tower. ठुलु, ठुल्हु.

A Towline. रसि.

A Town. शहरु, गोटु, गांउ, गामु, टंड़ो.

Of a Town. शहरतू, शहरेचो, गोठेचो, गोठाइतो.

The Town and lands attached, तरु; an inhabitant of these, तराई.

A fellow Townsman. गोठाई, ड़ेहाई.

A Toy. रांदीको, घोडोपटहलो.

A Trace. सगु, नीशानी, पेरो.

To Trace by tracking steps. पेरु -पेरो कढणु-खणणु.

To Trace (*outlines*). लीकणु, अंगारणु.

The Traces by which an animal is fastened in a water wheel, &c. कढ.

One who follows up Traces or Tracks. पेरो, पेरेवादी, पेणादी-ड्रो, पेराढू.

A Track. *See* Trace, Way.

To Track. *See* To Trace, Tow.

Trackless. रेवाटो, बेवाटो.

A Track rope. रसि.

Tractable. चएवारो, चएदारु, आग्याकारी, सुधातूरो, सधातूरो.

To be Tractable. चयो मञणु.

Trade, Trading. वापारु, वणिजु, वछाती, सौदो, सौदागरी.

A Trade (*profession*). कसबु, किर्ति, कमु.

To Trade. वापारु &c. करणु.

A Trader. वापारी, वणजारो, वछातु, सौदागरु.

A Tradition. ड़ंदकथा.
To Traduce. लेउ-ड़ोहु लाइणु.
A Traducer. लेभरू, लीभरू.
To Trail (*act.*). गिहिरणु, गिहिलणु.
To Trail (*neu.*). गिहिर्जणु, गिहिलिजणु.
A Trail. (*mark left*) गीसो, (*scent left*) धप. *See* Smell.
To be on the Trail. धपिजणु, धपाइजणु.
To Train. ड़मु करणु, सेखारणु.
A Train (*series q. v*). बहोर.
A Trait of character. अकानु, लछणु, पारू.
A Traitor. ड़्रोही, बेईमानु, वेसाहघाती.
To Trample. लतोड़णु, लताड़णु. *See* To Tread.
A Trample, Trampling. लतड़, लताड़, लतीड़.
Tranquil. सांति, ठहयों. *See* Quiet.
To Tranquillize. थहराइणु, ठारणु. *See* To Appease.
Tranquillity. थांहर, थँहर, ठहर, सांति, सांतीकाई.
To Transact. करणु, हलाइणु, रसाइणु, निबाहणु.
A Transaction. कमु, ग़ाल्हि, हाज.
To Transfix. आरोपारि कढणु-टुंबणु.
To Transgress (*neu.*). हुकुमु भञणु, ड़ोहु &c. करणु.
A Transgression. ड़ोहु, तक्सीर. *See* Fault, Sin.
A Transgressor. ड़ुहारी, गुनाही. *See* Offender.
Transient. खिणभंगु, थुक जो मुहर.
Transit duty. राहदारी.
Transitive (*in grammar*). सकर्मक, मुतद्दी.
To Translate into another tongue. ब्रिअ ब़ोलिअ करणु, तर्जिमो करणु.

A Translation. तर्जिमो.
To Transmit. ड़िआरे मुंजणु-मोकिलणु.
To Transplant. विहरणु, रोतणु, रूंबणु, थड़ारणु.
Transplantation, Transplanting. विहर, विहराड़ु, रोति, रूंब, रोंबो, विहुरो.
To Transport. *See* To Carry, Banish.
Transportation (*banishment*). ड़ेहनिकारो.
To Transpose. अगे पोइ करणु.
Transverse, Transversely. आड़ो.
A Trap. पिञिरो, कोड़्की, सिर्किणो. *See* Snare.
A Trap door. दरी.
The Trapping of a horse. पंज्संजो.
Trash. (*rubbish*) गंडुगोडु, गंडु, किचिरो, अंडुगंडु, (*improper food*) भलोमलो, भंडुगंडु.
To be in Travail. संभालणु.
To Travel. पंधु &c. करणु, ड़ेह घुमणु.
Travel, Travelling. पंधु, सफरु, मुसाफिरी.
A Traveller. पांधिरू, वाटहडू, वाटवहू, वाटावाहू, पांधी, मुसाफिरू.
A Tray. खूमूचो, थालु, थालु, पाठि.
Treacherous. ड़्रोही, बेईमानु, निमकहरामु. *See* Deceitful.
Treachery. ड़ोहु, बेईमानी, निमकहरामी, वेसाहघाती. *See* Deceit.
To Tread. (*step on, set the foot on*) पेरु रखणु- ड़िअणु, (*trample*) लताड़णु, लतोड़णु.
To Tread out grain. ग़ाहणु.
To lay a Treading floor. हलरि बंधणु.
The Treading out grain. ग़ाहु.

Treasure. खजानो.

A Treasurer. खजान्ची.

Treasury. खजानो.

To Treat (*behave towards*). फलाणे सां हलणु-करणु.

To Treat (*negociate*). ठाह-सुलिह जी गाल्हि करणु.

A Treaty. अहद्नामो,

Treble (*adj.*). ट्रीणो.

The Trebled or Threefold. ट्रीणि.

To Treble (*act.*). ट्रीणो करणु, ट्रीणाइणु.

A Tree. वणु; Trees or bushes in-general, वणराइ.

To Tremble. ड़कणु, कंबणु, थड़्कणु, फड़्कणु, धड़्कणु, धुडणु, सिभाटिजणु.

A Trembler, Tremulous. ड़किणो, कंबिणो.

A Trembling, Tremor. ड़किणी, कंबिणी, फड़्को, धड़्को, फड़्किणी, थड़्किणी.

Tremendous. ड़ाढो, आफात.

A Trench. कसी, चरी, खाही. *See* Drain.

A Trencher. पाट्रोडो.

Trepidation. कंबिणी, ड़िड़ु. *See* Trembling, Fear.

Trespass (*on lands*). भेल. *See* Transgression.

To injure by Trespass. भेलणु.

A Tress of hair. जुल्फ. *See* Lock.

A Trial. (*test*) कस, पर्ख, परीछा, आड्मुदो, (*judicial examination*) आचारु, अदालत, तड्वीज.

Triangular. टिकुंड़ो, टिकुंड़्यारो.

A Tribe. कोम, कुलु, कुरु, नुख, पथरु, जाति, निभाति. *See* Family.

Tributary. ढल भरींदडु, खिराजी.

Tribute. ड़नु, ढल, खिराजु.

A Trice. पलु. *See* Instant.

A Trick (*artifice q. v.*). मिखिरु, फंदु, फनु, फिकलु, बाजी, नखिरो, नाटु. *See* Habit.

Trickish. मिखिरेलो, नखिरेलो-लो.

To Trickle. टिमणु, झरणु.

A Trident. टिमूलु.

Tried. कय्लु, आड्मायलु.

Triennial. टिवर्हो.

A Trifle. थोरिड़ी-हल्की गाल्हि.

To Trifle. खेड़णु, खेड़ करणु, जख मारणु.

Trifling (*adj.*). नंढो. *See* Trivial.

The Trigger of a gun. माशो.

To pull the Trigger. माशो भीड़णु.

Trim (*adj.*). संजीलो, सिजिलाइतो. *See* Tidy.

To Trim. ठाहणु, सँवारणु, सिजिलाइणु.

To Trip (*act.*). आथुड़ाइणु, थाबिड़ाइणु, थेडणु, थेडाइणु.

To Trip (*neu.*). आथुडणु, थाबिड़्जणु, थिडणु, थिड़्कणु, आखुडणु, थाबो, &c. खाइणु.

A Trip, Tripping. थाबो, थुड़ो; methods of Tripping in wrestling, फिस्किणी, गोड़िडो, मुनिडी, विर्चो, जाठो, ब्रहडी, बिनाब्रहडी, रहडो, मकुडो, अडी.

A Trip (*journey to and from*). घुमिरो, दसु, पूरु, लिङ.

Tripe, the Tripes. ओझिरी.

Triple. ट्रीणो.

The Triplicate of a bill of exchange. परपाँउठि.

Triplication. ट्रीणाई.

Tripod. टिपेरो.

Trite. पुराणो.

To Triturate. गहणु, घोटणु.

Triumph. सोभ. *See* Victory.

Triumphant. सोभारो. *See* Victorious.

Trivial. हल्को, नंढो, थोरिडो.

A Troop. दफो, छुल्की. *See* Band.

A Trooper. सुआरू. *See* Horseman.

A Trot. डुग, ड़को.

To Trot. डुगाइणु, ड़काइणु.

To Trouble. अकाइणु, रंजाइणु, अँहँजाइणु, हलाखु करणु, कल्पाइणु, खिजाइणु, खपाइणु. *See* To Tease.

Trouble. हलाखी, अँहँजु, खेचरि, डुखु, ईजाउ, औखति, दिकत, कशालो, जाखोडो. *See* Difficulty, Distress, Perplexity.

Troublesome. (*person*) खेचिरो, खोदिरो, छितिरो, एथिरो, (*or matter*) अँहँजाइतो, डुखाइतो, ड़ाखिडांभों, डुखँदो.

A Trough. पाटोडो.

A Trowel. नारो, चूनालो.

A pair of Trowsers. सुथण, कांच, चनों.

Truant. रोलु, रोलाकु. *See* Vagabond.

True. सचो, खरो, सचु, सति, सोड़ोतु, बहालु, बहालु, वहवारू, सही, ठोकु, साभ्रां, सचाइतो.

Truely. सचु, तहकीकु. *See* True.

A Trumpet. तुरी, नसिंगो, कनाइ.

A Trumpeter. तुरीबाजु, कनांयो.

To Trundle (*neu.*). लेटणु. *See* To Roll.

The Trunk of a tree. थुडु.

The Trunk of an elephant. सूंढि.

A headless Trunk. धड़ु.

A Trunk (*chest*). संदूक.

Trust (*reliance*). वेसाहु, वेसहु, पति, पतीति, इतिबारू, सिदिकु, भावना, (*in God*) तौकल. *See* Faith, Tick.

A Trust (*thing deposited*). धरावत, अमानत.

To Trust (*place confidence in*). विसहणु, वेसाहणु.

Trusty, Trustworthy. वेसाही, वेसाहो, हथोको, पतिवारो, इतिबारी, मातिबरू.

Truth. सचु, सचाई, सचाणि, सचो, खराई, सचाराई, रास्ती.

To Try (*test*). कसणु, परखणु, आज़माइणु. *See* To Examine.

To Try (*attempt*). सायो-उद्मु करणु.

A Tube. नरो, नरो.

To Tuck in or up. खंजणु, उचांगणु, लांचणु, वरू खणणु.

Tuesday. अङारो, मंगलु.

A Tuft (*cluster*). छुगो, झुमकु; of hair, चग़, बुचु, मुचो, जाद; of grass, शुबो, शुबु.

In Tufts, Tufted. छुगारो.

To Tug (*act.*). ड़ाच्यो छिकणु.

A Tulip. लालो.

To Tumble (*throw down*). केरणु, केराइणु. *See* To Ruffle.

To Tumble (*neu.*). किरणु.

A Tumbler (*mountebank*). बाज़ींदो, बाज़ीगरू.

A Tumbler pigeon. लेटणु, तिखो.

A Tumour. ग़ोड़्हो, ग़ंढि, गंढो.

A Tumult. गोड़ु, लुड़ु, हुलरू, हंबसु, धूम, धम्चरू, बखेडो. *See* Clamor, Uproar.

A Tune. सुरू, गति, तानु, रागु, रागिणी.

To Tune. मिलाइणु.

A Turban. पग़, पाग़, पग़िडो, दस्तार, कआरासो; different kinds of Turbans, or methods of tying them, चोरो, पेची, शदो, फेंटो, ब्रचो,

मोल्हाटो, मोल्ह्यो, पट्को, पटिको; a cloth worn under the Turban, बतानो.

Turbid. लुडाटो, लुडु.

Turbulence. खलल, फिन्नो.

Turbulent. खलल्लो, फिन्नाई, फिन्नी.

A Turkois. पेरोजो, बुडो, (*small*) लिख.

Turmeric. हेडु.

Colored with Turmeric. हेडुंओ.

To Turn (*cause to move circularly*). घुमाइणु, फेराइणु, फेरणु.

To Turn (*cause to shift sides*). वराइणु.

To Turn inside out, or upside down. (*act.*). उबताइणु.

To Turn (*change q. v.*). मटणु.

To Turn away, out, or off (*act.*). तडणु, कढणु, लोधणु.

To Turn aside or off (*act.*). टारणु.

To Turn down (*fold*). भञ्जणु.

To Turn on a lathe. जंड्रिभ चड्हाइणु, चर्खि चाड्हणु.

To Turn over, or back. उथिलाइणु, वराइणु.

To Turn, or move, round (*neu.*). घुमणु, फिरणु.

To Turn or shift sides (*neu.*). वरणु.

To Turn back, or away (*neu.*). वरणु, फिरणु, मोटणु, उथिलणु.

To Turn aside or off (*swerve*). लडणु, मुडणु.

A Turn. (*revolution*) फेरी, फेरो, फेरू, फेराटो, घुमिरो, गेडो, पेडो, (*bend*) वरू, वराको, वकडु, वकुडु.

A Turn (*in rotation*). वारो, वारी, रव.

A Turn down, or dog's ear, in a book. भञ्ज.

By Turns. वारेवती, वाराइतो.

A Turner. जंड्रिभवाढो.

A Turnip. गोगिडू.

A Turret. *See* Tower.

A Turtle. कछँरुँ, कछूँ, कुमो.

A Turtle dove. कुमिरो, खुमिरी.

Tush (*inter.*). हुं, छो, छि.

A Tusk. ड्राठ, ड्राढ्ह, नेशु; of a boar, सिंघेर, सुंघेर.

Tusked, having Tusks. ड्राठिरू, सिंघिरू, सिंघारो, सुंघिरू, सुंघारो.

Tut. *See* Tush.

Tutty. तूतिओ.

A Twang, Twanging sound. छंणाटु.

A pair of Tweezers. नचिकणो.

Twelfth. ब्राहों.

The Twelfth day of the lunar fortnight. ब्रारिसि.

Twelve. ब्रारँहँ.

The name of the figure or number Twelve. ब्राहों.

Twentieth. वीहों.

Twenty. वीह.

About Twenty. वीहारो.

Twenty one. एकीह.

Twenty two. ब्रावीह.

Twenty three. ट्रेवीह.

Twenty four. चोवीह.

Twenty five. पंञ्वीह.

Twenty six. छवीह.

Twenty seven. सतावीह.

Twenty eight. अठावीह.

Twenty nine. उणटीह.

Twice. (*two times*) ब्र भेरा, दूबरि, दुराकत, (*a second time*) ब्रिहर, ब्रिहार, ब्रीहर, ब्रिभो भेरो.

To Twifallow (*plough a second time*). ड्रेलणु.

A Twig. चहो.

The Twilight. कारांझिडो, सुँहऊँधाई.

A Twin. जाडो, जाणों.

Twine (*string*). ड़ोरि, धागो, सग़ो, तंदो.

To Twine, Twist (*act.*) वटणु.

To Twine, Twist (*neu.*). वटिजणु.

To Twine, or Twist, round (*encircle*). वकोडणु.

To be Twined or Twisted together (*as trees*). अंगुडिजणु, वकुडिजणु.

Twining together (*intertwining, sub.*). अंगुडो, वकुडु, वकोड.

A Twinge. सूसटु, सूसाटु.

To Twinkle. *See* To Glitter, Wink.

A Twist. वटु, वरु, वकुडु, पेचु, वराको, (*as given to the leg, arm, &c.*) मोड, मरोड, मरोट.

To Twist or wrench (*one's arm, &c.*). मोडणु, मरोडणु, मरोटणु. *See* To Twine.

To Twitch (*jerk*). छिको &c. ड़िअणु-पाइणु. *See* To Snatch.

Two. ब्.

The name of the figure or number Two. ब्रिको.

The Two in cards or dice. दूओ.

And or with Two (*affixed to hundreds, &c*). ब्रिरोतर, ब्रिडो.

Two per cent. ब्रिरोतिरो सउ.

Two and a half. अढाई, (*reduplicating numeral*) अढूंणो, अढाऊणो, अढायो.

The Two and a half. अढूंणि, अढाऊंणि.

Two and a half per cent. अढाइतिरो सउ.

Amounting to Two and a half (*a share &c.*). अढांओं.

Two edged. ब्रिमुँहों.

Two headed. ब्रिमथो.

A Type (*emblem*). नोशानो. *See* Mark.

Tyrannic, Tyrannical. अंधेरो, कहरो, जुलिमी, कलूरो, जोरावरु. *See* Oppressive.

To Tyrannize. अंधेरु &c. करणु.

Tyranny. अंधेरु, कहरु, जुलिमु, बग्दादु, अलटु, कलूरु. *See* Oppression.

A Tyrant. जालिमु, बग्दादो. *See* Tyrannic.

A Tyro. नविलो, नवलु, नोलो, नँओं सेखाऊ-सेखिडाऊ.

U and V

Vacancy. (*from being unoccupied*) पाल्हाई, वांदाई, (*void space*) पोरु, सुञ, सुंन, (*a vacant place*) खालो जाइ.

Vacant (*unoccupied*). पाल्हो, वांदो, खालो. *See* Empty, Void.

To Vacate. पाल्हो &c. करणु.

Vacuity, Vacuum. *See* Vacancy.

A Vagabond, Vagrant. रोलाकडु, रोलाकु, रोलु, रोहिरूल्यो, फेटहडु, टोलाकडु; one without fixed habitation, बेहंधो, बेमागो, बेधुरो, बेथानोको. *See* Stationless.

A Vagary. पूरु, कुडु, टपो, तरंगु, उलेरु, उलेलु. *See* Fancy.

Vagrancy. टोलाको, रूलणु.

Vague, Vaguely. अणचिटो.

Vagueness. अणचिटाई.

Vain, Vainly (*unavailing*). अजायो, अकयार्थो, अबसु, बिर्थो, अविर्थो, बेफाइदो, निफलो, अवाडो. *See* Useless.

Vain (*conceited*). दिमागो, हठी. *See* Proud.

To grow Vain. आकिड्जणु.
A Valiant person. सूरिहु, वरनहु. *See* Brave, a Hero.
Valid. पको, पुख्तो.
A Valley. माथरि.
Valour. सूरिहाई, हिमथ. *See* Boldness.
Valuable. कीमती, अमुलु.
Value. मुल्हु, कीमत, कदुरू.
To Value (*appraise*). अघु विझणु -वंधणु. *See* To Esteem.
To Value (*be worth*). लहणु.
Valueless. बेकदुरो. *See* Worthless.
The Van of an army. मुहाड़ो, मुहड़ु, मुहुरो.
A Vane. गडगाहु.
To Vanish. गुमु-गैबु-गाइबु थिअणु.
Vanity. दिमागु, आकडि. *See* Pride.
To Vanquish. *See* To Conquer.
Vapid. फिको. *See* Insipid.
Vapour. बाफ.
Variable. फिरिणो, फेराइतो, अणथिरि.
Variance. *See* Difference, Disagreement.
Variation. फेरू. *See* Difference.
To Variegate. चिट्णु.
Variegated. चिट्कमिरो.
Variegation. चिट्, चिदिसाली, चिट्टिकारी.
Variety. *See* Kind.
Various, Variously, of Various kinds. जातीरो.
Various kinds. तरँहें तरँहें, घणी तरँहें.
Varnish. रोगनु.
To Varnish. रोगनु लाइणु.
To Vary (*change, neu.*). फिरणु, मटिजणु.
Vast. वड़ो, गडगाहु.
A Vat. कूनारू ; used by dyers of blue, कुनि.
A Vault, Vaulted roof. गुंबजु ; a kind of house with Vaulted roof, तजर.
To Vaunt. *See* To Boast.
Ubiquitous, Ubiquitary. सभ जाइ मौजूद, व्यापकु, सर्वव्यापी.
The Udder of Beasts. ओहु.
Veal. गाबे जो मासु.
To Veer. फिरणु. मटिजणु.
Vegetables. बकरू, तर्कारी.
Vegetable leaves. सागु, साओ सागु, भाज़ी, साई भाज़ी.
Vegetables sliced and dried. कचिरी.
A Vegetable field. पुडो, वाडी.
A seller of Vegetables. बाकिरो, कूंजिड्यो.
To Vegetate. अंगुर्जणु, मोर्जणु, अंगूरू कढणु.
Vehemence. जोरू, ड़ाढाई.
Vehement, Vehemently (*violent*). जोराइतो, जोरारो, ड़ाढो.
A Vehicle (*means of conveyance*). सुआरी ; beast of burden, वहिटु.
A Veil. (*for the face*) बुर्को, गुर्को, घुंघटु, (*curtain*) पड़दो.
To Veil the face. मुंहु ढकणु, बुर्को &c. करणु-कढणु.
A Vein. रग़, नस, नब्ज, नाडी.
To open a Vein. फस्त-सीर छोडणु.
Velocity. तिख, छोहु. *See* Swiftness.
Velvet (*sub.*). बखुमल.
Velvet, of Velvet. बखुमली.
Venal (*mercenary*). वढीखोरू, लबी, लबिरू, वढिरू रुश्वाती.
Venerable. वडो, कुर्बाइतो, मानाइतो, पूज़ु.
To Venerate. पूज़णु, मञणु.

Veneration. पूज़ा, मञ्जिता, कुर्बु, मानु.
The Venereal disease. पर्मेन्तु, गर्मी,
Venery (*of the sexes*). जमाउ, भोगु, जाड़ु. *See* Hunting.
A Venetian (*the coin*). मोतारामी, बुधिकी.
Venetians for windows. झिर्मिरी.
Vengeance. *See* Revenge.
Venom. विहु *f.* विखु *f.* जहरू.
Venomous. विसिहरू, विखिरू. *See* Poisonous.
A Vent. टुंगु, वाट, दरू.
To Ventilate. वाउखो करणु. *See* To Air.
Venture. *See* Hazard.
A Venturous person. हूडु.
Veracious. सचो, साऊ, सचारू. *See* True.
Veracity. सचाई, सचारी. *See* Truth.
A Veranda. दालानु, सुफो.
A Verb. क्रिया, फैलु.
The root of a Verb. धातु.
Verbal, Verbally. दातूणो, जबानो; verbally, वातवेणी.
Verbatim. अखरनि जा अखर.
Verbose, Verbosity. *See* Prolix, Prolixity.
Verdant. हर्यो, साओ.
A Verdict. निबेरो, फैसिलो. *See* Settlement.
Verdigris. जंगालु, कसु *f.*
Verdure. सब्जी, सब्जो, सावकि, सावकाई, वस, हर्यालि, हर्याणि, हर्याई.
Verge. *See* Mace, Edge.
To Verify. सचो-साभ्यो-साबितु करणु.
Verity. सचु.
Vermicelli. सेंयूं *plu.*
Vermillion. सिंगिरिफु, हिंगुलु.
Vermin. जीतु.
Vernacular. डेहाणो, डेही, डेसी.
Vernal. बसंती, बहारी.
Versatile (*variable q. v.*). घणमत्यो.
A Verse of a poem, &c. शिलोकु, बैतु, छंदु.
Verse (*poetry*). कविता, शाइरी.
Versed. हिर्यलु.
The Vertex. चोटी.
Vertigo (*giddiness q. v.*). भाणि, भांउटी.
Very (*in a great degree*). घणो, जोरू, तमामु, असहु, निपटु, अनानु, बेतरि.
Very (*the same, exact*). सागेो, सागूणो, सागी, उहोई.
A Vessel (*utensil*). थांउ, बासणु, बर्तणु, रछु. Some earthenware Vessels are, कूनारू, कूनरू, कूनारी, चाड़ो, जगन्नाथो, तसु, पारि, भागयो, माटो, माटी, कुनो, कुनिडो, दखी, साड्ही, डुझाई, किंगिरू, किंगिरी, तगारो. *See* Pot. Some Vessels of metal are, गडुं, चरू, चौंरि, झाझरि, झारी, तई, तभो, बाटी, पाउलो, मोर्यो, लोटो, बदिनो. Some water Vessels are, दिलो, दिलौं, मटु, मटिको, कौंरो, घडो, घडो, घागरि, घुघी, भभुई, छल, जम्नों, टिभेर, कुपिडो, नादौं, कुजो.
A stand for water Vessels. घडाम्जो.
A seller of metal Vessels. भान्सालो.
A trading Vessel (*varieties*). कोत्यो, दंगी. *See* Ship, Boat.
A Vestige. पेरो, निशानो. *See* Trace.
Vetch (*various kinds*). माँहिं कुल्ठी *or* कुल्ठो, मुङु, चौरो. *See* Pulse.
To Vex. खपाइणु, कल्पाइणु, ताइणु, तपाइणु. *See* To Anger, Tease.
Vexation. हलाखो, बेजारो, डुखु, रंजु, संकटु.

Vexatious. डुखयो, डुखाइतो, रंजाइतो.

Vexed. हलाखु, रंजि, डुखी, खस्तो, आतो, आजुजु.

To be Vexed. खपणु, कल्पणु, अर्मानिजणु.

Ugliness. बुछिडाई, कंझाई, बदिसूरतो.

Ugly. बुछिडो, बुछो, कोझो, बदिसूरत, कुरूपु.

A Vial. शीशी.

To Vibrate. लुडणु. *See* To Tremble.

A Vibration. लोडो, झुलो.

Vice. (*moral evil*) बदी, बुछिडाई, मैंदो, मैंदाई, (*fault q. v.*) अवगुण. *See* Failing.

A Vice (*the instrument*). जँबूरू.

Vicinity (*nearness q. v*). वेझाई, वेझिडाई. *See* Neighbourhood.

Vicious. बदि, बुछिडो, मैंदो. *See* Wicked.

Vicissitude. फेरू.

A Victim. कुर्बानु, सदिको, बलि.

Victorious, Victoriously. सोभारो, सोभाइतो, जीताइतो.

Victory. सोभ, फतिह, जीत, जैकारू, जइ.

Victuals. खेणु, खाइणु, खिअणु. *See* Food.

To Vie. रीस करणु, रीसाइणु.

To View. डिसणु. *See* To See.

View, Viewing. निगाह. *See* Sight, Prospect, Design.

Vigilance. सुचेतो, खबर्दारो, सुजागो, हुशिआरो.

Vigilant. सुचेतु, सुजागु-गो हुशिआरू.

Vigor. सघ, कुंअत, मर्दाना-न्गी. *See* Strength, Energy.

Vigorous. सघो, मर्दानो. *See* Strong.

Vile. बुछिडो, नीचु, खुआरू, ओछो, होछो.

Vileness. बुछिडाई, नीचाई ओछाई, होछाई.

To Vilify. लेउ-लोभ-ड़ोहु लाइणु, गिला करणु.

A Village. गोठु, गांउ, गामु, वसी, वसींह, वाँहणु, वहणु.

Of a Village, a Villager. गोठाणो, गोठाइतो.

A fellow Villager. गोठाई.

A Villain. लुचो. *See* Rascal.

Villainy. लुचाई. *See* Rascality.

To Vindicate. सचो-बेड़ोहो करणु.

Vindictive. वेरवठू, वेरू, खुंडो.

A Vine. डाख.

Vinegar. सुर्को.

To Violate (*infringe*). भञणु.

Violence. जोरु, ड़ाढाई, सबराई, जोरावरी, जोरो, दिगो.

Violent. जोरारो, ड़ाढो, सबरू, जोरावरू, जबरू, सब्राणो.

Violently, with Violence. जोराइतो, ड़ाढो, ड़ाढ्यां.

A Virgin. कुंआरी, कुमारी, कन्या.

Virgin, Virginal. कुंआरिको,

Virginity. कुंआराई.

The sign Virgo. कन्या.

Virile. मुर्साणो, मर्दाणो.

Virility. मुर्साई, मुर्सिपो-पाई-पणो, थूंम; to lose Virile powers, थथोथिअणु.

Virtue. (*moral goodness*) नेकी, धर्मु, पुञु, सीलु, सीरू, (*a good quality*) गुनु, गुण.

Virtuous. नेकु, धर्मी, सीलवानु, सबाबी, साधु, पुञी. *See* Chaste.

Virulent. जहरी.

A Visage. मुहांडो. *See* Face.

Viscid, Viscous. चीडालो, चीड़्हालो, चीड़्हारो, लेसिरू, लिग्लिग्यो.

Viscidity, Viscocity. चीडु, चीड़्हु, चीड़्हालाई, लेसु, लास.

Visible. ड़िसिणो, पधिरो, जाहिरू,
Vision (*sight q. v.*). नजर, निगाह.
Visionary. दिल्यों ठाहूपलु, खिआलो.
To Visit. गड़िजणु,-वञणु-अचणु,
A Visit. मुलाकाति, ड़िठि. *See* Meeting.
The Visiting an idol, gúrú, &c. दर्सनु.
To Vitiate. खारणु, फिटाइणु.
Vitriol. तूतिओ.
Vivacious. खुश्दिलि, खिलिणो.
Vivacity. खिलखुशी, खिलिणाई, मजो.
Vivà voce. वातवेणी, जबानी.
Vivid. तेजु, तिखो. *See* Bright.
Vividness. तेजी, तिखाई. *See* Brightness.
To Vivify. जिआरणु.
An Ulcer. नासूरू. *See* A Boil.
Ultimate. पोयों.
Ultimately. नेठांनेठि, पोयांपोइ. *See* At Last.
Umbrage. *See* Offence, Huff.
Umbrageous. छांवारो, छांववारो, छांइरू, छांवेलो.
An Umbrella. छटो, छटु.
An Umpire. ट्टिआकुडु, अमीनु, मुन्सिफु.
Un (*negative prefix*). अ, अण, बे, रे, ना, नि, न, म.
To be Unable. न सघणु.
Unaccomplished. अणपुनो, अणसर्यो. *See* Incomplete.
Unaccustomed. अणहिर्यलु-यों.
Unacquainted. असूंहो, अणसूंहो, अणवाकुफु, बेखबरो. *See* Ignorant.
Unadjusted. अणचुको.
Unadorned. अणसींगार्यो.
Unadvised, Unadvisedly. रे- अण -बे सलाहो.
Unaffected (*real q. v.*). अणठाह्यलु.

Unaided. *See* Unassisted.
Unalterable. अणमटु.
Unamiable. कुलछिणो, बेलछिणो.
Unanimity. बुधी, एको, हिक.
Unanimous, Unanimously. हिकमतो, हिकदिल्यो, हिकसलाहो.
Unapproachable. अणपहुचु.
Unapt. *See* Unfit, Stupid.
Unarmed. बेहथ्यारो, रेहथ्यारो.
Unasked. अणपुर्यो, अणपुछो.
Unassisted. बेहम्राहु-हो, बेपुठो, इकलो.
Unassuming. मजांतवारो, गरीबु.
Unattainable. अणलभु-भो, अलभु.
Unattended. रेनोकिरो, बेनोकिरो.
Unauthorised. रेहुकुमो, बेहुकुमो.
Unavailing. अजायो. *See* Vain.
Unawares. ओचितो, अजगैबी, अचानक, अणसुतें, अनासुतें, अचाचेति.
Unbathed. अणविहृतो.
Unbearable. अणसहिणो, अणसहू.
Unbearded. अणड़ाढ़्ह्यो-ह्यरू, रेड़ाढ़्ह्यो ; a beardless boy, गल्पटु.
Unbeaten. *See* Untrodden.
Unbecoming. बेवझो, अजोगु, नालाइकु-को, अणहतो, अणसुहँदो, अणजुगाइतो, अणठहू. *See* Unsuitable.
Unbelief. अणवेसाही, (*infidelity*), बेदीनाई-नी, बेधर्मी-माई, बेसिदिकी -काई.
An Unbeliever, Unbelieving. बेवेसाहो- सहो, अणवेसाहो - सहो. *See* Infidel.
Unbiassed. बेरिआउ-आओ, बेपछो.
Unbending. अमुडु. *See* Unyielding.
Unbidden. रेचयो, बेचयो.
To Unbind. *See* To Loose.
Unblamable. बेड़ोहु-हो.
Unblemished. बेऐबो, बेदागी-गो, बेवीको, अणदोको.

Unborn. अणज़ायलु.
Unbounded. बेहदि.
Unbridled. बेलगामो, बेक़ैदो.
Unbroken. अणभग़लु, सज़ो, (*as a horse*) जडु.
Unburied. अणदफन्यो.
Unburnt (*as a brick*). कचो.
To Unburden. बारु लाहणु.
To Unbutton. ब़ीडा लाहणु.
Unceasing, Unceasingly. हिकसारु, बराबरि. *See* Unintermitting.
Uncertain. शकी, शकाइतो, बेकाथो, बेकैतो, बेठोको, बेनेमो. *See* Capricious.
Uncertainty. शकु, संसो, संका, ड़िचिताई, बस्वसो, सुभो, शुबो.
Unchangeable. अणमटु, अणमोटु.
Unchecked. अझलु, अपलु, बेक़ैदो.
Uncircumcised. खोलेरो, अणतुहियो, बेसुन्नतो.
Uncivil. *See* Rude.
Unclaimed. निधणको. *See* Ownerless.
An Uncle. (*father's brother*) चाचो, ड़ाडो, (*mother's brother*) मामो, (*father's sister's husband*) फुफडु, (*mother's sister's husband*) मासडु.
Unclear. *See* Impure, Dirty. (*from a death in a family*) सूतको, (*from a birth*) पातको.
Uncleanness. *See* Impurity; (*from a death*) सूतकु, (*from a birth*) पातकु.
Uncomfortable, Uncomfortably. बेआरामो, बेसुखो.
Uncomfortableness. बेआरामी, बेसुखाई. *See* Discomfort.
Uncommon. विरिलो. *See* Rare, Strange.
Uncompounded (*simple*). निजातु, निरो, निखालिसु.
Unconcern, Unconcernedness. बेग़ंदिराई, बेपर्वाही, अलबेलाई.
Unconcerned, Unconcernedly. बेग़ंदिरो, अलबेलो, बेफिकिरो, बेदर्दो. *See* Indifferent.
Unconditional. बेशर्तो, बेक़ैदो, छड्यो.
Uncongenial. अणसुहाइंदो.
Unconquered, Unconquerable. अजीतु, अजइ.
Unconscious. बेखबरु, बेखबिरो, अणवाक़ुफु. *See* Insensible, Senseless, Ignorant.
Uncontrolled, Uncontrollable. अझलु, मगरु, बेक़ैदो.
Uncooked. कचो.
Uncounted. अणग़ण्यलु-ण्यो, रेग़ण्यो-ण्यलु.
Uncouth. अनाडो.
To Uncover. उघटणु, पटणु, उघाडो करणु.
Unction, Unctiousness. सणिभु, सणभाई-णि.
Unctuous. सणभो.
Uncultivated. गैरआबादु, अणवस्यो.
Uncurbed. *See* Unbridled.
Undaunted. बेभओ, निर्भउ, वड़ज़िगिरो. *See* Fearless.
To Undeceive. भोलो लाहणु, खबर्दारु करणु.
Undecided (*not settled*). अणनिबियो. *See* Irresolute, Undetermined.
Undefiled. पाकु, सुठो, पवितु, सुचि. *See* Pure.
Under. (*beneath*) हेठि, (*less than*) हेठि, घटि, (*in the time of*) में, ड़िहनि में.
Under, Undermost (*adj.*). हेठ्यों, हेठूंणो.

To Undergo. सहणु. *See* To Suffer.

Underhand (*adj.*). लिकोछपी.

To Undermine. सुरिंघ-सिरिंघ हणणु-करणु.

To Understand. समुझणु, पख्डणु, पुझंणु, लखणु, बुझणु.

The Understanding. समुझ, पख्ड, पुझं, अकुलु, होशु, होसिलो, वकूफु, बुधि, मति, ध्यानु, ग्यानु.

A sharp Understanding. उरू, जिहिनु.

Slow of Understanding. कुंदु.

Understood (*not expressed*). गुझो, लुमु, गुप्तु.

To Undertake. पँहँजे जिमे खणणु, पँहँजे हथि करणु.

An Undertaking. कमु, हाज.

To Undervalue. घटि लेखणु-गणणु.

Underwood. झनरि, (*of tamarisk*) लाइ.

Undeserved. नाहको, गैरवाजिबी.

Undeservedly. नाहकु.

Undeserving. नालाइकु. *See* Unworthy.

Undetermined. बेकैतो, बेकाथो. *See* Uncertain.

Undeviating. अणमुडु, अमुडु, अणलडु.

Undigested. अजोरणु.

Undiminished. अणघट्यो.

Undisciplined. अणसिखयलु, कचो.

Undiseased. निरोयो. *See* Well.

Undisputed. बेहुजतो.

Undistinguishable. अणलखो, बेमालूमु.

Undivided. अणवंड्यो. *See* Whole.

To Undo (*untie q. v.*). छोडणु. *See* Ruin.

Undoubted. बेशको, बेसुभो. *See* Certain, Positive, Sure.

Undoubtedly. बेशकि. *See* Certainly.

To Undress. अपिडो लाहणु.

Undressed. *See* Naked, Uncooked.

Undue. *See* Improper.

Undutiful, Undutifully. बेचयो, रेचयो.

Uneasiness. बेआरामी, लुछ्को, लोछि, लुछ, लुछकारो. *See* Restlessness, Anxiety.

Uneasy. बेआरामु, बेसुखो. *See* Restless.

Uneatible. अखाजु.

Uneducated. अणपढ्यो, अणपढ्हु.

Unemployed, Unengaged. निकमो, निवेकिलो, निखिमणो, बेकमो, बेकार्यो, बेकारू, रेकमो, पाल्हो, वेल्हो.

Unequal, Unequally. घटिवधि. *See* Uneven, Unfit.

Unequalled. अणमटु, अणजोडु, बेजोडु-डो, बेजोसु-सो, नपैदु, अणजोसु, बेनजीरू, बेमिसालु.

Unerring. (*faultless*) अभुलु, (*certain*) अगुसु.

Uneven (*not level*). हेठांओं मथांओं, डिंगो, हेठिमथे, घटिवधि.

Unevenness. हेठांई मथांई, डिंगाई.

Unexampled. बेमिसालु, बेनजीरू, बेबयानो.

Unexpectedly. ओचितो, अचानक, अचाचेति, अजगैबी, अनासुर्ति, अणसुर्ति.

To remain Unexpended. बचणु.

Unexperienced. अणहियलु, कचो, नवलु, नविलो.

Unexpressible. अणचइणो, बेबयानो.

Unfair. नाहको, गैरवाजिबु-बी.

Unfairness. नाहकु. *See* Cheating.

Unfaithful. कूडो, बेईमानु, बेवफा. *See* Faithless.

Unfaithfulness. कूडाई, बेईमानी. *See* Faithlessness.

To Unfasten. छोडणु.

Unfathomable. ओडाहु, अथाहु.

Unfavorable. अवलो, अणाओ.

Unfavorableness. अवलाई, अणाई.

Unfeeling. बेरहमु-मो, अवाझो, निर्दई, कठोरु.

Unfeigned. अणठाह्युलु, सचो.

Unfilled. अणभर्यलु, ऊणो.

Unfinished. अणपूरो, अधोखारो, अधोगाबिरो, अधोरो. *See* Half-finished.

Unfit. नालाइकु, अजोगु. *See* Improper.

Unfitting. *See* Unbecoming.

Unfitness. नालाइकी, अजोगाई.

Unfixed (*unsettled q. v.*). बेकैतो, बेनेमो. *See* Uncertain.

Unfledged. बेखंभो. *See* Featherless.

Unflinching. अमुडु, अटरु.

To Unfold (*act.*). उखेलणु, उखोलणु.

To Unfold (*neu.*). उखिलणु.

Unfordable. तारि.

Unforeseen. अणडिठो, अणरिथिओ.

Unforgiving. बेरहमु. *See* Unfeeling.

Unfortunate. निभागो, बेनसोबु-बो, बदिवख्तु-ख्तो, बदिनसोबु-बो, अभागी-गो.

Unfounded. देबुनिआदो-दो.

Unfriendly. बेनेहो, बेसंध्यो, अणसंध्यो, बेप्रोत्यो.

Unfruitful. निफरो, निफलो बेफरो. *See* Barren.

Unfulfilled. अणपुज्यलु.

To Unfurl. छोडणु, उखेलणु, उखोलणु.

Ungainly. बेड़ोलो, अनाडी.

Ungenerous. सोड़हदिल्यो, नंढदिल्यो.

Ungodliness. बेदीनाई–नी, अधर्मुमाई.

Ungodly. बेदीनो, अधर्मी.

Ungovernable. अझलु.

Ungraceful. बेड़ोलो.

Ungracefulness. बेड़ोलाई.

An Ungrateful person. बेगुणो, गुणचोरु, कुलालु, बेकदुरो,

Ungratefulness. बेगुणाई, गुणचोराई. कुलाली, बेकदुराई.

Unhandiness. खिर्विखिराई.

Unhandy. खिर्विखिरो.

Unhappiness. बेआरामी, नाखुशी, डुखु.

Unhappy. बेआरामु, नाखुशि, डुखी.

Unhealthy. रोगी, आजारी, रोगाइलो.

Unheard of. अणबुधलु, नँओं.

Unholy. *See* Impure, Wicked.

Unhurt. बेजोखो.

To be Unhurt. बचणु.

Uniform (*adj.*). हिकजिहडो.

Uniformity. हिकजिहडाई.

Unimportant. हल्को, नंढो, थोरो.

Uninformed. अणवाकुफु, अजाणु.

Uninhabitable. न विहण लाइकु.

Uninhabited. अणवस्यो, सुञो, सुञ. *See* Desolate.

Unintelligible. बेसमुझु.

Unintentionally. अणजाणो अणजातो–ते, ओचितो.

Uninterested. बेगर्जो-र्जु.

Uninteresting. अणसुहाइदो, अणवणंदो.

Unintermitting, Unintermittingly. हिकधडो, बरोबरि, बराबरि, हिकसारि-सरि-सारु.

Uninvited. बेसड्यो, अणकोठ्यो, बेदावतो, अणनेंडो.

Union. (*joining*) ग़ंढणु, ग़ंढु, (*concord q. v.*) मेलु, सूलु, पहति.
Unique. हेको, हिको.
Unison (*in music*). हिकतालु. *See* Union.
A Unit. एको. *See* One.
To Unite (*act.*). गडणु.
To Unite (*neu.*). गडिजणु.
United. गडु.
Unity. हेकिडाई, हिकिडाई, एकाई.
Universal. सभ-कुल जो.
The Universe. जहानु, दुना, जगतु, विशु *f.*
Unjust, Unjustly. नाहकी, गैरवाजिबो, अन्याई.
Unkind, Unkindly. बेब्राझो, अब्राझो, बेशर्यो, बेमिहिरो.
Unkindness. बेब्राझाई, बेमिहिरीं-राई.
Unknowing. बेखबरो, अणवाकुफु, अज़ाणु. *See* Ignorant.
Unknown. बेखबरो, अणवाकुफु, अणजातो-तलु.
Unlawful, Unlawfully. नाहकी, अरिहँदो.
Unlawfulness. नाहकु, अरिहँदाई.
Unlearned, Unlettered. अणपढ़ु -ढ़्यो.
Unleavened. बेखमीरो.
Unless. जेकड़हीं न.
Unlike. अणठहँदो, अणमाफकु.
Unlikely. अणथिभणो, न थिअण जिहडो.
Unlimited. बेसंधो, बेहदि, बेभंतु, अपारू.
To Unload. बारू लाहणु.
To Unlock. कुर्फु लाहणु.
To Unloose. छोडणु.
Unlucky. (*unfortunate q. v.*) निभाग़ों, (*bringing ill-luck*) निभाग़ो, नहसु, कुपेरो, कुभु, नास्तो.

Unmanageable. अझलु, बेलगामो, मवासु-सो.
Unmanlike, Unmanly. (*a person*) नामर्दु, कांइरू, गांडू, (*an act*) नामर्दाणो, कांइराणो, गांडुआणो.
Unmannerliness. बेढंगाई, अढंगाई, विललाई, बेललाई.
Unmannerly, Unmannered. बेढंगो, अढंगो, कुढंगो, बेढबो, बेललो, विललो, बेढँओ.
Unmarried. अणपर्ण्यो, कुंआरो.
Unmatched. अणजोडु, अणजोसु. *See* Unequalled.
Unmeaning. बेमतलबो, अजायो, बेमग़जो.
Unmeasured. अणकछो-छलु.
Unmeet. *See* Unfit, Unworthy.
Unmerciful, Unmercifully. बेब्राझो, अब्राझो, बेरहमु-मो, बेमरूअतो, बेरिआइतो, निर्दई, ड़ानउ, ड़ानासरू, ड़ईतु.
Unmercifulness. बेरहमी-माई, निर्दयाई.
Unmindful. *See* Careless, Unconcerned.
To Unmingle. धार धार करणु. *See* To Separate.
To Unmuffle. छिको लाहणु-छोडणु.
Unnatural. उबतो, जहान खां ब्राहरि-उबतो.
Unnecessary. अणजरूरी-रो, अजायो.
Unobserved. अणडिठो-ठलु.
Unobtainable. अलभु, अणलभु-भो.
Unoccupied. पाल्हो, वांदो, खाली. *See* Unemployed, Disengaged, Empty.
Unoffending. *See* Innocent, Inoffensive.
Unopened. अणपट्यो-ट्युलु.
Unopposed. अझलु, अणझल्यो-ल्यलु.

Unorderly. खिर्विंखिरो, बेड़ालो.
Unornamented. अणसोगायों, बुटो.
To Unpack. छोड़णु, कढणु.
Unpaid (*money*). अणगोतो-तलु, ड्रिअणो.
Unparallelled. *See* Unequalled.
Unperceivable. अलखु-खो.
Unperceived. *See* Unseen.
Unperformed. अणकिओ-किअलु.
Unpleasant, Unpleasing. अणसुहांईंदो, अणवणंदो.
Unploughed. अणखेड्यो-ड्यलु.
Unpolluted. *See* Pure.
Unpractised. अणहिर्यो-र्यलु,
Unprecedented. *See* Unexampled.
Unprejudiced. *See* Unbiassed.
Unprepared. अणतयारू.
Unprincipled. *See* Wicked, Dishonest.
Unproductive. नखटू, मखटू, भजायो. *See* Barren, Profitless.
Unprofitable, Unprofitably. भजायो. *See* Unproductive, Useless, Profitless.
Unpropitious. नहसु, भवलो, अणाओ, बुरो. *See* Unlucky.
Unpropitiousness. नहसाई, अवलाई.
Unprosperous. बदिनसीबो, अभागो. *See* Unfortunate.
Unprotected. बेवसीलो, बेवाहु-ह-हो, बेवाहर हुरू, बेराखो,
Unproved. अणसाबितु-ती.
Unpunished. रेसजा.
Unquiet. बेआरामो. *See* Uneasy.
Unquietness. बेआरामु. *See* Uneasiness.
To Unravel. उखेलणु, उखोलणु.
Unreadiness. अणतयारी.
Unready. अणतयारू.
Unreal. कूडो, कूडु, असति.
Unreconcilable. अणठहिणो.

Unrefined. अणसाध्यो-ध्यलु.
Unrelenting. बेरहमो. *See* Unmerciful.
Unremitting, Unremittingly. हिकधडो, हिकसारू. *See* Unintermitting.
Unreserved. *See* Frank.
Unresolved. बेकैतो. *See* Uncertain.
Unrestrained. अझलु, बेकैदो. *See* Uncurbed, Unchecked.
Unrighteous. बेदीनु-नो, बेधर्मी- मु-मों, अधर्मी.
Unrighteousness. बेदीनाई-नी, बेधर्माई-मीं, अधर्मु-माई.
Unrightful. अरिहिदो.
To Unrip. उड़ेड़णु.
Unripe. कचो.
Unripeness. कचाई
Unrivalled. बेजोसो, अणजोड़ु. *See* Unequalled.
To Unrol. उखेलणु, उखोलणु.
To Unroof. छति लाहणु.
Unruly. बेचयो, रेचयो, बेलगामो.
Unsafe, Unsafely. अणसोघो, अणपुख्तो, बेहथोको, जोखाइतो.
Unsatiable. बेढ़ओ.
Unsatisfactory, Unsatisfactorily. अणसुहाईंदो, नापसंदि.
Unsatisfied. नाराजो, नाखुशि, अरहो.
Unsavoriness. बेलजताई-ती, बेसवादु, लिसाई.
Unsavory. बेलजतो, बेसवादो-दी, लिसो. *See* Tasteless.
To Unseal. उखेलणु, उखोलणु.
Unseasonable, Unseasonably. बेमहलो, बेवख्तो, कमहलो, कुवख्तो, अवेरो, कुवेरो, कुवेलो.
Unseasonableness. कुमहलाई, कुवेलाई.
Unseemly. बेवडो, अपहतो, नालाइकु. *See* Unbecoming.

Unseen. अणडिठो.

Unserviceable. बेकमो. *See* Useless.

Unserviceableness. बेकमाई. *See* Uselessness.

Unsettled. बेकैतेा. *See* Undecided, Undetermined.

Unsettledness. बेकैताई.

To Unshackle. जंजीरू–निभरू &c. लाहणु – कढणु. *See* Fetters, Shackles.

Unshaken. अणधुडु, काइमु.

To Unsheath. कढणु.

Unsheltered. बेढको, बेछांओं.

Unshod. बेनालो.

Unshrinking. अणलडु-डो-डू.

Unsifted. अणछण्यो, अणछाण्यो-ण्यलु.

Unsincere. कूडो, खोटो.

Unskilful, Unskilled. अणपुख्तो, अनाडो, कचो.

Unskilfulness. अणपुख्ताई, कचाई.

Unsocial. एकांती.

Unsold. अणविकयो-क्यलु.

Unsolicited. अणघुर्यो-र्यलु.

Unsound. ऐबाइतो, ऐबदारू, बीकाइतो, बीकारो.

Unsoundness. बीक, ऐब.

Unspeakable. अणचइणो, बेबयानेा, चवण खां बाहरि.

Unspotted. बेदागेा-गो. *See* Spotless.

Unstable. हलिणेा, अणथिरि. *See* Irresolute, Variable, Fickle.

Unsteadiness. भुड़िणाई, अणपुख्ताई, हलहलि.

Unsteady. भुड़िणो, अणपुख्तेा. *See* Unstable.

To Unstitch. उड़ोडणु.

To Unstring. उखेलणु, उखोलणु.

Unsubdued, Unsubjected. अणजोर्यो.

Unsubstantial. पेरेा, खालो.

Unsuccessful, Unsuccessfully. अजायेा, निफलेा, अणभर्यो, बेमुरादेा. *See* Vain.

Unsuitable, Unsuited. अणठाहू, अणठहिणो, अणहतेा, नालाइकु, अणजुडंदेा.

Unsuitableness. नालाइकीअ, जोग़ इं.

Unsullied. बेऐबु-बेा. *See* Unblemished.

Unsupported. बेटेको, बेआधरेा, बेठ्ठो.

Unsurmountable. अणलंघिणेा.

Unsuspected. बेशको–की.

Unsuspecting, Unsuspicious. बेशको-की, साफुदिलि. *See* Simple.

Unswept. अणमेह्यो-ह्यलु.

Untainted. *See* Unblemished.

Untamed. अणहिर्यो-र्यलु.

To Untangle. समुझाइणु.

Untarnished. बेदागो–गेा.

Untempered. रे-बे-अणपाण्यो.

Unterrified. अणडिनलु-नो.

Unthankful, Unthankfulness. *See* Ungrateful, Ungratefulness.

Unthinking. बेग़ण्यो. *See* Thoughtless.

To Unthread. सग़ो कढणु.

Untidiness. अगलाई, खिर्विखिराई, बेसिजिलाई.

Untidy. अगलो, खिर्विखिरो, बेसिजिलो.

To Untie. छोडणु, उखेलणु, उखोलणु.

Until. ताईं, तोंईं, तोणी, तोडां, सूधो, सूधां, सीअ. *See* Till.

Untilled. *See* Uncultivated.

Untimely. बेमहलो, बोंईं. *See* Unseasonable.

Untired. *See* Unwearied.

Unto. *See* To.

Untold. अणचयो-यलु.

Untouched. अणछुह्यलु-ह्यो.

Untoward, Untractable. अदलो, जडु. *See* Obstinate, Unruly.

Untrained. अणसिख्यलु, जडु.

Untried. अणपरख्यो.

Untrod, Untrodden. रे-वे-अणपेरो.

Untrue, Untruly. कूडो, कूडु. *See* False.

Untrustiness. बेवेसाहो, बेइतिबारो.

Untrusty, Untrustworthy. बेवेसाहु, अणविसहू, बेइतिबारो-री.

An Untruth. कूडु.

To Untwine, Untwist. उखेलणु, उखोलणु.

Unvanquished. *See* Unconquered.

To Unvail. बुर्को उपटणु-पटणु-लाहणु.

Unused (*not put to use*). कतबि न आयो, अणहंड्यो-ड्यलु. *See* Unaccustomed.

Unusual. बेरीतो, बेदस्तूरो, नंर्भो.

Unutterable. *See* Inexpressible.

Unwarlike. अणवेड्हू.

Unwary, Unwarily. बेखबिरो. *See* Careless.

Unwashed. अणधोतो-तलु, अणधोयो-यलु.

Unwatered. अणरेजो, बेरेजो.

Unwearied. अणथक्यो-क्यलु.

Unweighed. अणतुर्यो-र्यलु.

Unwell. नाचङो, बेमजे, नाताजो.

Unwholesome. मर्जीलु, रोगो, जिआनी.

Unwieldy. अखजु, अणखजू.

Unwilling. नाराजी, अरहो; *or* Unwillingly, बेदिलि-ल्यो, अनमन्यो.

To be Unwilling. अरहाइणु, अरहिजणु.

Unwillingness. अरहाई, बेदिली, नाखुशी.

To Unwind. उखेलणु, उखोलणु.

Unwise. (*a person*) बेवकूफु, (*an act*) बेवकूफागो. *See* Foolish.

Unwittingly. बेखबिरो, अणज़ातो-ते. *See* Unintentionally.

Unworthiness. नालाइकी.

Unworthy. नालाइकु-की, अयहतो. *See* Unbecoming, Unsuitable.

Unwritten. अणलिख्यो-ख्यलु. *See* Oral.

Unyielding. खाहोडो, अटरू, अणटरू, अणलडु. *See* Firm, Resolute.

To Unyoke. छोडणु.

The Vocative (*in grammar*). संबोधनु.

Vociferous. शोरी, गोगाई, हुलिरो-रू, गोडो.

Voice. सुरू, आवाजु, तंवार, गलो.

Void. *See* Empty, Vain, Devoid.

Volatile. चलिवलो, चंचलु.

A Volley. दसु.

Voluntarily. पाण्हेंई, पाणहीं, पाणमुरादो.

A Volunteer. पाणमुरादो.

A Voluptuary, Voluptuous. ऐशी, अयाशी, विखई.

Voluptuousness. ऐश, अयाशु, विखइ.

To Vomit. ओकणु, ओगणु, कढणु, कइ करणु, मुहां वारणु.

Vomiting (*sub.*). ओक, कइ, मुहखाल, मुहफुल.

Vomative (*causing vomiting*). वातवारो.

Voracious. हब्छी, बुखमुभो. *See* Gluttonous.

Voracity. हबछ, बाठि, वांठि, डाझि, डाधि, डालड़ि

A Vortex. कनु. *See* Whirlpool.

A Votary. ब्रान्हो, दासु.

A Vote. मतु, सलाह.

To Vouch. साख-शाहिदी ड़िभणु.

A written Voucher. दस्तावेजु, सनद.

A Vow. सुखा, मञिता, मञति, खुणु.

To Vow. मञणु, बासणु, सुखा करणु.

The Vowel marks. लकना; the connecting the vowels with the consonants, कक्ि.

A Voyage. *See* Journey.

Up. (*aloft*) मथे, up to (*as far as*) ताईं, तोणी. *See* Until.

To Upbraid. ड़ोरापो &c. ड़िभणु.

An Upbraider. मिहिणेगोरू, तानो, तानिरू. *See* Taunter.

Upbraiding. ड़ोरापो, उभालो, मिहिणो. *See* Reproach.

To suffer Upbraidings. ड़ोरापिजणु.

To Uphold. *See* To Support.

Upon. ते, उते, (*with such a part downwards*) भर.

Upper, Uppermost. मथ्यों, उत्यों.

An Upper room. माडी, बालो.

Upright, Uprightly. (*erect*) उभो, खडो, संभों, उबाहो, (*honest q. v.*) संभों, सवलो, सलो, सूधो, सुपत्यो, साऊ, भलोलु, सवाटो.

Uprightness (*honesty q. v*). सवाई, सवति, सूधाई, सवलाई, सोरू.

An Uproar. गोडु, हुलु, लुडु, गोगाउ, शोरू, कगंलु, हंगामु-मो. *See* Outcry.

Uproarous. गोडो, गोगाई, शोरी, लुडाई-डाऊ, हुलिरी-रू.

To Uproot. पटणु, उखेडणु.

To be Uprooted. पटिजणु, उखिडणु.

To Upset (*act.*). उथिलाइणु, लेटाइणु, केराइणु.

To Upset (*neu.*). उथिलणु, लेटणु.

Upside down. उबतो, ऊंधो, उबतडि. *See* Topsy turvy.

An Upstart. नओं, बेबुनिआदी-दो.

Upward, Upwards. मथे.

Urbanity. माण्हिपो-पाई. *See* Politeness.

To Urge on. हुस्कारणु, चूंगणु, चोकणु.

Urgency. जरूरु, ताघ, छिक.

Urgent. जरूरी. *See* Importunate.

Urine. पेशाबु, मुटु; cow's urine, गौंटु.

Usage (*custom q. v.*). हलीचली, परि, रीति, चालि, दस्तूरु, धर्मु, रसम.

Use (*utility*). कमु, कतबु, कारि.

To Use (*apply to a purpose*). कमि &c. आणणु, हंडाइणु, चोडणु, वापिराइणु, बिले लाइणु.

To come into Use. कमि &c. अचणु, हंडणु, चुडणु, कमाइतो &c. थिअणु, वापिरणु.

Useful, Usefully. कमाइतो, काराइतो, कतबाइतो, सकार्थो, सक्यार्थो, सजायो.

Usefulness. *See* Utility.

Useless, Uselessly. निकमो, नाकामु-मो, बेकामु-मो, बेकारू-रो, निकारू-रो, बेकार्यो, रेकमो, फारकु, अजायो, अकार्यो अक्यार्थो, बिर्थो, अविर्थो, अबसु, बेफाइदो, अबाडो, अफिरादु.

Uselessness. निकमाई, बेकमाई, बेकारी-राई, निकाराई, नाकारी-राई.

Usual, according to usage. रीताइतो.

A Usurer. व्याजूखोरू, लाभिरू, लाभूखोरू.

Usurious. लाभाइतो.

To Usurp. खसणु.

Usury. व्याजूखोरी, लाभूखोरी.

On Usury. व्याजेरू, लाभेरू.

A Utensil. *See* Vessel.

Utility. कमु, कतबु, नफो, फाइदो. *See* Advantage.

The Utmost. पुज्ञाणी, ओड़कु, छेहु. *See* End.

To do one's Utmost. पुज्ञाणी &c. करणु.

Utter, Utterly. तमामु, सरासरि, सरोसरी. *See* Wholly.

To Utter. चवणु.

Utterance. चविणो.

Vulgar (*of the common people*). गारीबी.

A Vulture. गिझ.

The Uvula. काकिड़ो.

Uxorious. जोयो.

W

To Wabble. थिड़ाइणु.

A Wabbler, what Wabbles. गंगथिड़ों.

The Wad of a gun. लितो.

To Waddle. लुड़णु, लुड़णु लमणु, वांकणु.

To Wade. झागणु.

A Wafer. टिकी.

A Wag. चबाई, ठशाई. *See* Jester.

To Wag (*act.*). लोड़णु.

To Wage (*carry on war*). लाइणु.

A Wager. शर्त दाउ, बाजी.

To Wager. शर्त हणणु, दाउ &c. लाइणु-लगाइणु-रखणु, होड़ बंधणु.

Wages. मवाजिबु, वजिहु, पोह्यो. *See* Pay.

Waggery. खिलखुशी, चर्चो. *See* Raillery.

To Wail. आहूं-हाइहाइ करणु, रुअणु, पिटणु, रड़णु, बाड़ाइणु.

Wailing (*sub.*). हाइहाइ, भनणु, गिरिओ.

The Waist. चेल्हि, लकु, कमरि.

A cloth rolled round the Waist as a girdle. संधिरो, ड़ेढ़क, कुणिट, पेठि. *See* Girdle.

A Waistcoat. कमिरी.

A kind of Waist ornament of gold or silver. चेल्हिकी.

The Waist string of drawers. अगड़ु, पटहड़.

To Wait (*tarry*). विहणु. रहणु, तरसणु, ठहरणु, रखणु, थथिरणु, सबुरु करणु. *See* To Stop.

To Wait for. सोड़णु, ओसीड़णु, वाट ड़िसणु.

To be wearied with Waiting or wishing for any thing. उसिड़कणु.

To Wait upon (*serve*). नोकिरी &c. करणु.

To lie in Wait. छपि-छह मारे विहणु. *See* Ambush.

To Wake, Waken (*neu.*). जागणु, उथणु.

To Wake, Waken (*act.*). जागाइणु, उथारणु.

Wakeful. सुजागु-गो, सुजाखो.

Wakefulness. सुजागो-गाई, सुजाखाई. *See* Sleeplessness.

Waking, Waking state. जागु, ओजागो.

To Walk (*opposed to riding*). पेरें &c. हलणु. *See* Afoot. (*opposed to running*). विख हलणु, विख भरे हलणु.

To Walk about (*neu. as in taking an airing*). टहलणु, झंपूं साहणु, घुमणु. *See* Airing.

To Walk (*act. cause to go at a slow pace*). विख-कदमु हलाइणु.

To Walk about (*act. as in airing*). टहलाइणु, घुमाइणु, टोरो ड़िअणु.

A Walk, Walking (*airing*). टहल, टोरो, घोमि.

A Walker. पंधिड्यो, पेर्यो.

A Walking stick. लठि, लकुणु.

A Wall. भिति.

A Wall of sticks and mud. तेकी.

A Wallet. झोली, कश्कोलु, कंदील.

To Wallow. लेथिडणु, लेटणु.

A Walnut. अखिडोटु.

Wan. साभो. *See* Pale.

A Wand. बाम, चहो.

To Wander. घुमणु, फिरणु; idly and vainly, रूलणु, भट्कणु, भिट्कणु, भँवणु, भौंणणु, टुल्कणु, वतणु.

A Wanderer. घोमू, रोलु, रोलाकु-कड़ु, टुल्फाऊ, टोलाकड़ु, भोणो.

Wandering about (*sub.*). रोलो, टुल्को.

To Wane. घटणु. *See* To Lessen.

To Want (*have need of*). घुरणु, तलबणु.

To Want (*be deficient*). घटि &c. हुअणु.

Want. (*absence*) अणहूंदि, (*occasion for, need of*) गुर्ज. तांघ, तंघ, लुगोज, लोड़, गतो, गर्ज, भोखप, तडभोड़, तलब.

Want (*insufficiency*). ऊणि, ऊणाई, कमी. *See* Deficiency.

Want (*penury*). सोड्ह, तंगी, अणहूंदि, तडभोड़, सखिणाई. *See* Poverty.

Wanting. (*deficient q. v.*) घटि, ऊणो, (*without, devoid of*) रहितु. *See* Without.

Wanton. (*lascivious*) लांड़ारो, लंडो, (*unrestrained q. v.*) मइ, मवासु, मस्तु, मगु.

To grow Wanton (*as from pride, wealth, &c.*). मइजणु, मस्तिजणु, मवासिजणु, मगिजणु.

A Wanton. *See* Harlot.

Wantonness. (*lewdness*) लंड़ाई, लांड़ाराई, (*as from pride*) मस्ताई.

A War. जंगि, झेडो. *See* Fight.

To War. जंगि &c. करणु, विड़्हणु.

Of War, Warlike. जंगो, वेढ़ू.

To Warble. तँवारणु, ब्रोलणु.

Warbling (*sub.*). तँवार, ब्रोली.

Ward (*sub.*). *See* Watch, Quarter.

Ward (*affixed in composition*). ड़े, ड़ुहं. *See* Towards.

To Ward off. झलणु, टारणु, दफे करणु.

A Warden, Warder. राखो. *See* Keeper.

A Wardrobe (*room for clothes, jewels, &c.*). तोशाखानो.

The keeper of the Wardrobe. तोश्की.

Wares. मालु, सौदो, वखरु, वणिजु.

A Warehouse. कोठी, वखार.

Warfare. जंगाजंगी. *See* War.

Wariness. साड़ाह-ड़ह, ग़ण्ती, हुशिआरी.

Warm. कोसो, गर्मु, ततो, गमांऊ.

To Warm (*act.*). सेकणु, ताइणु, तइणु, तपाइणु.

To Warm (*neu.*). तपणु, कोसाइणु, गर्माइणु, सेकिजणु.

Warmness, Warmth. ताउ, तउ, ताति, तपसि, ताविड़ो, कोसाई-णि, गर्मी.

To Warn. अगुवारु ज़ाणाइणु, चेताइणु.

A Warning. तागीद.

To Warp (*neu.*). मुड़णु.

The Warp of a web. नाणो, नाणो.

To Warrant (*authorize*). मुख्त्यारु करणु, हुकुमु ड़िभणु.

A Warrant (*commission*). पर्वानो.

A Warrior (*a hero*). दोद्द, वर्यामु, सूरिहु, सूरो, सूमों, गोधो, जोधो, मांझी, गाजी, मथेरू, वरनहु, पहिल्वानु.

A Wart. भसो.

Wary. सुजाखो, खबर्दारु, साङाहू, गाणु, हुशिआरु.

To be Wary. सङाहणु, गाणणु.

To Wash (*act.*). धुअणु.

To Wash (*neu. perform ablution*). विहंजणु, भांइणु, सनानु-तडु करणु.

To Wash away (*act.*; *as the river does the bank*). पाइणु, खाइणु.

The Wash, Washing. धोपु, धोप, धुअप, धुअणी.

To be Washed. धोपणु, धोइजणु.

A Washerman. धोबी, परोटु, पर्टु, निओ, खट्री, खड्गु, खड्गखट्री.

Of a Washerman. धोबिको, खट्रिको.

A Washerwoman. धोबिणि-ड्याणी, खट्रिणि-ट्याणी.

The cost of Washing. धुआणी, धुआणीं.

Washy (*watery, weak q. v.*). खुंघो, खिंपो, फिको.

A Wasp (*different varieties*). चेलारो *or* चेलटु, ड़ेंभू *or* ड़ेंभू, घरेतिडी.

A swarm of Wasps. खखरि.

A Wasp's nest. मानारो, खखरि.

Wastage. खोटि, हुफो, सोसि.

To Waste (*act. expend uselessly*). विञाइणु, भजायो खर्चणु, उड़ाइणु, लुटणु, लुटाइणु.

To Waste (*time, strength, &c*). विञाइणु, गँवाइणु.

To Waste, lay Waste. उजाडणु, फिटाइणु, सुञ &c. करणु.

To Waste away (*dwindle away*). सुसणु, हपणु, हञमणु, हपाइजणु, गरणु, घटणु.

Waste. (*uncultivated q.v.*) गैरआबादु, (*desolate*) सुञ, सुञो, उजाड, उजडु, अरँडुँ, बरु, कंगराडि, वैरानु, चटु, चौड़ु, बिड़्यांड़ु, ढुफ, भुटु.

To become Waste. उजिडणु, फिटणु, सुञ &c. थिअणु.

Waste land, a Waste. सुञ, उजाड, अरँडुँ, कंगराडि, बरु, रिणु.

Waste (*wastage*). खोटि, हुफो, सोसि.

Waste, Wastefulness (*useless expenditure*). भजायो खर्चु, लुटि, फुरि.

A Waste book. खरिडो.

Wasteful, a Waster. विञाऊ, उड़ाऊ.

To Watch. (*not to sleep*) जागणु, (*to keep guard*) चौंकी &c. ड़िभणु, वाहिपो &c. करणु.

To Watch. (*regard closely*) निहारणु, तकणु, चकासणु, (*look after*) निहारणु, तातणु, टहोडणु, सांढणु, संभालणु, संभारणु.

To Watch for (*in expectation*). वाट ड़िसणु.

A Watch (*for telling time*). साइथ, घडी.

A Watch (*eighth part of the day*). पहरु.

Watch (*guarding, or a guard*). चौंकी, पहरो.

Watch, Watching. (*observing closely*) निहार, तक, निगाह, (*tending*) तात, ताइत, टहोड, मीट, रख, सांढ, संभार, संभाल, वाहिपो-प.

A Watch-house. नाको.

A Watchman. जागो, राखो, चौंकीदारु, याही.

A field Watchman. वाहो ; on the grain at harvest, काराभो.

The business or pay, of a field Watchman. वाहिपो-प ; of the Watchman on the grain at harvest, कारावत-तणि.

Watchful. सुजागु-गो, सुजाखो, खब-र्दारू, हुशिआरू, पुख्तो.

Watchfulness. सुजागी-गाई, सुजा-खाई.

Water. पाणी *m.* नीरू, जलु, जरू, आबु.

To Water, (*neu. as the mouth, eyes*). पाणी करणु.

To Water (*act.*). पाणी डिअणु, (*land before sowing*) रिजाइणु.

A Water-bag. सांदारो, ओई, मश्क.

A double Water-bag, carried on a beast. पखाल ; one side of it, खुर्थी.

A Water-carrier. पखाली.

A Water-course (*various kinds*). थड़, नाउको, नहरि, कसी, गुझ, वंझो, वाहुड़. *See* Canal.

Watered. (*flooded, land before sowing*) रेजाणो, रेजाइनो, (*after sowing*) पेज़ाणो, पेज़ाइतो.

To be Watered (*land before sowing*). रिजणु.

Water gruel. रबु, भतु, पिछ, पिछी, पेज़, पेज़ी.

The Watering or irrigating land before sowing. रेजु, रेजो, रेणी, रोणी, रौणी (*after sowing*) पेजु, पेज़ो.

Waterish. पट्टिड़ो, खुंघो, खिंघो, खुंगो, खिंगो, पंगो, छिड़ो, छिड़िड़ो, छिटो, छिट्टिड़ो. *See* Weak.

Waterishness. पट्टिडाई-णि, खुंघाई-णि, खिंघाई-णि, छिड़, छिड़ाई-णि.

Waterless, wanting water. रे-बे-अण पाण्यो.

A Water-lily. कूणी, कँवलु. *See* Lotus, Lily.

A Water-melon. हिंदाणो, छांहों.

A Water pit (*well, dug in the dry bed of a river*). वीरी, विअरि.

A Water-place, Watering place (*for watering, washing, &c.*). वडु.

A Water tax. इकाबो.

A Water-vessel. *See* Vessel.

A Water wheel. *See* Wheel.

Watery (*abounding with water*). पाण्यारो, पाण्यरू. *See* Waterish.

The Wattle of a cock. गुलू.

A Wattle (*stick*). छड़ो ; Wattles. लकड़ि.

A wall of Wattles and dab. तेको.

A Wave of the sea. लहरि, मौज, छोली, ओसाम, तरंगु.

To Wave (*play loosely*). लुड़णु, फड़कणु.

To Wave (*a weapon &c.*). घुमाइणु, फेराइणु.

To Waver. लुड़णु, दिलि लोड़हणु.

A Waverer, Wavering. बिचितो, *See* Uncertain.

Wavy. लहरिनि वांग्यां.

Wax of bees. मेणु.

Sealing Wax. ज़ड *f.*

Ear Wax. मरू *f.*

To Wax, (*act.*). मेणु लाइणु.

Wax cloth. मेण्तो.

A Way (*road*). वाट, रस्तो, राह, मारिख. *See* Path.

Way, Ways. (*manner q. v.*) दस्तूरू, रीति, तरहँ, गति, भाँति, भति, पारू.

In any Way. जिअँतिअं, जिएँतिएँ.

In the right Way. (*or road*) सवाटो, (*or manner*) सुरानो.

In the wrong Way. (*or road*) कुवाटे, (*or manner*) कुरीतो.

A Way-farer, Way-faring. वाटावाहू, वाटाहू, वाटवहू, वाटइडु. *See* Traveller.

Way-ward. होड़ि. *See* Perverse.

We. असीं.

Weak, Weakly (*feeble*). बेज़ोरो, अघो, बेसघो, बेसग़्गो-ग्गो, बेकुअतो, निसतो, निवलो, (*from emaciation*) ड़ुबलु, हीणो, (*though puffed out*) फेफो, फिल्हो, (*as the voice*) झीणो. *See* Gentle.

Weak (*not potent, as liquor*) मठो, झको, फिको, सादो, खुंघो, खिंघो, पंगो, झारो. *See* Waterish.

To Weaken (*act.*). बेज़ोरो &c. करणु.

Weakening (*adj.*). बेज़ोरो.

To Weaken (*neu.*). बेज़ोरो &c. थिअणु, अघाइणु.

Weakness (*feebleness*). बेज़ोरीराई, अघाई, बेसघाई, बेकुअतो-ताई, बेसग्गो-ग्गाई, निसताई, हीणाई, ड़ुबलाई.

Weakness (*as of liquors*). मठाई, झकाई, फिकाई, सादाई, खुंघाई.

A Weal (*mark from a stripe*). ड़ुनो, बनो. *See* Welfare.

Wealth. दुआ, दौलत, धनु, मालु, रिज़िकु, माया, लछिमी, ज़रि.

Wealthiness. वँझाई, दुआदारी, सावाई, साउभाई, साज़ाई.

Wealthy. दुआदारु, साओ, साऊ, वँझो, भाग्गो, साज़ो, शाहू, शाहूकारु, मालदारु, वहुडो, धनवानु, धनपात्रु.

To Wean. थञु-खीरु-बुबो छड़ाइणु.

A Weapon. हथ्यारु.

To Wear (*act. consume by attrition*). खाइणु.

To Wear (*act. as clothes*). पहरणु.

To Wear away (*neu. from attrition*). खाज़णु गसणु.

To Wear (*last*), or be in Wear. हंढणु, चुडणु. *See* To Last.

To Wear out (*act. render unserviceable by use*). हंढ़ाए खराबु करणु *or* विञाइणु, पाचाइणु, भीचाइणु.

To Wear out (*neu.*). हंढ़िजी-चुडिजी खराबु थिअणु, पीचणु, भोचणु.

Wear, Wearing. चोडु, हंढ़, चुडिणी, हंढ़िणी.

Weariness. थकु, चोकिडो, बेज़ारी, मांदाई, हलाखो.

Wearisome. थकाऊ, थकाइतो, विर्चाऊ.

Weary, Wearied. थको-कलु, ग़झो-झलु, बेज़ारु, बेरू, विरू, मांदो, हलाखु, फो, फसु, साणो, भातो.

To Weary (*act.*). थकाइणु, कुडाइणु, कडाइणु, विर्चाइणु.

To Weary, or be Wearied. थकणु, कुडणु, कडणु, विर्चणु, ओलिजणु.

A Weasel. नोरु.

The Weather. हवा.

To Weave. उणणु.

A Weaver. कोरी, गिराणो.

Of a Weaver. कोरिको.

A Weaver's beam. तुरि.

Weaving (*sub.*). उणावत, उणत, उणति, उणाति, उणिणी, ओज़.

The cost of Weaving. उणाणी.

A Web. नाको, नाकिओ, थानु, जोडी.

To Wed (*take in marriage*). पर्णणु. *See* To Marry.

Wedding (*adj.*). विहांइतो निकाहितो.

A Wedding, Wedlock. विहांउ, पर्णो, शादी, निकाहु.

A Wedge. चपर.

Wednesday. अर्बा, बुधरु.

Wee. नंढिड़ो. *See* Little.

A Weed, Weeds. रज.

To Weed. सोंइणु, रज कढणु.

Weeding. सोभ.

A Week. अठिड्यो, हफ़्तो.

Weekly. अठिड्ये अठिड्ये, हफ़्ते हफ़्ते.

To Weep. रूंअणु, ओछिंगारणु.

Weeping, a Weeper. रूंअणो.

Weeping(*sub.*). रोजु, ओराज़ा, रूंअणु, रूंअणाई, ओछिंगार.

A Weevil. घुणो, सोवी.

The Weft of cloth. पेटो.

To Weigh (*try weight of*). तोरणु, जोखणु, टरणु.

To Weigh (*equal in weight*). तोर &c. हुअणु.

To be Weighed. तुरणु.

A Weigher. तोरणवारो, वड्राई.

Weighing (*sub.*). तोर, धडु.

A scale full in Weighing. धडो.

Weight (*quantity weighed*). तोर, वजनु. *See* Burden, Importance.

A Weight for Weighing. तोरो, धडो, धडी, वटु, वटहडो.

Weightiness. ग़राई-णि, ग़ोराई-णि.

Weighty. ग़रो, ग़ोरो.

Weirs for catching fish. लँउं.

To Welcome. भलो-भले-जोउ-निचु चवणु *or* करे चवणु.

To be Welcome. भली-भले &c. अचणु *or* करे अचणु.

To Weld. ग़ंढणु.

Welfare. खैरु, खाँ, चङो, भलो, कल्याणु, मंगलु, सिधी.

A Well. खूहु, खुहो, वाइ, चूहो ; or water pit in the dry bed of a river, वोरी, विअरि.

The raised parapet round a Well. पग़.

A Well-digger. खूहाणो.

A instrument for cleaning out Wells. बेल.

Well (*in health*). चङो, निमिरो, चाकु, सखर, सखराइनो, ताजो, चङोभलो, ताजोतवानो, सज़रु, सरहो, राजी, मर्दानो, निरोयो.

Well (*in a good manner*). चङो, चङ्यां, चङे दस्तूरि.

Well (*in assenting*). चङो, भलो, खैरु.

Well-behaved, conducted, dispositioned, or mannered. सुवानूरो, सवानूरो, सुलछिणो, सुहाजो, सुग़टो, सुरोनो.

Well-born. घराणो, वडुघराणो, घराइनो. *See under* Family.

Well-cooked or ripened. सुपकु.

A Well-doer. सुकर्मी.

Well done. *See* Bravo.

Well formed or shaped. सुडौलो, डौलाइतो.

Well-informed. सुज़ाणु.

Well-known. पधिरो, जाहिरु, मशाहूरु, पर्धानु.

Well-off, Well to do. सधरु, सखर, ताजो.

A Well-wisher. घणघुरो, खैरखाहु,

The Welt of cloth. कनी, धडी. किनारि.

To Welter. लेथिडणु.

A Wen. ड़िपो, ग़ोड़हो.

The West. उलहँदो, ओलहु.

West, Westerly, Western. उलहँदो, ओलह्यो.

Westward, Westwardly. उलहँदे ड़े.

Wet. आलो, ह्यों, वटाइतो, पाण्याठो, पाण्यारो, पाण्यरु.

To Wet, make Wet. पुसाइणु, भिज़ाइणु.

To Wet, get Wet. पुसणु, भिज़णु.

Wet, Wetness. भान्हाई-णि, हयाँई-णि, हर्यालि, पाण्यठु, वट, पाणीभ. *See* Damp.

Injury from Wet. गर्की.

To be injured by Wet. गर्किजणु.

Wetted, injured by Wet. गर्की.

A Wet-nurse. दाई.

Wet weather. मोहोंगो.

A Whale. मांगमछु, मंगमछु.

A Whang of leather. कोर, वद्दी.

A Wharf. थलो.

What. (*which, interrog:*) केहों किहरो, केहरो, (*relative pro:*) जो, (*interrog.*) छा, कुञ्जाडो, कोडु.

Whatever, Whatsoever. जेको, जेकोको, जेकी, जेकोकी.

What like, What kind of. किहडो, किंअ.

Wheat. कणिक, गेहूं; some kinds are, ठोड्ही, कहणो, गाजि, खेरादिणो, पंबणु.

Wheat mixed with barley. गोजी, जवालो, करडि.

Wheaten. काणिकी.

To Wheedle. गल्थो&c. बुंभणु, चतिराइणु.

A Wheedler. गल्थाई, चटिरू, दाघराई, बमिरू.

Wheedling (*sub*). गल्थो, चट, दाधरि, चड्डु, चड्डाज, थन्नु. *See* Flattering, Enticing.

The Wheel of a cart, &c. फोंगे.

A potter's Wheel. चकु.

The Wheel of a water wheel. &c. चकरि, छटु.

To Wheel (*neu.*). फिरणु.

A Persian Wheel. अटु, (*large* नारू, चर्खो, (*small*) हुर्लो; there are three kinds of *hurlas*, viz. ड़ांदारू, गड़हिडो, चकिरांभों.

A Persian Wheel used for spring crops, and raised on wells or ponds. ढाको.

A water Wheel worked with the feet. पिड्डोटी.

A light term for a poor incomplete water Wheel. ढींगो.

A double Persian Wheel, or two Wheels working together. बिनारो, जुंगु.

A pair of Persian Wheels working one above and one below. बिहडि

The pit over which a Persian Wheel is fixed. खुहाड़ो, पड्हाड़ो, पडुहो, पड्हूडो, तड़ो.

A Persian Wheel with its bullocks and all apparatus complete. हल्टु

The principal parts of a Persian Wheel are. The cross beam on posts, forming the upper socket, काञणि; the piece of stick inclosing the socket, मकुडो; the upright beam or axle, मुहुरो; the cross beam below confining *muhuro*, and *dedho*, भारूनो; the socket hole in the *bhárúni*, गिड़ि; the beam or axle of the lower horizontal wheel, ड़ेढो, लठि; the handle or turning beam, to which the animals are bound, ग़ाधी; that part of the wheel over which the pots work, भांड़ो; the circular rope to which the pots are strung, माल्ह; the cross sticks in the *málh*, इरिडो; the pots, किंगिरी, किंगिरू, लोटे; the pieces of twine confining them, गुडिंदु; the trough receiving the water from the pots, पाडिछु; पाडिछो, the second trough receiving water from the *párich*, नेसरि ; a stick supporting the *párich*, कांउँ ; a stick keeping the *malh* in its place, माल्हाट्टो, माल्हारी ; a check stick preventing wheel running back, ठहकणु ; the smaller sticks used in making the wheels, ब्राइडु.

To Wheeze. सहकणु.

A Whelp. (*the young of any beast*) बुठिडो, (*of a dog*) गुलिरू.

When (*at the time that*). जड्हों, जड़्हों, जड़िहिं.

When (*at what time?*). कड्हों, कड़्हों, कड़िहिं.

Since When. कड्हाकुरू,-को ; *or also*, of when, or what time. कड्होंको, कड्डूंणिको.

Whence (*interrog.*). कि-का with थां-थों-थूं-थँऊं-थांई-थई-थांऊं-थांओं-थांहुं-थांहों-थहों-थाँहों - थांहूं-थांहिऊँ affixed, के-का with ड्हँ-ड्हों-ड्हूं-ड्हिऊँ-ड्हा-ड्हों-ड्हूं-ड्हों-ड्हूं-ड्हिउँ affixed.

Whence (*from such place as*). जि-जा with थां-थों &c. affixed as above, or also with the affixes तां-तों-तूं-तंउं &c. जे-जा with ड्हं-ड़्हों &c. as above.

Whence (*from which premises*). तँहिं-उन्हे-इन्हेकरे-मंझों-मों.

Whenever. जँहिं कँहिं महल, कहीं महल.

Where (*interrog.*). किथे, काथे, कथे, किते, काते, कते, केड़, काड़ि, के-का with ड़ांहों-ड़्हों-ड्हँ-ड्हों &c. as under Whence. कि-का with तांहों-तहों-थांहों-थहीं affixed.

Where (*to, or in, such place as*). जिथे, जिते, जाथे, जथे, जाते, जते, जेड़, जाड़ि, जिहां, जि-जा with तांहीं-हींत-थांहीं-थहीं affixed. जे-जा with ड़ांहीं-ड्हीं-ड्हँहीं - ड्हों, &c. as under Whence.

From any Where. जिथां तिथां, जांओं तांओं, जिहां तिहां.

Whereby. (*by which*) जँहिं करे-मंझों-मों, (*by what*) कँहिं-छा करे, &c.

Wherever. जिथे तिथे, जाथें ताथे.

Wherefore (*for this or that reason*). हिन-हुन-तँहिं करे-काणि &c.

Wherefore (*for what reason?*). छो, छाकाणि. *See* Why.

Wherein. (*in which*) जँहिं में -मंझि, (*in what?*) कँहिं-छा में &c.

Whereof (*of which*). जँहिं जो.

Whereupon. तँहिं ते, तिहां पोइ, तँहि खां पोइ.

To Whet (*sharpen*). लाइणु, तिखो करणु.

A Whet, Whetting छेरो.

A Whetstone. रॅहो.

Whether. तोड़े, जां. This word is seldom expressed; the second clause of the sentence gives its meaning.

Whey. धॅारे जो पाणो.

Which (*interrog.*). केहों केहो, किहड़ो; which number (*of several*). कांओं, कँओ.

Which (*relat.*). जो. (*fem.* जा).

A Whiff. फूक.

While, whilst (*during the time that*). जड्हों, जड़िहिं.

While (*as long as*). जेसीं, जासीं, जां, जांकी, जेसीं-जां-जांकी-जे with the affixes तांनांईं - तोणी. &c. *See* Till.

While (*time q. v.*). महल.

To While away (*pass*). विहाइणु, *See* To Spend.

A Whim. पूरू, रउ, रोचकु, लहरि, लहरो, दौरू, उलेरू, उलेलु, मौज, फुर्णो. *See* Fancy.

Whimsical. पूरारो, पूराइतो, रवाइतो, लहराइतो, रोचकी. *See* Fanciful.

To Whine. ऊंकारणु.

A Whine, Whining. ऊंकार.

A Whip. चहबुकु, चाबुकु, कमची.

To Whip. चहबुकु &c. हणणु-मारणु.

To Whirl (*act.*). सिघो फेरणु.

A Whirl, Whirling. भांइटो.

A Whirlpool. कुनु, निकूंजु, मेड़ु, घुमिरो भेरू.

A Whirlwind. वाचूडो, वाचूलो.

A Whirligig. भूंभूरी, फिर्णी.

A Whirr. भरे.

To Whirr. भरांइणु.

A Whisk, Whisking. झट्को.

A Whisker. कातियों.

To Whisper. भुण्कणु, सुस्सुसि &c. लाइणु, झुंगारणु.

A Whisper, Whispering. सुस्सुसि, भुण्भुणि, भुण्को, भुणिक, भुण्कार, झुंगार.

A Wisperer. सुस्सुस्यो, भुण्भुण्यो.

To Whistle. सीट &c. वज़ाइणु, करणु.

A Whistle, Whistling (*the sound and the instrument*). सीट, सींढ.

A Whistler. सींढिरू-ढाई, सीटिरू-टाई.

A Whit. कों, जरो, रती.

White (*adj*). अछो, बगो, सुफेदु, धौरो, (*complexion*) गोरो, भूरो, (*hair*) पर्यो, (*horse*) नोरो, (*bird*) होरो.

Somewhat White, Whitish. अछेरो, अछेरिडो.

To have a tendency to White. अछाइणु, धौराइणु.

The White of an egg. सुफेदी.

White, Whiteness. अछाई-णि, सुफेदी-दाई.

A White ant. उड़ोही.

To grow White-headed. पर्यांइणु.

White lead. सुफेदो.

To Whiten (*act.*). अछो &c. करणु.

To Whiten (*neu.*). अछो &c. थिअणु. अछाइणु.

Whither (*interrog.*). किथे, केडे, केड्हां. *See* Where.

A Whitlow. नँहथरू *f*.

A Whizz, Whizzing. सूसटु, सूसाटु.

Who (*interrog.*). केरू, (*fem.* केर).

Who (*relat.*). जो, (*fem.* जा).

Whoever. जेको, जेकोको.

Whole (*all*). सज़ो, सारो, समूरो, सर्बस्तो, सभु, सभोई, जुम्लो, जुमलु.

Whole (*entire, sound*). सज़ो, सारो, समूरो, सर्बस्तो. *See* Entire.

Wholeness. सज़ाई-णि, साराई-णि.

A Wholesale dealer. कोठीदारू.

Wholesome. चङो, निरोयो, गुणाइतो, गुणाकारी.

Wholesomeness. चङाई, निरोयाई, गुणु.

Wholly. तमामु, बिल्कुल, सरासरि, सरोसरि, पटिअ, बिनिह, निपटु.

A Whore. कस्बयाणी, कञ्जिरी, खोब्रिली, कुव्यांणी, जाभडि.

A Whore-monger. कञ्जिरीबाज़ु, रंडीबाज़ु. *See* Lecher.

Whoredom, Whoremongering. हरामु, लांगछोटाई, लंडाई, ज़ारी.

Whorish. लंडो, लांडारो, लांगछोटो. *See* Lecherous.

A Whoreshop. जभखानों, जाभड्खानो.

Whose (*interrog.*). कँहिं जो.
Whose (*relat.*) जँहिं जो.
Why. छो, छा with काणि-खां-खों &c. कुज़ाडे लाइ, कोहु.
The Wick of a light. वटि.
Wicked, Wickedly. बुछिडो, बुरो, मंदो, खराबु, जड़ो, पापी, गुनाहितो, पापाइतो, बदि, पिराछतो, शरीरु, दुष्टु.
Wickedness. बुछिडाई, बुराई, जड़ाई, पापीपणो, दुष्टाई.
A Wicker-worked frame, &c. किडी, किडो.
A Wicket. दरी.
Wide. वेकिरो, मोकिरो, कुशादो
To Widen (*act.*). वेकिरो &c. करणु.
Wideness. वेकिराई-णि, मोकिराई-णि, कुशादाई-णि.
A Widow. रन, रनड, फुलावंती, फुलांवती, ड़नी.
To Widow. ड़नणु.
To be Widowed. ड़निजणु.
A Widower. रनडु.
Widowhood. रनापणु.
Width. मोकरि, वेकरि, वेक, पेटु. *See* Wideness.
To Wield. हलाइणु.
A Wife. जोइ, जाल ; or the ladies of one's family, कबोलो, सापरि.
A rival or contemporary Wife. पहाज़, पहिज़.
One having a Wife. जोएतो.
A Wife's relations (*so called by her, or speaking of her*). पेका *plu.*
Wild. (*of a wilderness*) झंग्ली, (*not tame*) टहडु. *See* Untamed, Timorous.
Wild (*unmanegable q. v.*). बेकैदु -दो, मवासु. *See* Wanton.
A Wild beast. मिरूं.
Of a Wild beast. मिरूंआणो, मिरूं-अको.
A Wild, Wilderness. अरैडं, झंगु. *See* Waste.
Wildness. झंग्लीपणो, (*as being untamed*) टहडाई. *See* Timorousness.
A Wile. छंदु, फंदु, ड्रोहु. *See* Artifice, Deceit.
Wilful. होड़ो ; *or* wilfully, होड़ाइतो. *See* Obstinate.
Wilfulness. होड़्याई, हठीलाई.
Wiliness. छंदाई, फंदाई.
Will. (*choice*) इख्तियारु, वसु, (*pleasure*) मर्जी, खुशी, रजादिलि ; the divine will, भाणो.
To Will (*desire*). दिलि-इछा करणु.
A Will (*testament*). वासीनामो.
Willing. राजी, खुशि, कबूलु.
Willingly. दिल्यों, खुश्यों.
Willingness. खुशी, दिलि, खुशिदली.
Wily. छंदो, फंदो, छंदाइतो, फंदाइतो, ड्रोही. *See* Cunning.
To Win. खटणु, जीतणु.
To Wince. छिर्कणु.
The Wind. वाउ, हवा, पवनु, मोलिमु.
A hot Wind. लुक, झोलो, लूह.
A stroke of hot Wind. लुक &c. जो झडप.
A fair Wind. सणाई.
A foul Wind. अणाई.
An unsteady Wind veering to all quarters. चैवाओ.
To be blasted or injured by the Wind. वाउलिजणु, (*as a crop*) सणिकजणु.
To expose to the Wind (*to air*). वाउखाइणु.

The sound of the Wind. घूघाटु, घूघटु.
To Wind (*as a river, road, &c.*). वकुड़-वरुवकुड़ &c. करणु.
To Wind (*act. twine round*). वकोड़णु, वेड़्हणु, वकुड़णु.
To Wind or Wind up (*act. as thread*). वेड़्हणु.
To Wind up (*a watch, &c.*). फेरणु.
A Wind hole in the roof of a house. मँघ, बाद्गीरु.
Windiness (*flatulence*). वाई, वादी, बादु.
Winding, a Wind. वकुड़, वकड़, वरु, वराको.
Winding (*adj.*). वरारो, वराइतो.
A Winding sheet. खफणु.
A Windless. चर्खी.
Windless. निवाओ.
A Window. दरी, ग़िर्खी, गुड़्खो.
The Wind-pipe. निड़ो, निघंटु.
Windy, exposed to the Wind. वाउखो.
Wine. शराबु.
The Wing of a bird. खंभिडाटो, ढंभुड, परु.
To Wink. छिंभणु, अखि भञणु-टिपणु.
A Wink. छिंभ, रम्ज़.
A Winker. छिंभिरु.
A Winner. खटंदड़ु.
To Winnow. (*by shaking in a fan*) छंडणु, उपिणणु, (*in the wind*) वाउरणु, राइणु.
Winnowing (*sub.*). छंड़, छंड़्को.
A Winnowing fan. छज्जु, सुपु, गागिड़ो, कूंड़ो.
The Winter. सिआरो.
To Wipe. उघणु.
To Wipe out. मेसारणु.
Wiping, a Wipe. उघिणी.
The Wipings. ओघि.
A Wire. तारु, तंदु.
Wisdom. ड़ाहप, सिआणप, अकुलु, बुधि, होशु, चतुराई, ड़ाहि.
Wise, a Wise man. ड़ाहो, सिआणो, दानाहु, आकिलु, अकुलवंदु, होश्वंदु, होश्वरु, चतुरु, बुधिमानु, ग्यानी, अकुलाइतो, होशाइतो.
Wise, of a Wise man. ड़ाहाणो, चतुराणो; *or* wisely, अकुलाइतो, होशाइतो.
To Wish. दिलि &c. करणु, घुरणु, तरुषणु.
A Wish. दिलि, इछा, खाहिश, खाश, चाउ, चाहु, तलब, संकल्पु, निअत. *See* Desire.
Wishywashy. *See* Washy.
A Wisp of hay or straw. थबो.
Wistful. *See* Attentive, Thoughtful.
Wit, Wits. होसिलो. *See* Sense, Wisdom.
A Witch. ड़ाइणि, ड़ेणि.
Witchcraft. जादू, जादूगरी, सिहिरु, शिहिरु, इस्रारु, इश्रालु.
With. (*noting instrument*) साणु, सां, सें, सेणु, सीं, (*along with*) सूधां-धों, साणु, सां, सें, सी, (*in the hands of*) वटि, कोलि, कने, गि़ने, ग़रे, ग़रि, ग़ने, (*at the same time with*) सभों.
To Withdraw (*act.*). कढणु, मोटाए निअणु,
To Withdraw (*neu.*). निकिरणु, बाहरि वञणु, वञणु.
To Wither (*act.*). ग़ारणु, साड़णु.
To Wither (*neu.*). ग़रणु, सड़णु, कूमाइजणु, कूमाटिजणु, सुसणु.
To Withhold. *See* To Refuse, Restrain.

Within. अंदरि, मँझि.
From Within. अंदिरां-रों-हूं-रेंउ.
Without(*not within*). बाहरि, बहरि.
From Without. बाहरां-रों-हूं-रेंउ.
Without (*wanting*). बिना-नु-नूं, धारां-रों-हूं-रेंउ-रे, बाझां-झों झूं-झेंउ, सिवाइ, बिगरि, बे, रे, री, रिभ.
To Withstand. आड़ो बिहणु. *See* To Oppose.
Witness (*testimony*). साख, शाहिदी, ओग़ाही, गुहाई.
A Witness. साखी, शाहिदु, ओग़ाहु, गुहाउ.
To bear Witness. साख &c. डिभणु -भरणु.
Wittingly. *See* Knowingly.
Witty, Wittily. होसिलाइतो. *See* Sarcastic.
A Wizard. ड़ाइणु, डेणु, जादूगरु, इसरारी, कामिण्गोरु-रो.
Wo, Woe. डुखु, गमु, सोज़ु. *See* Grief.
Woeful, Woefully. डुखाइतो, गमाइतो, सोजाइतो. *See* Sorrowful.
A Wolf. बघडु, बघ्यडु, नाहरु.
A Woman. जाल, मिहिरी, औरत, नारी, इस्तिरी.
Womanhood. जालपणु.
Womanish. जालाणो, जनानो, जोयो.
Womanly, of a Woman. जालिको. जालाणो, जनानो.
The Womb. पेटु, गर्भु, कुड्हि.
Wonder. अजबु, अचुरजु, हैरत, इविरत, विस्मइ.
To Wonder. अजबु &c. लग़णु with agent in the dative.
Wonderful, Wonderfully. अजबु, अचुरजु, अजाइबु, अजोबु, अजबाइतो, अताई, अजब &c. जिहडो.
A Wonderful person or thing. आफात.

Wonderfulness. अजीबाई.
Wonder-striken (*stupified through amazement*). विसो, वाइडो, मे.ग़ो.
To Woo. इश्कु लाइणु.
Wood. काठु, काठी.
A Wood. बेलो, झंगु, बनु.
A Wood cutter or seller. काठ्यरु, काठ्यारो.
Wooden. लाकूड्यो.
A Wood man (*forester*). बेलाई, बेलारी.
Wood work. काठग़ड्हु.
The Woof of cloth. पेटो.
Wool. उन, पशम.
Woollen, Woolly. ओनो.
Woollen cloth. बनात.
A Word. अखरु, लब्जु, पदु, शब्दु.
The Word of God. खुदा जो कलामु
Wordy. घणभखिरो, अछिरो, डिघो. *See* Prolix.
Work (*employment*). कमु, काजु' कारि, कमुकाजु-कारि, हाज, धंधो, कर्तउ. *See* Labour.
To Work (*make*). करणु, जोडणु घडणु.
To Work, make to Work. कमाराइणु.
To Work hard (*act.*). ग़ाहणु, ग़हाइणु, वहाइणु.
To Work up. *See* To Excite, Knead.
To Work, perform Work. कमु &c. करणु, कमाइणु.
To Work (*or act, as a purgative*). पेटु छोडणु.
To Work hard (*neu.*). ग़हणु, वहणु.
A Workfellow. कमभाई.
A Workman (*labourer q. v.*). कमो.
A good Workman. कारीगरु. *See* Artificer.

Workmanlike, Workmanly. कारीगराणो, कस्ब्याणो, कसबाइतो.

Workmanship. घड़िणी, घड़िति, घड़िप, घाड़ेटो.

A Workshop. दुखानु, कार्खानो.

The World. दुनिआ, दुआ, जहानु, जगु, जगतु, जगटु, लोकु, विशु, संसारु, स्रिष्टि.

Worldliness. दुअवी.

Worldly. दुआई, दुअवी, संसारी, जहानी.

Worldly life or concerns. संसारु; *or* manners of men, दुआदारी, जहान्दारी.

A Worm. किँऑं.

An intestinal Worm. डुमंदु, डुमो.

Worms (*maggots*). किँअड़ि, किँआड़ि.

Wormy. किँअरो, किआँरो.

To be Worn away, or injured by wear (*as clothes*). खुसणु.

To be Worried (*harassed*). अड़णु, अकणु, आतो-तालां-ककि थिअणु.

To Worry (*tear and mangle*). चिथेड़णु, चिचिरणु. *See* To Tease.

Worse, Worst. लाभो. *See* Bad.

Worship. इबादत, बंदगी, पूज़ा, सेवा, भज़नु, भगति.

To Worship. पूज़णु, सेवणु, भज़णु, सुमरणु, इबादत &c. करणु.

A Worshipper. इबादती, पूज़ारो, सेवकु, भज़नीकु, भगतु.

To Worst. *See* To Defeat.

Worsted yarn. ओनो धागो.

Worth (*value*). कदुरु, कीमत, मुल्हु.

One who recognizes another's Worth. कदुराइतो, कदुर्दानु.

To be Worth. लहणु.

Worthiness. चङाई, लाइकी.

Worthless. की न जिहड़ो, निकमो. *See* Useless, Unworthy.

Worthlessness. निकमाई. *See* Uselessness.

Worthy, Worthily. चङो, लाइकु, जोगु, वडाइतो, कदुराइतो, पात्रु. *See* Suitable.

Would that. शाल, छाल.

A Wound. फटु, जखमु, घाउ, धकु, वाढोड़ु.

To Wound. फटणु, जखमणु, घाइणु, वाढोड़णु.

Wounded. जखमी, घायलु.

To be Woven. उज़णु.

A Wrangle, Wrangling. रग़िड़ो, झग़िड़ो, ब्राएतालु, रदबदलि. *See* Squabble.

To Wrangle. झग़िड़णु, रग़िड़ो &c. करणु.

A Wrangler. रग़िड़ाई, झग़िड़ाई. *See* Sqabbler.

To Wrap. वेढ़्हणु. To Fold.

A Wrapper, cloth for Wrapping. वेठणु, बुक्को.

Wrath. काविड़ि. *See* Anger.

Wrathful, Wrathfully. काविड़ीलु, काविड़ाइतो, ड़मिरीलु, ड़मिराइतो.

A Wreath of flowers &c. (*for the head*). सिहिरो.

To Wreath. वेढ़्हणु.

To Wrench. (*twist*) मरोटणु, मरोड़णु, मोड़णु, (*wrest from by violence*) मरोटे &c. वठणु.

A Wrench (*violent twist*). मरोड़, मरोट.

To Wrest. *See* To Wrench.

To Wrestle. मल्ह विढ़्हणु.

A Wrestler. मल्लु.

Wrestling (*sub.*). मल्ह.

A Wrestling yard. मलाखिड़ो.

A Wretch. निंदोरो, निंधकु, निजसु, नामुरादु.

Wretched, Wretchedly. डुख्यो, डुखी, डुल्यो, डुखाइतो, डुखभर्यो.

To be Wretched. डुऌणु, डुखिजणु.

Wretchedness. ड़ोलो, डुखु, डोखिडोकष्टु.

To Wriggle. टिलणु, लुड़णु लमणु.

To Wring. (*twist violently*) मरोडणु, वटणु, (*force out by contortion*) निपूडणु. *See* To Wrench.

To Wrinkle (*act.*). घुंजाइणु, गुञाइणु.

A Wrinkle. घुंजु, गुञु.

The Wrist. कराई, ब्रचो.

To Write. लिखणु.

A Writer. लेखारी, लिखणहारो.

To Writhe. तड़फणु, फथिकणु.

The act of Writing. लिखिणी, लिखति.

A Writing, or Written paper. लिख्यो, लिखति, अखरु.

Contracted Writing. पेची अखर.

The cost of Writing. लिखाणी.

A Writing board. पटी, फरही.

A Wrong (*injustice q. v.*). नाहकु; the being wrong, the wrong side, उबति, उबताई.

Wrong, Wrongly. (*erring*) भुलाइतो, भोलाइतो, गलति, ड़धि, असुधि (*reverse*) उबतो, ऊंधो, (*improper, q. v.*) बेदडो, नालाइकु. *See* Injury.

To Wrong. हकु न ड़िभणु.

Wrongful. *See* Wrong.

Wroth. *See* Wrathful.

Wry (*distorted*). मोडाइतो, मेछिरु.

Y

A Yam. सूरणु.

A Yard (*courtyard*). अङणु, आंगु.

The Yard of a ship. आड़, पिमांणु.

Yarn. *See* Worsted.

To Yawn. उबासी ड़िभणु.

A Yawn. उबासी.

A Yawner, Yawning. उबासिरु.

Ye. *See* You.

Yea. *See* Yes.

A Year. वर्ह्यु, सालु, संबतु, सनु.

This Year. हेल.

Of this Year. हेलेको.

Last Year. परु, पार्सालु.

Of last Year. परोको.

Yearly, every Year. वर्ह्योसिर्वर्हि, वर्ह्योवर्हि.

Yearly, of a Year. वर्ह्योको.

Yearly pay. सालिआनो, बारँहँमाँहीं.

To Yearn. सिखणु; also छिकणु -ताणणु with दिलि as nominative.

A Yearning. छिक, ताण, सिक.

To Yell. कीकणु, कीकाइणु. *See* To Scream.

A Yell, Yelling. कूक, कीक, रडि, कीह. *See* Scream.

Yellow. जर्दु, जर्दो, पिअरो, पीलो, साओ, कैसिरी, हेडुंओं, बसंती.

Yellowish. जर्देरो, जर्देरिडो.

To be Yellowish, have a tendency to Yellow. जर्दाइणु, पिअराइणु, पीलाइणु.

Yellowness. जर्दी - दांई, पिअराई, पीलाई.

To Yelp. कूकणु.

Yes. हां, आँईं, थाँईं, थांहि, हओ, हाओ.

Yesterday. कल्ह, काल्ह.

Of Yesterday. कल्हीको, काल्हूणो, काल्हेको, काल्हूणो.

Yet (*nevertheless*). त बि, तड़ी बि, पर.

Yet, as Yet (*still*). अजा.

To Yield. (*act. give, produce*) ड़िअणु, करणु, (*admit*) मञणु, कबूलणु, (*surrender*) छड़णु, ड़िअणु.

To Yield (*neu. submit q.v.*). दबिजणु, तातो थिअणु.

A Yoke. पांजारी, पाञारी, जुहरू.

The outside pin of the Yoke. ड़ोरिणो.

The inside pin of the Yoke. थंभिड़ी.

The lower cross stick of a Yoke. तरहट.

The rope fastening the Yoke to the plough. नाड़ो.

A Yoke of oxen. जोग़.

To Yoke. जोटणु, बंधणु.

The Yolk of an egg. जर्दी.

Yonder. हुते. *See* There.

You. अहीं, अव्हीं, तहीं, तव्हीं, अँईं, आंईं.

Young (*not old*). नंढो, नंढिअ-थोरिअ उमिरि जो.

The Young of man or any animal. ब़ाचि.

To be with Young. (*brutes*) फरणु, फर्जणु, (*as an ewe*) पुर्जणु, (*as a goat*) बोकिजणु. *See* To be Pregnant.

A Young man. जुआनु, जुआणु, कूंधु, कूंधरू. *See* Youth.

Of a Young man. जुआनिको-नाणो-नाइनेा, जुआणिको.

To become a Young man, or appear so. जुआनाइणु.

A Youngster. *See* A Youth.

Your, Your's. अहां-अव्हां-तव्हां जो.

Youth, Youthfulness. नंढपणु-पाई, नंढेपो-पाई, जुआणो, जोभनु, लास्यारी.

A Youth. लास्यारू, ग़भिरू. *See* A Young man.

Youthful. *See* Youth.

Z

Zeal. सायो, गोरश-शो, उजमु, उदमु, जुहदु, धुनि.

Without Zeal. उतिरिथो, उछातिरो, मथाछिरो.

Zealous. सायाइतेा, गोरशो, उजमो, उदमी, जुहदी, खफ्ती, उज़माइतो, हिकादिल्यो.

Zealously. दिल्यां-ल्यों, सायाइतेा, उज़माइतो.

To work Zealously. सतणु.

Zedoary. जद्वार, कपूरकचिरी.

A Zenana. जनानखानो, ड़ेउढो, ड़ेढी, देरी.

The Zenith. चोटी, कापारू.

Zest (*relish q.v*). साउ, सवादु, सवाड़ु, रुचि.

The Zodiac. रासिचक्रु.

A sign of the Zodiac. रासि.

A Zone. *See* Girdle.

ERRATA.

3 page	16 line	for "Adhesion"	read Adhesive.
10	last „	इशरो	इशारो
13	14	गल्हो	गह्लो
16	15	चिभाटणु	चीभाटणु
17	8	साणु	सानु
22	21	मिटणु	मीटणु
24	23	दत्रीजणु	दत्रिजणु
27	33	राणो	रानो
31	20	लुड़इणु	लुड़ाइणु
44	5	आ सु	आब्नूसु
46	20	enjoin	enjoy
47	25	लिलाइणु	लीलाइणु
„	28	लिल्डी	लील्डी
49	26	पखिडणु	पखिडणु
51	12	झूलीणो	झूलिणो
54	6	वछेडो	वछेरी
55	21	पंजूँणो	पंजूँणि
59	11	सामुद्री	सामुड़ी
67	32	Gysum	Gypsum
75	13	मड़ाहिको	माड़िहिको
„	18	मण्हिपो	माण्हिपो
78	14	लांडरो	लांड़ारो
80	5	तक्तिरो	तल्किरो
„	30	उधाडा	उधारो
90	39	अर्कं	इर्कं
105	38	गाफिलाइ	गाफिलाणो
112	25	दवारु	दब्गरु
122	12	बीजु	वेंजु
125	24	सरदाइणु	सरहाइणु
126	30	शइारी	शाइरी
134	36	फूखणु	फूकणु
143	8	लाढ़ाणि	लाड़णि
145	17	भाभर्यो	भावभर्यो
148	1	दिन्दारी	दीन्दारी
157	22	जामिनि	जामिनी
167	20	*let*	*set*
170	20	सहडणु	सहडणु
173	12	शीक	शीख
180	3	खोठी	कोठी
182	15	मिन्हती	मिह्नती
189	20	गुतूफार	गुफ्तार
202	37	रव	वार